I libri di Viella
Arte

Angelica Federici

Convents, *Clausura* and Cloisters

Religious Women in Late Medieval Rome and Latium

viella

Copyright © 2022 - Viella s.r.l.
All rights reserved
First published: September 2022
ISBN 979-12-5469-106-9

FEDERICI, Angelica
    Convents, clausura and cloisters : religious women in late medieval Rome and Latium / Angelica Federici. - Roma : Viella, 2022. - 217 p., [16] c. di tav. : ill. ; 24 cm. - (I libri di Viella. Arte)
    Bibliografia: p. [191]-207
    Indici dei nomi e dei luoghi: p. [209]-217
    ISBN 979-12-5469-106-9
    1. Donne - Monachesimo [e] Vita religiosa - Lazio - Medioevo   2. Conventi - Lazio - Medioevo
    271.90022 (DDC 23.ed)   Scheda bibliografica: Biblioteca Fondazione Bruno Kessler

viella
libreria editrice
via delle Alpi 32
I-00198 ROMA
tel. 06 84 17 75 8
fax 06 85 35 39 60
www.viella.it

Table of contents

Preface   7

1. Major Themes
    1. Space, Gender and Politics: Reframing the Female Religious Experience   9
    2. Contemporary Readings of the Cloister   17
    3. Idealised Realities: The Onset of Nunneries in Rome   26

2. Roman Nunneries
    1. Female Power and Prestige:
       The Extraordinary Case of Sant'Agnese fuori le Mura   33
    2. Icons in *Clausura*: Domenico Guzmán
       and the Nuns at San Sisto Vecchio   51
    3. Assisi in Rome? Clare's Influence
       at Santi Cosma e Damiano in Mica Aurea   65
    4. Baronial Authority and Identity in Rome:
       The Colonna at San Silvestro in Capite   72
    5. Interpreting Medieval Vestiges:
       Rediscovering San Lorenzo in Panisperna   81
    6. Comparing Roman Conventual Communities in Context:
       A Few Considerations   90

3. The Benedictines in Latium
    1. Forlorn Latium: Medieval Nunneries in the Region   93
    2. Women's Place and Space:
       Introducing Benedictine Art and Architecture   99
    3. Between Rome and Naples:
       Artistic Presence at Santa Maria del Monacato, Castrocielo   102
    4. Rediscovering Forgotten Identities: San Luca, Guarcino   110
    5. Hidden Gems: San Pietro, Montefiascone   114
    6. Off the Beaten Tracks:
       Sant'Angelo di Orsano, Trevi nel Lazio   121
    7. Comparing Benedictine Conventual Communities: A Few Considerations   127

4. The Mendicants in Latium
   1. Game Changers and Puzzling Absences:
      The Ascent of the Clarissans in Latium ... 131
   2. Female Patronage or Baronial Intervention? San Sebastiano, Alatri ... 135
   3. Shedding New Light on Neglected Sites:
      San Michele Arcangelo, Amaseno ... 145
   4. A New Manifesto for the Mendicant Order: San Pietro in Vineis, Anagni ... 149
   5. Treasures under Water:
      The Nunnery of Santa Filippa Mareri, Borgo San Pietro ... 159
   6. Comparing Clarissan Conventual Communities: A Few Considerations ... 167

Epilogue ... 169

Appendix
   Benedictine Convents in Latium (ca. 1200-1400) ... 177
   Clarissan Convents in Latium (ca. 1200-1400) ... 186

Bibliography ... 191
Index of Names ... 209
Index of Places ... 215

Preface

Despite the popularity of academic research devoted to religious women, Rome and Latium have yet to be the object of an extensive survey on medieval conventual art and architecture. Yet there is a tangible presence of women's artistic output in the city and region during the late medieval period. Perhaps the attention of scholars may have moved to Avignon along with the papacy, and, with few convents from the period surviving to present times, research is problematic, which may dissuade further investigation. This study begins filling this gap by collecting thirteen case studies, some of which have only been published by local historians, which provide insight into the importance of female patronage pre- and post-Avignon. It will hopefully be a resource for fellow researchers interested in convents in Rome and Latium in the thirteenth and fourteenth centuries.

Given the breadth of the topic and the lack of a resource examining the region as a whole, in compiling this study it was important to take a holistic approach. This book is the result of extensive fieldwork and scrutiny of artistic, architectural and documentary data conducted for the greater part during my PhD at the University of Cambridge. Everything from the art on the walls to surviving evidence such as economic registries, visitation records, and chronicles, was taken into consideration while composing these case studies. This organic methodology allows us to view these sites as organisms, and forces us to consider their artistic, architectural, social and historical elements in their integrity. Perhaps even more interestingly, the lack of information available prompted one of the most important aspects of this study: the development of AutoCAD floor plans for the convents that were examined. This allowed objects, and their liturgical uses, to be truly studied in their original context, and put hypotheses previously drawn from archival documents to the test. The material presented in this book will also hopefully prove to be a useful tool for further research.

Convents, much like monasteries, were recruitment centers for women of the ruling classes. Members of families such as Bonamazza, Caetani, Cenci, Colonna and Orsini feature consistently in their registries, a testament to their wealth and social status, of which artistic patronage represents only a fragment of a complex social history. This collection of case studies begins introducing the importance of female monasticism as a culturally defining element in Roman society during the Middle Ages, providing data and research that future studies may build upon.

I would like to express my deep gratitude to Professor Manfredi Merluzzi, Head of the Humanities Department at the Università degli Studi di Roma Tre and Professor Giulia Bordi for her enthusiastic guidance and support. A special thanks also to Professor Maria Chiara Giorda, my post doc supervisor.

This book originates from my PhD dissertation at the University of Cambridge under the patient guidance, enthusiastic encouragement and continuous advice of Dr. Donal Cooper

I am grateful for the endless assistance provided by the staff members of the Bibliotheca Hertziana, the Archivio Apostolico Vaticano and the Archivio di Stato di Roma.

A profound gratitude to my friends and family for providing the moral strength and support to carry out this project.

1. Major Themes

1. *Space, Gender and Politics: Reframing the Female Religious Experience*

> There is still no overreaching study of female monasticism in medieval and early Renaissance Rome[1]

Although the past two decades have witnessed a substantial rise in the study of conventual art, no comprehensive, in-depth study has ever been devoted to Rome and Latium. Yet, evidence of female presence in the city and the region during the late medieval period is conspicuous; its neglect may be a consequence of the perceived dominance of both the papacy and the noble families in this scenario. While single case studies on Roman and Latium convents do exist, there has been no attempt to investigate female religious art in a broader artistic, political and social context. This investigation will examine women's religious art in Rome and Latium during the late medieval period and contextualize these convents within a political, social, and historical framework for the first time.

The survival of documentary and artistic testimony including epigraphy, sculpture, architecture and funerary monuments bears witness both to an uninterrupted artistic production in Rome throughout the Avignon period, and to the role of nuns as key players in the promotion of these commissions. Indeed, in opposition to the 'black hole' scenario advanced by existing historiography – and critiqued early on by Angiola Maria Romanini – the gathered evidence underscores both the political agency and extensive patronal activity of female monastic communities in this somewhat overlooked, but artistically vibrant period.[2] Thus, although the first decades of the fourteenth century were characterized by an absence of major papal projects, artistic commissions by single congregations (Tre Fontane, Aracoeli, San Lorenzo, San Sisto Vecchio and Sant'Agnese fuori le Mura); by cardinal bishops (Santa Maria Maggiore, Aracoeli); and by private

---

1. A. Dunlop, "Dominicans and Cloistered Women: The Convent of Sant'Aurea in Rome", *Early Modern Women*, 2 (2007), p. 49.

2. A.M. Romanini, "Introduzione", in S. Romano, *Eclissi di Roma. Pittura murale a Roma e nel Lazio da Bonifacio VIII a Martino V (1295-1431)*, Rome, Electa, 1992, p. 7.

individuals (Santa Balbina, *Madonna of the Porta Iudicii* and *Madonna della Bocciata* in the Vatican Grottoes of San Pietro) abound.[3] While Rome undoubtedly lost some of its brightness as a result of the Avignon papacy, this absence left space for other agencies.

Alfonso Marini, an expert on the Franciscans, revised the catalogue of female monasteries present in Rome between the thirteenth and fifteenth centuries.[4] The scholar's objective was to provide the groundwork for different disciplines to develop future research in the field. The author acknowledges that inventories of this sort already exist, but argues that their content is either imprecise or lacks important details.[5] Marini lists a total of twenty-nine nunneries, of which seventeen followed a Benedictine rule. The remaining twelve adhered to the newly established monastic orders, namely the Dominicans, the Clarissan, the Augustinians, the Cistercians, and the Humiliate.[6] By examining surviving statistics and single case studies, Marini presents a brief survey on the religious fervour, life-style, wealth and social status of convents in Rome. The numbers point towards the great popularity of the new monastic families. Indeed, the Dominican house at San Sisto Vecchio was the largest nunnery during these centuries, recording a total of seventy nuns in the year 1320.[7] The Clarissans followed with three nunneries totalling ninety nuns (San Silvestro in Capite, San Lorenzo in Panisperna and San Cosimato). Although the Benedictine nunneries maintained an overall numerical majority, the order witnessed a rapid decline in vocations with the advent of the new congregations.[8] According to Giulia Barone, at the beginning of the fourteenth century, women of noble lineage were principally adhering to the new monastic families. These include the convents of San Silvestro in Capite and San Lorenzo in Panisperna (both Clarissan), whose abbesses came from the Colonna, Conti and de Prefectis families.[9] Cristina Carbonetti Vendittelli maintains that this trend also applied to the monastery of

---

3. Romano, *Eclissi di Roma*, p. 10.

4. A. Marini, "Monasteri femminili a Roma nei secoli XIII-XV", *Archivio della Società romana di storia patria*, 132 (2010), pp. 81-108.

5. According to Marini the *Monasticon Italiae*, 1, *Roma e Lazio*, 1, ed. by F. Caraffa, Cesena, Centro Storico Benedettino, 1981, is the most complete record but contains information only on Benedictine monasteries.

6. Marini, "Monasteri femminili", pp. 84-85.

7. These numbers derive from *Il Catalogo di Torino* published in "Il Catalogo di Torino delle chiese, degli ospedali, dei monasteri di Roma nel secolo XIV", ed. by G. Falco, *Archivio della Società romana di storia patria*, 32 (1909), pp. 411-433; M. Armellini, *Le chiese di Roma dal secolo IV al XIX*, Vatican City, Tipografia Vaticana, 1891, pp. 45-55; C. Carbonetti Vendittelli, "Il registro di entrate e uscite del convento domenicano di San Sisto degli anni 1369-1381", in *Economia e società a Roma tra Medioevo e Rinascimento. Studi dedicati a Arnold Esch*, ed. by A. Esposito and L. Palermo, Rome, Viella, 2005, pp. 96-97.

8. Marini, "Monasteri femminili", p. 93.

9. G. Barone, "Margherita Colonna e le Clarisse di San Silvestro in Capite", in *Roma anno 1300. Atti della IV settimana di studi di storia dell'arte medievale all'Università di Roma "La Sapienza"*, ed. by A.M. Romanini, Acts of the conference (Rome, 19-24 May 1980), Rome, L'Erma di Bretschneider, 1983, p. 800.

San Sisto Vecchio.[10] Her study is based on the economic registry (*liber bursarie*, 1369-1381) preserved at the Archivio Vaticano in the *fondo* of Santi Domenico e Sisto.[11] Using Marini's survey as a starting point, this research was expanded into the greater Latium areas in order to create a comparative framework between urban and regional nunneries.

I conducted a gazetteer on surviving conventual complexes pertaining to the Benedictine and Mendicant orders outside of Rome; selecting and performing a more in-depth analysis of the convents which had the most promising collection of archival, artistic and architectural evidence. This survey, whose findings are summarised in the Appendix, lists a total of seventy-one Benedictine, Clarissan and Dominican nunneries in Latium (excluding Rome) active between 1200-1400: forty-nine Benedictine, twenty-one Clarissan and one Dominican. While Rome offers a variety of documentary evidence and resources, nunneries in the wider Latium region act as a local comparative context for these metropolitan artistic and architectural commissions. Roman nunneries were divided according to territorial divisions of familial power; a trend that extended to convents in Latium.[12] Five or six well-known influential families prevailed inside Rome and across Latium: the Annibaldi, the Colonna, the Orsini, the Savelli and by the end of the thirteenth century, the Caetani.

The thirteen convents selected for this research represent the best documented (artistic, architectonic, documentary, epigraphic) conventual complexes for this period. While some have been comprehensively published upon, others remain unknown; thus generating an uneven relationship to the pre-existing literature. This book provides a thorough summary and critical analysis of existing publications, but ultimately aims to advance research on less known nunneries. It is this combination of the well-studied and unstudied which gives this investigation its value as an overview of the region's nunneries. This survey also attested to the relative absence of Dominican female communities outside of Rome. As far as female Dominican settlements are concerned, the most comprehensive list is provided by a small manuscript preserved in the Archive at Perugia; a codex which offered essential information to the prior of the Provincia Romana.[13] This region originally extended beyond present-day Latium including parts of Tuscany and Umbria. Sixteen female convents are listed for the thirteenth century with an additional seven nunneries for the Trecento. As Joanna Cannon rightly points out, there is an objective lack of documentation as far as these female foundations are considered.[14]

10. Carbonetti Vendittelli, "Il registro", p. 98.
11. The registry is archived at the Archivio Apostolico Vaticano, Monasteri femminili soppressi, SS. Domenico e Sisto, 191, 192. The San Sisto inventory has been published by S. Pagano, *L'archivio del convento dei SS. Domenico e Sisto di Roma. Cenni storici e inventario*, Vatican City, Archivio Vaticano, 1994; Carbonetti Vendittelli, "Il registro", pp. 96-97.
12. S. Carocci, *Baroni di Roma*, Rome, École française de Rome, 1993.
13. Archivio di Stato di Perugia, Corporazioni religiose soppresse, S. Domenico Miscellanea, 66; J. Cannon, *Religious Poverty, Visual Riches. Art in the Dominican Churches of Central Italy in the Thirteenth and Fourteenth Centuries*, London-New Haven, Yale University Press, 2013, p. 9.
14. *Ibid.*, pp. 9-16.

Ultimately, this selection also stemmed from the objective of reconstructing the medieval *facies* of these nunneries. The analysis of architectural space is mostly centred around the church area – and in particular on the position of the choir. Reconstructions were attempted through a multidisciplinary analysis of available primary and secondary resources. Spatial reconstructions also contributed to further the understanding of the female religious experience in Central Italy and to contextualize artworks in their original context. The assembled data is significant due to its great variety, which extends from painted crosses to frescoes, bells to liturgical apparatus. Conventual spaces were frequently embellished by leading painters in the latest styles. Names including Pietro Cavallini, Bartolomeo Pisano, Lello and the Maestro di Anagni testify to the role of these nuns in a substantial operation of artistic renewal in Rome and across Latium more generally. When present, images of patrons have been duly noted and examined. These donor images share a striking resemblance to images of the deceased in tomb monuments; and although he does not specifically address conventual realities, Ingo Herklotz argues that this iconographic link derives from a conceptual analogy between funerary art and the eschatological function of the donation act inherent to patronage within a religious setting.[15]

As stated above, convents have been selected in accordance to the presence of solid artistic, architectural, or documentary data. Surviving evidence such as economic registers, visitation records, and chronicles emphasise that, just like their male counterparts, these institutions acted as 'recruitment' centres for women from the Roman aristocracy and upper middle classes. Names such as Boccamazza, Caetani, Cenci, Colonna, and Orsini figure prominently in these documents. This testifies to the wealth and social status of these convents, of which artistic commissions represent only individual *tesserae* of an intricate mosaic. It is unquestionable that, as in other Italian centres, female monasticism was a culturally defining element in Roman society between the thirteenth and fourteenth centuries.[16] The material collected here indicates that female religious patronage did not act as a substitute to the vacated papal seat, but rather maintained a continuity throughout a period that has generally been regarded by mainstream historiography as artistically insignificant. We shall attempt to deconstruct this apparent segregation and examine works of art in their original context where possible. Is it correct to assume that an artwork's location within the space of nunneries determines both its function and a visual lexicon for its recipient? This is one of the greatest challenges this study faces. Addressing the viewers' gaze in the deconstruction of artistic content is not new to scholarship in the field.[17] However, as far as nunneries are concerned

---

15. I. Herklotz, *Sepulcra e monumenta del Medioevo*, Naples, Liguori, 2001, p. 139.

16. G. Barone, "La presenza degli ordini religiosi nella Roma di Martino V", in *Alle origini della nuova Roma. Martino V (1417-1431)*, ed. by M. Chiabò, G. D'Alessandro, P. Piacentini and C. Ranieri, Acts of the conference (Rome, 2-5 March 1992), Rome, Nuovi Studi Storici, 1992, pp. 353-365: 357.

17. C. Bruzelius, "Nuns in Space: Strict Enclosure and the Architecture of the Clarisses in the Thirteenth Century", in *Clare of Assisi: A Medieval and Modern Woman. Clarefest Selected Papers*,

it offers greater insight into the patron's/matron's decision-making. Indeed, what has come to be defined as *matronage*[18] (as a gendered alternative to patronage) by current research cannot always be conclusively substantiated.[19]

Today, it is unanimously accepted that the study of religious women was jeopardized more by cultural stereotyping than what is usually ascribed to a general loss of material evidence. Here, the study of artistic testimonies alongside architectural remains (through ground plans, axonometric views and sections on AutoCAD) have been considered in relation to their function and gendered identity. Today it is unanimously accepted that the study of religious women was jeopardized more by cultural stereotyping than what is usually ascribed to a general loss of material evidence. Methodological advancements in the field are at least partially the product of innovations in digital technologies like mapping, modelling and interpreting spatial data. A three-dimensional visualization of space has undoubtedly encouraged a variety of new interpretations. For the purpose of this research, reconstructions on AutoCAD facilitated both the detection of architectural patterns which were not immediately discernible and studying artworks in their original context. These, however, are only the first steps towards digitally recording historical data with the use of three-dimensional visualization techniques. Furthermore, this field is destined to undergo major transformations with the advent of GIS, photogrammetry, laser scanning and building information modelling. This approach is indebted to the pioneering work of *Atlante: Percorsi visivi*[20] which offers the first recontextualization of wall paintings and mosaics in Rome's churches with the aid of floor plans and axonometric views. These are outlined with the main objective of showcasing the original medieval decorations which predominantly survive in a fragmentary state today. Ultimately, the aim was to recreate original architectural contexts which were altered during the course of time. The iconographic set of the 31 monuments covered in this volume consists of 163 plans and 595 images, 72 of which were two-dimensional views obtained from three-dimensional virtual models. The latter enabled a precise spatial analysis and simulation possibilities exceeding the analogue and descriptive limit of photographic reproductions.

---

ed. by I. Peterson, New York, Columbia University Press, 1996, pp. 53-74; M. Caviness, *Visualizing Women in the Middle Ages: Sight, Spectacle and Scopic Economy*, Philadelphia, University of Pennsylvania Press, 2001; J. Lacan, *The Seminar. Book XI. The Four Fundamental Concepts of Psychoanalysis*, London, Hogarth Press - Institute of Psycho-Analysis, 1977; L. Mulvey, "Visual Pleasure and Narrative Cinema", in *Film Theory and Criticism. Introductory Readings*, ed. by L. Braudy and M. Cohen, New York-Oxford, Oxford University Press, 1999, pp. 833-844; L. Cartwright, M. Sturken, *Practices of Looking. An Introduction to Visual Culture*, Oxford, Oxford University Press, 2009.

 18. T. Martin, "Exceptions and Assumptions: Women in Medieval Art History", in *Reassessing the Roles of Women as 'Makers' of Medieval Art and Architecture*, ed. by T. Martin, Leiden, Brill, 2012, p. 1.

 19. *The Ashgate Research Companion to Women and Gender in Early Modern Europe*, ed. by J. Couchman and A.M. Poska, Farnham, Ashgate, 2013.

 20. M. Andaloro, *La pittura medievale a Roma 312-1431. Atlante. Percorsi visivi*, 1, *Suburbio, Vaticano, Rione Monti*, Milan, Jaca Book, 2006.

This study has placed particular attention on the position occupied by choirs inside conventual churches. Caroline Bruzelius' research on the "implications of strict enclosure for the architecture of women"[21] has been a methodological guiding light for this research. As stated by Emanuele Zappasodi, "the nuns were marginalized in their own choir, which represented the true heart of the liturgical life [...] affecting the distribution of conventual spaces".[22] The use of this area was manifold, but most importantly it had distinguished, separate and independent regulations from the main church. This influenced it profoundly both in its arrangement and decorative choices, thematised around the subject of Christ, the Virgin and the Eucharist. Bruzelius claims that the nuns had no visual access to the high altar and the Eucharistic ritual. Nevertheless, we need to remember that the elevation of the Host was commonly reserved to a select few, usually only the officiating clergy. The altar inside the choir created a sort of church within the church with its own distinctive prescriptions and specific set of artworks. As liminal secluded spaces on the margins of the established church area, we may identify choirs as *heterotopias*. Etymologically this term signifies, other place, or, on the edge, and as theorised by Michel Foucault these are spaces that have multiple layers of signifiers.[23]

After the *Periculoso* decree (1298) issued by Pope Boniface VIII (1294-1303), and confirmed in 1309 by the encyclical *Apostolicae sedis* of Pope Clement V (1305-1314), all female monastic communities were subject to strict enclosure. This meant that nuns could not leave the convent under any circumstance. This measure also applied to the Benedictine *moniales* whose rule did not require formal *clausura* and who were previously allowed to journey outside their nunneries. Especially after the *Periculoso*, most convents found themselves on the psychological margins of society. To a certain extent, their experience resembled the asceticism of medieval mystics. Forced enclosure was undoubtedly also a way in which the clergy controlled female waves of mysticism, popular in Central Italy during the late Middle Ages.

While a gap always existed between the ideal and the reality of forced *clausura*, this obviously affected nunneries both on a symbolic and practical level. As Saundra Weddle rightly observes, "the exploitation of architecture's affective capacity was especially useful for the projection of a particular image of religious women".[24] It is generally recognised that the end of Boniface's papacy marked something of a revolution in the arrangement of conventual complexes. The impact of forced

---

21. C. Bruzelius, "Hearing is Believing. Clarissan Architecture, ca. 1213-1340", *Gesta*, 31, 2 (1992), pp. 83-91: 83.

22. E. Zappasodi, *Sorores reclusae. Spazi di clausura e immagini dipinte in Umbria fra XIII e XIV secolo*, Florence, Mandragora, 2018, p. 11: "Come morte al mondo, come recluse e incarcerate le monache erano marginalizzate nel proprio coro vero cuore pulsante della vita liturgica. Per la sua funzione, la sua disposizione rivestiva un'assoluta centralità nella distribuzione degli spazi monastici".

23. M. Foucault, "Of Other Spaces: Utopias and Heterotopias", in *Rethinking Architecture: A Reader in Cultural Theory*, ed. by N. Leach, New York, Routledge, 1997, pp. 330-336.

24. S.L. Weddle, "Women in Wolves' Mouths", in *Architecture and the Politics of Gender in Early Modern Europe*, ed. by H. Hills, Aldershot, Ashgate, 2003, p. 113.

enclosure (after 1298) profoundly affected space on practical and symbolic stances. Indeed, it is more problematic to make distinctions between orders based on architectural observations, as enclosure emerged as the essential characteristic of the good nunnery.[25] Julian Gardner rightly states that in many European languages cloister signifies enclosure, highlighting the strategic communication of female religious space.[26] The archaeology of female piety has effectively demonstrated how the implications of *clausura* changed widely according to practical limitations. These were usually imposed both by the inheritance of building complexes originally inhabited by monks or friars and by women's sparse economic means. Bruzelius also observes that several architectural solutions in response to the need of enclosure were lost as a result of the perishable nature of building materials.[27]

Our knowledge on religious women is still extremely impressionistic. While patronage encompasses fundamental criteria of creativity exposing practices tied to the conception, funding, and fabrication of an artwork or an architectural ensemble; the study of space allows us to deconstruct power relations bound to gender roles. Henri Lefebvre's social considerations on space state that it

> represents the political use of knowledge, […] it implies an ideology […] and employs at best a technological use […] as for representations of the relations of production, which subsume power relations, these too occur in space: space contains them in the form of buildings, monuments and works of art.[28]

Architectural spaces sometimes act as negotiators between individuals creating gendered stereotypes. This statement is particularly true in the context of nunneries, especially in the immediate aftermath of the *Periculoso*.

To a certain extent the analysis of space is analogous to the deconstruction of language semiotics, reflecting a complex symbolic communication system of signs. Indeed, "space is a medium through which social relationships are negotiated";[29] and while it does not define, create, or predict gender relations, it determines a specific iconography for female medieval religious architecture. When envisaging space as a complex social construction, we also need to acknowledge its subtleties of meaning, which demand an attentive multivocal interpretation. As far as architectural practices and divisions of space within the medieval convent are concerned, their roots are to be sought in the axioms established by Benedict at Montecassino.[30] These had a reverberating effect

---

25. J. Gardner, "Nuns and altarpieces agendas for research", *Römisches Jahrbuch der Bibliotheca Hertziana*, 30 (1995), pp. 27-57.

26. *Ibid.*

27. Bruzelius, "Nuns in Space".

28. H. Lefebvre, *The Production of Space*, Oxford, Blackwell, 1991, pp. 8-10.

29. R. Gilchrist, *Gender and Material Culture. The Archaeology of Religious Women*, New York, Routledge, 1994, p. 3033.

30. "Benedictine Architecture", in *The Oxford Dictionary of the Middle Ages*, ed. by R.E. Bjork, Oxford, Oxford University Press, 2010; *Monasticon Italiae*; M. Righetti Tosti-Croce, "Architettura monastica: gli edifici. Linee per una storia architettonica", in *Dall'eremo al cenobio. La civiltà monastica in Italia dalle origini all'eta di Dante*, ed. by G.C. Alessio, Milan, Garzanti, 1987,

across all of Europe and well into the Counter Reformation years. As Roberta Gilchrist rightly asserts:

> Nunneries observed the standard monastic layout in which a central complex of buildings was grouped around a cloister. The cloister provided a community with the maximum seclusion, accessibility between principal structures, and order. [...] Instead of individual spaces, nunneries more often splintered in smaller groups within the house.[31]

Spatial frameworks that regularised encounters in the nunnery between different genders and religious groups living in the same convent had a decisive impact on the layout of these buildings. Once again, Gilchrist:

> Space as a form of material culture is fundamental in constituting Gender. It determines the contexts in which men and women meet; it assists in defining a sexual division of labour; it reproduces attitudes towards sexuality and the body. [...] Space becomes a map in which personal identity and boundaries between social groups are expressed.[32]

The scholar works her definitions of space around Pierre Bourdieu's theories on *habitus*, conceptualising the convent as a social space which is affected by a symbolic power of relations.[33] Furthermore, she argues that "archaeology may be seen as central to a discourse of space and the body, since space reproduces social order and sometimes acts as a metaphorical extension of the body", making space and social behaviour mutually dependant.[34] The medieval female body, however, is both problematic and polysemic; too often interpreted by feminist and gendered historiography as an enantiosemy, and pushing interpretations towards a virgin-whore dichotomy. At times simplistic, this reading may hold a certain degree of truth, especially in so much as the religious female body was interpreted by medieval contemporaries. Reassessments of female religious experiences are still lacking a thorough survey. Women's place and space is often devalued as a result. While the limited evidence for conventual communities has been associated with women's sparse economic and cultural resources, our knowledge is still largely imprecise. This hinders any generalisation on the use of sacred enclosures. The study of religious women is still based on male standards, and rarely considers the private and liminal characteristics of these complexes. Accumulated evidence –

---

pp. 486-575; H. Houben, "Le istituzioni monastiche medioevali dell'Italia meridionale all'epoca di Bernardio di Clairvaux", in *I Cistercensi nel Mezzogiorno medioevale. Atti del convegno internazionale di studio in occasione del IX centenario della nascità di Bernardo di Clairvaux*, ed. by H. Houben and B. Vetere, Galatina, Pubblicazioni del Dipartimento di Studi Storici dal Medioevo all'Età Contemporanea, 1994, pp. 73-87.

31. Gilchrist, *Gender and Material*, p. 3069.
32. *Ibid.*, p. 4011.
33. P. Bordieu, *Outline of a Theory of Practice*, Cambridge, Cambridge University, 1977.
34. R. Gilchrist, "Medieval Bodies in the Material World: Gender, Stigma and the Body", in *Framing Medieval Bodies*, ed. by S. Kay and M. Rubin, Manchester-New York, Manchester University Press, 1994, pp. 43-61.

tied to the feminine agency of these commissions – aims to identify the role of women in the making of religious art.[35] In this sense, contextualising artmaking and artworks is fairly problematic and often speculative. Indeed, it reveals that the intended audience was more often than not the lay public rather than the conventual community, and that iconographic programs were also influenced by their recipients.

This is particularly significant when we treat altarpieces considering that they were hosted by architectural prescriptions that reinforced precise physical reminders of women's segregation, such as grates, doors, *rote*. Ultimately, the objective is to contribute to a larger scholarship that refutes the idea of treating female patronage as an exception.[36] The integrated methodology adopted here broadly aims to situate these nunneries in a local and comprehensive context. Therefore, rather than re-evaluating female patronage as a category, our primary objective is to connect the dots and potentially conceive of convents as social, political and economic networks for the first time. I will explore the role of matronage as a vehicle for a strategic aesthetic discourse and as a testimony of nuns' agency in medieval society. This study will hopefully support future research on a vibrant period, which has been overlooked by current art historiography.

2. *Contemporary Readings of the Cloister*

A vast literature on the subject of female religious art already exists. However, in spite of earlier contributions by pioneering scholars such as Eileen Power[37] and Lina Eckenstein,[38] studies on female spirituality and women's place and space within the convent only gathered pace during the early 1980s.[39] In 1982, Caroline Bynum's *Jesus as Mother* reassessed the twelfth-century use of maternal images to describe God and Christ.[40] Although the book did not explore the role of religious women in medieval society, it introduced specific categories of gender analysis into the academic debate. Five years later, the publication of Bynum's *Holy Feast, Holy Fast* (1987) established the scholar as one of the leading voices on the subject.[41] As stated in the "Introduction", the book's aim was to examine female spirituality "through the implications of food related religious practices and texts [...] to show the manifold meaning of food and its pervasiveness in religious

---

35. R. Dressler, "Continuing the Discourse: Feminist Scholarship and the Study of Medieval Visual Culture", *Medieval Feminist Forum*, 43, 1 (2007), pp. 15-34: 19.

36. Martin, *Reassessing the Roles of Women*, p. 1.

37. E. Power, *Medieval English Nunneries c. 1275-1535*, Cambridge, Cambridge University Press, 1922.

38. L. Eckenstein, *Women under Monasticism*, Cambridge, Cambridge University Press, 1896.

39. S.G. Bell, "Medieval Women Book Owners", *Signs*, 4 (1982), pp. 742-768.

40. C.W. Bynum, *Jesus as Mother. Studies in the Spirituality of the High Middle Ages*, Berkeley, University of California Press, 1982.

41. C.W. Bynum, *Holy Feast, Holy Fast. The Religious Significance of Food to Medieval Women*, Berkeley, University of California Press, 1987.

symbolism".[42] Contemporaneously to Bynum's publications, scholars such as Susan Bell assessed female spirituality from a very different perspective. In her 1982 article, "Medieval Women Book Owners", she examined female lay piety as the catalyst for the production of religious manuscripts. Here, she described how "book-owning women substantially influenced the development of lay piety and vernacular literature in the later Middle Ages".[43] Bell's acknowledgement of women's role as "ambassadors of culture" was a catalyst for new important contributions on the subject of female piety and religious patronage.[44]

Another major factor in the establishment of medieval studies from a female perspective was the emergence of gender as a new element for historical examination. In "Gender: A Useful Category of Analysis", Joan Scott argues that its definition "rests on an integral connection between two propositions: gender is a constitutive element of social relationships based on perceived differences between the sexes, and gender is a primary way of signifying relationships of power".[45] The gender debate aimed to rehabilitate figures, which were traditionally ignored by academia, and excluded from so-called "power relations" in general. This included both lay and religious women in all aspects of the social historical framework. More recently, as Elizabeth L'Estrange and Allison More rightly observe, there has been

> a shift away from the dichotomy in which 'empowerment' discourses were countered by those that stressed the inevitable reassertion of patriarchy, and thus 'women's' inevitable victimization. Attention to women's varied social roles – different combinations of, for example marital statuses (single, married, widow), lifestyle choice (nun, beguine, the decision to remain a widow), profession, religion and class – can shed new light on the position of women in society without casting them in the role of victims of patriarchy or as exceptions overcoming the odds.[46]

The establishment of the Society for Medieval Feminist Scholarship at the 1984 congress in Kalamazoo (University of Western Michigan) by Jane Burns, Roberta Krueger and Elizabeth Robertson not only encouraged this line of inquiry, but also intensified communications amongst feminist medievalists. This led to the foundation of the Medieval Feminist Newsletter, first published in 1986. However, a thorough investigation into medieval artistic contexts was not carried out until the founding of the Medieval Feminist Art History Project by Paula Gerson and Pamela Sheingorn at the 1991 Kalamazoo congress.[47] Based on the talk delivered by Sheingorn at Kalamazoo, the MFAHP's objective was to "use cultural approaches to analyse subjects such as the body, gender, and sexuality. Within this theoretical framework situate art associated with sub-groups like the

---

42. *Ibid.*, pp. 4-5.
43. Bell, "Medieval Women", p. 743.
44. *Ibid.*
45. J.W. Scott, "Gender: A Useful Category of Historical Analysis", *The American Historical Review*, 91, 5 (1996), pp. 1053-1075: 1067.
46. E. L'Estrange, A. More, "Introduction", in *Representing Medieval Genders and Sexualities in Europe*, ed. by E. L'Estrange and A. More, Farnham, Ashgate, 2011, pp. 279-280.
47. Dressler, "Continuing the Discourse", p. 19.

female mystics, or the Beguines, [...] and recuperate artefacts that have been devalued as crafts".[48]

To a certain extent Gerson and Sheingorn provided a platform for medieval art historians to compare findings and investigation.[49] According to Dressler "throughout the decade of the 1980s and the first half of the 90s the MFAHP served a crucial function for those art historians engaged in investigating the role of women in the production of medieval art".[50] This was surely the case for the Kalamazoo session *Case Studies in the Convent* sponsored by the group in 1992.[51] Participants included Marilyn Dunn (*The Nuns of Argenteuil and Chelles as Patrons of twelfth-century Sculpture*), Jeffrey F. Hamburger (*The Curious Case of Venturino da Bergamo: Images, Flagellation, and Self Control in the Cloister Context*) and Kathleen Nolan (*The Trecento Altarpiece of Beata Umiliata*), who presented their findings based on visual testimonies, thus addressing the recurrent presence of female patrons in a religious setting.[52] To a certain extent these experiences bridged the existing gap between studies devoted to women's spirituality and female monasticism. Indeed, scholars such as Hamburger reconciled these two lines of inquiry by focusing on the artistic production of nunneries. That same year, at the Binghamton conference in New York, the MFAHP sponsored a series of essays on themes of commemoration and innovation within female aristocratic commissions. This did not primarily focus on nuns, and included Elizabeth Valdez del Alamo's contribution on Doña Banca of Najera's sarcophagus.[53]

The project's decline was possibly linked to the imposition of a marked feminist stamp and to its "informal procedures – there was no membership fee, newsletter or publication to consolidate and support the organization's functions".[54] This may have discouraged the adhesion of traditional academic bodies. There was an undeniable rise in the number of publications relating to women's space in the convent during the 1990s. Nevertheless in 1998, Hamburger affirmed: "there is still nothing approaching a survey of the art and architecture of female monasticism in medieval art, [at present] any attempt to write one would be somewhat premature given the lack of research".[55] As far as the 1990s were concerned, the key players in shaping the literature on female medieval monasticism were Hamburger (mainly manuscripts) and Bruzelius (mainly architecture). While there was a significant increase in publications on single case

---

48. P. Sheingorn, "The Medieval Feminist Art History Project", *Medieval Feminist Newsletter*, 12, 1 (1991), pp. 5-10: 7.

49. Dressler, "Continiung the Discourse", p. 20.

50. *Ibid.*, p. 21.

51. Online Archive of the International Congress on Medieval Studies at Western Michigan University, Kalamazoo, http://wmich.edu/medieval/congress/ (last accessed 01/11/2021).

52. *Ibid.*

53. E. Valdez de Alamo, "Lament for a Lost Queen: the Sarcophagus of Doña Blanca in Nájera", *The Art Bulletin*, 78, 2 (June 1996), pp. 311-333.

54. Dressler, "Continuing the Discourse", p. 21.

55. J.F. Hamburger, *The Visual and the Visionary. Art and Female Spirituality in Late Medieval Germany*, New York, Zone Books, 1998, p. 14.

studies and on the patronage of laywomen, these two scholars were responsible for addressing the question of female spirituality as a catalyst for the creation of religious art.[56] In 1992, their studies appeared in volume 31 of *Gesta*.[57] The articles in this issue originated as papers read at the session of the 1991 meeting of the College Art Association *Medieval Women and their Patrons. Architectural Space and Problems of Design*.[58] This publication was highly significant and marked out the scholars' respective research areas.

Hamburger's studies primarily focused on religious illuminated manuscripts, German nunneries and their visual production. In his ground-breaking book, *Nuns as Artists. The Visual Culture of a Medieval Convent*, Hamburger examined manuscripts, textiles, prints, metalwork, and other media from Benedictine nunneries in late medieval Germany.[59] He claimed that "often condemned as the naïve expression of a supposedly unsophisticated spirituality, the material culture of convents has made little headway on the high road of art history, a fate that tells us more about the discipline than about the artefacts themselves".[60] In the *Visual and the Visionary. Art and Female Spirituality in Late Medieval Germany*, published only a year later, Hamburger affirmed women's fundamental role in the construction of devotional art and the shaping of often different and contradictory visual cultures.[61] As he brilliantly summarized in this volume: "it is easy enough to romanticize female voices from the Middle Ages but it is also cynical to ignore them".[62]

While Hamburger focused on German speaking territories, Bruzelius' 1992 article in the journal *Gesta* anticipated her research on female spirituality in Italy with a particular focus on Clarissan architecture. As Carola Jäggi rightly points out in her review article, in *Hearing is Believing* Bruzelius first addressed the "thematised effect of regulations on claustration, which became increasingly rigid in the course of the thirteenth century, on the architecture and decoration of late medieval churches in women's cloisters".[63] In *Clare of Assisi. A Medieval and Modern Woman*, edited by Ingrid Peterson, Bruzelius published one of her most renowned essays entitled "Nuns in Space", a survey on the physical position occupied by nuns during the celebration of the mass.[64] However, given that nuns were often settled inside pre-

---

56. *The Cultural Patronage of Medieval Women*, ed. by J. Hall McCash, Athens, The University of Georgia Press, 1996; C. King, *Renaissance Women as Patrons Wives and Widows in Italy, 1300-1550*, Manchester, Manchester University Press, 1998.

57. Bruzelius, "Hearing is Believing", pp. 83-91; J.F. Hamburger, "Art, Enclosure and the *Cura Monialium*: Prolegomena in the Guise of a Post-Script", *Gesta*, 31, 2 (1992), pp. 108-134.

58. *Gesta*, 31, 2 (1992).

59. J.F. Hamburger, *Nuns as Artists. The Visual Culture of a Medieval Convent*, Berkeley, Berkeley University Press, 1997.

60. *Ibid.*, p. 213.

61. *Ibid.*, p. 15.

62. *Ibid.*, p. 16.

63. C. Jäggi, "Review of J. Elliott and C. Warr, eds., *The Church of Santa Maria Donna Regina. Art, Iconography and Patronage in Fourteenth-Century Naples*; C. Bruzelius, 'The Stones of Naples: Church Building in Angevin Italy, 1226-1343'", *Speculum*, 81 (2006), p. 507.

64. Bruzelius, "Nuns in Space", pp. 53-74.

existing buildings, she acknowledged the limits and the challenges entailed in the construction of a history of female conventual architecture.[65] Bruzelius, however, did advance the claim that, "the one common feature of all these churches is that generally the sisters could not obtain a full and clear view of the liturgical celebration and usually had no view at all. Thus, the religious experience consisted of hearing rather than viewing, the involvement primarily an auditory one".[66] The author reconstructed women's engagement with spirituality from a strictly physical perspective and maintained a solid archaeological basis throughout the article. Her influence is apparent in the work of other scholars such as Jeryldene Wood, who that same year published a volume on the art of the Clarissan offering a "multifaceted view of Clarissan art and spirituality".[67] While Anabel Thomas' book *Art and Piety* examines central Italian regions, namely Tuscany and Umbria in order to address the "art produced for the female gaze within an enclosed religious space [...] seeking to establish the nature of such institutions and the place of art within them".[68] Alongside Janis Elliott and Cordelia Warr, Bruzelius has also been key in reshaping the literature around the architecture of female convents in Angevin Naples (especially in relation to Santa Chiara and Santa Maria Donna Regina).[69]

More recently, as far as the architecture of female Mendicant orders is considered, Jäggi has been a major contributor in the field. Her 2006 book, *Frauenkloster im Spätmittelalter*, offers a comprehensive survey of 140 buildings across Switzerland, Germany, Italy, Slovakia, Hungary, Austria, Poland and the Czech Republic.[70] As Judith Oliver rightly points out in her book review, the volume "is meticulously researched and documented, synthesizing numerous earlier archaeological studies, monographic work on individual sites and studies of related decorative arts".[71]

The 2005 exhibition *Krone und Schleier. Kunst aus mittelalterlichen Frauenklösten* held in Bonn and Essen is generally considered a milestone for female conventual studies.[72] Defined by Corine Schleif as a "blockbuster exhibition

---

65. *Ibid.*, p. 57.
66. *Ibid.*, p. 61.
67. J.M. Wood, *Women, Art, and Spirituality. The Poor Clares of Early Modern Italy*, Cambridge, Cambridge University Press, 1996, p. 14.
68. A. Thomas, *Art and Piety in the Female Religious Communities of Renaissance Italy*, Cambridge, Cambridge University Press, 2003, p. XXIII.
69. C. Bruzelius, *The Stones of Naples. Church Building in Angevin Italy, 1266-1343*, New Haven, Yale University Press, 2004; *The Church of Santa Maria Donna Regina. Art, Iconography and Patronage in Fourteenth-Century Naples*, ed. by J. Elliott and C. Warr, Aldershot, Ashgate, 2004.
70. C. Jäggi, *Frauenklöster im Spätmittelater*, Petersberg, Michael Imhof Verlag, 2006.
71. J. Oliver, "Review of C. Jäggi, *Frauenklöster im Spätmittelater*", *Speculum*, 83, 1 (2008), p. 204. In the Italian academic context, Alfonso Marini published a survey of Clarissan houses in Latium during the thirteenth century in the journal *Collectanea Franciscana*, but did not analyse artistic or architectonic trends in these settlements, A. Marini, "Le fondazioni francescane femminili nel Lazio nel Duecento", *Collectanea Franciscana*, 63 (1993), pp. 71-96.
72. *Krone und Schleier. Kunst aus mittelalterlichen Frauenklöstern: Ruhrlandmuseum: Die frühen Klöster und Stifte 500-1200. Kunst – und Ausstellungshalle der Bundesrepublik Deutschland: Die Zeit der Orden 1200-1500*, ed. by J. Gerchow and F. Jutta, Munich, Hirmer, 2005.

with a beautifully produced catalogue", the initiative was largely responsible for bringing together for the first time an immense corpus of artistic objects produced within the space of the convent.[73] Undoubtedly, the artistic quality of these objects contributed to re-shaping and re-assessing the perception of nuns both as artists and patrons. In 2008, Columbia University Press published the revision of the 2005 exhibition catalogue in English as *Crown and Veil. Female Monasticism from the Fifth to the Fifteenth Centuries* edited by Jeffrey F. Hamburger and Susan Marti.[74] Meghan Callahan maintains that the book is very different from the catalogue, "the focus being on the history of the nuns and convents where such works were created and used" as opposed to the objects displayed in the exhibition.[75] Although largely based on the German speaking territories rather than focusing on single case studies or artefacts, the book aims to create a "broader history of convents".[76] Far from being an exhaustive survey on the agency of the convent, this work is extremely informative as it reflects both a complex and productive collaboration between pre-eminent scholars in the field (i.e. Bynum, Jäggi, Hamburger, Marti etc.).

Although the last decade has witnessed the emergence of multiple studies devoted to the analysis of female medieval spirituality, scholars such as Therese Martin are still claiming that "despite the advances of recent decades, the field continues to be, for the most part, a history of men. That is, medieval art is not approached from a position of neutrality but rather presumed to be masculine in origin and intent".[77] Gender based approaches have now been thoroughly absorbed by mainstream historiography. Martin is debating whether we can treat female patronage as an exception altogether. Indeed, the term *matronage* is gaining currency as a gendered alternative to patronage.[78]

Moving into the early modern period, Sharon Strocchia's work on Florentine nunneries and Mary Laven's on Venetian ones has contributed to a detailed portrayal of the female patronage scenario in the two artistically vibrant centres of Florence and Venice.[79] As Anna Esposito rightly points out, the past few years have witnessed a slow but steady rise in the study of medieval female agency within the space of the convent by Italian scholars.[80] This is the result

---

73. C. Schleif, "Review of *Krone und Schleier. Kunst aus mittelalterlichen Frauenklöstern*", *Speculum*, 82 (2007), p. 456.

74. *Crown and Veil. Female Monasticism from the Fifth to the Fifteenth Centuries*, ed. by J.F. Hamburger and S. Marti, New York, Columbia University Press, 2008.

75. M. Callahan, "Review of *Crown and Veil. Female Monasticism from the Fifth to the Fifteenth Centuries*", *The Burlington Magazine*, 151, 1275 (June 2009), pp. 400-401.

76. *Ibid.*, p. 401.

77. Martin, *Reassessing the Role of Women*, p. 1.

78. *Ibid.*

79. M. Laven, *Virgins of Venice*, London, Penguin Books, 2004; S. Strocchia, *Nuns and Nunneries in Renaissance Florence*, Baltimore, Johns Hopkins University Press, 2009.

80. A. Esposito, "Il mondo della religiosità femminile romana", *Archivio della Società romana di storia patria*, 132 (2009), pp. 149-172: 149. For the purpose of this section I will take into account only scholars who have focused directly on Rome. I believe this will give greater insight on the state of the research that exists on roman female religious patronage. For this reason I have

of a scholarly effort to recover the history of women's identity in late medieval society. As far as the Roman context is considered, research is still extremely fragmentary.[81] Literature on the subject is usually confined to single case studies, as the nunneries of San Cosimato and San Sisto Vecchio – investigated by Joan Barclay Lloyd and Karin Bull-Simonsen Einaudi – demonstrate.[82]

Due to the greater availability of documents and sources,[83] investigations linked to the Renaissance and the early modern period attract more attention.[84] The publications by Alessia Lirosi and Emily Dunn on conventual culture in post-Tridentine Rome are a clear example of this.[85] The 2008 conference at the Università degli Studi di Roma La Sapienza, organised by the Medieval Studies Department, was the first systematic anthology of studies dedicated to the Roman female religious experience during the late medieval period. These contributions were edited by Anna Esposito and Giulia Barone and published in the journal of the *Archivio della Società romana di storia patria* in 2009-2010.[86]

As far as Latium is concerned, San Sebastiano at Alatri was comprehensively published under the initiative of a group of fellows at The American Academy in Rome in 2005.[87] These studies share a meticulous analysis of the different building phases of the complexes with a particularly thorough survey of the masonry structure. While presenting this material to a broader audience, these collaborative works also push scholarship on medieval conventual studies towards an interdisciplinary methodology. This contributes to an exhaustive interpretation of the examined material. San Sebastiano at Alatri is also examined in Zappasodi's *Sorores reclusae. Spazi di clausura e immagini dipinte in Umbria fra XIII e XIV*

not taken into account the work of scholars like Xavier Barral i Altet, Giovanna Valenzano, Zuleika Murat, and Gabriella Zarri.

81. *Ibid.*, p. 150.

82. J. Barclay Lloyd, "The Medieval Benedictine Monastery of SS. Cosma e Damiano in Mica Aurea in Rome, c. 936-1234", *Tjurunga. An Australian Benedictine Journal*, 34 (1988), pp. 25-35; "SS. Cosma e Damiano in Mica Aurea. Architettura, storia e storiografia di un monastero romano soppresso", ed. by J. Barclay Lloyd and K. Bull-Simonsen Einaudi, *Miscellanea della Società romana di storia patria*, 38 (1998); J. Barclay Lloyd, "The Architectural Planning of Pope Innocent III's Nunnery of S. Sisto in Rome", in *Innocenzo III: Urbs et Orbis*, ed. by A. Sommerlechner, Acts of the conference (Rome, 1998), Rome, Nuovi Studi Storici, 2003, pp. 1292-1311; J. Barclay Lloyd, "Paintings for Dominican Nuns: A New Look at the Images of Saints, Scenes from the New Testament and Apocrypha, and Episodes from the Life of Saint Catherine of Siena in the Medieval Apse of San Sisto Vecchio in Rome", *Papers of the British School at Rome*, 80 (2012), pp. 189-232.

83. T. Lazzari, *Le donne nell'alto medioevo*, Milan, Mondadori, 2010, p. 9.

84. Esposito, "Il mondo della religiosità femminile", p. 150.

85. M. Dunn, "Roman Nuns, Art Patronage, and the Construction of Identity", in *Wives, Widows, Mistresses and Nuns in Early Modern Italy. Making the Invisible Visible through Art Patronage,* ed. by K.A. McIver, Farnham, Ashgate, 2012, pp. 183-224; A. Lirosi, *I monasteri femminili a Roma tra XVI e XVII secolo*, Rome, Viella, 2012.

86. *Archivio della Società romana di storia patria*, 132-133 (2009-2010).

87. *Walls and Memory. The Abbey of San Sebastiano at Alatri (Lazio) from Late Roman Monastery to Renaissance Villa*, ed. by E. Fentress, C.J. Goodson, M.L. Laird and S.C. Leone, Turnhout, Brepols, 2005.

secolo. However, as suggested by the title, the focus of his investigation is on the female religious experience in Umbria, rather than Latium.[88] The author's methodological enquiry centres around the position occupied by the choir space inside conventual churches.[89] This leads him to a comprehensive analysis of nunneries in the peninsula with a particular focus on Central Italy. He identifies three typological solutions, namely choirs *a latere*, on the counter-façade, and behind the altar.[90] Instances of "architectural experimentalism" within this context are also taken into account and as far as Latium is concerned, San Pietro in Vineis at Anagni and San Sebastiano at Alatri are examined in further detail.[91]

Issues of conventual patronage and women's place within the space of the nunnery continue to attract scholarly attention. The 2021 conference *Royal Nunneries at the Center of Medieval Europe. Art, Architecture, and Aesthetics* (11th-14th centuries) organised by the Bibliotheca Hertziana - Max Planck Institute for Art History, Rome, Czech Academy of Sciences and the University of Ostrava curated by Klára Benešovská, Tanja Michalsky, Daniela Rywiková and Elisabetta Scirocco testified to the abundance and diversity of medieval material on the subject. Until now royal monastic art and architecture has been studied according to the organisers «mostly within national academic schools resulting in separate parallel narratives of phenomena which in most cases were, in fact, related on a trans-regional scale thanks to dynastic and diplomatic connections, and also to female networks based on ties of faith and blood».[92] The conference aimed to challenge these readings and was undoubtedly responsible for generating a broader scholarly dialogue across regional and temporal barriers while exploring the manifold aspects of conventual art on a diachronic and synchronic scale. Sessions examined a number of different topics, such as networking and communications, architecture, liturgy, representation and their royal patrons. Both the diversity of, and the reference to specific internal factors avoided any generalization regarding vague references to gendered spaces and reception theories (passive enclosed communities) and to top down regionalised readings of the cloister.

Although archival material is fragmentary and information on conventual communities sparse, there is a meagre but solid body of documentary/artistic evidence on female autonomy within the space of the convent. Volumes 4 and 5 of *La pittura medievale a Roma 312-1431. Corpus e Atlante* edited by Serena Romano feature several artistic commissions both during and prior to the centuries examined in this book, which testify towards this claim.[93] The Last Judgment

---

88. Zappasodi, *Sorores*.
89. *Ibid.*, pp. 15-38.
90. *Ibid.*, pp. 15-24.
91. *Ibid.*, pp. 26-34.
92. https://events.biblhertz.it/event/43/ (last accessed 01/01/2021).
93. S. Romano, *La pittura medievale a Roma 312-1431. Corpus e Atlante*, 4, *Riforma e tradizione 1050-1198*, Milan, Jaca Book, 2006; S. Romano, *La pittura medievale a Roma 312-1431. Corpus e Atlante*, 5, *Il Duecento e la cultura gotica (1198-1280)*, Milan, Jaca Book, 2012. The author addresses this issue in section 4 "Questione di donne" of the "Introduction" to volume 5, p. 23: "Trovare informazioni su monasteri femminili romani è un'impresa ardua: a tutt'oggi, non solo

panel (1061-1071) – currently located at the Pinacoteca Vaticana of the Vatican Museums and originally found in the oratory of San Gregorio Nazianzeno – provides an invaluable testimony.[94] The painting, whose controversial chronological aspects will not be explored here, is quite exceptional in many respects.[95] It was financed and commissioned by the female religious community of Santa Maria in Campo Marzio, specifically by Constantia *abbatissa* and *domina* Benedicta *ancilla Dei*. Constantia and Benedicta are represented in the lower rectangular predella-like portion of the panel, outside the gates of heavenly Jerusalem.[96] In addition, Constantia is depicted holding a model of a small oratory, while Benedicta is represented holding a candle – a common oblation in medieval donor portraits. Not only does this artefact attest to the wealth and social status of female patrons, it also suggests their autonomy from male intermediaries. Indeed, it was highly uncommon for female patrons to be depicted on their own, in the absence of male counterparts.[97] Although this was especially true for laywomen whose portraits are almost always accompanied by those of their husbands; nuns too – as in the celebrated thirteenth-century painted cross from the monastery of Santi Domenico e Sisto in Rome – were often depicted alongside male intermediaries.

This research aims to survey female religious patronage during the late medieval period through an interdisciplinary and comprehensive analysis of both primary and secondary sources. The selected thirteen case studies include extensively published and unknown convents making this research a valuable overview of a region that has been largely neglected in the context of conventual studies. The methodology adopted here ultimately aims to showcase the role of nuns as political, social and artistic agents during the Middle Ages. This multifaceted approach will also address the role of conventual architecture in response to stricter enclosure. Planimetric reconstruction on AutoCAD will hopefully reveal and reconstruct a historical past which is no longer accessible. This process of drawing and designing plans is indebted to the pioneering work of Caroline Bruzelius on the physical implications of *clausura* during the Middle Ages. Finally, this exercise will also push forward our understanding of nunnery art in a physical space and allow us to address themes of patronage, gaze, and gender.

---

manca un panorama d'insieme sufficientemente dettagliato, ma mancano anche le indagini preliminari, in un deserto in cui spuntano soltanto casi fortunati".

94. Romano, *Riforma e tradizione*, pp. 45-55; R. Suckale, "La tavola del Giudizio Universale da Santa Maria in Campo Marzio a Roma", in *Alfa e Omega*, ed. by V. Pace, Castel Bolognese, Itaca, 2006, pp. 99-101.

95. E. Garrison, "Dating the Vatican Last Judgement Panel: Monument *versus* Document", *La bibliofilia*, 70 (1970), pp. 121-160. This is the most recent publication on the subject prior to Romano, *Riforma e tradizione*.

96. Garrison, "Dating the Vatican", p. 130.

97. F. Gandolfo, "Il ritratto di committenza", in *Arte e iconografia a Roma da Costantino a Cola di Rienzo*, ed. by M. Andaloro and S. Romano, Milan, Jaca Book, 2000, pp. 175-192; F. Gandolfo, "Il ritratto nobiliare di committenza", in *La nobiltà romana nel medioevo*, ed. by S. Carocci, Rome, École française de Rome, 2006, pp. 279-290.

3. Idealised Realities: The Onset of Nunneries in Rome

The fourth century marks the most ancient – or first recorded – group of women in the house of the Roman patrician Marcella on the Aventine.[98] According to Saint Jerome (347-420), she introduced female monasticism to the city and convinced other rich noblewomen to follow her.[99] This primitive form of monasticism took place within a domestic environment and was exclusively based on the initiative of private individuals.[100] Following the Barbarian migrations and invasions, the foundation of both male and female religious institutions close to basilicas and burial grounds became increasingly common.[101] The study of Gregory the Great's (540-604) letters is crucial to the understanding of primitive models for nunneries in Rome.[102] These documents confirm that during the sixth century, as many as 3,000 ancillae Dei were financially subsidized by the Holy See, and organized in religious communities by Pope Gregory's aunts Tarsilla, Emiliana and Gordiana.[103] An inscription dated to 514, commemorating the burial of Serena abbatissa, likely testifies that Sant'Agnese fuori le Mura was one of the earliest convents in the city.[104] During the seventh century, the Iconoclastic controversy caused the flight of many religious men and women from the Byzantine Empire, some of whom sought asylum in Rome.[105] These circumstances account for the number of Greek nunneries in the area around Campo Marzio. The displacement of Basilian nuns may also explain the presence of Byzantine icons and relics of Greek saints spread

98. *Monasticon Italiae*, 1, p. 24.
99. G. Penco, *Storia del monachesimo in Italia dalle origini alla fine del Medioevo*, Rome, Edizioni Paoline, 1961, pp. 15-21.
100. O. Bertolini, "Per la storia delle diaconie romane nell'Alto Medio Evo sino alla fine del secolo VIII", *Archivio della Società romana di storia patria*, 70 (1947), pp. 1-147.
101. *Monasticon Italiae*, 1, p. 20; G. Ferrari, *Early Roman Monasteries. Notes for the History of the Monasteries and Convents at Rome from the V through the X Century*, Vatican City, Pontificio Istituto di Archeologia Cristiana, 1957, p. 31.
102. Lirosi, *Monasteri femminili*, p. 25.
103. Gregorii I Papae, *Registrum epistolarum*, t. 2, post P. Ewaldi obitum edidit L.M. Hartmann (*Monumenta Germaniae Historica, Epistolae (in Quart)*, t. 2), Berolini, apud Weidmannos, 1899; Lirosi, *I monasteri femminili*, p. 25; P.H. Schmitz, "La première communautè de Vierges a Roma", *Revue Bénédictine*, 38 (1926), pp. 189-195.
104. V. Forcella, *Le iscrizioni delle chiese e d'altri edifici di Roma dal secolo XI fino ai nostri giorni*, XI, Rome, Cecchini, 1877, p. 346.
105. F. Antonelli, "I primi monasteri di monaci orientali in Roma", *Rivista di archeologia cristiana*, 5 (1928), pp. 105-121; F. Burgarella, "Presenze greche a Roma: aspetti culturali e religiosi", in *Roma fra Oriente e Occidente*, Spoleto, Centro Italiano di Studi sull'Alto Medioevo, 2002 (Settimane di studio del Centro Italiano di Studi sull'Alto Medioevo, 49), pp. 943-988; C.J. Goodson, *The Rome of Pope Paschal I. Papal Power, Urban Renovation, Church Rebuilding and Relic Translation, 817-824*, Cambridge, Cambridge University Press, 2010, pp. 187-192; M. McCormick, "The Imperial Edge: Italo-Byzantine Identity, Movement and Integration", in *Studies on the Internal Diaspora of the Byzantine Empire*, ed. by H. Ahrweiler and A. Laiou, Cambridge, Harvard University Press, 1998, pp. 17-52; A. Ekonomou, *Byzantine Rome and the Greek Popes*, Plymouth, Lexington Books, 2007; J.M. Sansterre, "Les moines grecs et orientaux à Rome aux époques byzantine et carolingienne (milieu du VIe s.-fin du IXe s.)", *Mémoires de la classe des lettres*, 2, 661 (1983).

throughout the churches of Rome.[106] The translation of bodies inside the city walls from the Catacombs, called for the renovation and construction of both male and female monastic enclosures.[107] By the ninth century, ten nunneries existed inside the Aurelian walls.[108] Apart from their mention in the *Liber pontificalis*, under the papacy of Leo III (795-816), very little is known on their origins and traditions.[109] To a certain extent, the tenth century marks what is generally viewed as the turning point for both male and female monasticism. This change came about with the visit of Odo of Cluny (878-942) in the summer of 936. Under the aegis of Count Alberic II (932-954), ruler of Rome, Odo of Cluny reformed several nunneries.[110] Although the eleventh and twelfth centuries witnessed the emergence of new forms of religious spirituality, as far as Rome was concerned, the majority of female convents remained faithful to the Benedictine rule.[111]

During the thirteenth century Roman nunneries underwent a period of extensive transformation.[112] The IV Council of the Lateran (1215) summoned by Innocent III (1198-1216) forbade the creation of new religious orders, a decree which was only partially followed in view of the establishment of both the Franciscans (Clarissan) and the Dominicans.[113] Additionally, it was under Innocent's pontificate that enclosure emerged as the essential characteristic of a good nunnery.[114] According to Vladimir Koudelka, the lax lifestyle enjoyed by most Roman monasteries caused frequent scandal amongst high-ranking ecclesiastics at the beginning of the thirteenth century.[115] Innocent envisaged a *coenobium universalis* to gather all nuns from existing Roman convents.[116] To a certain extent, this was also a quick-fix to the problem of the Bizoke, women who conducted a semi-religious lifestyle

---

106. G.D. Gordini, "Origini e sviluppo del monachesimo a Roma", *Gregorianum*, 37 (1956), pp. 220-260.

107. C.J. Goodson, "The Relic Translation of Paschal I (817-824): Transforming City and Cult", in *Roman Bodies*, ed. by A. Hopkins and M. Wyke, Rome, British School at Rome, 2005, pp. 123-141: 123-125; 135-136.

108. *Monasticon Italiae*, 1, pp. 22-23; Lirosi, *I monasteri femminili*, p. 25.

109. *Ibid.*

110. *Monasticon Italiae*, 1, p. 25.

111. *Ibid.*, p. 26; R. Manselli, "Certosini e cistercensi", in *Il monachesimo e la riforma ecclesiastica (1049-1122)*, Acts of the conference (Passo della Mendola, 1968), Milan, Vita e Pensiero, 1971, pp. 79-104.

112. S. Sibilia, *Bonifacio VIII*, Rome, Edizioni Paoline, 1949, p. 35.

113. R. Foreville, *Latran I, II, III et Latran IV*, Paris, Editions de L'Orante, 1965, pp. 225-317; *The History of Medieval Cannon Law during the Classical Period (1140-1234)*, ed. by W. Hartmann and K. Pennington, New York, The Catholic University of America Press, 2008; E. Petrucci, *Ecclesiologia e papato*, Rome, Carocci, 2001, p. 45.

114. F. Accrocca, *L'identità complessa*, Padua, Centro Studi Antoniniani, 2014, p. 24; V.J. Koudelka, "Le 'monasterium Tempuli' et la fondation dominicaine de San Sisto", *Archivum Fratrum Praedicatorum* (1963), p. 47; J. Sayers, *Innocenzo III*, Rome, Viella, 1997, p. 23.

115. Koudelka, "Le 'monasterium Tempuli'", p. 47.

116. Barclay Lloyd, "Paintings for Dominican Nuns", p. 190; Koudelka, "Le 'monasterium Tempuli'", p. 44; R. Spiazzi, *Cronache e fioretti del monastero di San Sisto all'Appia*, Bologna, Edizione Studio Domenicano, 1993, pp. 109-114.

and were enjoying great popularity in Central Italy.[117] Amongst others, this is testified by Benedetto da Montefiascone, a Dominican chronicler who composed the *Registrum notabilium rerum ac negotiorum monasterii Santi Sixti de Urbe*, a collection of papal bulls regarding the aforementioned nunnery at the turn of the thirteenth century.[118] Although Innocent died before completing his ambitious project of unification, his legacy was carried out by Pope Honorius III (1216-1227).[119] Likewise, in a papal bull from 1232, we learn that Gregory IX (1227-1241) also thought that Roman nunneries were in need of serious reform.[120] For this reason, he instructed the archbishop of the church of Santi Ciro e Giovanni to visit and reform the nunneries of Sant'Agnese, Santa Bibiana, Sant'Andrea de Biberatica, Santi Ciriaco e Niccolò in Via Lata, Santa Maria de Maxima and Santa Maria in Campo Marzio. Furthermore, Pope Nicholas III (1277-1280) called for a similar reform in 1278.[121] Throughout this century, the thrive and popularity of Mendicant orders made their female counterparts centres for aristocratic recruitment.[122] Out of the three communities in Rome two (San Lorenzo in Panisperna and San Silvestro in Capite; Santi Cosma e Damiano in Mica Aurea originally male Benedictine became Clarissan only after a papal decree promoted by Gregory IX) were founded by the powerful Colonna family.[123] However, the thirteenth century was not only characterized by the rise of the Mendicant orders. Indeed, the Benedictines, under an unexpected revival carried out by Santuccia Carabotti, which eventually gave rise to the *Congregatio Servarum Beatae Mariae Virginis*, also enjoyed a period of great reform and prosperity.[124] Santuccia was in charge of various congregations, and in 1287 established herself in Santa Maria in Iulia. Under the concession from the Master of the Temple of Rome, Fra Giacomo Malleio, her nuns were allowed inside the monastery around 1290.[125] She died in 1305 and Santa Maria in Iulia was instituted as the residence for the supreme abbess of the congregation.[126] In Rome, the *Santucce* were in charge of other monasteries including Santa Maria in

---

117. B. Bolton, "Daughters of Rome: All One in Christ Jesus!", in *Women in the Church*, ed. by W.J. Sheils and D. Wood, Oxford, Blackwell, 1990, p. 106.

118. "Innocentius papa III monasterium Sancti Sixti cum devotione animi de bonis Ecclesiae aedificare cepit, ut mulieres Urbis et moniales aliorum monasteriorum Urbis per diversa vagantes possenti bi sub arcta clausura et diligenti custodia Domino familari", in Koudelka, "Le 'monasterium Tempuli'", p. 39; T. Kaeppeli, "Dalle pergamene di S. Maria in Gradi di Viterbo", *Archivum Fratrum Praedicatorum*, 33 (1963), p. 250.

119. J. Claussen, *Papst Honorius III (1216-1227)*, Hildesheim, Olms, 2004; P.N.R. Zutshi, "Letters of Pope Honorius III Concerning the Order of Preachers", in *Pope, Church and City*, ed. by F. Andrews, B. Brenda and C. Eggar, Leiden, Brill, 2004, pp. 269-286.

120. *Monasticon Italiae*, 1, pp. 22-23.

121. *Ibid.*, p. 27.

122. G. Barone, "Federico II e gli Ordini Mendicanti", in *Federico II e l'arte del Duecento italiano*, ed. by A.M. Romanini, Lecce, Congedo, 1981, p. 179; Marini, "Monasteri femminili", p. 90.

123. S. Romano, "I Colonna a Roma", in *La nobiltà romana nel Medioevo*, pp. 291-312.

124. *Monasticon Italiae*, 1, p. 28.

125. *Santità femminile nel Duecento*, Acts of the conference (Cingoli, 1999), ed. by G. Avarucci, Ancona, Studia Picena, 2001.

126. *Ibid.*, p. 74.

Isola (which after the suppression of San Giovanni Battista by order of the papal decree issued by Urban V (1362-1370) in 1381, eventually became San Giovanni Calibita), Sant'Ambrogio della Massima, Sant'Eufemia inside the church of Santa Pudenziana and Santa Maria Liberatrice.[127]

The end of the thirteenth century is marked by the *Periculoso* decree (1298) and the enforcement of a rigid *clausura*.[128] This was confirmed by the encyclical *Apostolicae sedis* of Pope Clement V in 1309.[129] Marilyn Dunn affirms that enclosure was long-established practice dating back to patristic times.[130] Women's morality had to be protected through spiritual perfection, which was practically ensured via the use of architecture. Indeed, the nuns' purity guaranteed their effectiveness as intercessors with God. Although frequently disobeyed, especially by the members of those orders (like the Benedictine) that did not prescribe it formally, *clausura* became the prevailing characteristic for nunhood. While there was always a gap between the ideal and the reality of forced enclosure, it obviously affected nunneries both on a symbolic and practical level.[131]

According to *Il Catalogo di Torino*, an anonymous manuscript compiled around 1320, currently found at the University of Turin (code EV 17): in Rome, 470 nuns were spread out between 14 monasteries: Sant'Andrea de Biberatica (15 nuns), Sant'Urbano (18 nuns), Sant'Agnese fuori le Mura (40 nuns), Santi Ciriaco di Camilliano (40 nuns), Santa Maria in Campo Marzio (17 nuns), Santa Maria de Cella (8 nuns), Santa Caterina (8 nuns), Sant'Eufemia (4 nuns), Santa Maria in Petrochia (15 nuns), Sant' Anna di Marmorata (4 nuns), Sant' Erasmo (16 nuns), Santa Bibiana (18 nuns), Santa Maria in Iulia (40 nuns), Santa Maria di Massima (12 nuns), and San Pancrazio (35 nuns).[132]

---

127. *Monasticon Italiae*, 1, p. 28.

128. "Periculoso et detestabili [...] praesenti constitutione perpetuo irrefragabiliter valitura sancimus, universas et singulas moniales, praesentes atque futuras, cuiuscumque religionis sint vel ordinis, in quibuslibet mundi partibus exsistentes, sub perpetua in suis monasteriis debere de cetero permanere clausura" [Dangerous and accursed [...] in perpetuity, without the possibility of alteration, all and single nuns, present and future of any congregation and order, in any part of the world they reside, must observe perpetual enclosure], *Corupus Iuris Canonici*, 1, Graz, Akademische Druck- u. Verlagsanstalt, 1959, pp. 1053-1054; J.A. Brundage, E. Makowski, "Enclosure of Nuns: The Decretal *Periculoso* and Its Commentators", *Journal of Medieval History*, 20 (1994), pp. 143-155. According to Zappasodi, *Sorores*, p. 10: "Le nuove disposizioni rendevano ora gli spazi claustrali impenetrabili, tanto alle monache che non potevano più abbandonarli, quanto agli esterni a cui interdetto l'accesso senza licenza speciale: i passaggi furono chiusi, le finestre ferrate, la sola porta di accesso serata perennemente con due differenti serrature. [...] Le conseguenze della *Periculoso* furono notevoli. Le religiose a indirizzo eremitico furono costrette ad abbandonare I propri romitori per trasferirsi all'interno della cerchia ubica e si rese necessaria e vincolante un'architettura monastica che permettesse una vita comunitaria nel pieno rispetto della clausura rigorosa".

129. G. Paolin, *Lo spazio del silenzio. Monacazioni forzate, clausura e proposte di vita religiosa femminile nell'età moderna*, Pordenone, Biblioteca dell'Immagine, 1996, p. 12.

130. Dunn, "Roman Nuns", p. 151.

131. C. Rendina, *I papi*, Rome, Newton & Compton, 1990, p. 79.

132. "Il Catalogo di Torino", pp. 411-439.

In addition to the enforced enclosure imposed amongst Roman nunneries, at the death of Pope Benedict XI (d. 1304) the papal seat was vacated from the city for more than seventy years. The return of the pope from Avignon to Rome in 1377 with Gregory XI contributed to a massive crisis amongst the college of cardinals. Until the election of Martin V in 1417 the Church of Rome had two and sometimes three spiritual leaders. The palpable tensions inside the Curia were not the only cause for social instability in Trecento Rome. Indeed, the Black Death of 1348 was a major factor in shaping fourteenth-century mentality. However, the major social crisis caused by the plague is interpreted by contemporary scholarship in different and contrasting ways. Through the analysis of fourteenth-century wills Samuel Cohn argues for a greater attachment to material goods.[133] In contrast, Barone identifies a greater spirituality and a major adhesion to religious congregations as ultimately contributing to the popularity of Tertiary movements.[134] Barone nevertheless claims that Rome underwent a period of profound religious crisis characterized by spiritual incertitude and tragic political lacerations.[135] From an economic standpoint, both the Black Death and the residence of the papal seat in Avignon implied a lower availability of funds for female monastic institutions in Rome.[136] This, however, was likely compensated by the greater influence exercised on these institutions by local baronial families, who guaranteed sizeable dowries to female members joining these communities. Nuns received a monthly allowance from their families, owned property and were allowed to travel outside the convent (this matter was of great controversy among the Dominicans who required nuns to observe a strict *clausura*).[137] Whether this money was also destined for the embellishment of the convent will be discussed further on in this investigation.

However, recent scholarship has re-evaluated the general misconception that Rome fell into a cultural paralysis as a result of the Avignon period.[138] According to Claudia Bolgia there is a veritable absence, «a missing link in a chain of continuity and change, one that can no longer be overlooked». While this study aims to salvage this long-lost history, it also acknowledges the objective fragmentation of primary sources, which has produced an uneven relationship to secondary literature, both

---

133. S.K. Cohn, "Renaissance Attachment to Things: Material Culture in Last Wills and Testaments", *Economic History Review*, 65 (2012), pp. 984-990; S.K. Cohn, *Cultures of the Plague*, Oxford, Oxford University Press, 2010.

134. G. Barone, "Chierici, monaci, frati", in *Storia di Roma dall'antichità a oggi*, 2, *Roma medievale*, ed. by A. Vauchez, Rome-Bari, Laterza, 2001, pp. 187-212: 211.

135. *Ibid.*, p. 211.

136. Romano, *Eclissi di Roma*, p. 12.

137. Carbonetti Vendittelli, "Il registro", p. 97.

138. S. Carocci, "Barone e podestà. L'aristocrazia romana e gli uffici comunali nel Due-Trecento", in *I podestà dell'Italia comunale. Reclutamento e circolazione degli ufficiali forestieri (fine XII sec.-metà XIV sec.)*, ed. by J.C. Maire Vigueur, Rome, École Française de Rome, 2000, p. 865; A. Rehberg, "Roma Docta? Osservazioni sulla cultura del clero dei grandi capitoli romani del Trecento", *Archivio della Società romana di storia patria*, 122 (1999), pp. 164-167; Romano, *Eclissi di Roma*, p. 7.

in the pre- and post-Avignon years.[139] Sandro Carocci too pushes back against this interpretation, advocating against the inadequacy of an old stereotype of a brutal and uncultivated baronage now obvious, but rather the surprising vastness of its cultural interests and knowledge.[140] Nunneries acted as recruitment centres for these powerful baronial families. In contrast to Angevin Naples where the royal family economically supported female monasticism, Roman nunneries were divided according to territorial divisions of familial power. This trend extended to convents in the greater Latium area too. By the second half of the thirteenth century, the baronial centre was made up of a few lineages and to a certain extent, "convents of this era remained largely – though not exclusively – the preserve of the upper classes".[141]

The selection of five Roman case studies stems from the intention of showcasing the high level of both artistic and architectonic sophistication in the pre- and post-Avignon years. Although these convents are not new to the secondary scholarship, I analysed them in an interdisciplinary fashion with a view to organically reason around their original medieval *facies*. I have also visualised these spaces through architectural reconstructions on AutoCAD. This has deepened my understanding of these foundations and simultaneously enabled me to contextualize art objects. Unfortunately, given Rome's complex architectural stratification this was not always possible. Ultimately, the data gathered throughout the analysis of architectural, artistic and archival remains contributes to the research on Rome in two crucial centuries of its history. The second chapter of this book will open with the convent of Sant'Agnese fuori le Mura. This nunnery was selected for my first case study for a number of reasons. These include, its early foundation date, its complex history, and its recent pictorial findings. San Sisto Vecchio will follow as the first female Dominican house in Rome. The survival of an abundant corpus of documentary and artistic evidence makes this one of the most compelling case studies in terms of reconstructions. The Roman section will close with the analysis of San Cosimato, San Silvestro in Capite and San Lorenzo in Panisperna, all belonging to the Clarissan order. San Lorenzo in Panisperna and San Silvestro in Capite were both endorsed by Giacomo Colonna, brother of the beatified Margherita Colonna, while San Cosimato was entrusted to the Poor Clares by Pope Gregory IX. It is significant that these three convents were originally Clarissan, bearing witness to the popularity of the Mendicants in the late medieval period, as recently exemplified in Bolgia's monographic study on Santa Maria on the Aracoeli in Rome.[142]

139. C. Bolgia, "The "Long" Trecento: Rome Without the Popes, c. 1305-1420", Members' Research Report Archive, Washington DC, National Gallery of Art, 2016-2017, pp. 61-63.
140. Carocci, *Baroni di Roma*, p. 114.
141. E. Lehfeldt, "The Permeable Cloister", in *The Ashgate Research Companion*, p. 14.
142. C. Bolgia, *Reclaiming the Roman Capitol: Santa Maria in Aracoeli from the Altar of Augustus to the Franciscans, c. 500-1450*, London, Routledge, 2017.

2. Roman Nunneries

1. *Female Power and Prestige:*
The Extraordinary Case of Sant'Agnese fuori le Mura

The monumental complex of Sant'Agnese fuori le Mura abuts over a small hilltop off the Via Nomentana on the outskirts of central Rome. Originally the site of a proto-Christian cemetery and of the burial of Saint Agnes herself, the area underwent a period of extensive development during the transition of the Roman Empire from paganism to Christianity.[1] The initiative – undertaken via imperial patronage – was promoted both by Emperor Constantine (272-337) and his daughter Constantia (307-354) during the first half of the fourth century (ca. 337-350). The site originally included the Constantinian basilica, the mausoleum of Santa Costanza, and a *sacellum ad corpus* on the burial grounds of the saint.[2] Given the popularity of this female martyr and the political agenda of Christianization of the *Urbis Romae* promoted by the Emperor, the impressive scale of this enterprise is not surprising. Indeed, a substantial number of suburban basilicas,

---

1. Armellini, *Le chiese di Roma*, p. 858; G. Fabricius, *Roma. Antiquitatum libri duo*, Basel, Oporin, 1550, p. 214; H. Brandenburg, *Die frühchristlichen Kirchen in rom von 4. bis zum 7. Jahrhundert. der Beginn der abendländischen Kirchenbau- Kunst*, Regensburg, Schnell & Steiner, 2013; A.P. Frutaz, *Il complesso monumentale di Sant'Agnese*, Vatican City, Tipografia Poliglotta Vaticana, 1960.

2. F.W. Deichmann, "Die Lage der konstantinischen Basilika der heiligen Agnes an der Via Nomentana", *Rivista di archeologia cristiana*, 22 (1946), pp. 213-234; S. Corbett, W. Frankl, R. Krautheimer, *Corpus basilicarum christianarum Romae. The Early Christian Basilicas of Rome (4.-9. cent.)*, 1, Vatican City, Pontificio Istituto di Archeologia Cristiana, 1937, pp. 14-38; O. Panvinio, *Schedae de Ecclesiis Urbis Romae*, Biblioteca Apostolica Vaticana (hereafter BAV), Vat. lat. 6780, fol. 278r (transcription in S. Pesarini, *Appunti, copie, estratti e schede riguardanti in massima parte le chiese di Roma*, BAV, Vat. lat. 13127, fol. 454r); P. Ugonio, *Compendio del Theatro della città di Roma*, BAV, Barb. lat. 2160, fols. 129v, 130r (transcription in Pesarini, *Appunti, copie, estratti e schede*, BAV, Vat. lat. 13127, fols. 456r, 456v); P. Ugonio, *Theatrum Urbis Romae*, 1594, Ferrara, Biblioteca Comunale Ariostea, Classe I. 161, fol. 966 (transcription in Pesarini, *Appunti, copie, estratti e schede*, BAV, Vat. lat. 13127, fol. 458r); P. Ugonio, *Theatrum Urbis Romae*, 1594, Ferrara, Biblioteca Comunale Ariostea, Classe I. 161, fol. 966 (transcription in Pesarini, *Appunti, copie, estratti e schede*, BAV, Vat. lat. 13127, fol. 458r). For a tentative reconstruction of the Masoleum of Santa Costanza see Andaloro, *La pittura medievale a Roma. Atlante. Percorsi visivi*, 1.

such as San Lorenzo fuori le Mura on Via Tiburtina or Santi Pietro e Marcellino on Via Casilina testify to the popularity of early Christian shrines outside the city walls.[3] By the beginning of the seventh century, both the basilica and mausoleum lay in a state of semi-abandonment, and were deemed unfit to fulfil daily cultic practices by Pope Honorius I (625-638).[4] This is what appears to have motivated Honorius to build a new and comparatively smaller edifice over the saint's burial shrine. According to Richard Krautheimer, the original building on top of Agnes' tomb had a rectangular plan terminating in a semi-circular apse.[5] This was confirmed by early twentieth-century excavations conducted by Augusto Bacci. While Bacci's findings were rather inconsistent with the actual remains of the original funerary shrine, his observations were crucial in unveiling the complex stratification of the semi-hypogeum basilica on site.[6] Today the edifice unfolds on a rectangular plan divided into three naves terminating in three apses (only the central one survives to date). The internal space is articulated on two floors with suspended galleries along the three sides of the perimeter. These two levels were not connected by an internal passage or staircase but were accessed directly from the exterior at street level. Indeed, although the present-day basilica has been heavily affected by the seventeenth-century radical restorations undertaken by Cardinal Alessandro Medici (1535-1605) – who literally exhumed the church from its tufa block – we need to keep in mind that it originally only surfaced above ground up to the second gallery level. Therefore, the suspended galleries over the side aisles, or *matroneum*, were originally destined for the pilgrims as a deambulatory around the martyr's tomb, and possibly functioned as the female religious community's choir from the thirteenth century onwards. The model held by Honorius in the apsidal mosaic commissioned by the pope himself gives us an idea of the church's seventh-century appearance.[7] As Antonella Ballardini rightly observes: "the immersion of the building in the hill is realistically evoked even in the apse mosaic, where the model presented by Pope Honorius is partially hidden by the chasuble, emerging only at the height of the galleries and clerestory".[8] A proud Saint Agnes stands next to the pope wearing a purple tunic and *maniàkion*

---

3. R. Krautheimer, *Rome. Profile of a City, 312-1308*, Princeton, Princeton University Press, 1980.

4. *Le Liber pontificalis. Texte, introduction et commentaire par l'abbé L. Duchesne*, 3 vols., Paris, de Boccard, 1981, I, p. 323; C. Cecchelli, *Sant'Agnese fuori le mura e Santa Costanza*, Rome, Danesi, 1961; R. Valentini, G. Zucchetti, *Codice topografico della città di Roma*, 4 vols., Rome, Istituto Storico Italiano per il Medioevo, 1940.

5. Krautheimer, *Corpus basilicarum*, p. 32; A. Bacci, "Ulteriori osservazioni sulla basilica nomentana", *Rivista di archeologia cristiana* (1906), pp. 77-87; A. Bosio, *Roma sotterranea*, Rome, appresso Guglielmo Facciotti, 1632, p. 312.

6. Bacci, "Ulteriori osservazioni"; A. Bacci, "Scavi nel cimitero e nella basilica di S. Agnese", *Rivista di archeologia cristiana* (1902), pp. 222-297.

7. Krautheimer, *Corpus basilicarum*; L. Covello, "Ipotesi ricostruttiva dei sistemi di accesso della Basilica Onoriana di Sant'Agnese fuori le mura", *Augustinianum*, 58, 2 (2018), pp. 511-531.

8. A. Ballardini, "*Habeas Corpus*: Agnese nella basilica di via Nomentana", in *«Di Bisanzio dirai ciò che è passato, ciò che passa e che sarà». Scritti in onore di Alessandra Guiglia*, ed. by S. Pedoni and A. Paribeni, Rome, Bardi edizioni, 2018, p. 258.

over the preciously adorned gemmed *loros*.⁹ As far as the identification of the pope to Agnes' left is considered various hypothesis have been put forward. These range from Gregory the Great (540-604) to Symmachus (498-514), who was responsible for the previous restoration of the saint's burial site.[10]

Despite being heavily restored in the sixteenth century, the monumental staircase connecting the basilica to the monastery today was already in place from the onset. This has been demonstrated by recent studies undertaken by Emanuele Gambuti.[11] It served as a passageway between the different levels of the monumental complex, namely the Constantinian basilica (the so called *circiforme*) and the tomb. Through careful reading of the *Gesta Innocentii* (ca. 1220) and Onofrio Panvinio's accounts of the basilica, Gambuti identifies the steep passage with a *porticus ecclesiae* richly adorned with "pavimenta marmorea tesselatea et porphyreticis orbibus ornata".[12] This passaged corridor guaranteed direct access to the ground floor of the Honorian basilica. Indeed, it formed an integral part of the new construction fulfilling processional and liturgical functions.[13] As we shall examine later on in this study, the church and the adjacent monastery underwent a period of extensive restoration and lavish reconstruction during the thirteenth century. It is possible that the mosaic carpet cited by Panvinio indicated a path which wound from the female medieval Benedictine nunnery to the staircase, into the narthex and then, turning ninety degrees along the main nave, through the *schola cantorum* and beyond the *pergula*, around the altar to the papal chair at the bottom of the apse.[14] The 1256 renovations should, in my opinion, be read in light of these recent findings. In fact, the planimetric dispositions of the Honorian basilica and the pictorial, sculptural and liturgical testimonies of the 1256 "re-consecration" of the church grant us the rare opportunity of reconstructing a female Benedictine convent almost in its integrity over several centuries of its history. We shall therefore proceed by providing a detailed analysis of the Benedictine female occupation of the complex including its living monastic quarters.

During the fifth century, the basilica's daily religious functions were officiated by a college of canons under the title of Vestina or San Vitale (the sources are unclear on this point) while a group of Greek nuns acted as the keepers of the relics and the tomb.[15] This claim is possibly corroborated by a sixth-century

9. *Ibid.*, p. 271.
10. For the most recent and comprehensive analysis on the matter see M. Gianandrea, "Il doppio papa nelle decorazioni absidali del Medioevo romano", in *Le plaisir de l'art du Moyen Âge*, ed. by R. Alcoy, D. Allios and X. Barral i Altet, Paris, Picard, 2012, pp. 637-643.
11. E. Gambuti, "*Porticus Ecclesiae Sanctae Agnetis:* lo scalone di accesso alla basilica onoriana", *Quaderni dell'Istituto di Storia dell'Architettura* (2015), pp. 5-18. E. Gambuti, "Ricondurre all'ordine un'antica fabbrica: l'opera del cardinale Alessandro de' Medici in Sant'Agnese fuori le mura", *Palladio. Rivista di Storia dell'Architettura*, 65-66 (2020), pp. 123-146.
12. Gambuti, "*Porticus Ecclesiae Sanctae Agnetis*", p. 8; Anon., *Gesta Innocentii III*, in *Spicilegium Romanum*, ed. by A. Mai, VI, Rome, typis Collegii urbani, 1841, pp. 300-312; Panvinio, *Schedae de Ecclesiis Urbis Romae*, BAV, Vat. lat. 6780, fol. 278r.
13. Ballardini, "*Habeas Corpus*", p. 260; Gambuti, "*Porticus Ecclesiae Sanctae Agnetis*", p. 8.
14. *Ibid.*, p. 13.
15. Frutaz, *Il complesso monumentale*, p. 93.

funerary inscription, which testifies to the burial of Serena *abbatissa* in 514.[16] The replacement of a Greek nunnery by a Benedictine one during the papacy of Paschal I (817-824) is not supported by substantial evidence. However, coeval documents do mention Pope Leo III's (795-816) donation of a silver *canistrum* to the female religious community of Sant'Agnese, thus confirming that by the ninth century there was an active female community on site.[17] In 1112, Paschal II (1099-1118) installed a group of Benedictine nuns who occupied the complex for over three and a half centuries until they were replaced by a community of monks in 1480.[18] Today the monastery is officiated by the Canons Regular of the Lateran. Throughout the centuries, the basilica has been the subject of extensive restoration plans. Its present form therefore reflects the radical overhauls that the complex underwent during the sixteenth and nineteenth centuries.

The monastery of Sant'Agnese abuts the southwestern side of the present-day basilica. It is comprised of five distinct bodies: the dormitories, the rectory of Pius IX, the medieval wing, the original stairway from the burial site to the Constantinian basilica, and a tower (Fig. 1).[19] The planimetric disposition of the buildings creates two cloisters respectively destined for the public and private use of the religious community today. In the Middle Ages, particularly during the thirteenth and fourteenth centuries, the monastery's fabric underwent major constructive changes.[20] This was partly due to Frederick II's (1194-1250) turbulent relationship with the Holy See, which gave rise to political unrest around the city of Rome, and called for an adequate defence system.[21] Indeed, in an image by Baldassare Peruzzi (1481-1537), the exterior of Sant'Agnese resembles a citadel incorporating a defensive tower and crenelated walls.[22] The political instability that characterized medieval Rome transformed most rural monasteries into fortified complexes.[23] Today, the convent of the Santi Quattro Coronati on the Caelian Hill offers a unique insight into the medieval structural and architectural trends of these monasteries.[24] Patrizia Saini and Davide Ravignani, who worked on the 2004 restorations funded by the Ministry of Culture, agree that the important renovations at Sant'Agnese that culminated in the 1256 consecration came as a result of the political and military instability of this extra-mural site.[25] The radical

---

16. Forcella, *Le iscrizioni delle chiese e d'altri edifici di Roma*, p. 346.
17. Frutaz, *Il complesso monumentale*, p. 94.
18. *Ibid.*, p. 34.
19. A.P. Frutaz, *Le piante di Roma*, 3, Vatican City, Tipografia Poliglotta Vaticana, 1962.
20. P. Saini, D. Ravignani, "Il Convento di S. Agnese: origini ed età medievale", in *La basilica costantiniana di S. Agnese. Lavori archeologici e di restauro*, ed. by C. Magnani Cianetti and C. Pavolini, Milan, Electa, 2004, p. 58.
21. D. Abulafia, *Federico II*, Turin, Einaudi, 2006, p. 83.
22. Saini, Ravignani, "Il Convento di S. Agnese", p. 58.
23. P. Venturini, "La descrizione dell'edificio: la lettura del rilievo e delle sue componenti geometrico-proporzionali", in *La basilica costantiniana*, p. 37.
24. P. Manzi, *Il convento fortificato dei SS. Quattro Coronati nella storia e nell'arte*, Rome, Arma del Genio, 1968, p. 150.
25. Saini, Ravignani, "Il Convento di S. Agnese", p. 59.

refurbishments inside the basilica are reported by an inscription, originally found in the choir but currently sited in the stairway that connects the church to the convent.

In the year of the Lord 1256 on the declaration of the 14th indiction on that day in which the terrestrial burial of the blessed Vitalis is celebrated [28 April] Pope Alexander with the entire Curia consecrated in the church of Sant'Agnese three altars, and precisely/namely the altar of John the Baptist in which the relics of many saints are reposed/hidden/covered, the altar of the blessed John the Evangelist where there is his sepulchre which preserves/released manna and the relics of many saints, the altar of the blessed Emerenziana in which there are the relics of the Saints Saturnino and Sisinio and of many others. Conceding [by Pope Alexander] to all who are truly penitent and confessed and that annually visit this site three years and three quadragenes of indulgences. At this consecration were the cardinal-bishop Stefanus [Stefano Vancsa] of Prenestnus [Prenestino], the cardinal-bishop [Eudes of Châteauroux] of Tusculunus [Tuscolano], Ugo [of St Cher] cardinal priest Santa Sabina, Iohannes [John from Toledo] cardinal priest San Lorenzo in Lucina, cardinal-deacon Iohannis [Giovanni Gaetano Orsini] San Nicòla in Carcere Tulliano, Petrus [Pietro Capocci] San Giorgio al Vello Aureo, Octavianus (Ottaviano Ubaldini) Santa Maria in Via Lata, cardinal-deacon Octobonis [Ottobono Fieschi] San Adriano, bishop Sclavinensis [of the Slavs?], bishop Marocensis [Orthodox/Maronite?][26] and many other religious and honest men. Resident Domna Lucia abbess of this monastery, Theodora prioress domna Jacoba devout sacristan with the entire convent were also present and left/opened their monastery to those honest/pure at heart/soul.[27]

The inscription declares that in 1256, three altars were consecrated in the presence of Pope Alexander IV (1254-1261) and a large group of senior ecclesiastics (Figs. 2-3). The solemnity of the celebration was indicated by the presence of the

---

26. To date with my current research I was not able to identify San Adriano, bishop Sclavinensis and bishop Marocensis; future investigations could possibly clear this point.

27. ANNO DOMINI MCCLVI INDICTIONE XIV EO DIE QUO STATIO BEATI VITALIS CELEBRATUR DOMINUS ALEXANDER PAPA IV CUM TOTA CURIA CONSECRAVIT IN HAC ECCLESIA SANCTE AGNETIS TRIA ALTARIA VIDELICET ALTARE BEATI IOHANNIS BAPTISTE IN QUO RELIQUIAS MULTORUM SANCTORUM RECONDIDIT ALTARE BEATI IOHANNIS EVANGELISTE IN QUO EST DE MANNA SEPULCRI EIUS CUM RELIQUIIS MULTORUM SANCTORUM ALTARE BEATE EMERENTIANE IN QUO SUNT DE RELIQUIIS SANCTORUM SATURNINI SISINII ALIORUM MULTORUM CONCEDENS OMNIBUS VEREPENITENTIBUS ET CONFESSIS ANNUATIM AD HUNC LOCUM ACCEDENTIBUS USQUE AD TRES ANNOS TRES QUADRAGENAS HUIC CONSECRATIONI INTERFUERUNT STEFANUS EPISCOPUS PENESTRINUS EPISCOPUS TUSCULNUS UGO TITULI SANCTE SABINE IOHANNES SANCTI LAURENTII IN LUCINA PRESBITERI CARDINALES IOHANNIS SANCTI NICOLAI IN CARCERE TULLIANO PETRUS SANCTI GEORGII AD VELLUM AUREUM OCTAVIANUS SANCTE MARIE IN VIA LATA OCTOBONIS SANCTI ADRIANI DIACONES CARDINALES LAURENTIUS EPISCOPUS SCLAVINENSIS EPISCOPUS MAROCENSIS CUM ALIIS PLURIBUS RELIGIOSIS VIRI HONESTIS RESIDENTE DOMNA LUCIA ABBATISSA HUIUS MONASTERII THEODORA PRIORISSA DOMNA JACOBA DEVOTA MONIALI SACRISTA CUM TOTO CONVENTU IPSIUS MONASTERII RELASARUNT RECTIS CORDE: Forcella, *Le iscrizioni delle chiese*, 9, p. 350; P.C. Claussen, *Die Kirchen der Stadt Rom im Mitterlater, 1050-1300. A-F (Corpus Cosmatorum II, 1: Forschungen zur Kunstgeschichte und christlichen Archaeologie)*, Stuttgart, Steiner, 2002, p. 55; S. Romano, "Agnese e le altre donne. Marmi e pitture del Duecento romano", in *Attorno al Cavallini. Frammenti del gotico a Roma nei Musei Vaticani*, ed. by T. Strinati, Milan, Jaca Book, 2008, p. 23.

future Popes Giovanni Gaetano Orsini (later Nicholas III) and Ottobono Fieschi (later Adrian V), the powerful Cistercian cardinal John of Toledo, the influential Roman noble Pietro Capocci, and all the cardinals (excluding Riccardo Annibaldi) promoted during the rule of Innocence IV.[28] The inscription goes on to state that the entire female monastic community was present and mentions three members by name: Lucia, Theodora and Jacoba. Serena Romano rightly observes that there is no mention of a *presbyter* or a *praepositus*, nor indeed of any male intermediary between the monastic community and senior representatives of the Roman Curia.[29] Although this may seem surprising, it was not an uncommon practice during the twelfth and thirteenth centuries. Like their German counterparts, female monastic communities in Rome were less reclusive than is generally understood today.[30] This is especially true in the case of nunneries that were aristocratic foundations. As the monasteries in Via Lata or the area around Campo Marzio demonstrate, women were allowed private apartments, servants as well as a monetary maintenance, and could freely circulate outside the convent's walls.[31]

When considering the consecration of the basilica of Sant'Agnese fuori le Mura in 1256, one should never lose sight of the political authority of conventual communities in Roman society. According to Peter Cornelius Claussen and Romano, this enterprise was possibly financed by Jacoba, a noble matron as the epithet *domna* would suggest.[32] These assumptions are largely based on two other inscriptions that record her name and allegedly indicate that she financed the construction of the *schola cantorum* (fragments of which survive in the stairway connecting the basilica to the monastery, incorporated in the altar of the left side chapel and in the present-day refectory), the Cosmatesque pavement and the enclosure surrounding the presbytery.[33] The first inscription was transcribed by Onofrio Panvinio in his commentary on the church written around the 1550s. Today, it survives in an extremely fragmentary state in the stairway connecting the basilica to the convent. Although Panvinio did not record the inscription's exact location he reported the text in its integrity: ODERICUS STEPHANI FECIT HOC OPUS. DOMNA JACOBA DEVOTA SACRISTA.[34]

The presence of the Cosmatesque master Odericus highlights the quality of this commission. A personality of international prestige, Odericus would soon leave Rome for London to execute the great pavement of Westminster Abbey, which bears his signature and the date, 1268.[35]

28. *Ibid.*, p. 24.
29. *Ibid.*
30. This has been advocated both by Hamburger, *The Visual and the Visionary*, p. 14; and Romano, "Agnese e le altre donne", p. 15.
31. Romano, *Riforma e tradizione*, p. 15.
32. Romano, "Agnese e le altre donne", p. 25; Claussen, *Die Kirchen*, p. 55.
33. Romano, "Agnese e le altre donne", p. 25; Claussen, *Die Kirchen*, p. 60.
34. Panvinio, *Schedae de Ecclesiis Urbis Romae*, BAV, Vat. lat. 6780, fol. 278r; Claussen, *Die Kirchen*, p. 64.
35. P. Binski, *Westminster Abbey and the Plantagenets. Kingship and the Representation of Power, 1200-1400*, New Haven-London, Yale University Press, 1995, p. 133.

Regrettably, however, the only surviving portion of the inscription now reads: FECIT.HOC. / TA SACRISTA.

The second inscription cited by Romano and Claussen allegedly located in the choir area, was already in a fragmentary state when Pompeo Ugonio recorded it in 1594. Unfortunately, it has since been lost but according to Ugonio it read: …EST…UT…DEDITOPHOCDEVOTARCSITA[SACRISTA?]…SISSACUDG…ERE…OLET…E …EG…TU …HONORE.[36]

Judging from Ugonio's transcription, the text did not include Jacoba's name but only the epithet *devota sacrista*, as in the dedicatory inscription of 1256. A 16th century plan of the complex (ca. 1550s) drawn by Alberto Alberti (1525-1598) displays the original extent of the *schola cantorum*.[37] This occupied almost all of the central nave and was divided from the presbytery by a transept or an *architrabe tesselatis* as described by Panvinio. Finally Alberti's map also confirms the location of the Sant'Emerenziana altar on the counterfacade reported in Ugonio's acount of the church.

Given these circumstances it is difficult to build a case for the real decisional power of *domna* Jacoba in the church's thirteenth-century refurbishment. Although we do know of instances where large scale refurbishments were financed by female members of religious congregations,[38] we cannot corroborate this claim further on the basis of surviving inscriptions. Moreover, Isa Lori Sanfilippo, who has studied the monastery of Sant'Agnese in great detail, does not agree with Claussen's and Romano's arguments. Rather she claims that Jacoba's noble ancestry would have been identified in the 1256 consecration inscription either through a patronymic, or, a surname.[39] Lori Sanfilippo claims that, in medieval inscriptions, it was quite common for the names of the abbess and prioress to be mentioned alongside that of the eldest member of the community.[40] In fact, nuns were commonly referred to as *domina* or *ancillae Dei* until the first half of the twelfth century; terms later replaced in common usage by *moniales* and *monachae* during the later Middle Ages.

The impressive 1256 "re-consecration" of Sant'Agnese marked a larger refurbishment of the basilica and the convent that probably extended over a considerable period of time, and included fresco cycles both in the church and in

---

36. Ugonio, *Theatrum Urbis Romae*, fol. 966; Claussen, *Die Kirchen*, p. 65.

37. Gambuti, "Ricondurre all'ordine un'antica fabbrica", p. 124; G.M. Forni, *Monumenti antichi di Roma nei disegni di Alberto Alberti*, Rome, Accademia Nazionale dei Lincei, 1991.

38. Constantia at San Gregorio Nazianzeno; Iacopa Cenci at Santi Cosma e Damiano in Mica Aurea; Angelica Boccamazza at San Sisto Vecchio; Sopphia de Sant'Eustachio at San Sisto Vecchio.

39. I. Lori Sanfilippo, "Le più antiche carte del monastero di Sant'Agnese sulla Via Nomentana", *Bollettino dell'Archivio Paleografico Italiano*, 2-3 (1956-1957), pp. 65-97. Her study analysed the surviving documentation up to the twelfth century. In this article she affirms that a publication with the remaining thirteenth- and fourteenth-century material would follow. This was published as a monograph by the Archivio della Società romana di storia patria in 2015: I. Lori Sanfilippo, *Il monastero di Sant'Agnese sulla Via Nomentana. Storia e Documenti (982-1299)*, Rome, Società romana di storia patria, 2015.

40. Private communication with Lori Sanfilippo, 09/08/2015, before the 2015 article, was published by the Archivio della Società romana di storia patria which bears witness to this claim.

the nuns' conventual spaces.[41] Surviving documentary evidence indicates that the nunnery underwent a period of economic prosperity from the second half of the thirteenth century to the 1320s. From the *Catalogo di Torino*, we are aware that the community was composed of forty nuns. This would have made Sant'Agnese fuori le Mura the largest female community in Rome after the convent of San Sisto Vecchio.[42] The presence of this large community and of the surviving pictorial decorations are proof of the nunnery's wealth and stability. The existence of these paintings was reported by sixteenth- and seventeenth-century chronicles of the basilica.[43] While the lower portion of the frescoes originally found in the aisles and the pendentives of the central nave were lost; the fragments of mural paintings in the upper galleries – above the suspended ceilings of both the basilica and the convent have been preserved. The chronological span of these frescoes, based exclusively on stylistic evidence, makes Romano's claim for Jacoba's patronage both in the church and the convent highly unlikely. We cannot dismiss the possibility of a commission financed both by nuns and private donors. Indeed, as previously stated, by examining the documents from Sant'Agnese held at the Archivio di San Pietro in Vincoli we can determine that the nunnery enjoyed a certain degree of economic wealth and stability. Nevertheless, these also indicate that Sant'Agnese was not the recepient of noteworthy donations from the laity. Moreover, with regard to our chronological time frame, the convent does not seem to have attracted female members of the local nobility or baronial classes. Unlike San Silvestro in Capite or San Lorenzo in Panisperna, this convent was not a family foundation and fell directly under papal patronage. This determined the influence first, of the Conti di Segni, and later by the Savelli family.

In addition to a vineyard, their estate comprised a number of land holdings in Rome and beyond. These were located across the Via Nomentana and the Via Salaria with direct access to the river Aniene and in the area around Tivoli and Monte Soratte.[44] These documents indicate that the community's economic independence was guaranteed by numerous land holdings through papal donations.[45] It is particularly noteworthy to highlight the absence of a guarantor or a bursar responsible for the convent's financial savings.[46] This appears to

---

41. Romano, "Agnese e le altre donne", p. 27.

42. The congregation amounted to 70 nuns; this number is based on the *Catalogo di Torino* (1320): "Il Catalogo di Torino", pp. 411-439.

43. In addition to Ugonio, Panvinio and Bartolini also by M. Milesius Sarazanius, *Commentarius de Basilica S. Agentis Gallicani et Constantini in Via Nomentana*, Naples, Biblioteca Nazionale di Napoli, Ms. Brancacciano I F. 1.

44. The documentary archive of the monastery of Sant'Agnese is held at the Archivio di San Pietro in Vincoli. These claims are made on a series of documents: Posiz. 400P 554, Id. 5407 1: Venditio-a Leone Angelo Ioannis-vineae extra portam Noment. 2. Locatio-ab abbatissa S. Agnetis-vineae extra portam Salariam 9 octobris 1267; Posiz. 402.1 P606, Id. 5507: Condemnatio capituli et clericorum S. Mariae in monasterio super quasdam pedices terrae ad favorem abbatissae S. Agnetis 21 februarii 1348.

45. Lori Sanfilippo, *Il monastero di Sant'Agnese*, p. XXIII.

46. Lori Sanfilippo, "Le più antiche carte del monastero", p. 68.

indicate that the nuns exercised autonomous authority over their patrimony. Was the abbess in complete control of the convent's finances and savings? We cannot be certain. However, if we compare these documents with the registers from other monasteries (like that of San Sisto Vecchio held at the Archivio Apostolico Vaticano), which cite the presence of male intermediaries, this absence is worthy of mention. As in other ecclesiastical institutions of similar calibre and prestige to San Sisto Vecchio, nuns were usually of noble lineage and were required to guarantee a sizeable dowry upon entering the monastery. Although, we cannot account for the familial origin of Sant'Agnese's residents we may assume that there were able financial administrators among the nuns.[47]

Until recently, only two fresco cycles were known to the public. These depict scenes from the lives of Saint Catherine and Saint Benedict.[48] Originally located in the upper galleries of the basilica, they were detached in 1856 during the restoration works carried out by Pope Pius IX (1846-1878). The Saint Catherine cycle was found in the northern gallery, extending on the area above the narthex; while the Saint Benedict stories were situated on the southern side of the *matroneum*.[49] At present, they are preserved in the deposits of the Pinacoteca Vaticana. Formerly ascribed by Fritz Volbach to the last quarter of the thirteenth century, scholars now date the Saint Catherine cycle to around 1300 and the Saint Benedict series to the 1320s, the latter with a solid attribution to Lello.[50] Given their location in the upper galleries of the basilica, we may hypothesize that these frescoes were destined for the nuns. The subject matter seems particularly appropriate: on the one hand, the stories of the founding member of the order; on the other, those of a female virgin martyr, a subject particularly suited to a female conventual community. The frescoes are, in my opinion, further proof that the congregation's choir was located , by the end of the thirteenth century, in the upper galleries and that the arched openings were possibly fitted with wooden screens to protect the nuns from being seen by the officiating clergy and laity. The presence of Lello confirms the high quality of this commission. This is especially true if we consider that these paintings were, in all likelihood, solely visible to the conventual community.

These cycles only represent a small portion of the original decorative plan of the basilica, most of which was irrevocably lost during the nineteenth-century restorations. Other surviving frescoes were only known through black and

---

47. Lori Sanfilippo, *Il monastero di Sant'Agnese*, pp. V-LVI.

48. For the *Sante Principesse*, the detached frescoes of two female saints originally found in the narthex and preserved at the Pinacoteca Vaticana dating to the eleventh century, see G. Bordi, "I pannelli staccati con due figure di sante già in Sant'Agnese fuori le mura", in *Riforma e tradizione*, pp. 63-65.

49. Frutaz, *Il complesso monumentale*, pp. 164-167; S. Romano, *La pittura medievale a Roma 312-1431. Corpus e Atlante, 6, Apogeo e fine del Medioevo (1288-1431)*, Milan, Jaca Book, 2017, pp. 108-113; 303-307.

50. F. Larcinese, "Il ciclo delle Storie di santa Caterina" and "Il ciclo delle Storie di san Benedetto", in *Attorno al Cavallini*, pp. 46-117; Romano, *Apogeo e fine del Medioevo*, pp. 108-113, 303-307.

white photographs taken by the Soprintendenza ai Monumenti di Roma in the 1930s, published by Romano in the 1989 *Fragmenta Picta* exhibition catalogue and more recently in the last volume of the *Corpus e Atlante*.[51] These pictures included a Crucifixion, a Last Supper, a scene with a group of figures identified by Romano as a Pentecost, and the image of two peacocks facing each other. The existence of the Peacocks fresco, however, was well documented by nineteenth-century sources. It was described by Domenico Bartolini in 1858 and reproduced in an engraving by Virginio Vespignani.[52] Additionally, in 1960, Pietro Frutaz stated that "a small portion of the medieval decoration is still visible above the panelled ceiling."[53] Only the Peacocks were found inside the suspended ceiling of the basilica. The Crucifixion and the other scenes were only recently discovered in the medieval wing of the convent, over the hall commonly referred to as the Baptistery of Pius IX (Figs. 4-5).

Although not previously mentioned, the first one to acknowledge their existence was Mariano Armellini in the nineteenth century. In his words: "a Crucifixion was recently discovered in the portion between the ceiling and the suspended roof of the convent".[54] After the damage sustained by the monastery in the 2009 L'Aquila earthquake, the frescoes were re-discovered (previously only known through photographic testimonies of the Istituto Centrale per il Catalogo e la Documentazione), consolidated and restored under the direction of Andreina Draghi. In addition, a completely unknown painting depicting an *Enthroned Christ* was found above the suspended ceiling of the medieval wing of the convent. The painting, likely dating to the turn of the thirteenth century, maintains a strong stylistic and iconographic relationship to Cavallini's *Last Judgment* in Santa Cecilia. These were only recently published in December 2017, in the last volume of Romano's *Corpus e Atlante* and dated 1310.[55] The first floor of the medieval wing where the frescoes are located is currently divided into three separate chambers, architect Barbara Rossetti, in charge of the recent restorations, claims that it was originally one large rectangular hall with the Crucifixion, Last Supper and Pentecost on one side and the Enthroned Christ axially opposite.[56]

---

51. S. Romano, "I cicli a fresco di Sant'Agnese fuori le mura", in *Fragmenta Picta. Affreschi e mosaici staccati del Medioevo romano*, ed. by M. Andaloro, A. Ghidoli, A. Iacobini, S. Romano and A. Tomei, Exhibition catalogue (Rome, Museo di Castel Sant'Angelo, 15 December 1989-18 February 1990), Rome, Electa, 1989, p. 257; Romano, *Apogeo e fine del Medioevo*, pp. 242-244; 277-279.

52. Bartolini, *Gli atti del martirio della nobilissima vergine*, p. 122; Romano, "Agnese e le altre donne", p. 25.

53. Frutaz, *Il complesso monumentale*, pp. 63-64.

54. "Recentemente, all'intercapedine fra un soffitto ed il tettto della canonica annessa, si trovarono altri affreschi esprimenti la Crocefissione": Armellini, *Le chiese di Roma*, p. 1066.

55. Romano, *Apogeo e fine del Medioevo*, pp. 242-244. Romano dates them to the first years of the fourteenth century, she identifies an adjourned *maniera cavalliniana* with "giottesque" influences streaming in from Assisi and Padua.

56. This information comes from a personal communication with architect Barbara Rossetti on 9 March 2015.

Given its location and dimensions, this area is likely to have been one of the major conventual spaces – possibly functioning as either a Chapter house, or, a refectory.

The Sant'Agnese Crucifixion is found on the upper western portion of the rectangular hall above the Baptistery of Pius IX beneath a bricked-up window. This opening is decorated at its sides by a refined red vegetal motif of spiralling branches on a white background framed by a thin blue border. The window is flanked by the prophets David and Isaiah holding scrolls. The two haloed and bearded figures are represented at half-length in front of a blue backdrop. Although symmetrical, there is a significant attempt to distinguish them on a physiognomic level. The inscription held by David is in Gothic capitalized script with uncial letters and a number of abbreviations. Unfortunately, the inscription does not offer any clear chronological indications on the dating of the fresco. Very similar examples of this can be found as early as the 1250s, for instance, in the Calendar frescoes at the Santi Quattro Coronati. It reads: [PARTITI]I S[UNT] [SIBI] VESTIMTA MEA [ET SUPER VESTEM] MEAM MISERUNT SORT[ES] (Psalms 21:19).

This text, best known from the Good Friday liturgy, directly refers to the Crucifixion scene. By contrast, the scroll on the right is too damaged to offer an accurate reading, but one may hypothesize that its content likely referred to Christ's suffering on the cross (probably taken from Isaiah 52:13-53:12).

The Crucifixion scene is bordered by three bands of colour, while the background is rendered in pale blue. The palette is generally characterized by the use of brown, blue, green, purple and blue tones. The scene is dominated by the figure of a lifeless Christ depicted hanging from the cross with his side fatally pierced. A pelican and its nest is situated above the cross. His closed eyes are characteristic of the *Christus patiens* iconography. His head gently tilted to the left is circumscribed by a cruciform halo with indented rays around the entire circumference. An analogous rendering of the halos can be observed in the surviving panels of the Saint Benedict cycle in the Pinacoteca Vaticana. The *patiens* formula spread across Italy during the first half of the thirteenth century due to the advent of the Mendicant orders and eventually replaced the tradition of the *Christus Triumphans*.[57] Anne Derbes' definition of the *patiens* mode is particularly well suited to this Crucifixion. She offers an accurate synthesis of Christ's physiognomy stating that the *Christus patiens* is that "in which Christ as suffering human replaces the triumphant saviour: his eyes are closed, his head bowed, and his body begins to lose its upright stance, sagging to the left".[58] Above the cross is a pelican and its nest. In medieval Europe, the pelican came to symbolize the Passion of Jesus and the Eucharist. In his Eucharistic hymn *Adoro te Devote*, composed in 1264, Thomas Aquinas (1225-1274) describes Christ as the

---

57. M. Gaeta, *Giotto und die "croci dipinte" des Trecento Studien zu Typus, Genese und Rezeption; mit einem Katalog der monumentalen Tafelkreuze des Trecento (ca. 1290-ca. 1400)*, Münster, Rhema, 2013, pp. 34-46; A. Derbes, *Picturing the Passion in Late Medieval Italy. Narrative Painting, Franciscan Ideologies, and the Levant*, Cambridge, Cambridge University Press, 1996, pp. 1-9; E. Sandberg, *La croce dipinta italiana e l'iconografia della passione*, Rome, Multigraf, 1980, p. 89.

58. Derbes, *Picturing the Passion*, p. 3.

Lord Jesus, Good Pelican,
Wash me clean with your blood,
One drop of which can free
The entire world of all its sins.[59]

To my knowledge, the earliest surviving Crucifixions representing a pelican identified to date can be found in the churches of San Felice in Piazza and San Marco in Florence dated ca. 1315,[60] that of San Silvestro in Tuscania dated by an inscription to 1315, and the one in the border medallion above the Crucifixion by Pietro Lorenzetti in the Lower Church of San Francesco at Assisi – usually dated to the late 1310s, possibly 1316-1317.[61] If Romano's dating (1310 ca.) is correct, this would make the Sant'Agnese Crucifixion the first one representing a *Christus patiens* with a pelican above the cross. Directly below the pelican's nest one can still read the sign identifying Christ as the king of the Jews in Gothic script: IESUS NAZARENUS REX IUDAEORUM. Two flying angels can be observed on either side of the cross. The one on the left is clad in a green tunic; the one to the right, donning a brown/orange tunic, points towards the crucified Christ. Both angels are rendered with great attention to detail especially in the portrayal of their plumage and drapery folds. The one on the left is clad in a green tunic; the one to the right donning a brown/orange tunic points towards the crucified Christ. A comparable rendition of angelic wings can be observed in the detached fresco, *The Death of Saint Benedict* (inv. 40471), from the Sant'Agnese Saint Benedict cycle at the Pinacoteca Vaticana. In addition to the angels, the two thieves are painted to the sides of Christ. They both display a significant sculptural quality in the modelling of the upper part of the torso analogous to that of the Saviour. One can also notice a comparable portrayal of the facial features including the elongated brow and the eye contour. This characteristic portrayal of the eyes is also apparent in the two fresco cycles originally found in the suspended galleries of the basilica. Unfortunately, the thief on the right has been badly damaged, however the surviving iconographic features are coherent with the other two figures in the composition. Finally, the abundance of spears in the background and the presence of the two thieves suggest that the lower part of the painting was crowded with figures. One can confidently assume the presence of Longinus, Roman soldiers (given the SPQR flag), the Virgin, Saint John, the dolenti and other key players of the Crucifixion narrative.

---

59. "Pie Pelicane, Jesu Domine, Me immundum munda tuo sanguine: Cujus una stilla salvum facere Totum mundum quit ab omni scelere": H. Hugh, "Adoro Te Devote", in *The Catholic Encyclopedia*, 1, New York, New Advent, 1907, online.

60. A. De Marchi, "Un cadre béant sur le monde. La révolution giottesque à travers le developpement de nouveaux types de croix et de retable monumentaux", in *Giotto e compagni*, ed. by D. Thiébaut, Exhibition catalogue (Paris, Louvre, 18 April-15 July 2013), Paris, Louvre, 2013, p. 64.

61. E. Carli, "La pittura gotica in Italia", in *La pittura gotica*, ed. by E. Carli, J. Gudiol and G. Souchal, Milan, Mondadori, 1964, pp. 7-30; De Marchi, "Un cadre béant", pp. 49-66; Romano, *Eclissi di Roma*, p. 59; Romano, *Apogeo e fine del Medioevo*, dates the Crucifixion panel to the 1310, making it virtually the first example of a crucified Christ with pelican nest on top of the cross.

In order to frame the painting chronologically, we can draw iconographic parallels with other representations of the crucified Christ in the Roman area. Although some of these frescoes cannot be dated with absolute certainty, they offer a useful stylistic comparison for the Sant'Agnese Crucifixion. A series of Crucifixions dating from the third quarter of the thirteenth century in the convents of Santa Balbina and San Silvestro in Capite may serve as a broad chronological *post quem* after which the Sant'Agnese fresco was executed.[62] In these earlier images Christ is depicted dead with his head slightly tilted to the side and his body sagging from the cross. At the turn of the century, this iconographic trend is maintained in other frescoes, such as Santi Simone e Giuda[63] and San Marco.[64] On the outskirts of Rome, analogous tendencies can be observed in the murals in San Flaviano at Montefiascone and Santa Maria in Trasponte in Fiano Romano.[65] On the contrary, the greater naturalism and attention to physiognomic detail which characterizes a series of Crucifixions dating to the 1320s (San Saba in Rome, San Pietro in Tivoli) likely set the chronological limit for the dating of our painting.[66] As previously stated, Romano dates the frescoes ca. 1310 on the basis of stylistic comparisons with the Crucifixion of San Saba, the frescoes of Santa Passera and the paintings in the apse of San Sisto Vecchio. She states that, although the frescoes are tied to painterly models from the last two decades of the thirteenth century, they are stylistically cursive and softened compared to their earlier prototypes.[67]

The Sant'Agnese Crucifixion is flanked at its sides by two scenes framed by Solomonic columns with Corinthian capitals. A depiction of the Last Supper survives to the left in relatively good condition. The scene unfolds in front of a red/orange curtain with blue-white geometrical patterns decorated by a white and green band on the upper border. The former is adorned with a fictive inlay pattern of green and red squares, while the latter is framed by a similar frieze of red circles enclosed in rectangles. Christ is portrayed in the act of announcing his betrayal by one of the apostles. Although damaged, one cannot deny the pictorial quality of this painting, evident in the facial and gestural characterization of each character. This is especially true for the group to the far right. Their features are rendered through attentive and minute brush strokes, and sharing the characteristic elongated brow. Once again, the palette is dominated by earthy colours predominantly brown, yellow, orange accompanied by a limited use of blue and green.

Previously identified by Romano as a *Pentecost*, in the *Corpus e Atlante,* the author describes it as a Washing of the Feet.[68] In the background, one can notice

---

62. J.S. Gaynor, P. Toesca, *San Silvestro in Capite*, Rome, Danesi, 1963, p. 114; Romano, *Il Duecento*, pp. 296-299; 376-377.

63. Romano, *Eclissi di Roma*, p. 49.

64. F. Hermanin, *San Marco*, Rome, Danesi, 1932, p. 18; Romano, *Eclissi di Roma*, p. 67.

65. G. Matthiae, *Pittura romana del Medioevo, sec. XI-XIV*, ed. by F. Gandolfo, 2 vols., Rome, Palombi, 1988, II, p. 352.

66. *Ibid.*, p. 352; P. Toesca, *Storia dell'arte italiana. Il Trecento*, Turin, UTET, 1951, p. 119; Romano, *Apogeo e fine del Medioevo*, p. 277.

67. *Ibid.*, p. 278.

68. Romano, "Agnese e le altre donne", p. 28; Romano, *Apogeo e fine del Medioevo*, p. 277.

a series of arcades with projecting rectangular pilasters supporting the beams beneath the ceiling of the edifice. As in the Last Supper, the curtain is skilfully used as a backdrop for the crowded scene. The group of haloed figures on the right likely represents the apostles, while the isolated figure on the left possibly depicts Christ. The arrangement of the figures is noticeably unusual for a Pentecost. In fact, while this scene would provide a narrative progression from the Last Supper and Crucifixion, other iconographic solutions should be considered. As in the late twelfth-century painted cross from the church of San Sepolcro in Pisa, currently held at the Museo Nazionale di San Matteo, the representation of the Washing of the Feet could have been juxtaposed with the Last Supper.[69] On a strictly iconographic level, the Washing of the Feet commonly takes place indoors and is characterized by the isolated figure of Christ surrounded by the group of dismayed apostles. This would account for the left side of the composition possibly being occupied by the remaining disciples, as in other representations of the Washing of the Feet (like Giotto's in the Scrovegni chapel). Indeed, one may argue that the scenes were not arranged in a straightforward narrative sequence and that the Crucifixion acted as an *intermezzo* between the lateral registers. Another possibility is that it represented the Appearance of Christ to the Apostles at Supper as portrayed in the celebrated *Maestà* by Duccio.[70] This is undeniably a rare subject and the Washing of the Feet represents a far more pertinent iconographic solution.

A lettered frieze dating to the nineteenth century runs across the wall where the frescoes are found, cutting the lower extremity of all three scenes. The former currently measure approximately 2x1 m each. Today the total height of this wall measures exactly 8,7 m, although the architect Barbara Rossetti claims that the original medieval flooring of the room was considerably higher than it is today. Given the presence of the tops of the spears in the Crucifixion, one can safely assume that the central fresco extended downwards. On the contrary, if one examines the lateral scenes (Last Supper and Washing of the Feet), it would appear that they have been preserved almost in their integrity. As in the refectory fresco in Santa Croce, Florence, by Taddeo Gaddi depicting the Crucifixion or *Lignum Vitae* surrounded by four narrative scenes, I would suggest that at least two painted registers were present to the sides of the Sant'Agnese Crucifixion.[71] Although the paintings did not necessarily cover the entire surface, it is possible that they were frescoed with other Christological scenes or with hagiographical narratives.

The survival of the Enthroned Christ opposite and almost axially aligned with the Crucifixion as well as a very small and deteriorated portion of painted ceiling on the right wall depicting lilies, presents us with the concrete and tantalizing possibility that a fresco cycle covered all four sides of the hall.[72] A narrative cycle,

69. Derbes, *Picturing the Passion*, p. 5.

70. This hypothesis was suggested to me during my last visit by father Edoardo, Sant'Agnese's parish priest until 2018.

71. B. Nardini, *Il complesso monumentale di S. Croce*, Florence, Nardini, 1983, pp. 307-314.

72. Romano, *Apogeo e fine del Medioevo*, p. 277: Romano suggests that the "mysterious" scene depicting lilies possibly represents an Ascension or a Dormition.

depicting the life of Christ, would have been extremely well-suited to either a Chapter hall or a refectory. Although extremely damaged, the Enthroned Christ is high quality, possibly superior to that of the Crucifixion and likely belonging to a different artist altogether. Christ is encircled by a red *mandorla*, bordered by an interlacing pattern of yellow, white and green diamonds. The throne is extremely elaborate, with a decoration characterized by the use of inlay-coloured stones and marbles. The arm is the only surviving portion of Christ's body, elegantly clad in a blue tunic with a golden geometric rim. Only four angels survive from the heavenly court that was undoubtedly present around the figure of the Saviour. They distinguish themselves both in pose and attire. The surviving angel on the left is portrayed with golden-brown hair and polychrome wings, while the ones on the right are depicted with a blue triangular headpiece. One of the angels on the right has been preserved almost in its entirety. His figure is draped by a green and yellow embroidered toga. The figure of Christ was undoubtedly encircled by an angelic court. Although the resemblance to Cavallini's Last Judgment in Santa Cecilia is striking we cannot determine with absolute certainty whether the apostles were present at Christ's side on the basis of the surviving fragment. Indeed, other well-known representations of the *Majestas Domini* in Rome are characterized by the depiction of the Enthroned Christ exclusively surrounded by an angelic court. This includes the one located in the *Sancta Sanctorum*, or, on the façade of Santa Maria Maggiore by Filippo Rusuti. Given the grandeur of this enterprise, the possibility that an Ascension, or indeed a Last Judgment covered the entire surface of this wall as in Santa Cecilia should not be excluded.

As far as the Sant'Agnese Enthroned Christ is considered, a little-known fresco cycle found in the apsidal vault of San Sisto Vecchio displays analogous tendencies in terms of patronage, style and chronology.[73] As in Sant'Agnese, the survival of these frescoes testifies to the agency of the convent in the promotion of artistic patronage in Rome. According to Barclay Lloyd, who has studied the frescoes extensively, "it is likely that these nuns played an important role in planning and commissioning the frescoes, which thereby constitute an interesting example of convent art or paintings that were specifically designed for the Dominican sisters in Rome".[74] She dates the paintings between 1295 and 1314 ascribing them to an artist influenced by Cavallini.[75] It is my opinion that the Enthroned Christ present at Sant'Agnese shares a similar chronology and attribution.[76]

By considering the presence of a Crucifixion, an Enthroned Christ and other Christological scenes, one can account for the original function of this room. The pictorial prototypes for these frescoes should be sought in other monasteries and private apartments reserved for the clergy's use. When taking

---

73. Romano, *Apogeo e fine del Medioevo*, p. 278: stylistic analogies with San Sisto Vecchio are also identified by Romano.

74. Barclay Lloyd, "Paintings for Dominican Nuns", p. 193.

75. *Ibid.*, p. 210.

76. Romano, *Apogeo e fine del Medioevo*, p. 242: Romano dates these paintings to the "primi anni del XIV secolo".

the iconography of the Sant'Agnese frescoes into account, it would appear that the various activities that occurred inside a Chapter house were particularly well suited to our decorative scheme. Miklos Boskovits maintained that in "the Trecento the more common type of decoration is that which presents a series of large compositions at both sides of the Crucifixion as well as on other walls of the Chapter hall".[77] Additionally, Julian Gardner's analysis of the Santa Maria Novella Chapter house hypothesizes the existence of an evolutionary pattern in the frescoes that characterized these halls.[78] He claims that "it can be seen how the earlier, more iconic 'monastic' programme was progressively extended: probably at first by accepting an amplified Crucifixion, and subsequently by importing narratives from the history of the order in place of the earlier order saints".[79] This claim is also corroborated by William Hood who asserts that there were two major pictorial components in Chapter house decorations in Italy by the twelfth century: the Crucifixion and the order's titular saints, as witnessed in the Chapter room in the Benedictine abbey of Pomposa painted by Pietro da Rimini in 1320.[80] Additionally, although uncommon, we know of at least one example of a Roman nunnery where the Chapter house and the church were found on opposite sides of the cloister, the convent of Santa Maria in Campo Marzio.[81]

Although Heidrun Stein-Kecks asserts that "as a visible sign of the *imitatio Christi* in the chapter, the symbol of the cross became the standard ornament of the Chapter house";[82] she also acknowledges the architectural affiliation that existed (and that at Sant'Agnese seems to be missing) between the cloisters and Chapter houses. Indeed, in contrast to Sant'Agnese where the paintings are found on the first floor of the medieval wing of the convent, the Chapter house usually had a door directly onto the cloister walk. Moreover, in Chapter houses the Crucifixion invariably faced the doorway leading in from the cloister. However, refectories were usually oriented in parallel with one of the cloister walks with the Crucifixion at one end. Therefore, at Sant'Agnese, the position, the rectangular dimensions of the room (approximately 8x20 m), and the location of the frescoes within that space all seem to indicate this room's function as a refectory. Additionally, by taking into account the disposition of other Benedictine nunneries in Rome such as San Cosimato, which transferred to the Clarissan in the thirteenth century, we can observe that the Chapter house was usually adjacent to the church,

---

77. M. Boskovits, "Insegnare per immagini: dipinti e sculture nelle sale capitolari", *Arte cristiana*, 78 (May-June 1990), p. 123.

78. J. Gardner, "Andrea di Bonaiuto and the Chapter House Frescoes in Santa Maria Novella", *Art History*, 2 (June 1979), p. 128.

79. *Ibid.*, p. 129.

80. W. Hood, *Fra Angelico at San Marco*, New Haven-London, Yale University Press, 1993, p. 170.

81. F. Borsi, "L'antico convento di S. Maria in Campo Marzio", in *Santa Maria in Campo Marzio*, ed. by N. Iotti, Rome, Editalia, 1987, p. 67.

82. H. Stein-Kecks, "Claustrum and capitulum: Some Remarks on the Façade and Interior of the Chapter House", in *Der mittelalterliche Kreuzgang*, ed. by P.K. Klein, Regensburg, Schnell & Steiner, 2004, pp. 157-189: 171.

while the refectory was found on the opposite side of the courtyard.[83] This was standard practice across monastic architecture and may well indicate that the hall at Sant'Agnese functioned as a refectory. As Joanna Cannon has observed, the presence of a Crucifixion inside a refectory hall is testified in a predella panel by Fra Angelico representing the Miracle of the Loaves.[84] According to Creighton Gilbert, "to judge from the few examples we have, these early refectories seem to have their own standard theme, namely the Crucifixion".[85] Finally, as in Santa Croce in Florence, Last Suppers and Crucifixion scenes were often combined. Romano points out that a *Maiestats Domini* decorated the refectory in the abbey of Chiaravalle Milanese.[86] However, she claims that the chronological discrepancies between the paintings (namely that of the Crucifixion and the *Maiestas Domini*) at Sant'Agnese likely testify to the division of the hall into two different spaces.[87] She asserts that these rooms functioned as a refectory and Chapter house or as reception rooms. Given the size of the congregation, I believe that this was one large room, which could accommodate all the nuns.

The congregation's private apartments were also decorated by a set of fifteenth-century frescoes, originally located in the nuns' dormitory, and presently found in the sacristy and in the basilica.[88] These paintings, recorded by Domenico Bartolini and published by Raimond Van Marle, were known through sketches by Seroux d'Agincourt.[89] They were likely commissioned during the papacy of Martin V (1417-1431) in order to celebrate the translation of the Saint Agnes' relics from a wooden case to a silver one and offer further proof of female religious

---

83. J. Barclay Lloyd, "L'architettura medievale di S. Cosimato in Trastevere", in Barclay Lloyd, Bull-Simonsen Einaudi, *SS. Cosma e Damiano in Mica Aurea*, pp. 101-112.

84. Cannon, *Religious Poverty, Visual Riches*, p. 198.

85. C.E. Gilbert, "Last Suppers and their Refectories", in *The Pursuit of Holiness in Late Medieval and Renaissance Religion*, ed. by H.A. Oberman and C. Trinkaus, Leiden, Brill, 1974, p. 375.

86. Romano, *Apogeo e fine del Medioevo*, p. 244.

87. *Ibid.*, p. 242.

88. These paintings include a depiction of the *Saints Cosmas and Damian*, *Four Standing Saints*, *Adoration of the Magi*, *Saint Leonard*, *Madonna Lactans*, *Enthroned Madonna* and *Saint Ansanus* detached and now in the second left chapel of the basilica, and an *Enthroned Madonna*: Romano, *Eclissi di Roma*, p. 394; W. Angelelli, L'Adorazione dei Magi e Quattro Santi, I Santi Cosma e Damiano e San Leonardo *nel convento di Sant'Agnese fuori le mura*, and Id., *La Madonna Lactans e la* Madonna in trono col bambino e Sant'Ansano *in Sant'Agnese fuori le mura*, in Romano, *Apogeo e fine del Medioevo*, pp. 373-374 and 409-411; S. L'Occaso, "Osservazioni sulla pittura a Roma sotto Martino V", *Archivio della Società romana di storia patria*, 125 (2002), pp. 42-51; A. De Marchi, "scheda 16", in *Il Quattrocento a Camerino*, ed. by A. De Marchi and M. Giannatiempo Lopez, Milan, Motta, 2002; A. Cavallaro, "Roma 1420-1431. La pittura al tempo di Martino V", in *La storia dei giubilei*, ed. by J. Le Goff, G. Fossi and C. Strinati, Rome, BNL Edizioni, 1997, p. 314; A. Cavallaro, "Recensione. *Osservazioni sulla pittura a Roma sotto Martino V* di S. L'Occaso", *Archivio della Società romana di storia patria*, 125 (2005), pp. 146-148.

89. J.B. Seroux d'Agincourt, *Histoire de l'art par les monumens depuis sa décadence au IVe siècle jusqu'à son renouvellement au XVIe siècle*, II, Paris, Treuttel et Würtz, 1823, p. 118; Bartolini, *Gli atti del martirio*, pp. 140-141; R. Van Marle, *The Development of the Italian Schools of Painting*, 8, Hague, Nijhoff, 1927, p. 436.

agency in the realm of patronage.[90] A stylistic analysis indicates that they were probably executed in two different campaigns. *The Saints Cosmas and Damian*, *Four Standing Saints*, *Adoration of the Magi*, *Saint Leonard* at an earlier date, while the *Virgin Lactans* and the *Enthroned Virgin with Saint Ansanus* and the *Annunciation* later on.[91] This claim is disputed by Walter Angelelli who pushes the chronology of these frescoes to the 1430s and questions the intervention of a Marchigian painter *tout court*.[92] The subject of these paintings, which are mostly tied to Marian themes, appears to be particularly well suited to the nuns' private apartments.

In conclusion, these large-scale refurbishments confirm the status of the conventual spaces within the nunnery and the high quality of their interior decoration. Moreover, Sant'Agnese fuori le Mura presents the opportunity to witness the renovation of public and private spaces inside a nunnery over a considerable period of time. Furthermore, it enables us to re-evaluate female agency within the space of the convent and more generally in the context of patronage during the Middle Ages. Undoubtedly, the different cycles present within the complex are of exceptional quality, and represent a rare survival of Roman painting inside conventual communities. The existence of these frescoes helps us reassess the artistic output in Rome destined for a female audience. In absence of documentary evidence pertaining to these commissions, we may nevertheless state that the nunnery's prestige is testified by the presence of the pope and the curia during the 1256 "re-consecration" of the basilica.[93] The extent to which the female community acted as a catalyst for the renovations in the complex remains impossible to determine. However, it is evident that the sisters made sure that their own private conventual spaces were decorated by leading painters and in the latest style.

Sant'Agnese fuori le Mura also allows us to reason around architectural forms and the contextualisation of artworks in space. The extent of the *schola cantorum* drawn in Alberti's plan possibly indicates that the nuns initially attended mass here.

90. B. Beverini, *Vita e culto di Sant'Agnese V. e M. con addizione di note*, Naples, Festa, 1856, p. 46: "Trascorsero da questo tempo 457 anni, quando sotto il governo del Vescovo Federigo Blachenheimio furono di nuovo le sacre reliquie di s. Agnese ai 2 di Settembre trasferite dall'arca antica di legno in una nuova di argento con molta pompa e celebrità. Fu istituita la festa di questa traslazione nel giorno medesimo dei 2 di Settembre, come apparisce dai Breviari di quella Chiesa, solennizzando nel giorno stesso l'altra traslazione ancora che accadde ai 31 di Marzo, per esser quel giorno per lo più impedito dalla memoria della Passione del Signore. Della qual seconda traslazione parlano il Molano, e i Certosini di Colonia nelle addizioni ad Usuardo, inoltre Andrea Saussay nel Martirologio Gallicano, un antico Martirologio detto il Florario, e finalmente Tommaso da Kempis Canonico Regolare nella Cronica del suo Monastero del Monte di s. Agnese, sebbene quest'ultimo varia nel tempo, riferendo che seguì non l'anno 1421, ma 1414"; L'Occaso, "Osservazioni sulla pittura a Roma", pp. 43-45.

91. L'Occaso, "Osservazioni sulla pittura a Roma", p. 45: "Ne fosse incaricato il pittore di maggiore rilievo presente a Roma in quel momento". Although this fresco is detached we can be fairly sure it came from the convent's apartments.

92. Angelelli, *Apogeo e fine del Medioevo*, pp. 410-412.

93. See 1256 inscription.

However, as suggested by the extensive fresco cycle, the community's choir likely moved to the suspended galleries by the end of the thirteenth century. When it comes to Benedictine architecture, we tend to have a greater standardisation in the planimetric disposition of conventual complexes; however, the existence of a *matroneum* inside the church points towards a broader and more eclectic architectural arrangement than what is generally theorised. The iconographic analysis of the surviving paintings in the convent's large rectangular room supported the hypothesis that this space functioned as a refectory. Overall, the combined study of architecture, art, and epigraphy offers a tantalising glimpse of witnessing a largescale operation of artistic renewal in Rome over the course of several centuries. This was possibly promoted by the nuns showcasing the high level of artistic and architectonic sophistication in the pre- and post-Avignon years.

2. *Icons in* Clausura*: Domenico Guzmán and the Nuns at San Sisto Vecchio*

San Sisto Vecchio on the Via Appia is distinguished by its vast array of surviving documentary, artistic and architectonic evidence, which characterises it as one the most compelling case studies in Rome. Envisaged by Innocent III (1161-1216) as a *coenobium universalis*, large enough to accommodate all Roman nuns, the project was part of the greater *renovatio Romae* undertaken by the pope at the beginning of the thirteenth century.[94] By imposing a rigid *clausura*, enforced by the presence of the Gilbertine order, Innocent wanted to counteract the lax lifestyle seemingly enjoyed by convents in Rome.[95] The enclosure of all religious women in one nunnery was clearly in accordance with the pope's reformation of the Church, and with the attempt to unify an increasingly challenged institution.[96] As outlined by Brenda Bolton, it is apparent

94. The following works have been consulted: Armellini, *Le chiese di Roma*, pp. 315-318; Barclay Lloyd, "The Architectural Planning of Pope Innocent", pp. 1292-1311; Barclay Lloyd, "Paintings for Dominican Nuns", pp. 189-232; J.J. Berthier, *Chroniques du monastère de San Sisto et de San Domenico e Sisto à Rome écrites par trois religieuses du même monastère et traduites par un religieux dominicain*, 2 vols., Levanto, Imp. de l'Immaculée, 1919-1920; Bolton, "Daughters of Rome", pp. 101-115; H. Brandenburg, *Le prime chiese di Roma. IV-VII secolo*, Milan, Jaca Book, 2004, pp. 152-153; Carbonetti Vendittelli, "Il registro", pp. 83-121; C. Hulsen, *Le chiese di Roma nel Medioevo*, Florence, Olschki, 1927, pp. 234-237; Romano, *Eclissi di Roma*, pp. 67-70; Koudelka, "Le 'monasterium Tempuli'", pp. 2-81; Matthiae, *Pittura romana*, II, pp. 109-114; G. Ronci, "Antichi affreschi a San Sisto Vecchio a Roma", *Bollettino d'arte*, 36 (1951), pp. 15-26; F. Vitali, "Gli affreschi medievali di S. Sisto Vecchio in Roma", in *Roma anno 1300*, pp. 433-447; A. Walz, "Die 'Miracula beati Dominici' der Schwester Caecilia, Einleitung und Text", *Lateranum*, 15, 1 (1948), pp. 293-326.

95. Foreville, *Latran*, pp. 225-317; *The History of Medieval Cannon Law*; Petrucci, *Ecclesiologia e papato*, p. 45; Barclay Lloyd, "The Architectural Planning of Pope Innocent", p. 1294; Bolton, "Daughters of Rome", p. 104; Romano, *Il Duecento e la cultura gotica*, p. 43.

96. "Innocentius papa III monasterium Sancti Sixti cum devotione animi de bonis Ecclesiae aedificare cepit, ut mulieres Urbis et moniales aliorum monasteriorum Urbis per diversa vagantes possent bi sub arcta clausura et diligenti custodia Domino famulari": Koudelka, "Le 'monasterium

that the diversity in religious practice was a cause of great concern for Innocent. Indeed, this effort at merging experiences was not only applied to women in Rome but also to the Mendicants (forcing Saint Dominic, for example, to adopt the Augustinian rule).[97] By centralizing communities and standardising norms of *clausura* Innocent was hoping to neutralise the waves of heresies in southern Europe, facilitate the conversion of pagans in the Balkans, and offset the charges of clerical immorality.[98] Ultimately, presenting the Church of Rome as a cohesive front would, in Innocent's view, mitigate the rising upheaval and scandal in the Catholic world.

Scholars usually associate the imposition of *clausura* with the *Periculoso* decree, issued by Pope Boniface VIII in 1298, or, with the Council of Trent in 1563; however, it was already expected to be followed by all convents during Innocent's papacy. These measures were met with great resistance and very rarely respected. In fact, women who refused to give up their freedom could appeal to the *Regula Aquensis*, a reformed version of Saint Benedict's rule established at the Council of Aachen.[99] Nevertheless, enclosure was eventually even imposed on orders whose statutes did not formally prescribe it. As previously stated, the reason behind this was likely tied to the profound reform the church underwent during Innocent's papacy. Moreover, it is likely that the pope sought a quick fix to the problem of the Bizoke, groups which enjoyed great popularity in Central Italy.[100] They were allowed to live communally and were expected to observe a regime of chastity.[101] This was not always possible, in part due to a secular lifestyle which made strict chastity hard to sustain, in part by family pressure for marriage.[102]

Although Innocent did not live to see his ambitious project realised, it was brought to completion by his successor Honorius III.[103] The nunnery's development was transferred to the Dominican order and was personally overseen by Saint Dominic (1170-1221) who, as contemporary sources indicate, was particularly concerned with the proper education of religious women.[104] By this time, Dominic

Tempuli'", p. 39; Kaeppeli, "Dalle pergamene di S. Maria in Gradi di Viterbo", p. 250; Barclay Lloyd, "The Architectural Planning of Pope Innocent", p. 1295; Bolton, "Daughters of Rome", p. 106.

97. Bolton, "Daughters of Rome", p. 106.

98. *Ibid.*

99. Romano, *Il Duecento e la cultura gotica*, p. 44.

100. J. Coakley, *Women, Men and Spiritual Power*, New York, Columbia University Press, 2006, p. 257.

101. M. Sensi, "Le bizzocche di S. Anna a Foligno, Torre degli Specchi a Roma, S. Elisabetta a Venezia, tre storie a confronto", in *Francesca Romana. La santa, il monastero e la città alla fine del Medioevo*, ed. by A. Bartolomei, Florence, Edizioni del Galluzzo, 2009, pp. 36-40.

102. Coackley, *Women, Men and Spiritual Power*, p. 257; Sensi, "Le bizzocche di S. Anna a Foligno", p. 40.

103. J. Claussen, *Papst Honorius III (1216-1227)*, Hildesheim, Olms, 2004; P.N.R. Zutshi, "Letters of pope Honorius III concerning the order of preachers", in *Pope, Church and City*, ed. by F. Andrews, B. Brenda and C. Eggar, Leiden, Brill, 2004, pp. 269-286; Barclay Lloyd, "The Architectural Planning of Pope Innocent", p. 1295; Bolton, "Daughters of Rome", p. 106; Koudelka, "Le 'monasterium Tempuli'", p. 64.

104. Zucchi, *Roma domenicana*, 1, p. 259.

had managed the foundation of the nunnery of Prouille in France – a sort of double community which followed the Augustinian rule.[105] The friars provided spiritual and temporal sustenance to the newly established convent. This would guarantee the preservation of strict enclosure while also providing for an adequate *cura monialium*. The abdication of Abbess Eugenia from the convent of Santa Maria in Tempuli marked the formal establishment of San Sisto in 1221.[106] Aside from the convent of Santa Bibiana, the project was received with very little enthusiasm from other female communities in Rome.[107]

Like their French counterparts, the nuns of San Sisto were expected to follow the Augustinian rule. The convent was self-sustained by a rich patrimony of land holdings across Rome and in the area around Tivoli. Additionally, members of the community were drawn from the Roman baronial class and aristocracy. Their dowries constituted an important contribution to the convent's patrimony. From the letters of Innocent IV, we understand that the pope left a wide margin of choice to the abbess in the selection of her novices. Starting at least from the mid-thirteenth century, nuns from wealthy Roman families are listed in the convent's records. This is demonstrated by the presence of Margarita de Palumbara, Constancia Malabrance, Andrea de Sancto Eustachio, Maria Boboni, Margarita Consolini, Paola and Eufrosina Orsini, Prospera and Giovanna Colonna, and Artemia Pierleoni in the registries.[108] Additionally, this practice sustained an intricate pattern of relations between the nunnery and powerful Roman families, a factor of great influence in San Sisto's daily affairs. Although the economic register (the so-called *liber bursarie*) for the period 1369-1381, preserved at the Archivio Apostolico Vaticano in the *fondo* of Santi Domenico e Sisto, only covers twelve years,[109] it suggests that this aristocratisation trend continued into the fourteenth century. The register confirms the steady presence of numerous members of both the old baronial families and of the new emerging middle classes. By keeping a detailed record of the income and expenses of the convent, it also demonstrates how certain nuns had a monthly allowance to tailor their needs. This guaranteed them a greater independence than what we would normally expect from an enclosed community.[110]

---

105. Barclay Lloyd, "The Architectural Planning of Pope Innocent", p. 1295; Bolton, "Daughters of Rome", p. 106; Koudelka, "Le 'monasterium Tempuli'", p. 64.

106. Spiazzi, *Cronache e fioretti*, pp. 109-114.

107. Walz, "Die 'Miracula beati Dominici'", pp. 307-309: Suor Cecilia – member of the female community at Santa Maria in Tempuli – in the prologue to the chronicle on the miracles of Saint Dominic recounts that the saint had to obtain three professions of adherence to the Dominican order before convincing the congregation to move to San Sisto. It was essential given the possession of the precious icon of Saint Luke for this community to adhere to the project. Their establishment in San Sisto would have guaranteed the adherence of other nunneries.

108. *Ibid.*

109. The registry is archived under the title *Monasteri femminili soppressi, SS. Domenico e Sisto*, 191, the San Sisto inventory has been published by S. Pagano, *L'archivio del convento dei SS. Domenico e Sisto di Roma. Cenni storici e inventario*, Vatican City, Archivio Vaticano, 1994; Carbonetti Vendittelli, "Il registro", pp. 96-97.

110. *Ibid.*, pp. 98-99.

The archive of San Sisto is perhaps one of the most emblematic cases of the processes of dispersal and above all dismemberment to which many Roman ecclesiastical records have been subjected, to a greater or lesser extent, since the beginning of the nineteenth century. The reasons are, at least partially, directly or indirectly linked to the profound political upheavals that brought disorder, concealment and consequently loss and fragmentation of this heritage. Nevertheless, thanks to the pioneering work of Vladimir Koudelka and Cristina Carbonetti Vendittelli, a large part of these documents has either been published or indexed.[111] Koudelka has traced the convent's history and the events which led to the abdication of Abbess Eugenia from the Monasterium Tempuli; Carbonetti Vendittelli has meanwhile examined the internal organisation of the convent and the proceedings tied to its landholdings.

Surviving documentary evidence testifies that the foundation of San Sisto in 1221 was witnessed by Ugolino of Ostia (the future Pope Gregory IX), Nicholas of Tusculum and Stephen of Fossanova.[112] Ugolino, responsible for the enforced *clausura* of proto-Clarissan, likely had an influence over the convent's internal organisation. In contrast to primitive Mendicant architecture very little survives from the early female Dominican context. Unfortunately, early Dominican nunneries like Notre-Dame at Prouille, Santo Domingo in Madrid and Sant'Agnese in Bologna have been heavily reconstructed and therefore do not offer a solid base for comparison. For the purpose of this survey, in addition to examining San Sisto Vecchio in a comparative, trans-regional architectural context, we shall cross-reference this material with archaeological surveys and surviving artefacts. Chronicles on the nunnery have also been taken into account as precious testimonies of the original conventual architectonic makeup. This investigation will also account for surviving fourteenth-century documentary evidence from the destroyed Dominican convent of Sant'Aurea on Via Giulia.[113] Additionally, it will consider the nunnery's internal design within the context of *clausura* in relation to the growing devotion towards the Eucharist.[114]

---

111. Carbonetti Vendittelli, "Il registro delle entrate", pp. 98-99; C. Carbonetti Vendittelli, S. Carocci, "Le fonti per la storia locale", *Rassegna degli Archivi di Stato*, 44 (1984), pp. 68-148, pp. 68-148; Koudelka, "Le 'monasterium Tempuli'".

112. W. Maleczek, *Papst und Kardinalskolleg von 1191 bis 1216. Die Kardinäle unter Coelestin III. und Innozenz III*, Vienna, Historisches Institut beim Österreichischen Kulturinstitut, 1984, pp. 126-133.

113. It is worth noting that the community at Via Giulia joined San Sisto in the sixteenth century.

114. In accordance with the promulgations of the Fourth Lateran Council, we may assume that religious women wanted a greater degree of participation in the Eucharistic rite, especially in so far as the elevation of the Host was considered. The first decree of the Lateran Council sanctioned the word *transsubstantiatio* as the correct expression of Eucharistic doctrine. Bruzelius, "Hearing is Believing"; A.J. Duggan, "The Legislation of the Four Councils of the Lateran", in *The History of Canon Law in the Classical Period, 1140-1234: From Gratian to the Decretals of Pope Gregory IX*, ed. by W.Hartmann and K. Pennington, Washington,, The Catholic University of America Press, 2008, pp. 318-366.

The medieval nunnery of San Sisto was built over the Roman Basilica of Crescentiana erected by Pope Anastasius (399-401) between 399 and 410.[115] Two epigraphs, now lost but transcribed by Pompeo Ugonio and Alberto Zucchi, record how this early Christian shrine became the site for the preservation of numerous suburban Christian relics.[116] The church was heavily restored during the papacy of Innocent III and completed under Honorius III with the installment of the female community by 1222.[117] The monumental complex of San Sisto Vecchio is comprised of five distinct bodies: church, bell tower, cloister, Chapter house and refectory. The nunnery is located in what is currently named the Parco di Porta Capena or Passeggiata Archeologica, between the western portion of the Caelian Hill and the Circus Maximus in front of the church of Santi Nereo e Achilleo. The complex is parallel to the street, therefore the apse of the church points towards the North. Although the original early Christian basilica had three aisles (the central one higher with a clerestory) preceded by a narthex and terminating in a semi-circular apse, the medieval church was reduced to one nave and its pavement was raised by at least two metres.[118] The right nave was occupied by a portion of the nunnery's cloister, while the left one was divided into several spaces, whose original function is still unclear. Archaeological investigations conducted in the 1960s have shown that the apse was clearly reinforced on its southwestern side, and a triangular enclosure was added to the south.[119] This space, the use of which has still not been clarified, was accessed by a long, vaulted corridor which led to rooms adjacent to the left side of the church. A seventeenth-century stuccoed interior now masks the thirteenth-century church.[120] This makes the reconstruction of the nuns' sacred space all the more challenging. The erection of the bell tower, which is found in the space of the central nave behind the church's façade, was coeval to the medieval refurbishments. The medieval kitchen and refectory, covered by a low vaulted ceiling, still survive to the right of the church along with the entrance to the Chapter house on the south-eastern portion of the complex. This was decorated with *spolia* columns from the original fifth-century basilica. The Dominican friars lived in a building which extended from the apse of the basilica in the direction of the church of Santi Nereo and Achilleo, destroyed when Via di Valle delle Camene was built (ca. 1910).[121] This building was large enough to accommodate a fairly big community. Towards the end of the century, thanks to the liberal donations of Cardinal Giovanni Boccamazza (1285-1309), both the dormitory and Chapter house were likely enlarged.

115. See bibliography for this case study.
116. S. Corbett, R. Karutheimer, "San Sisto Vecchio", in Spiazzi, *Cronache e fioretti*, p. 200; Zucchi, *Roma domenicana*, 1, p. 319; P. Ugonio, *Historia delle Stationi di Roma*, Rome, appresso Bartholomeo Bonfadino, 1588.
117. Koudelka, "Le 'monasterium Tempuli'", p. 81.
118. Corbett, Krautheimer, "San Sisto Vecchio", p. 213.
119. H. Geertman, "Ricerche sopra la prima fase di San Sisto Vecchio in Roma", in Spiazzi, *Cronache e fioretti*, p. 230.
120. At present the church is undergoing renovations and cannot be accessed by the public.
121. Corbett, Krautheimer, "San Sisto Vecchio", p. 220.

From the *Catalogo di Torino* of Roman churches, we know that in 1320 the convent housed seventeen friars and seventy nuns. These numbers are very significant in terms of explaining the organization of the liturgical space inside the presbytery. The church's internal structure has been studied by Barclay Lloyd (Fig. 6). The scholar states that a *tramezzo* screen divided the nave into two, and separated the space reserved for the nuns from that of the officiating clergy and the laity.[122] She places this division at three quarters length inside the main body of the nave, and claims that the nuns occupied the portion towards the apse. Her reasoning is based on the written testimony provided by Sister Cecilia, possibly from the Frangipane, Malabranca or Cesarini families, who was approximately seventeen years old in 1222, the year San Sisto was reformed. She died in 1290 at the convent of Sant'Agnese in Bologna and her memoirs were collected by another nun named Angelica around 1288. The chronicle entitled *Miracula beati Dominici* represents a valuable testimony of San Sisto's founding years.[123] Cecilia describes the last days of the female community of Santa Maria in Tempuli and the events behind the transfer of their precious icon in great detail. Indeed, although Dominic was anxious to persuade the nuns to join the Dominican order and live under the supervision of the friars of San Sisto Vecchio, he realized "that their stability in the new home depended on the transfer and the subsequent stability of the Icon".[124]

Barclay Lloyd provides evidence for the existence of the tramezzo and a choir in the northern side of the church (namely the presbytery) from Cecilia's account of two miracles performed by Dominic in the church of San Sisto Vecchio (the expulsion of the seven demons from a possessed woman and the miracle of the wine).[125] On both occasions Cecilia describes viewing the saint through a rota, a device used in female communities, which allowed women to participate during mass and receive the sacrament of the Holy Communion.[126] In her view, further proof is provided by the thirteenth-century fresco cycle in the apse designed for a female audience. According to Barclay Lloyd, Bruzelius' survey of Clarissan choirs in the article "Hearing is Believing" is contradicted by evidence provided in San Sisto, which indicates that the Dominican nuns could not only hear the service but also witness the liturgy.[127] These claims are disputed by Mercedes Perez Vidal in her study on choirs from Dominican convents in the Spanish region of Castile. She refutes this hypothesis by stating that the internal disposition of the church was flipped, in so much that the paintings inside the apse were destined for the friars.[128] She determines this by claiming that, in the

---

122. Barclay Lloyd, "Paintings for Dominican Nuns", p. 192.
123. Walz, "Die 'Miracula Beati Dominici'", pp. 5-45.
124. Cannon, *Religious Poverty, Visual Riches*, pp. 72-73.
125. Barclay Lloyd, "The Architectural Planning of Pope Innocent III", p. 1299.
126. *Ibid.*, pp. 1308-1309; Waltz, "Die 'Miracula Beati Dominici'", pp. 313-315.
127. Bruzelius, "Hearing is Believing", pp. 83-91.
128. I am grateful to Dr Perez Vidal for sending me her forthcoming article "Estavan todas no coro e ben cantand' e Leendo. Tipologie e funzioni dei cori nei monasteri delle Domenicane con particolare riferimento alla Castiglia dal XIII al XVI secolo" in advance of publication.

Catalogo di Torino, seventeen friars are listed against seventy nuns. Perez Vidal maintains that the female community could not fit inside the alcove of the apse, which according to the scholar was likely destined for the celebration of the service by the friars and therefore housed the church's main altar.[129] Perez Vidal's hypothesis only works if the nuns' choir occupied a portion of the nave, so that during the celebration of the liturgical service the friars could distribute the sacraments to the lay congregation (most definitely present given the church housed the revered icon of Santa Maria in Tempuli) without passing through the women's enclosure (Figs. 7-9).

In accordance with Cecilia's account, we know that there was an opening, *rota*, or some sort of grated window through which the female community could witness the elevation of the Eucharist.[130] Archaeological analysis has brought to light a passage between the church and the cloister at the height of the apse.[131] Is it possible that this was the passage referred to in the *Miracula Beati Dominici*? Choirs adjacent but external to the main body of the church were extremely popular in female Mendicant churches, San Damiano being the most celebrated case and point.[132] This disposition would definitely reconcile the need for enclosure with the accommodation of the male religious community while simultaneously allowing the distribution of sacraments to the lay population. In addition, this layout would guarantee enclosure whilst granting the laity access to the precious Madonna Advocata icon from the Monasterium Tempuli, and the thirteenth-century painted panel Crucifix from the nunnery. These two works are frequently mentioned side by side in later sources and historiographies.[133] An analogous disposition was found in the church of Santa Chiara in Assisi. Here, on the *tramezzo* before the presbytery, the *Triumphal Cross* was framed by the images of the *Maestà* and the *Santa Chiara Vitae* retable. Zappasodi suggests that crucifixes and Marian images were a recurrent typology in nunneries in Central Italy.[134] Indeed, this pair or tandem (to use Luciano Bellosi's terminology) is also present in the fresco depicting the Verification of the stigmata inside the Upper Basilica at Assisi as

129. Forthcoming in Perez Vidal, "Estavan todas".
130. "Stabat ad fenestram, ita quod sorores poterant eum videre et audire, et verbum domini fortiter predicabat [...] in ecclesia Sancti Sixti ad fenestram, presente sorore Cecilia et ceteris": Waltz, "Die 'Miracula Beati Dominici'", p. 313; Spiazzi, *Cronache e fioretti*, published an Italian edited translation of the text; this passage is referred to at pp. 64-65.
131. Barclay Lloyd, "Paintings for Dominican Nuns", p. 190.
132. Zappasodi, *Sorores*, pp. 16-19.
133. Domenica Salomonia, "Memorie del Monastero dei SS. Domenico e Sisto 1652-1656", in Berthier, *Chroniques du monastère de San Sisto*, II, p. 13; Zucchi, *Roma domenicana*, 1, p. 354; Romano, *Il Duecento e la cultura gotica*, pp. 274-277.
134. E. Zappasodi, "Intus Dictum Monasterium Prope Cratem: La croce e il coro delle monache", in *Francesco e la croce di San Damiano*, ed. by M. Bollati, Milan, Edizioni Biblioteca Francescana, 2016, pp. 133-155; E. Zappasodi, "La croce dipinta in Umbria al tempo di Giunta e di Giotto, tra eleganza dolorosa e coinvolgimento emotivo", in *Francesco e la croce dipinta*, Exhibition catalogue (Perugia, ottobre 2016-gennaio 2017), Milan, Silvana Editoriale, 2016, pp. 69-101.

proof for his argument.[135] Can we opt for a similar arrangement at San Sisto on the basis of this testimony? Romano asserts that the Marian cycle depicted in the apse should be connected to the precious icon.[136] These elements could indicate that both were positioned in the apse space. The icon might have been placed on the main altar, while the crucifix suspended from the ceilings via ropes or chains (the dimensions of the crucifix would indeed suggest this). Alternatively, the crucifix may have been supported by a beam, which separated the presbytery from the main body of the church with the *Icona Tempuli* on the main altar. Having the choir of the nuns outside the main church could facilitate access to the icon at least during mass.[137] This spatial arrangement is also recorded for the church of Sant'Aurea founded in 1346, the female Dominican community that was originally located on Via Giulia and which joined San Sisto in the sixteenth century.[138]

The lost convent of Sant'Aurea, originally on Via Giulia, offers an insightful case study for our understanding of female religious communities and their church design in the context of *clausura*. Through surviving documents, which testify to lay commissions within the church space, we may tentatively reconstruct its internal disposition. This in turn may offer a valid point of comparison with the convent of San Sisto Vecchio. Two surviving altarpieces respectively found at the church of Santi Domenico e Sisto in Rome and at the Walters Art Museum in Baltimore, shed new light on the use of liturgical space by the nuns and officiating clergymen. As with the Colonna hegemony in San Silvestro in Capite and San Lorenzo in Panisperna, Sant'Aurea thrived under baronial patronage, in this case enjoying the support of the Orsini until its suppression in 1514 (Figs. 10-11).[139]

Although the convent has been completely destroyed, we may reconstruct its exterior through the 1593 map of Rome by Antonio Tempesta. If we draw the outer lines of the conventual complex from the Tempesta map, we gain a fairly accurate idea of what its outer shell looked like. The entrance to the church was preceded by an open court and a narthex, which probably had two, or possibly, three openings. The gabled façade had a central *oculus* and the church likely had one nave (this was the case at San Sisto Vecchio). The interior furnishings of the *ecclesia monialium* may be partially reconstructed through a commission dated 1368. On 10 April 1368, Agnese, widow of Pucciarello de Puccio Boviis, entrusted Francesca and Francesco

---

135. L. Bellosi, "The function of the Rucellai Madonna in the Church of Santa Maria Novella", in *Italian Panel Painting of the Duecento and Trecento*, ed. by V. Schmidt, Washington, National Gallery of Art, 2002, pp. 146-159.

136. Romano, *Eclissi di Roma*, p. 231.

137. We know that given Dominic's imposition of a strict enclosure on the nuns of San Sisto Vecchio, the relocation of the painting was not well received by the Roman populace, forcing him to transfer the icon at night: Cannon, *Religious Poverty, Visual Riches*, p. 73.

138. Please refer to the local historian friar Emilio Panella's website (http://www.etheca.net/emiliopanella/governo/vade24.htm, last accessed 12/06/2021); Romano, *Apogeo e fine del Medioevo*, pp. 329-330.

139. A. Dunlop, "Dominicans and Cloistered Women: The Convent of Sant'Aurea in Rome", *Early Modern Women*, 2 (2007), p. 55; P. Pecchiai, *La Chiesa dello Spirito Santo e l'antica chiesa di Sant'Aurea in via Giulia*, Rome, Ugo Pinnarò, 1953; Zucchi, *Roma domenicana*, 1, p. 167.

Count of Anguillara with 400 florins to build a chapel inside the convent. The chapel is described as being behind the main altar, on the opposite side of the choir, and was intended to grant the nuns visual access to the main altar, which they could not view from the grate of their choir.[140] The community had specifically complained about this, and had requested the construction of the altar in front of their enclosure.[141] We may therefore deduce that they could probably hear but not witness the celebration of the liturgical service. According to Antonio Zucchi, Pio Pecchiai and Anne Dunlop, the triptych with the Virgin and saints by Lippo Vanni dated 1358 should be linked to this commission.[142] The dimensions of the painting suggest that it was destined for the main altar (172x208 cm). In my opinion, it is more likely that another triptych by Lippo Vanni (dated 1350-1359[143] or 1374-1375,[144] 49x45 cm), currently in the Walters Art Museum, was part of this commission. The larger work by the Sienese painter may be linked to Andrea di Orso Orsini's testamentary bequest of fifty gold florins to the church in 1348.[145] The triptych by Lippo Vanni records the date of its execution to 1358, while the bequest by Agnese, widow of Pucciarello, is dated to 1368 and specifically prescribes for the construction of a chapel. On the basis of chronological evidence, it would appear more likely considering its prestige that the testamentary bequest of Andrea was destined for the large triptych by Lippo Vanni. Therefore, if we assume that this altarpiece was intended for the main altar (given its size and importance this seems like a valid possibility) we cannot tie its realization to Pucciarello's donation recorded ten years after the execution of this altarpiece. Three reasons come into play: the importance of its patron, chronology, and prestige of its location (namely the main altar). On the contrary, Beatrice Cirulli suggests that the larger Lippo Vanni may have been commissioned by the Orsini possibly by someone named Bartolomeo.[146] She reasons behind the choice of including Saint Bartholomew, as opposed to the more evident choice of Thomas Aquinas.[147] Although this may well be a valid point no documentary proof is provided to corroborate this hypothesis (Figs. 12-14).

---

140. From Pecchiai, *La Chiesa dello Spirito Santo* also cited in Dunlop, "Dominicans and Cloistered Women", Archivio della Curia Generalizia dei Padri Predicatori a S. Sabina in Roma, 1368 April 10, M4: "[…] monialium dicti monasterii elegit singnanter altare et locum altaris intus dictam ecclesiam, videlicet in respect gratis ferree dicti monasterii iuxta et prope altare magnum Sancte Auree, per quam gratem dicta domina priorissa et moniales valeant habiliter et ex aspect oculorum videre et audure canere missam at canere et celebrare divina officia et alia sollempnia que requiruntur facere in aliis alataribus consacratis aliarum ecclesiarum".

141. Dunlop, "Dominicans and Cloistered Women", p. 68: the document is transcribed in this article.

142. *Ibid.*, p. 48; Pecchiai, *La Chiesa dello Spirito Santo*, p. 57; Zucchi, *Roma domenicana*, 1, p. 45.

143. Walter's Art Museum Website, https://art.thewalters.org/detail/12489/reliquary-with-madonna-and-child-with-saints/, last accessd 09/09/2018.

144. Romano, *Apogeo e fine del Medioevo*, p. 330.

145. Testamento di Andrea Orsini, Rome, Archivio Storico Capitolino, Archivio Orsini II, A 005, n. 007, 12 June 1348.

146. B. Cerulli, "Lippo Vanni. Il Trittico di Santa Aurea", in *Apogeo e fine del Medioevo*, p. 330.

147. *Ibid*.

The analogy of Sant'Aurea offers a strong case for positioning the nuns' choir at San Sisto Vecchio outside the main body of the church. However, we may also hypothesise that it was found in the presbytery enclosed on three sides, and opened towards the apse where the precious *Icona Tempuli* was possibly on display. The friars could have occupied the space around it, accessed by the passage to the left of the nave. A *tramezzo* screen possibly separated the *ecclesia* into two, and the large wooden crucifix (almost 2 m tall and 1,60 m wide) could have been placed on top of it or hung from the ceiling. This reconstruction would reconcile both the double community and the artworks, and presents a viable solution to the problem of *clausura*.[148]

Moreover, I would suggest that the internal layout of San Sisto resembles the arrangements of male Mendicant churches. Indeed, a similar display has been hypothesized for the Dominican monastery of Santa Maria Novella in Florence by Marcia Hall, and would in fact also account for the liturgical use of the images and church furnishing.[149] Donal Cooper maintains that although most rood screens were removed during the sixteenth century, especially in so far as the churches of Mendicant orders are accounted for, these were more popular than has been generally been considered.[150] *Tramezzo* screens offered a viable solution to the problem of separating the laity from the congregation in single nave churches so popular in Dominican and Franciscan houses.[151]

As previously stated, the painted cross at San Sisto is extraordinarily significant because in early sources it is frequently mentioned alongside the *Madonna Advocata* from the Monasterium Tempuli.[152] Along with the revered icon, it is one of the most compelling artistic vestiges to have survived from the first Roman female Dominican community. The blue cross with red boarders is depicted over a gold background and represents Christ in the *patiens* formula. The inscription in Gothic capitalized script reads IH(ESU)S NAZA/RENUS REX / IUDEORUM. Above the inscription, at the centre of the *cimasa*, is the figure of Christ encircled by a mandorla delimited by two angels at half-length. Two other angels may be viewed at his sides. Christ's lifeless body is flanked by the figures of the Virgin and Saint John. At the bottom of the cross, two kneeling portraits of Dominican friars on the left are mirrored by two nuns on the

148. I. Hueck, "Review of M. Bigaroni, H.R. Meier and E. Lunghi, *La Basilica di Santa Chiara in Assisi* (Quattroemme: Perugia, 1994)", *Kunstchronik*, 50 (1997), pp. 287-292; Donal Cooper has envisaged this model for the church of Santa Chiara at Assisi positioning the Abbess Benedicta crucifix between the *Vita* retable of Saint Clare and the *Virgin and Child* panel. D. Cooper, J. Robson, *The Making of Assisi. The Pope, the Franciscan and the Painting of the Basilica*, New Haven-London, Yale University Press, 2013, p. 73, image 74.

149. M.B. Hall, "The Ponte in S. Maria Novella: The Problem of the Rood Screen in Italy", *Journal of the Warburg and Courtauld Institutes*, 37 (1974), pp. 157-173.

150. D. Cooper, "Recovering the lost rood screens of medieval and Renaissance Italy", in *The Art and Science of the Church Screen in Medieval Europe*, ed. by S. Bucklow, R. Marks and L. Wrapson, Woodbridge, The Boydell Press, 2017, pp. 221-223.

151. Cooper, "Recovering", pp. 235-236.

152. Berthier, *Chroniques du monastère de San Sisto*, 1, p. 354; Romano, *Il Duecento e la cultura gotica*, pp. 274-277.

right. In contrast to the Franciscan order, which frequently represented supplicants or titular saints at the foot of the cross, this practice was quite uncommon amongst the Dominicans.[153] The presence of the friars testifies to the double community that was installed at San Sisto Vecchio. In this case it is probable that they represent the prior and the *oeconomus*, while the nuns are most likely the abbess and the sacristan. It is important to push this analysis forward, and underline how all four figures are presented on the foreground with no demarcation of status in terms of size. Are we meant to understand that both men and women are equal in the face of Christ's sacrifice? Is this equality of the sexes also possible in view of the religious habit? In a context where we would expect gender to be a particularly significant element, this visual uniformity between the friars and the nuns is noteworthy. What we may state objectively is that no part of the community is specifically favoured over the other. In fact, the nuns and friars are specular and therefore interchangeable. While there are other instances of female patrons portrayed at the foot of a monumental cross – examples including the *Benedicta crucifix* in Santa Chiara in Assisi – the San Sisto crucifix is particularly striking in view of the friars' presence.

In addition to the painted cross, a little-known fresco cycle found in the apsidal vault of San Sisto Vecchio displays another important testimony of Roman conventual medieval art of which so little has survived. These frescoes may well represent conventual agency in the promotion of artistic patronage in Rome at the turn of the century. The paintings were restored in two campaigns, between 1990 and 1992, by Silvana Franchini.[154] According to Barclay Lloyd, who has studied the frescoes extensively, "it is likely that these nuns played an important role in planning and commissioning the paintings, which thereby constitute an interesting example of convent art or paintings that were specifically designed for the Dominican sisters in Rome".[155] Located in the medieval apse of the church of San Sisto Vecchio, the frescoes were executed in two distinct phases. The first phase of the apse decoration likely dates to the turn of the thirteenth century, while the later one possibly between 1380 and 1411.[156] A depiction of Saints, Martyrs Angels, a Pentecost and a Presentation of the Virgin and one of Christ characterizes the former paintings. In terms of attribution, Toesca was the first to identify them as a product of the *scuola cavalliniana*.[157] Matthiae confirmed this but also stated that they were reminiscent of Cavallini's late style, as witnessed in the paintings of Santa Maria Donna Regina in Naples.[158] According to the

---

153. Cannon, *Religious Poverty, Visual Riches*, p. 67.
154. Barclay Lloyd, "Paintings for Dominican Nuns", p. 190; H. Geertman, M.B. Annis, "San Sisto Vecchio: indagini topografiche e archeologiche", in *Roma dall'antichità al medioevo, 2, Contesti tardoantichi e altomedioevali*, ed. by L. Paroli and L. Vendittelli, Milan, Electa, 2004, pp. 517-541. Currently these paintings are inaccessible because restoration works are being carried out in the convent.
155. Barclay Lloyd, "Paintings for Dominican Nuns", p. 193.
156. *Ibid.*, p. 228; Ronci, "Antichi affreschi a San Sisto", p. 20; Romano, *Apogeo e fine del Medioevo*, p. 264.
157. Toesca, *Storia dell'arte italiana*, p. 684.
158. Matthiae, *Pittura romana*, II, p. 350.

aforementioned economic register, and to a seventeenth-century chronicle on the foundation years of San Sisto by Sister Domenica Salomonia (who entered the nunnery in 1612 and died in 1672) entitled *Narratione historica del monastero dei SS. Domenico e Sisto*, the frescoes were mostly financed by the nuns' families including the Colonna and the Boccamazza.[159] In this chronicle, Sister Domenica claims that Angelica Boccamazza, prioress of the convent in 1290, and possibly the niece of Pope Honorius IV, was responsible for attracting large donations from the Curia and old baronial families.[160] The surviving documents at San Sisto Vecchio testify to the nuns' economic and political agency within the space of the convent.[161] The high-quality decorative program may confirm the nuns' role as catalysts for a significant operation of artistic renewal. Following Federica Vitali, Barclay Lloyd dates these paintings between 1295-1314 ascribing them to an artist influenced by Cavallini.[162] While in volume VI of *Corpus e Atlante*, Daniela Sgherri further restricts the chronology granting the frescoes an execution date that falls between the death of Cardinal Boccamazza in 1309 and the period of great destitution underwent by the community in 1314.[163]

As far as the paintings from the second phase are concerned, a series of standing saints including Saint Peter Martyr, Saint Dominic, Saint John the Baptist, Saint Paul, and Saint Catherine with a nu*n* are represented. In the upper portion of the apse on the left-hand side, one may still read the inscription B(EA)-TA KATHERINA DE SENIS.[164] This inscription has proven extremely insightful for a variety of reasons. On the one hand, it has helped identify Catherine of Siena in the two scenes on the far left; on the other it has restricted the chronology for the dating of the paintings.

159. The manuscript is preserved in the archive of the Santissimo Rosario at Montemario (Rome); the complete title is: *Narratione historica del monastero dei SS. Domenico e Sisto et sua origine cavata dalle Cronache di San Domenico da varie traditioni et alter scritture autentiche raccolte da sor Pulcheria Carducci et sor Domenica Salomonia monache in detto monastero, l'anno MDCXXXVIII sotto il priorato della molto R. sor Maria Tenaglini* and has been only partially published.

160. "[Cardinal Boccamazza] accordò immediatamente un larghissimo aiuto in denaro, poi indusse altri pii benefattori romani ad imitarlo, e così furono messi insieme i mezzi per rifare e ingrandire il dormitorio bruciato": Spiazzi, *Cronache e fioretti*, pp. 114-120.

161. This is particularly evident if we take into account the *Liber depositarie seu bursarie* 1369-1391 (Archivio Apostolico Vaticano, Monasteri femminili soppressi, SS. Domenico e Sisto, 191) which lists the nuns' personal possessions. This registry also includes the *Libro dell'inventario delle monache morte* where we learn for example that Palotia Grassa (1376) owned a *domus minor* and a *domus magna* which guaranteed her a fixed revenue: Carbonetti Vendittelli, "Il registro", pp. 97-99. Additionally, in this documentation it is quite common to find *pro anniversario* or *pro anima* donations from the nuns to the convent – these are listed as entries for the nunnery in the *Liber depositarie*. Finally, this also testifies to the status of the community where names such as Boccamazza, Savelli, Grassi, Annibaldi appear regularly. The high status of these nuns would have guaranteed them a sizeable dowry when entering the convent. As we have seen this was partially administered autonomously by the community.

162. Barclay Lloyd, "Paintings for Dominican Nuns", p. 210.

163. D. Sgherri, "La decorazione ad affresco nell'antica abside e nella navata di San Sisto Vecchio", in *Apogeo e fine del Medioevo*, p. 269.

164. Tommaso de Senis, *Sanctae Catharinae Senensis Legenda Minor*, ed. by E. Franceschini, Milan, Bocca, 1942; Ronci, "Antichi affreschi a San Sisto Vecchio", p. 25.

According to Gilberto Ronci, who assigns these paintings to the *scuola senese*, Saint Catherine was beatified in 1411, *terminus ante quem* for dating the frescoes.[165] The term 'Beata' is consistent with the rays of light with which the saint is depicted in the frescoes, and reinforces a chronology, which falls between Saint Catherine's death in 1380, and her canonisation in 1411. In the lower portion of the representation of Catherine's vision of Christ, the portrait of a Dominican nun, possibly the patron of the paintings, can be seen. The standing saint to the right of these paintings has been identified by the Sant'Eustachio coat of arms as the family's titular saint.[166] Ronci assumes that the nun in the frescoes should be identified as a member of the Sant'Eustachio family. In Sister Domenica Salomonia's chronicle, two nuns are recorded with the name Andrea di Sant'Eustachio. They respectively entered the convent in 1280 and the last quarter of the fourteenth century.[167] In another document from the Tivoli archives, which is dated 1386, there is a reference to another nun at San Sisto named Sopphia de Sancto Eustachio.[168] While Ronci makes no mention of this document, Barclay Lloyd (citing the work of Carbonetti Vendittelli) asserts that the nun present in the frescoes is either the later Andrea, or, Sophia. Like the Boccamazza, the nuns from the Sant'Eustachio family gathered similar prestige in the convent's affairs during the fourteenth century.[169]

The apse was covered by a fresco cycle on all its surfaces. Indeed this likely continued towards the walls of the central nave. Given the strict enclosure imposed upon the order, Barclay Lloyd hypothesizes that they were only visible to the nuns. She states that an iconographic program was designed *ad hoc* for the female community. In her conclusions, she asserts that with the endowment from Cardinal Boccamazza, the prioress, prior and perhaps nuns whose families had paid for the paintings were in charge of the decorative programme.[170] Romano goes as far as stating that the nuns exclusively used the cardinal's legacies to embellish the church with fresco decoration.[171] Should we concur with Barclay Lloyd's claim that these frescoes "may represent an interesting example of late medieval convent art, that is art planned specifically by and for nuns"?[172] As we have seen, this statement is largely based on the reading of secondary literature by Romano, Vitali, Ronci and

165. *Ibid.*, p. 31; Beatrice Cirulli in *Apogeo e fine del Medioevo* changes the *terminus ante quem* to 1395 for stylistic reasons, B. Cirulli, "Gli affreschi nella navata di San Sisto Vecchio", in *Apogeo e fine del Medioevo*, p. 347.
166. Barclay Lloyd, "Paintings for Dominican Nuns", p. 212; Ronci, "Antichi affreschi a San Sisto Vecchio", p. 31; U. Salvini, *Raccolta di stemmi di famiglie di Ancona, Firenze, Montemignaio, Recanati, Roma, Senigallia, Tolentino*, Florence, 1954.
167. *L'Archivio Tiburtino di S. Giovanni Evangelista*, ed. by V. Pacifici, Subiaco, Tipografia dei Monasteri, 1922, pp. 62-65.
168. Barclay Lloyd, "Paintings for Dominican Nuns", p. 215; Ronci, "Antichi affreschi a San Sisto Vecchio", p. 36; *L'Archivio tiburtino di S. Giovanni*, p. 65.
169. *Le più antiche carte del convento di San Sisto in Roma (900-1300)*, ed. by C. Carbonetti Vendittelli, Rome, Società romana di storia patria, 1987; Barclay Lloyd, "Paintings for Dominican Nuns", p. 229; Ronci, "Antichi affreschi a San Sisto Vecchio", p. 39.
170. Barclay Lloyd, "Paintings for Dominican Nuns", p. 215.
171. Romano, *Eclissi di Roma*, p. 102.
172. Barclay Lloyd, "Paintings for Dominican Nuns", p. 211.

on documents published in the works of Berthier, Carbonetti Vendittelli, Koudelka and Spiazzi. Although the possibility that Boccamazza financed the fresco program is viable and has been previously advanced by Romano, Vitali and Ronci, we cannot be certain that the nuns' choir was found in the apse. Even if we refute the possibility of the apse as the choir's location, these paintings still offer a valid testimony of medieval female conventual art of which so little survives in Rome. Romano's claim that the Marian scenes should be tied to the presence of the *Icona Tempuli* is worth considering, and seems to be a more valid hypothesis. Indeed, contemporary accounts of the Icon highlight its great prestige both for the Roman people and for the nuns at the Monasterium Tempuli. Its presence inside the apse of the presbytery would have easily justified a targeted iconographic programme.

San Sisto Vecchio is one of the most compelling case studies for our understanding of female conventual life in Rome and the greater Latium area. Although it is not possible to determine the patronage of the frescoes from the first phase inside the apse with absolute confidence, they certainly do testify to high-level commissions in Rome during the Avignon period. Nunneries across the city did not act as substitutes for the vacated papal seat but still presented viable alternatives of patronage for artists working in Central and Southern Italy. Moreover, San Sisto demonstrates that when it comes to female monastic complexes, a standard architectural practice does not exist. For this reason, I have attempted to reconstruct its medieval facies by integrating the liturgical study of space with the surviving artefacts present in the church. These tentative planimetric drawings were challenged by the loss of a great part of the original medieval furnishing. By integrating Barclay Lloyd's reconstructions and architectural elements with written testimonies left by Sister Cecilia in the *Miracula beati Dominici*; the CAD plans were used as a visual map to reason around the various architectural solutions in order to account for the use of space and the re-positioning of artworks in their original context. The main challenge in these reconstructions was to factor in the notion of space as an element which regularized encounters between different genders and religious groups in the nunnery. Indeed, in this regard *clausura* acted as a *fil rouge* of analysis for the different solutions presented in the disposition of the choir inside the church. By considering its rich historiography and comparing it to other nunneries, this case study hopefully exemplifies the interdisciplinary integrated methodology advanced by this research.

Additionally, San Sisto Vecchio fosters debates on questions of bias established when scholarship is forced into a gendered reading of primary sources. Although it is fair to underline that spaces inside convents were conceived with a clear destination for women, should we think of these in a more permeable fashion? This is not likely, however, one must also be cautious when forcing predetermined reasoning based exclusively on a contemporary reading of the medieval past. Is the representation of nuns and the friars as equals designed for a lay public? Is Innocent's agenda of presenting the Church of Rome as a cohesive front pushed forward with this iconography? And finally, should we treat this artefact as an exception? As far as conventual art is considered, it might be wiser to set new research agendas. For example, understanding the liturgical use of images and church furnishing within the larger context of conventual spaces, as I have attempted to do for the monumental cross, the icon, and the frescoes in the apsidal vault.

3. *Assisi in Rome? Clare's Influence at Santi Cosma e Damiano in Mica Aurea*

The monastery of Santi Cosma e Damiano in Mica Aurea, commonly known as San Cosimato, is in Trastevere, one of Rome's oldest suburban areas.[173] San Cosimato has been studied extensively by secondary literature. Alongside Gemma Guerrini Ferri[174] and Karin Bull-Simonsen Einaudi,[175] Barclay Lloyd edited two separate monographs on the complex, which cover the nunnery's intricate building history and extensive archival record. The latest survey on the convent was recently published as a collection of essays edited by Anna Maria Velli.[176] Contributions by Guerrini Ferri and Barclay Lloyd are also present in this volume. In addition to providing a historical context for the convent, the monograph sponsored by the *Associazione di volontariato culturale Mica Aurea* aims to expand the 2013 proceedings of the conference on the nunnery which resulted in the aforementioned edition by Guerrini Ferri and Barclay Lloyd. San Cosimato is unquestionably one of the most extensively studied foundations in Rome. We will, however, push forward the findings by reasoning around questions of space, function and gender inside the church and the conventual complex.

The *Mica Aurea* region covered almost half the perimeter of the *Transtiberim* neighbourhood, and extended from the banks of the Tiber all the way up the Janiculum hill. The Benedictine monastery was founded during the first half of the tenth century between 936 and 948 by Benedictus Campaninus – a loyal collaborator of Alberic II, Count of Tusculum and *de facto* ruler of Rome from 932 until his death in 954. Benedictus laid the foundations of the church on his property and invited Venerando, a monk from the imperial abbey at Farfa, to join the monastery as its

---

173. Barclay Lloyd, "The Medieval Benedictine Monastery", pp. 25-35; Barclay Lloyd, Bull-Simonsen Einaudi, *SS. Cosma e Damiano*; *San Cosimato*, ed. by F. Caraffa and L. Lotti, Rome, Nardini, 1971; P. Fedele, "Carte del monastero di SS. Cosma e Damiano", *Archivio della Società romana di storia patria*, 21 (1898), pp. 459-534; L. Gigli, *Rione XII. Trastevere*, Rome, Edizioni storiche, 1987; *"San Chosm'e Damiano e 'l suo bel monasterio..."*: *il complesso monumentale di San Cosimato ieri, oggi, domani. Un itinerario tra le memorie ed i tesori del Venerabile Monastero dei Santi Cosma e Damiano in Mica Aurea*, ed. by G. Guerrini Ferri and J. Barclay Lloyd, Rome, Testo e Senso, 2013; K.J.P. Lowe, "Franciscan and Papal Patronage at the Clarissan Convent of San Cosimato in Trastevere 1440-1560", *Papers of the British School at Rome*, 68 (2000), pp. 217-239; K.J.P. Lowe, *Nuns' Chronicles and Convent Culture in Renaissance and Counter-Reformation Italy*, Cambridge, Cambridge University Press, 2003; G. Sicari, "Il monastero di SS. Cosma e Damiano in Mica Aurea: sue proprietà in Roma", *Alma Roma*, 23 (1982), pp. 30-44.
174. *"San Chosm'e Damiano"*.
175. Barclay Lloyd, Bull-Simonsen Einaudi, *SS. Cosma e Damiano*.
176. *Nuovi studi su San Cosimato*, ed. by A.M. Velli, Rome, Graphofeel Edizioni, 2017.

new abbot. A bull issued by Pope John XVIII (1004-1009) in 1005 provides us with a valuable description of the monastery itself.[177] The main church was dedicated to Saint Benedict, while a small oratory was entitled to Saint Nicholas. Several living quarters destined for the monks were provided with fireplaces, while the exteriors were characterized by the presence of a cloistered portico, a vineyard, an orchard and several acres of farmland on the banks of the Tiber. The extent of this large site may be seen on the map drawn by Mario Cartaro in 1576.

The tenth-century phenomenon of monastic foundations by private individuals came as a result of the secularization of cloistered culture. After the collapse of the Carolingian Empire, the reformation of ecclesiastic culture was principally promoted by Cluny.[178] The latter fostered a spirit of reform, which transformed the monastery as a religious, but more importantly, social and political institution under the direct protection of the Holy See. Indeed, the influence exercised by Cluny over the monastery of Santi Cosma e Damiano in Mica Aurea is unquestionable, and took place under the aegis of Odo of Cluny (878-942). He was, in fact, specifically invited to Rome by Alberic II in order to reform and revive monastic life in Central Italy.[179] The foundation of Santi Cosma e Damiano in Mica Aurea came at a time when the Roman aristocracy was attempting to broaden its political power through the newly found socio-political role of monastic institutions.[180] San Cosimato was officiated by Benedictine monks for almost three centuries. Given its state of advanced decline and the accusations of simony that fell upon the congregation, the monastery was suppressed and passed to the female branch of the Franciscans during the thirteenth century. Gregory IX personally established a Clarissan nunnery in 1234.[181] San Cosimato was the first Clarissan community in the city of Rome. The Franciscan First Order was already established in the neighbourhood at the Chapel of San Biagio (the later San Francesco a Ripa, originally also part of the Benedictine community at San Cosimato). It appears that Gregory, encouraged by the noble matron Jacopa de Settesoli, wished to create a concentration of Franciscan foundations in the area. The Franciscan tertiary, Jacopa, was a Roman noblewoman possibly from the Frangipane family. It is generally believed that she met Saint Francis in Rome in 1222 during the pontificate of Honorius III. As stated by numerous Franciscan sources, she had a very special relationship with the saint and was granted the privilege of burial inside the basilica at Assisi.[182] Even

---

177. The main church was dedicated to Saint Benedict, while a small oratory was devoted to Saint Nicholas. Several of the monks' living quarters were provided with heated rooms, while the exteriors included a cloistered portico, a vineyard, an orchard and several acres on the banks of the Tiber. The site's significant dimensions figures on the map drawn by Mario Cartaro in 1576.

178. G. Antonelli, "L'opera di Odone di Cluny in Italia", *Benedictina*, 4 (1950), pp. 19-40; G. Constable, *Cluny from the Tenth to the Twelfth Centuries. Further Studies*, Aldershot, Ashgate, 2000.

179. Antonelli, "L'opera di Odone di Cluny", p. 33.

180. *"San Chosm'e Damiano"*, p. 45.

181. L. Wadding, *Annales minorum seu Trium Ordinum a S. Francisco institutorum*, 6, Rome, Rochi Bernabò, 1733, p. 578.

182. Bernanrdo da Bessa, Thomas from Celano and Saint Bonaventure all speak fondly of her: G.E. Lovrovich, *Jacopa dei Settesoli*, Marino, Tipografia Santa Lucia, 1976, p. 18.

during her lifetime and without ever leaving the secular world Jacopa was seen as an influential model of piety and devotion.[183]

In his survey on Clarissan nunneries in Latium during the thirteenth century, Marini claims that nuns from the community at San Damiano in Assisi came to oversee the foundation of the new Roman convent.[184] Given the special ties between Pope Gregory IX and Saint Clare (1194-1253) (who was still alive at the time of the Roman foundation), this assumption may hold a certain degree of truth. These considerations are particularly noteworthy in relation to the architectural reconstruction of the complex, the division of space inside the church and the position occupied by the nuns' choir. The Clarissans resided in the nunnery until 1874, when it was seized by the Italian state and transformed into the hospital Nuovo Regina Margherita.[185]

As testified by a copy of a sixteenth-century parchment preserved at the Archivio di Stato di Roma, the new Clarissan church was consecrated in 1246 by the bishop of Ascoli.[186] Although Abbess Iacopa Cenci is not mentioned in this parchment, we know she headed the massive reconstruction of the complex in the 1240s.[187] Iacopa's role as the promoter of this large-scale renovation is documented by the sixteenth-century chronicle of the convent written by the three times abbess, Orsola Formicini, who entered the nunnery in 1558 at the age of eight and resided there until her death in 1614.[188] Today the nunnery is comprised of a portal, two large cloisters – one medieval, the other dating to the fifteenth century – former living quarters, a small church dating originally to the ninth century but refurbished by Abbess Iacopa in the 1240s and then in 1475 under Pope Sixtus IV (1471-1484). The "Romanesque" bell tower present today likely followed the reconstruction of the church by Pope Sixtus. Here, we shall only consider thirteenth- and fourteenth- century refurbishments, or at least what can be safely identified as such.

---

183. *Ibid.*

184. Marini, "Le fondazioni francescane femminili", pp. 71-96. Unfortunately, the scholar does not provide any bibliographical reference for this claim.

185. Given the rigid *clausura* observed by nuns, the nunnery has only been studied in the last century when the local archive was moved to the Archivio di Stato di Roma (*fondo* santi Cosma e Damiano) and published by Pietro Fedele in Fedele, *Carte del monastero.*

186. Archivio di Stato di Roma (hereafter ASR), Collezione Pergamene, Clarisse in SS. Cosma e Damiano in Mica Aurea, cassetta 17 bis, n. 261: "In Nomine Domine Amen. Anno dominicae incarnationis Millesimo duecentesimo quadragesimo Sexto, temporibus domini Innocentij Pape tertij die secda p dominica de passione Domine Theodinus Episcopus Aclan de mandato Venerabilis domini Stephani cardinalis tunc temporis vicarij domini pape Urbis consecravit hoc altare in honore Sanctorum Cosmi et Damiani ubi reconduntur reliquias sanctorum subscriptas". The citation and the text are published in Barclay Lloyd, Bull-Simonsen Einaudi, *SS. Cosma e Damiano*, p. 135.

187. Romano, *Riforma e tradizione*, p. 23.

188. This chronicle is currently preserved at the Biblioteca Nazionale Centrale of Rome (hereafter BNCR). The codices Ms. Varia 5 and Ms. Varia 6 at the BNCR collect the first and the second edition of the *Liber monialum.* O. Formicini, *Liber monialum sancti Cosmati de Urbe in regione Transtiberim de observantia sub regula sancte Clare* […], Rome, BNCR, Fondi Minori, Ms. Varia, 6; G. Guerrini Ferri, *I libri di suor Orsola Formicini*, in *"San Chosm'e Damiano"*, pp. 89-100.

According to Formicini, under Iacopa's guidance the nunnery underwent a period of extensive transformation and remodelling of the earlier Benedictine complex. On the basis of Formicini's testimony and from the analysis of *spoliae* still present on site, Romano claims that the former cloister was enlarged and remodelled with columns and capitals from coeval construction sites such as San Paolo fuori le Mura and San Giovanni in Laterano.[189] This process of adapting existing buildings to the needs of a new conventual community parallels the work undertaken at the original Clarissan house at Assisi.[190] The use of *spoliae*, so common in medieval Rome, may in this instance be specifically linked to this Franciscan ideology of reuse. The employment of Roman stonemasons is also testified by a number of graffiti on column capitals which can be traced back to the *magistri doctissimi romani*.[191] The original medieval cloister extends on the southern side of the present-day church; an analysis of the cloister's masonry in *opus saracinescum* indicates that the western range was enlarged and refurbished during the first half of the thirteenth century.[192] A series of pilasters were inserted between the set of binary columns to sustain the blind arches and accommodate the new floor. While the cloister's existing southern range, and the adjoining portion of the western side were entirely constructed in the first half of the fourteenth century. Likewise, this appears to be the case for the southern part of the west wing of the cloister.[193] Under Iacopa, the new cloister possibly measured 34,1 m from north to south and 30,5 m from east to west.[194]

The rigid *clausura* imposed a set of predetermined structures designed to guarantee the nuns' security, but this need only partially drove Abbess Iacopa's large-scale renovation. In addition to the structural changes noted above, it also encompassed a lavish Cosmati *schola cantorum*, which survives as fragments in the medieval cloister, and the commission of a church bell from the famous Bartholomeus from Pisa.[195] Bartholomeus was responsible for casting the bells at San Francesco in Assisi and at the Aracoeli in Rome.[196] His commission testifies to the prestige of this large-scale renovation undertaken by Iacopa Cenci and likely overseen by Pope Gregory IX.

189. Romano, *Il Duecento e la cultura gotica*, p. 33.
190. J. Barclay Lloyd, "L'architettura medievale di S. Cosimato in Trastevere", in Barclay Lloyd, Bull-Simonsen, *SS. Cosma e Damiano*, pp. 77-126: 115; Bruzelius, "Hearing is Believing", p. 83; *Francesco, il francescanesimo e la cultura della nuova Europa*, ed. by I. Baldelli and A.M. Romanini, Rome, Istituto della Enciclopedia Italiana, 1986, pp. 181-195; Zappasodi, *Sorores*, pp. 24-26.
191. Romano, *Il Duecento e la cultura gotica*, p. 33.
192. Barclay Lloyd, "L'architettura medievale di S. Cosimato in Trastevere", pp. 109-110; V. Danesi, "Il chiostro medievale a San Cosimato a Trastevere: una nuova proposta di lettura", in *Domus sapienter staurata. Scritti di storia dell'arte per Marina Righetti*, ed. by A.M. D'Achille, A. Iacobini, P.F. Pistilli, Rome, Silvana Editoriale, 2021, pp. 244-252.
193. P. Tomei, *L'architettura a Roma nel Quattrocento*, Rome, Palombi, 1942, p. 161.
194. Barclay Lloyd, "L'architettura medievale di S. Cosimato in Trastevere", p. 106.
195. Inscription on bell: A.D.M.C.C.XXXVIII BARTHOLOMEUS PISANUS ME FECIT.
196. J. Gardner, "For Whom the Bell Tolls: A Franciscan Bell Founder, Franciscan Bells and a Franciscan Patrons in Late Thirteenth-Century Rome", in *Medioevo. I committenti*, ed. by A.C. Quintavalle, Acts of the conference (Parma, 2010), Milan, Electa, 2011, pp. 460-468.

Unfortunately, the church was entirely refurbished during the fifteenth-century restoration carried out by Pope Sixtus IV. Today, it is divided into two by a thick masonry wall which separates the *ecclesia monialium* from the *ecclesia laicorum*. As testified by nineteenth-century plans of the complex, the former terminated in an apse. This possibly formed part of the nuns' choir and probably hosted the precious Marian icon, currently preserved at the Istituto Centrale del Restauro and commonly referred to as *Madonna del Coro* (Figs. 15-17).[197] We are not certain whether this disposition reflects the original thirteenth-century medieval layout of the church. Retro-choirs made their first systematic appearance in female Mendicant churches during the fourteenth century. Zappasodi, however, identifies a series of Clarissan convents with retro-choirs that pre-date the celebrated example of Santa Chiara in Naples (ca. 1310).[198] Nevertheless, while the Neapolitan complex qualifies as a double community, we know from the *Catalogo di Torino* that San Cosimato was composed of thirty-five nuns with only two officiating friars.[199] Even the Clarissan community of San Silvestro in Capite likely housed a choir behind the presbytery, however, its foundation also comes at a later date (1280s). Having said this, we may argue that the nuns in Rome were modelling their church on San Damiano with a choir behind and adjacent to the presbytery. This could indeed be a valid possibility if we accept Marini's claim that nuns from Assisi came to oversee the construction of the Roman convent.

Analysing contemporary chronological time frames and local regional areas may also shed light on the the choir's location inside the church. An examination of coeval Clarissan settlements in Latium may provide invaluable insight on the original layout of this Roman nunnery. The lost complex of Borgo San Pietro was founded by Saint Filippa Mareri when Clare was still alive. Plans and archival material collected by the Genio Civile during the construction of the Salto Lake dam in the province of Rieti allow us to reconstruct the original layout of the convent.[200] The medieval nunnery had a north-west/south-east orientation, which applied both to the church and the conventual spaces. The Chapter hall and the refectory were located around the square cloister on the south-eastern side, the kitchens and the deposits on the south-western portion, while a fortified entrance which opened across the bell tower was found on the north-eastern perimeter. The nuns' cells

---

197. Rome, Archivio Centrale dello Stato, AABBAA, II, II, busta 402, All.B.13; Lowe, *Franciscan and Papal Patronage*, p. 238.

198. Zappasodi, *Sorores*, pp. 21-24. Zappasodi states that before 1310 retro-choirs were already popular. Outside the Mendicant sphere, other celebrated examples of convents with retrochoirs are Santa Marta in Siena and San Gaggio in Florence. Additionally in E. Zappasodi, "Ambrogio Lorenzetti 'Huomo di grande ingegno': un polittico fuori canone e due tavole dimenticate", *Nuovi Studi. Rivista di arte antica e moderna*, 19 (2013), pp. 5-22: through the reconstruction of a disemembered altarpiece by Ambrogio Lorenzetti the author suggests that large-scale polyptychs were sometimes used to frame the *fenestra monialium* of retrochoirs, examples cited by the author are, however, all later than the refurbishments which took place at San Cosimato in Rome.

199. Falco, *Albori d'Europa*.

200. For Borgo San Pietro, see Chapter 4,§5, *Treasures under Water: The Nunnery of Santa Filippa Mareri, Borgo San Pietro*.

were on the south-eastern and south-western sides whereas the side adjacent to the church was occupied by a choir. It is highly possible that this was the choir's original location.

This would not be the first example of a Clarissan nunnery in Latium with a choir overlooking the church laterally. Indeed, other examples such as San Pietro in Vineis[201] in Anagni testify to this practice. The church itself, and the extension on the right, are the only surviving portions of the medieval nunnery today. The section adjacent and overlooking the cloister consists of two floors. Today, there is a corridor at ground level, which extends across the length of the church's exterior nave and opens into one of the arms of the modern cloister. The walls are decorated with devotional paintings, dating from the thirteenth to the fifteenth centuries. The choir itself is located in a recessed room on the upper floor, directly above the right nave, to the left of this corridor. From an architectonic standpoint, San Pietro in Vineis testifies to a series of trends, which are frequently used in Clarissan conventual complexes throughout Latium and which may offer further insight into the proto Clarissan nunnery at San Cosimato.

At San Sebastiano at Alatri the choir is located in a suspended room adjacent to the church, while at San Michele Arcangelo it can be found in the counter-façade. This scheme recalls that of Santa Maria Donna Regina in Naples. Indeed, from surviving evidence collected at San Pietro in Vineis, Borgo San Pietro, San Pietro at Tuscania, San Michele Arcangelo at Amaseno, and San Sebastiano at Alatri – we may assert that in Latium, the order's choirs were frequently positioned in a room overlooking the church. The only surviving example of a choir located at ground level that I am aware of in this region is Santa Rosa at Viterbo.

As far as San Cosimato is concerned, we may also hypothesize that the choir was positioned outside the church, possibly on the southern side and either on the first, or, the second floor.[202] This would have facilitated access to the convent's apartments or to the cloister itself. Alternatively, the choir might have been positioned at right angles with the apse as in San Damiano at Assisi. Unfortunately, due to the construction of the fifteenth-century cloister by Pope Sixtus IV this cannot be determined with absolute certainty. Formicini informs us that Iacopa was responsible for doubling the height of the church (the estimate is by at least 5 m), constructing the portico and possibly building the dormitory or a suspended choir over the portal of the church.[203] The influence imparted by the church of San Damiano on San Cosimato is undeniable, but unfortunately without further archaeological investigations it is impossible to determine the latter's original disposition.

---

201. For the Anagni convent, see Chapter 4, §4, *A New Manifesto for the Mendicant Order: San Pietro in Vineis, Anagni*.

202. Bruzelius, "Hearing is Believing", pp. 83-91; Hamburger, "Art, Enclosure and the *Cura Monialium*", pp. 108-134.

203. Barclay Lloyd, "L'architettura medievale di S. Cosimato in Trastevere", pp. 83, 122.

As in San Sisto Vecchio, the large-scale refurbishments served both to guarantee enclosure and possibly to allow the lay congregation to access the revered Marian icon. These considerations have put forward different spatial arrangements inside the church. This is especially the case in relation the choir. These solutions considered the spatial frameworks that regularised encounters between different genders and religious groups in the nunnery. Most importantly, at San Cosimato we witnessed the influence San Damiano at Assisi exercised over conventual complexes in Central Italy. As the first Clarissan house, it was likely seen as an ideal model to replicate. This is the case for several other settlements in Latium. In this particular instance, it is significant both for the arrangement of the choir but most importantly for the position of the dormitory over the main body of the church, emphasising the importance of architectural forms in the iconography of female religious piety.

In conclusion, rigid *clausura* imposed a set of predetermined structures to guarantee the nuns' security. This did not deter the large-scale renovation promoted by Abbess Cenci, which resulted in the construction of the cloistered garden, the Cosmati *schola cantorum* and the commission of a church bell manufactured by Bartholomeus from Pisa in 1238. These large-scale refurbishments during the mid-thirteenth century appear to be a fairly common trend in Roman nunneries during the late medieval period. A similar pattern of patronage is also present in the Benedictine convent of Sant'Agnese fuori le Mura. It is likely that something comparable occurred at the nunnery of San Cosimato where the massive restoration of the existing monastic complex was promoted by an abbess under the auspices of the Holy See. Although no traces of thirteenth-century decorations survive, small fragments of fifteenth-century paintings representing Saint Sebastian remain in the presbytery, while representations of the Saints Cosmas and Damian may be observed in the wall adjacent to the apse. These indicate that the church was likely embellished by a fresco cycle. Indeed, as in the Dominican nunnery of San Sisto, it is likely that the presence of the Marian icon alone would have prompted some sort of decorative program, at least as far as the apse was concerned. In fact, we should not underestimate the "restoration" of the Marian icon in the first quarter of the thirteenth century.[204] Was this operation part of Iacopa's general refurbishment of the conventual complex? We may not know for sure.

---

204. G. Leone, *Icone di Roma e del Lazio*, Rome, L'Erma di Bretschneider, 2013; O. Panciroli, *I tesori nascosti dell'alma citta' di Roma*, Rome, per gli Heredi di A. Zanetti, 1600, p. 289; R. Scognamiglio, L. Speciale, "L'altra Madonna di Trastevere. La tavola della Vergine di San Cosimato", in *L'officina dello sguardo. Scritti in onore di Maria Andaloro*, ed. by G. Bordi, I. Carlettini, M.L. Fobelli, M.R. Menna and P. Pogliani, Rome, Gangemi Editore, 2014, pp. 359-354; G. Guerrini Ferri, "La Madonna del coro", in *"San Chosm'e Damiano"*, pp. 225-239. Guerrini Ferri states that: "sotto la supervisione del prof. Giuseppe Basile [...] questa icona fu oggetto di un raffinato lavoro di restauro [...] opera di un autore anonimo del XIII secolo, e non si tralascio di notare come essa fosse a sua volta sovrapposta ad un altro dipinto più antico, del quale, tuttavia non restano che minime trace, percettibili ai bordi", *ibid.*, p. 226. Suor Orsola states that a certain Pope Leo venerated this icon, unfortunately, she does not offer further insight as to the dating of the original painting, however, given that Formicini mentions that it was originally found the chapel of Saint Processus

Nevertheless, given that it was originally preserved in an altar at Saint Peter's, commissioned by Pope Paschal I (817-824) and dedicated to Saint Martinian and Processus, both its importance and prestige should be acknowledged. Its presence at San Cosimato under the Benedictine occupation is testified both by Formicini and by Ottavio Panciroli's *Tesori nascosti dell'alma città di Roma*.[205]

Santi Cosma e Damiano in Mica Aurea both reinforces and defies specific patterns of conventual patronage in Rome. Although nunneries were frequently subject to external endowments, it would seem that the nuns at San Cosimato were in charge of overseeing a significant operation of artistic and architectonic renewal internally. While the involvement of the female community in the 1256 re-consecration of the basilica ultimately remains speculative at Sant'Agnese, at San Cosimato, Abbess Iacopa's large-scale intervention is confirmed by the 1558 chronicle of the convent by Orsola Formicini. Given a similar chronological time frame, is it safe to assume that something similar also occurred at Sant'Agnese fuori le Mura under the aegis of Abbess Lucia? The possibility is viable but impossible to confirm with the evidence collected to date. Ultimately, San Cosimato underpins the active role played by popes in Roman convents, especially in so far as the Mendicant orders were concerned. For the time period accounted for in this book, the Mendicants enjoyed great popularity among curial circles. This claim is reinforced by Gregory IX's 1234 instalment of the Clarissan nunnery. As in San Sisto Vecchio, it possibly points to the Mendicant's understanding of the importance of female communities as centres to showcase their power and influence in the city of Rome. Yet San Cosimato pushes this statement forward by highlighting the role of lay women, possibly Jacopa de Settesoli, in creating a Franciscan stronghold in Trastevere. Was this also motivated by the desire to expand her familial presence in the neighbourhood? Although this claim is purely hypothetical and has not emerged from the surviving documentation; we are aware that Roman convents were divided according to territorial divisions of baronial power, a trend that possibly also applied to this nunnery.

4. *Baronial Authority and Identity in Rome: The Colonna at San Silvestro in Capite*

As with other female monastic institutions in Rome, San Silvestro in Capite furthers our understanding of Roman nunneries beyond a purely art historical context. The evidence collected not only underscores the extensive prestige of this female monastic community, but also its significance in a more complex socio-historic scenario. As far as this case study is concerned, our objective will not be to revaluate women's agency in the context of matronage, but rather to contextualize this community as a centre of power for one of the leading baronial families in Rome,

---

and Saint Artignanus in Saint Peter's a ninth-century date has been put forward by Guerrini Ferri in *"San Chosm'e Damiano"*, pp. 230-233.
  205. Panciroli, *I tesori*, p. 289; *"San Chosm'e Damiano"*, pp. 225-239.

the Colonna. This will hopefully contribute to the understanding of nunneries in a broader social, political and economic network. Given its complex nature, we shall proceed with a very brief historical introduction. A detailed analysis of the Colonna family takeover will follow, and finally, we shall corroborate our thesis through the rich documentary corpus preserved in Rome's Archivio di Stato.

The monastery of San Silvestro in Capite or San Silvestro e Stefano is found in the south-eastern region of the Campo Marzio area.[206] It is unclear whether the church was built over a Roman theatre, a stadium, or a thermal complex, but excavations have proven that it was indeed constructed over a pre-existing ancient Roman building.[207] As stated by the *Constitutum* and by the biography of Paul I (757-767) in the *Liber pontificalis*, San Silvestro in Capite was constructed over the residence of the pope's father during the eighth century to preserve relics and bodies from the suburban catacombs.[208] The first monograph on the convent, written by Giovanni Giacchetti in 1629, asserts that the monastery was developed on two levels.[209] The lower one consisted of a *confessio*, while the ground floor followed a rectangular plan with a central altar, which preserved the bodies of Saint Silvester and Saint Stephen.[210] A few vestiges of the early medieval eight-century phase still survive in the foundations of the building, which may be observed in portions of the peripheral walls and in a series of *cipollino* marble columns. Other churches, such as Santa Prassede or Santa Maria in Domnica built by Pope Paschal I during the ninth century, may give us a sense of its original form. The description given in the *Liber pontificalis* does indeed confirm this hypothesis. It also confirms that the church was composed of three naves and had a *confessio* to preserve the numerous relics from other suburban basilicas outside the city walls.[211] The monastery was originally officiated by Greek monks.[212] In his monograph *Early Roman Monasteries*, Guy Ferrari claims that a Greek *scriptorium* existed at San Silvestro.[213] Archival documents, preserved at the Archivio di Stato di Roma, and

---

206. The most recent and comprehensive publication on the complex is by E. Kane, *The Church of San Silvestro in Capite in Rome*, Genoa, Marconi, 2005. Marilyn Dunn has also published on the convent but only on its post-Tridentine years: M. Dunn, "Nuns agents and agency", in *Patronage, Gender and the Arts in Early Modern Italy*, ed. by K.A. McIver and C. Stollhans, New York, Italica Press, 2015, pp. 127-151; after Giacchetti, cited later in this volume, the oldest historic account on the complex is by G. Carletti, *Memorie istorico-critiche della chiesa, e monastero di S. Silvestro in Capite di Roma*, Rome, Pilucchi Cracas, 1795, p. 9: this source identifies the choir revetments at Santi Nereo and Achilleo as part of the *schola cantorum* originally present at San Silvestro.

207. Armellini, *Le chiese di Roma*, pp. 341-343; Huelsen, *Le chiese di Roma*, pp. 129-130; Gaynor, Toesca, *San Silvestro in Capite*; A. Rehberg, *Kirche und Macht im römischen Trecento. Die Colonna und ihre Klientel auf dem kurialen Pfründenmarkt (1278-1378)*, Niemeyer, Tübingen, 1999.

208. *Le Liber pontificalis*, 1886-1892, 1, p. 464.

209. G. Giacchetti, *Historia della venerabile chiesa, et monastero di S. Siluestro de capite di Roma*, Rome, appresso Giacomo Mascardi, 1629, p. 9.

210. *Ibid.*, p. 11.

211. *Le Liber pontificalis*, 1886-1892, 1, p. 464.

212. C. Baronio, *Annales Ecclesiastici*, Rome, 1588-1607, ad. Ann. 818, n. 13; Armellini, *Le chiese di Roma*, pp. 341-343: "monaci greci"; Gaynor, Toesca, *San Silvestro in Capite*, p. 26.

213. Ferrari, *Early Roman Monasteries*, p. 15.

edited by Costantino Corvisieri and Vincenzo Federici confirm that the community had converted to the Benedictine rule by the twelfth century.[214] The only trace of the Benedictine phase is the bell tower and fragments of a Cosmatesque pavement in the main body of the church. Both likely date to the last decade of the twelfth century when the monastery underwent a general refurbishment.[215] A document from the convent's archive dated 1267, cited by Giovanni Giacchetti's seventeenth-century *Historia del monasterio*, describes relics from the altar of Saint Dionisus as being traslated to the altar dedicated to the Saints Nicholas and Paul.[216] The year 1256 should be considered the *terminus ante quem* for the century long refurbishment undergone by the monastery. In order to adapt the existing structures to the needs of an enclosed female community, the convent was also subject to some major changes during the Clarissan occupation in the thirteenth and fourteenth centuries. Surviving descriptions and plans from the sixteenth and seventeenth century testify to the later refurbishments promoted by the nunnery which we shall examine in this case study. At present, the church maintains its sixteenth/seventeenth-century shell, while the conventual apartments were transformed into a Post Office by 1879.

Arnolfo, the last Benedictine abbot, was transferred to the abbey of San Lorenzo fuori le Mura in 1285. Due to a papal petition and to political pressures from the Colonna family the monks were forced to vacate San Silvestro.[217] The monastery was transformed into a Clarissan nunnery and donated to a group of religious women from Palestrina, who were moved to San Silvestro after the death, in 1284, of their spiritual leader Beata Margherita Colonna.[218] The petition presented by Margherita's successor Abbess Erminia to Pope Honorius IV was positively received; and with the bull *Ascendit fumus aromatum* the nuns gained control over the monastery's possessions and adopted the Clarissan Isabelline rule first approved by Pope Alexander IV in 1259 and subsequently by Pope Urban IV in July 1263.[219] Along with San Lorenzo in Panisperna, another Colonna foundation, this was the only nunnery in Italy which was allowed to adhere to the rule of the *Sorores Minores*. It is no coincidence that this rule was more lenient on the rigorous pauperism promoted by Saint Clare, thus allowing

---

214. V. Federici, "Regesto del Monastero di S. Silvestro in Capite"; *Archivio della Società romana di storia patria*, 22 (1899), pp. 213-300; 498-538; 23 (1900), pp. 67-128; 411-439; E. Casanova, "Le carte di Costantino Corvisieri", *Archivi Italiani*, 7 (1920), p. 20; E. Montefusco, "Secondo: non conservare. Per una ricostruzione dell'archivio di San Silvestro in Capite a Roma", *Archivio della Società romana di storia patria*, 135 (2013), pp. 5-29.

215. Kane, *The Church of San Silvestro in Capite*, p. 10.

216. Giacchetti, *Historia della venerabile chiesa*, pp. 47-48.

217. G. Barone, "Margherita Colonna e le Clarisse di San Silvestro in Capite", in *Roma anno 1300*, p. 799.

218. "Le due vite scritte dal fratello Giovanni Colonna, Senatore di Roma, e da Stefania monaca di S. Silvestro in Capite, testi inediti illustrati e pubblicati", ed. by L. Oliger, *Lateranum*, 1, 2 (1935); A. Cadderi, *Beata Margherita Colonna. Le due vite scritte dal fratello Giovanni, senatore di Roma e da Stefania, monaca di San Silvestro in Capite; testo critico, introduzione, traduzione italiana a fronte da un manoscritto latino del XIV secolo*, Palestrina, ITL, 2010.

219. Barone, "Margherita Colonna e le Clarisse", p. 801.

the convent to secure a considerable number of landholdings previously owned by the Benedictine community. As exemplified by Emily Graham:

> the Rule also ensured that Giacomo's sister's followers were reliably ministered to by Franciscan friars, rather than placing that into the hands of the Pope or Cardinal Protector – which was, at the time, a position held by the Orsini family or Franciscan hierarchy, traditionally opposed to committing friars to the care of female religious. Given the family's continued interest in the Order and affinity for Franciscan spirituality, Giacomo may well have sought to ensure that the community would remain within the Franciscan orbit by imposing a Rule otherwise unused in all of Italy.[220]

The Clarissan order occupied the nunnery until 1876 when the community was suppressed and its assets transferred to the Italian state.[221] In 1885, the monastery was newly consecrated and passed to the Society of the Catholic Apostolate (Pallotines).[222]

From a political standpoint, the death of Margherita Colonna in 1280 came as an opportunity for her brothers, Senator Giovanni and Cardinal Giacomo, to leverage the Holy See and exercise control over one of the most ancient and powerful monastic institutions in Rome.[223] Indeed, the monastery accounted for the greater part of its property inside the *Rione* Colonna and the north of the city where the family had strong expansionistic ambitions.[224] From Margherita's biography, it seems very unlikely that she envisaged her community in this setting.[225] Although Margherita had a considerable following, even during her lifetime she had expressed the desire to join the sanctuary of the Mentorella (close to Tivoli east of Rome) as an oblate.[226] This sanctuary was found in a Conti fief and given the political resonance of her social standing, both her brothers and their powerful enemies forbid her to join the community.[227] Scholars including Barone have interpreted Margherita's desire to enter the Mentorella as a rejection to her family's political control.[228] Indeed, by the thirteenth century, the feudalization of the Church especially in Rome and in greater Latium had transformed churches and nunneries into the property of the

---

220. E.E. Graham, "Memorializing Identity: The Foundation and Reform of San Lorenzo in Panisperna", *Franciscan Studies*, 75 (2017), pp. 467-495: 481.

221. Gaynor, Toesca, *San Silvestro in Capite*, p. 56.

222. Kane, *The Church of San Silvestro in Capite*, p. 1.

223. Barone, "Margherita Colonna e le Clarisse", p. 802; Montefusco, "Secondo: non conservare", p. 10.

224. P. Toubert, *Les structures du Latium médiéval*, Rome, Ecole française de Rome, 1973, p. 632: "La structure même de son patrimonie explique l'intérêt quelle portait à la region tiberine, qui commandait tout le trafic fluvial de Rome avec le Nord du Latium"; Barone, "Margherita Colonna e le Clarisse", p. 804: "Era questa una zona in cui i Colonna erano fino ad allora penetrati a fatica e in cui erano invece potenti gli Orsini. Di qui l'interesse dei Colonnesi per San Silvestro e di qui, forse, anche il divampare dell'inimicizia con gli Orsini".

225. "Le due vite scritte dal fratello", p. 40.

226. Cadderi, *Beata Margherita Colonna*, p. 23.

227. Barone, "Margherita Colonna e le Clarisse", p. 802.

228. *Ibid.*, p. 803.

great noble families.[229] The latter supervised these institutions closely both from a hereditary and a spiritual standpoint. In the *Vita Prima*, Giovanni Colonna affirms that Margherita had also expressed her willingness to join the community at San Damiano, or alternatively build her own nunnery in the family's fief in Palestrina.[230] She ended up doing neither. Assuming that the Colonna did not lack the means to fund the latter, we may therefore deduce that her desire to become an oblate or a penitent was probably superior to that of becoming the abbess of a community. Moreover, it is likely that the Colonna brothers had already conceived the possibility of acquiring a monastery for her followers at her death. Barone goes as far as to affirm that the *Vita Prima* was written with the intent of pressuring the pope to find a suitable location for Margherita's disciples.[231] This was fulfilled under Pope Honorius IV, who granted the privileged location of San Silvestro in Capite in 1285 to Abbess Erminia, leader of Margherita's followers at her death.

If we consider that the pope required the newly established community to follow the *regula sororum minorum inclusarum*, which granted the nunnery the privilege of owning property, it seems evident that there was a larger scheme at play. This of course takes us into the complex socio-political equilibrium of late thirteenth-century Rome. By the second half of the thirteenth century, the baronial centre was dominated by a handful of lineages. Inside Rome and across Latium, four or five well-known influential families prevailed: the Annibaldi, the Colonna, the Orsini, the Savelli and by the end of the thirteenth century, the Caetani too.[232] Nunneries acted as recruitment centres for the *pulzelle* of these powerful clans, with Roman nunneries fractured according to the territorial divisions of familial power.

As demonstrated by the economic registries preserved at the Archivio di Stato di Roma, San Silvestro in Capite had extensive landholdings both in the *Rione* Colonna and in the region north of the Tiber beyond Ponte Milvio, which controlled the river's traffic to northern Latium.[233] The Colonna had had difficulty penetrating this region, which was historically controlled by the Orsini. Obtaining a sphere of influence over San Silvestro meant that these lands were automatically secured. According to Etienne Hubert, who published the convent's *Liber Instrumentorum* covering the period 1300-1383 for the *Archivio della Società romana di storia patria*, the nunnery's real estate portfolio was comparable in scale to that of Saint Peter's or the Lateran.[234] It counted at least 180 houses (most

---

229. Main publication on the subject but see introduction for a more detailed bibliography in Carocci, *Baroni di Roma*.
230. Cadderi, *Beata Margherita Colonna*, p. 27.
231. *Ibid.*, p. 33.
232. Carocci, *Baroni di Roma*.
233. Barone, "Margherita Colonna e le Clarisse", p. 804 (in particular footnote 49); Montefusco, "Secondo: non conservare", p. 12; Tourbet, *Le structure du Latium*, p. 632.
234. E. Hubert, "Un censier des biens romains du monastère S. Silvestro in Capite (1333-1334)", *Archivio della Società romana di storia patria*, 111 (1988), p. 93. Hubert's survey is based on the fourteenth-century *liber intrumentorum* in the ASR, Corporazioni religiose femminili, Clarisse di S. Silvestro in Capite, busta 4996/1.

of which were concentrated in the *Rione* Colonna, while a quarter of the properties in the neighbouring *Rioni* of Campo Marzio and Trevi) and numerous lands in the regions of Tuscia (specifically in the town of Orte in the castro of Bassanello, Palatitiolu and Vaccua), the Sabina and Tiburtina (strategically the area and the road that led to the Colonna feuds in Tivoli and Palestrina).[235] This real estate had been accumulated over the centuries and consolidated by the Benedictines prior to the arrival of the Clarissans. Taking indirect possession of these massive holdings allowed the Colonna to secure one of the most central and prestigious areas of Rome without the need for compromising alliances.

This grand scheme was seriously undermined by the election of Pope Boniface VIII, and the turbulent relations that developed between the Colonna and the Caetani both in Rome and in the greater Latium area. Abbess Giovanna, daughter of Senator Giovanni Colonna, was deposed from the nunnery by the pope in December 1297. The excommunication text refers to Giovanna in terms of her inability (*inhabilem*) to pursue her office and ordered her immediate suspension.[236] In addition, the community was forced to embrace a new rule, that of the *Ordo Sanctae Clarae regulae Urbani IV*.[237] The nuns passed under the jurisdiction of the Franciscan cardinal Matteo d'Acquasparta (1240-1302) who was a close ally of the Caetani. Moreover, the convent was also deprived of the church of San Terenziano in the proximity of Bagnoregio, where the Colonna had recently built a fortress. These hostile measures only abated with the death of Boniface VIII in October 1303 and the election of his successor Benedict XI.

It is somewhat challenging to gain a precise idea of the medieval appearance of San Silvestro, before the sixteenth-century refurbishments (1595-1601) that gave the church its current structure. Remains of the medieval walls still survive to a considerable height in the transept (right side of the left arm) and on the outer wall on the side of Via del Gambero. The medieval structure remains under the sixteenth-century brickwork. This is clearly visible from the bell tower, which seems to indicate that the original basilica extended to the present front courtyard, and as indicated by the moulding, it had walls that surpassed the roof of the rear of the church in height. It is also possible that the early Christian sanctuary had a different orientation. The three naves were likely altered over the centuries in order to create more space for the side chapels. We may assume that when the Clarissans succeeded the Benedictines with the help of the Colonna, their sponsors did not fail to modify and improve the church. Unfortunately, no trace of these refurbishments survives in the documents preserved at the Archivio di Stato di Roma. Furthermore, architectural elements which were visible until the nineteenth century have now been completely lost due to the transformations that took place with its suppression. This is particularly true for the monastic complexes that originally surrounded a courtyard adjacent to the church. The

---

235. Hubert, "Un censier des biens romains", p. 77.
236. Giacchetti, *Historia della venerabile chiesa*, p. 45.
237. Barone, "Margherita Colonna e le Clarisse", p. 803.

living apartments reserved for the nuns have now been transformed both externally and internally to fulfil their function as office spaces.

The only surviving architectural plan with which we may reconstruct the appearance of the church prior to the renovations of 1595-1601, is the sketch sent on the 2 November 1518 by the sculptor Antonio Tanghero to Michelangelo, who had been asked to submit a project for the main altar. In this drawing, the intersection of the church in front of the courtyard and the access to the nunnery are traced in a very schematic way. Measurements, however, are indicated with extreme precision and allow a precise comparison with the 1591 reconstruction. From Antonio Tanghero's design, we may conclude that the church measured 33,51 m in length, its central nave 10,70 m wide, and ended with a rectangular choir 7,30 m deep until the sixteenth century. As can still be witnessed today, the basilica itself was preceded by an irregular quadrangular courtyard that was accessed from a small passage on Via del Gambero. The façade was characterized by the presence of three doors, now reduced to one after the two lateral portals were walled up in 1595. Originally, there was a porch supported by four columns instead of pillars. It is reasonable to presume that the nunnery's exterior, in particular the church's façade, was similar to those of other Roman shrines such as San Lorenzo fuori le Mura or Santa Prassede. On entering there was a small chapel with an altar on the left portion of the central nave. Scholars like Kane have put forward the possibility that the chapel of Saint John the Baptist, where the relic of the saint's head was preserved, was originally found in this corner.[238] The left nave had no other chapels and was divided from the central one by pillars alternating with columns.

The main altar at the end of the central nave was probably covered by a canopy, as the four columns marked at the corners would seem to suggest. We are not aware of its chronology possibly being either a Benedictine or Clarissan initiative. A *confessio* was reached by a double ramp composed of seven steps under the main altar. The sanctuary part of the church was raised and preceded by an arch at the entrance to the choir. From Piero Rosselli's letter to Michelangelo dated 2 November 1518, we learn that the nuns did not want to use the old choir and had requested to move it over the entrance of the church.[239] There are other examples of this type of arrangement in Latium at Amaseno and Tuscania.[240] The new oratory was likely terminated around 1520, and the high altar was probably completed at the same time (Figs. 18-20).

Beyond the main altar there was an ample rectangular space on the right side of the church. This was marked by the presence of four columns in Tanghero's plan, suggesting that this space was covered by a cross vault. This is likely the

---

238. Kane, *The Church of San Silvestro in Capite*, p. 60.
239. G. Scaglia, "Antonio del Tanghero in Rome with Pietro Rosselli, Michelangelo Buonarroti and Antonio da Sangallo il Giovane", *Mitteilungen des Kunsthistorischen Institutes in Florenz*, 38 (1994), pp. 218-245.
240. Zappasodi, *Sorores*, pp. 19-21. The author claims that this solution was particularly popular in Germany and that in Italy "il coro sospeso in galleria […] rappresenta un risultato architettonico più maturo", p. 19.

chapel commissioned by the papal chaplain Pietro Colonna in his testament dated 18 June 1290.[241] This chapel was altered and possibly enlarged shortly after Margherita's followers entered the monastery to adhere to the needs of a claustral community.[242] Unfortunately, we cannot reconstruct its structure or decorative programme, but it is very likely that it was an impressive chapel in the latest Gothic style. This chapel was followed by the Palombara and Tedalini family shrines.[243] Given that these two maintain their original layout in the present-day church, we may assert (even due to the presence of the Colonna coats of arms visible today in the side chapel to the left of the main altar possibly in their original location) that the Colonna sanctuary was indeed located next to the main altar. This underscores both the power and authority the family had over this institution. Indeed, thanks to the Colonna clan San Silvestro and San Lorenzo in Panisperna became the flagship female Mendicant nunneries in Rome by the end of the thirteenth century and throughout the *Trecento*.

Regrettably, very little has survived from the early Clarissan settlement as previously stated. This was due to the radical sixteenth-century refurbishments and the expropriation of the convent by the Italian State in 1876. A few fragments of painted fresco are still visible and are mostly preserved in the church's sacristy. These include a *Madonna Advocata*, a *Madonna Lactans*, a Flagellation and a Crucifixion. The Crucifixion is now detached and displayed in the chapel to the right of the entrance but was originally located in the nuns' choir.[244] This fresco represents the crucified Christ in the patiens formula flanked by the Virgin Mary and the Magdalene to the left, while Saint John the Evangelist appears on the right. It is evident that the painting was originally larger with figures depicted in full length, and that it was subsequently cut. As previously stated, the Clarissan order had a special devotion towards the Crucifix. Therefore, the survival of this Crucifixion reinforces how the choir functioned as a space of meditation for the nuns. Evident comparisons may be drawn between San Silvestro and the Passion cycle in the choir of San Pietro in Vineis at Anagni. The latter, however, which is one of the largest pictorial cycles to have survived inside a choir in the region during the thirteenth century, curiously does not include a Crucifixion scene. San Silvestro testifies to the practice of embellishing sacred spaces exclusively

---

241. Federici, "Regesto del monastero", pp. 426-428; Gaynor, Toesca, *San Silvestro in Capite*, p. 59.

242. Indeed, San Silvestro is thought of as a family foundation.

243. Gaynor, Toesca, *San Silvestro in Capite*, pp. 40-41; p. 60, n. 11; ASR, Corporazioni religiose femminili, Clarisse di S. Silvestro in Capite, busta 4996, ins. 3, p. 42 and busta 5225, p. 5, n. 11, Miscellanea Corvisieri 208/20; L. Cangemi, P. Trivelli, *Roma. Chiesa di S. Silvestro in Capite: lo stato attuale*, Rome, International Maxpress, 1995 (Materiali per la storia e il restauro dell'architettura: scheda per le esercitazioni), pp. 8, 20.

244. Rome, Archivio Centrale dello Stato, Ministero dei Lavori Pubblici, Roma Capitale, busta 33: *1876-1878: Ritrovamento del dipinto nel corso dei lavori di adattamento dell'edificio del convento a Posta Centrale da parte del Genio Civile; stacco e deposito nella chiesa di San Silvestro*; Gaynor, Toesca, *San Silvestro in Capite*, pp. 30, 114; Romano, *Il Duecento e la cultura gotica*, pp. 376-377.

reserved for women. Romano goes as far to suggest that the "pathetism" expressed by Christ's physiognomy may be a direct product of this.[245]

The documentary *fondo* produced by this important and long-standing monastic institution is one of the richest preserved in the Archivio di Stato di Roma. The *Fondo Diplomatico* contains 298 parchments[246] so that it is only second to that of San Cosimato. In the 1899 publication of the *Archivio della Società romana di storia patria*, which indexed the 117 parchments before 1299, Vincenzo Federici claimed that the archive had suffered a serious depletion and that it was reduced to a third of its original size.[247] This was based on the *Inventario di tutti gli atti e le scritture esistenti nell'archivio del venerabile monastero di San Silvestro in Capite* preserved at the Archivio di Stato di Roma and likely compiled by Costantino Corvisieri, historian, palaeographer and founder of the *Archivio della Società romana di storia patria*. Between 1871-1872, Corvisieri headed the team responsible for cataloguing the contents of Roman archives immediately after the incorporation of Rome into the Italian state. According to Federici, by 1899 at least 500 parchments had gone missing from the *fondo* San Silvestro. The nuns were possibly responsible for this, given that they had strongly resisted the nineteenth-century confiscations by the Italian authorities. Indeed, the case for the missing documents at San Silvestro was well known and led to an official investigation.[248]

In order to understand the socio-political implications of this nunnery within the Colonna sphere of influence, the economic aspects of its history must be explored. This historical analysis may be reconstructed thanks to the aforementioned documentary corpus. Although Federici's claims regarding the loss of documents must be kept in mind, we still have sufficient material to advance certain hypotheses. San Silvestro was among the great Roman landowners who benefited from the concession of large plots of uncultivated land in the northern part of the city (in the Campo Marzio, Trevi, and Colonna *Rioni*).[249] At the same time, its property holdings also expanded north of the city into the region of the Sabina where the Colonna had little or no control. Moreover, during the thirteenth century, San Silvestro benefitted from a massive restructuring of the agrarian landscape along the Via Flaminia next to the catacombs of San Valentino which transformed these plots into vineyards.[250] The monastery did not gain any significant new estates

---

245. *Ibid.*, p. 377. This claim must be advanced with caution, this was more likely tied to a stylistic trend in Rome during the thirteenth century, for example the Sancta Sanctorum which had little to do with nuns.

246. ASR, cassetta 12: parch. 1-181, 9th-13th cent.; cassetta 13: parch 182-298, 13th-18th cent.; ASR, Corporazioni religiose femminili, Clarisse di San Silvestro in Capite, buste 4988-5226, registri 5610-5631, 13th-19th cent.; Gaynor, Toesca, *San Silvestro in Capite*, p. 54.

247. Federici, "Regesto del Monastero", p. 236; Montefusco, "Secondo: non conservare", p. 8.

248. *Ibid.*, p. 9.

249. Hubert, "Un censier des biens", pp. 100-101; ASR, Corporazioni religiose femminili, Clarisse di San Silvestro in Capite, busta 4996/1.

250. Montefusco, "Secondo: non conservare", p. 12; Hubert, "Un censier des biens", p. 104; G. Tomassetti, *La campagna romana antica, medievale e moderna*, 3, Rome, Loescher, 1913, pp. 292-294.

when it came under the influence of the Colonna clan. Indeed, it was already well endowed thanks to the donations of Paul I in 761 and Sergius II in 844, later confirmed by Agapitus II and John XII in the tenth century.[251] Presumably, it was this huge territorial and extra-mural patrimony that contributed to the Colonna's interest as they sought to counterbalance the economic power of the Orsini.

Overall, San Silvestro in Capite provides the opportunity to study the socio-political implications of conventual complexes in Rome during the late Middle Ages. Indeed, although almost nothing has survived in terms of the medieval fabric, documentary evidence is sufficient to account for its status, wealth, power and prestige in the city. This trend was likely also reflected in its patronal activities. This case study, however, has a deeper significance, which evades art historical research and places this investigation within an interdisciplinary framework. This broadens and furthers our understanding of nunneries within networks of familial divisions of power, political balances, and territorial presence. San Silvestro testifies to the expansionistic aims of the Colonna family which secured the nunnery's landholdings from the pope by adopting the Isabelline rule. The significance of San Silvestro is not reflected in the high quality of its interior decoration, but rather in its strategic role as a socio-political and economic asset both in the city and the region. This corroborates our thesis that nunneries acted as centres of political prestige and power between the thirteenth and the fourteenth centuries. In the absence of a tangible patronal activity, documentary sources are a viable proof of conventual wealth and status in medieval society. Roman nunneries were seen as privileged outposts by leading baronial families to secure their status and position across the city and in greater Latium. This is true not only for San Silvestro in Capite but also for other convents including San Lorenzo in Panisperna and San Sisto Vecchio on the Via Appia. Given the extensive architectural restorations carried out over the centuries, it is challenging to study these complexes from an art historical perspective. The AutoCAD reconstructions are tentative and serve more as a visual map than as a definitive rendering of the church space. Once again, the rich archival corpus was a determining factor to draw conclusions on the convent's medieval *facies*. I have attempted to trace the original position of the choir and the detached fresco of the Crucifixion. The choir's position above the altar evokes San Damiano's oratory. As we have witnessed at San Cosimato, this nunnery acted as an ideal model emphasising the importance of architectural norms at Assisi in the iconography of Clarissan convents in Latium.

5. *Interpreting Medieval Vestiges: Rediscovering San Lorenzo in Panisperna*

Until recently, the Clarissan nunnery of San Lorenzo in Panisperna had attracted next to no scholarly attention. As of 2014, Alfonso Marini from the Università di Roma "La Sapienza" established a small team of researchers from

---

251. Gaynor, Toesca, *San Silvestro in Capite*, p. 61.

the Department of Religious and Medieval Studies to analyse the parchment collection from the convent. This is currently preserved at the Archivio Storico Generale dell'Ordine dei Frati Minori at Santi Apostoli. Along with Marini, Simone Guido and Ivana Ait have been working on the documents from the *Fondo Panisperna*. These consist of 200 parchments, juridical and notarial acts, some dating from before the Clarissan presence with a time span from 1140 to 1900. The *Fondo Panisperna* was indexed in the nineteenth century, a brief description being provided for each entry. The Archivio was entrusted by the nuns of San Lorenzo in Panisperna to the Franciscan friars of Santa Maria Mediatrice in 1924.[252] Two fifteenth-century parchments, consisting of a testament (5 January 1407) and a selling agreement (3 February 1420), survive in the Archivio Colonna in Subiaco. Finally, in the Archivio Storico Capitolino, in addition to the *Fondo Orsini* which preserves eight parchments from the convent's archive; the protocols of the celebrated notary Nardus de Venectinis (*busta* 756 bis) contain a donation act dated 12 June 1426. This is of extreme interest and has been included as part of this case study's findings. The document provides a full list of nuns and although it only offers a snapshot of the year 1426, it does to a certain extent testify to the socially elevated status of this community at that date. Part of the reason for San Lorenzo in Panisperna's slim publication record is the fact that, until recently, the *Fondo Panisperna* was untraceable. To date, I am aware of only one extensive survey on the nunnery published by Salvatore Fallica in 2015.[253] Fallica, now an architect, wrote his B.A. thesis on San Lorenzo in Panisperna at the Università di Roma La Sapienza, Department of Architecture, in 2000 and later published an extract of his dissertation in the journal *Studi Romani*.[254] Simone Guido presented his research findings at the Istituto Storico Germanico in 2014 and published an extract of his thesis (La Sapienza) in the journal *Frate Francesco* in 2015.[255] Unfortunately, the latter lacks a cohesive structure and does not present a review of pertinent findings from the Archivio Storico Generale dell'Ordine dei Frati Minori. In addition to these contributions, San Lorenzo in Panisperna is briefly mentioned in an article by Giulia Barone as part of the acts of the international conference on Martin V[256] and in a survey dated 1908 on bell towers by Virgilio Burti in the journal *Emporium*.[257] Guides to

---

252. P.G. Munoz, *Archivio Storico dei Francescani*, Congress *Memoria fidei: Archivi ecclesiastici e Nuova Evangelizzazione*, accessible online, http://www.memoriafidei.va/content/dam/memoriafidei/documenti/12%20Gil%20-%20Comunicazione.pdf, p. 11, last accessed 02/02/2021.

253. S. Fallica, "Sviluppo e trasformazione della chiesa di San Lorenzo in Panisperna a Roma", *Studi romani*, 148 (2015), pp. 117-148.

254. S. Fallica, *Il complesso edilizio di San Lorenzo in Panisperna a Roma*, Tesi di laurea in Storia dell'architettura moderna, Sapienza Università di Roma, 2000.

255. S. Guido, "Il monastero di San Lorenzo in Panisperna in Rione Monti a Roma", *Frate Francesco*, 81 (2015), pp. 185-195.

256. Barone, "La presenza degli ordini religiosi nella Roma di Martino V", p. 357 and footnote 22.

257. V. Burti, "I campanili di Roma e le loro decorazioni", *Emporium*, 28 (1908), pp. 123-130.

the complex, such as the one by Pietro Tomassi[258] or that by Patrizia de Crescenzo and Antonio Scaramella,[259] offer little if no insight into the nunnery's medieval fabric. What seems to be the source (apart from the more obvious citations taken from Armellini, Huelsen, and Forcella) is the monograph by Padre Andrea da Rocca di Papa published in 1893.[260] Recently, Emily Graham has analysed the convent as a manifestation of Giacomo Colonna's adherence to the reformation within Franciscan circles. Although her findings are exclusively analysed in a historical framework, the scholar makes some interesting contributions to the understanding of the convent's past and *raison d'être*.[261]

This brief, but necessary literature review on San Lorenzo in Panisperna, serves to justify the inclusion of this case study as part of our survey on female religious patronage in late medieval Rome. From a medievalist's perspective – as at San Silvestro in Capite – very little survives in terms of artistic or architectural vestiges from the convent's early days. However, the existing documentary corpus allows us to trace the importance of this complex through a broader socio-political framework. By the end of the fourteenth century, San Lorenzo in Panisperna replaced San Silvestro as the "ideal" nunnery for the *pulzelle* of the Roman baronial class.[262] Archival material not only testifies to the presence of women from the leading aristocratic families (Colonna, Savelli, Prefectis) but also to a dynamic and versatile control of a significant real estate portfolio. Indeed, we should not treat the role of Cardinal Giacomo Colonna (brother of Margherita and driving force behind the foundation of San Silvestro), who endowed San Lorenzo in Panisperna in 1308, as purely coincidental. Once again, we find a link between this powerful family and a newly founded Clarissan community, destined to become a leading voice in the city's conventual experience. Barone goes as far as to compare San Lorenzo in Panisperna to its Franciscan counterpart at the Aracoeli.[263] Indeed, the nunnery's consistent holdings in the area around Tivoli may have largely been the real motive behind Cardinal Colonna's munificence. The family's expansionist aims in the territory around Palestrina, where their stronghold was based, shall be examined later on in this case study. We shall proceed by providing a necessary historical introduction on the complex and then turn to the surviving documents.

The nunnery of San Lorenzo in Panisperna is found behind the Ministry of the Interior on the Viminale, in the area known to the ancient Romans as the *suburra*, and today part of the *rione* Monti. The complex rises prominently on Via Panisperna, overlooking the Esquiline Hill and the basilica of Santa Maria Maggiore. The nunnery was transformed into the Museo della Fisica e Centro studi e ricerche

---

258. P. Tomassi, *Chiesa di San Lorenzo in Panisperna*, Rome, Tipografia Giammarioli, 1967.
259. P. Crescenzo, A. Scaramella, *La chiesa di San Lorenzo in Panisperna sul Colle Viminale*, Rome, Ministero dell'Interno-Direzione generale degli Affari dei culti, 1998.
260. Andrea da Rocca di Papa, *Memorie storiche della chiesa e monastero di San Lorenzo in Panisperna*, Rome, Tipografia Editrice Romana, 1893.
261. Graham, "Memorializing Identity", pp. 467-495.
262. Barone, "Presenza degli ordini", p. 357.
263. *Ibid.*, pp. 357-358.

dedicated to Enrico Fermi in 1999. This is also true for the church, which survives in its sixteenth-century renovated form and to parts of the conventual complex. Although it is difficult to imagine San Lorenzo in Panisperna as a thriving female Mendicant community today, it was founded in one of Rome's most prestigious early Christian pilgrimage areas. Indeed, according to legend this was where Saint Lawrence was martyred on 10 August 258.[264] The site where the martyrdom took place is identified with the *forno* inside the church's crypt.[265] It is unclear whether Constantine or Sergius I erected a shrine in commemoration of the saint.[266] Nevertheless, its presence is ascertained by the tenth century in the chronicle of the Archbishop of Canterbury's trip to Rome dated 990.[267] Although we know that a male Benedictine community was already on site by the tenth century, the first document which explicitly speaks of San Lorenzo in Panisperna as an abbey is dated 1119.[268] Under Pope Honorius III, the monastery received a conspicuous donation with which restoration works were carried out.[269] The monastery fell into a state of decline during the course of the thirteenth century. Boniface VIII took measures against this by affiliating the church and all its possessions to the Lateran Chapter which was entrusted with the management of its clerical community and with the necessary measures to reform it.[270] The Lateran Canons, however, demonstrated discontent and disobeyed the orders of the Pontiff to such a degree that the monastery was left in ruin. Later, Cardinal Giacomo Colonna moved by particular devotion towards the holy martyr, and by the convent's convenient location in front of Santa Maria Maggiore (where he had been reinstated by Clement V both as Cardinal and Deacon) offered to restore the church at his own expense provided that it was granted to him with the adjacent buildings.[271] The Chapter accepted the project and on the 26 or 27 April 1308, during the pontificate of Clement V, the notary Martino Francesco Paduli signed a donation agreement between the cardinal and Pietro Capoccia, vicar of the archpriest of the Lateran Basilica.[272] Immediately after, Francesco, priest of the church of Sant'Egidio, took possession of the church on behalf of Giacomo Colonna, subsequently entrusted to the care of the newly established Clarissan Community.[273] Nuns from the convent of San

---

264. Armellini, *Le chiese di Roma*, p. 199; Huelsen, *Le chiese di Roma*, p. 293.
265. Tomassi, *Chiesa di San Lorenzo in Panisperna*, p. 5.
266. *Le Liber pontificalis*, 1, 1886-1892, pp. 371-382; Crescenzo, Scaramella, *La chiesa di San Lorenzo*, p. 7.
267. E. Pesci, "L'Itinerario romano di Sigerico e la lista dei papi portati in Inghilterra (anno 990)", *Rivista di archeologia cristiana*, 13 (1936), pp. 43-60.
268. Fallica, "Sviluppo e trasformazione", p. 147.
269. Guido, "Il monastero di San Lorenzo", p. 190.
270. Andrea da Rocca di Papa, *Memorie storiche della chiesa*, p. 8.
271. Rome, Archivio Storico Generale dell'Ordine dei Frati Minori (hereafter AGOFM), D/8; Andrea da Rocca di Papa, *Memorie storiche della chiesa*, p. 8; Fallica, "Sviluppo e trasformazione", p. 120.
272. AGOFM, D/4-53; Andrea da Rocca di Papa, *Memorie storiche della chiesa*, p. 8; Fallica, "Sviluppo e trasformazione", p. 120.
273. Andrea da Rocca di Papa, *Memorie storiche della chiesa*, p. 10.

Martino ai Monti were transferred to the convent.[274] In addition to restructuring the premises, the fixed contract fee was established at two pounds of wax which had to be paid to the Lateran Chapter on Saint John the Baptist's feast day. The Colonna had a particular devotion towards the Baptist whose head was preserved in the other family foundation of San Silvestro in Capite. Furthermore, Giacomo was, in fact, portrayed next to him in the apsidal vault of Santa Maria Maggiore by Jacopo Torriti.[275] The generous donations imparted by Cardinal Giacomo may have been prompted by the desire to rehabilitate his ecclesiastic career in Franciscan circles after the political crusade that had been undertaken by Boniface VIII against his family. According to Graham, Giacomo may have

> founded San Lorenzo in Panisperna as a personal project. [...] Rather than seeking to replicate his familial success with San Silvestro – already flourishing, and in no need of replacement – Giacomo Colonna sought to use a familiar template, the Rule of Isabella, as the bedrock of a far more intriguing experiment.[276]

In 1303, Pope Benedict XI partially revoked the convictions imposed by his predecessor on Giacomo Colonna, however his cardinal's posts and the socio-economic benefits that came with them were not restored.[277] Giacomo and his nephew Pietro appealed to King Philip IV of France (1268-1314), former opponent of Boniface VIII, but nothing had been decided when Pope Benedict XI died in 1304.[278] His successor, Clement V, proceeded to return the cardinalate to Giacomo and to his nephew (14-15 December 1305); while a general revocation of the sentences against the family followed in 1306.[279] In the same year, the Cardinal received the proceeds from the Benedictine house of San Pietro in Perugia from Pope Clement V. His archbishopric of Santa Maria Maggiore, provisionally returned on 4 April 1306, was confirmed on the 5 November 1312.[280] During this period, Giacomo Colonna stayed in Rome, where one of his most important tasks was organising the restoration work of the Lateran Basilica after the severe fire of May 1308.[281] Although some of the normal curial activities were entrusted to him, it is clear that he was not reinstated into a position of primacy by Clement. Therefore, the endowment of San Lorenzo in Panisperna may be interpreted as a means of re-establishing himself in the complex balance of power and influences within the Curia and more generally in Rome during the years that followed the reign of Boniface VIII and the subsequent move to Avignon.

---

274. Fallica, "Sviluppo e trasformazione", p. 121.
275. Guido, "Il monastero di San Lorenzo", p. 190.
276. Graham, "Memorializing Identity", pp. 494-495.
277. A. Coppi, *Memorie colonnesi*, Rome, Salviucci, 1855, p. 75.
278. D. Waley, "Colonna, Giacomo", in *Dizionario Biografico degli Italiani*, 27, Rome, Istituto della Enciclopedia Italiana, 1982, online.
279. Waley, "Colonna, Giacomo".
280. Coppi, *Memorie colonnesi*, p. 75; Graham, "Memoriallizing Identity", p. 472; Waley, "Colonna, Giacomo".
281. Carocci, *Baroni di Roma*, p. 119.

The donation of San Lorenzo in Panisperna was confirmed by John XXII with a bull dated 3 November 1318. This was issued in the basilica of Santa Maria Maggiore by the notary Tommaso di Bartolomeo di Tommaso di Obbiccione in the presence of numerous witnesses.[282] This document, delivered the monastery's full possession to the Clarissan community in the person of Abbess Francesca di Sant'Eustachio di Giacomo del Signore Oddone Penestrina, and the nuns Margarita, Maddalena, Angela, Giovanna, Agata, Agnese, Mattea, Giovannola, Lucia, Lorenza, and Andrea.[283] The nuns also came into ownership of the rural church of Sant'Angelo in the Arcese valley and part of the diocese of Tivoli.[284] In the space of a decade, Cardinal Giacomo Colonna was responsible for creating one of the most important female religious institutions in fourteenth-century Rome. Indeed, documents from the Archivio Storico Generale dell'Ordine dei Frati Minori testify to its granaries, vineyards, towers and houses in the city; while Sandro Carocci's survey of Tivoli during the medieval period confirms its extensive landholdings in this area.[285] Carocci claims that, from the first half of the fourteenth century well into the fifteenth, the nuns of San Lorenzo in Panisperna dynamically managed their holdings which amounted to several hundreds of acres.[286] These lands were largely used to cultivate crops, especially grain, which was subsequently exported and sold in Rome. On more than one occasion, the historian states that in contrast to other Roman ecclesiastic patrimonies in the area around Tivoli and more generally the Tiburtino, which were characterized by stagnant yields and often short-term ownership of land, the nuns of San Lorenzo in Panisperna administered these assets with great efficiency.[287] He emphasises that this competence was also translated to the administration of their real estate portfolio in Rome itself.[288] This does not seem like a coincidence and one cannot fail to notice several analogies with the convent of San Silvestro in Capite. Indeed, we may speculate that the Colonna were administering strategically located outposts both in Rome and the area north of Palestrina, through these monastic institutions.

According to Barone, by the end of the fourteenth century, San Lorenzo in Panisperna acted as a recruitment centre for the daughters of the Roman aristocracy (similarly to San Silvestro in Capite at the beginning of the century).[289] It is no coincidence that when Saint Bridget of Sweden died in 1373, she was buried in the nunnery.[290] Her presence is documented in the city from the jubilee year of 1350. She lived in the convent (although we do not know exactly when she

---

282. AGOFM, D/8 D; Andrea da Rocca di Papa, *Il convento di S. Lorenzo*, p. 8; Fallica, "Sviluppo e trasformazione", p. 120.
283. Armellini, *Le chiese di Roma*, p. 199; Wadding, *Annales minorum*, p. 578.
284. S. Carocci, *Tivoli nel basso Medioevo: società cittadina ed economia agraria*, Rome, Istituto Storico Italiano per il Medioevo, 1988, p. 427.
285. AGOFM, D/4-53; Carocci, *Tivoli nel basso Medioevo*, p. 489.
286. AGOFM, D/4-53; Carocci, *Tivoli nel basso Medioevo*, p. 489.
287. AGOFM, D/4-53; Carocci, *Tivoli nel basso Medioevo*, p. 489.
288. AGOFM, D/4-53; Carocci, *Tivoli nel basso Medioevo,* p. 493.
289. Barone, "Presenza degli Ordini", p. 357.
290. P. Giovetti, *Brigida di Svezia. Una santa europea*, Rome, San Paolo Editore, 2002.

became a part of the community) and received burial there. A parchment from the *Fondo Panisperna* at the Archivio Storico Generale dell'Ordine dei Frati Minori testifies that a sepulchre made of marble and decorated with angels was built to commemorate her passing and establish a shrine.[291] When her body was moved to Sweden in the 1380s, Steffana Savelli commissioned a chapel in Rome in gold and stucco to preserve her relics.[292] Like Saint Catherine of Siena, Saint Bridget was considered as one of the great mystics of her time, and her burial in the convent of San Lorenzo in Panisperna undoubtedly had a great resonance for the community.[293]

The 1426 donation act preserved at the Archivio Storico Capitolino, signed by Nardus de Venectinis, provides a list of the entire community present at San Lorenzo in Panisperna at the beginning of the fifteenth century.[294] The notary registers all its members including: the Abbess Gregoria de' Prefetti, and the nuns Anastasia di Sant'Eustachio, Palozia del fu Pietro de' Cinciis, Margherita Sclavi di Giovanni Angelo, Cefalella di Cola Stinchi, Vannozza de' Mancini, Caterina di Cola Papa, Santa di Angelo Blasi, Marta di Gaeta, Maddalena di Gaeta, Caterina di Petruccio Sabba, Sicilia di Pietro Nisci, Renza and Nicolia (presumably sisters) di Lorenzo Benintendi, Angelozza di Angelo, Caterina di Iacobello Paloni, Clara di Rieti, Angilella di Iacobo, Vannozza di Menico Gentile, Vannozza di Isaia, Margherita Moritoni, Iacobella del signor Pietro de' Busco, Filippa del signor Pietro and Margherita di Giovanni Grassi.[295] In addition to being one of the most complete lists of nuns with surnames from medieval Rome, this document is extremely significant for a number of reasons. Abbess Gregoria, from the influential Prefetti family, and daughter of Francesco di Vico prefect of Viterbo is associated with an inscription (unfortunately now lost) which recorded HOC OPUS FIERI FECIT DOMINA GREGORIA DE PRAEFECTIS ANNO MCCCCXX.[296] According to Armellini and Fallica, this should be associated with a small chapel originally found in the cloister.[297] Others such as Burti claim that Gregoria was responsible for building the bell tower which was subsequently replaced during the sixteenth-century refurbishment of the church.[298] The act notifies the receipt by the community of a donation consisting in a series of houses by Perna widow of Cristoforo Nardini. Perna's donation leads us into another historiographical line of enquiry, which is tied both to wills and *pro-redemptione anima* endowments as a cultural *topos* for medieval women. The medieval *post-mortem* preoccupation with the after-life caused a substantial change in the writing of donations, which resulted in women leaving their belongings to churches and pious foundations. According to Samuel Cohn

---

291. AGOFM, D/4-53; Fallica, "Sviluppo e trasformazione", p. 122.
292. Armellini, *Le chiese di Roma*, p. 199.
293. AGOFM, D/4-53; Fallica, "Sviluppo e trasformazione", p. 122.
294. Rome, Archivio Storico Capitolino, busta 756 bis.
295. *Ibid.*
296. Armellini, *Le chiese di Roma*, p. 199; Fallica, "Sviluppo e trasformazione", p. 122.
297. *Ibid.*, pp. 122-123.
298. Burti, "I campanili di Roma", p. 125.

"these aspirations changed fundamentally after the Black Death, when testators began to reverse tack, devising ever more complex legal strategies to govern the future flow of their goods".[299]

Finally, it is also significant to investigate where the donation takes place, something which is specified in the document more than once. The text recites "[professe/members?] of the nunnery, assembled at the sound of the bell in the Chapter hall, that is, in front of the iron grate in front of the main altar of the nunnery".[300] This leads to some speculation on the disposition of the church before the sixteenth-century refurbishment, placing the Chapter hall adjacent to the main body of the church. According to Padre Andrea from Rocca di Papa, writing at the end of the nineteenth century, the sixteenth-century church, completed in 1574, was rebuilt at a higher point on the hill, and underwent substantial transformations. Thus, the side naves were renovated into conventual apartments and the church was reduced to only the central nave (Figs. 21-23).[301] The original lateral naves terminated with two doors on the façade with the main central entrance to the church in the middle. Padre Andrea also provides evidence for the earlier structure of the church. Based on his observations, the primitive church (before the Clarissan occupation) originally consisted of three parts: the narthex for penitents and catechumens, the naos for the communicators, and the bema for the clerics who performed their duties. The external narthex was likely composed of a porch, an atrium and a vestibule. However, the church certainly consisted of three aisles. According to Padre Andrea, the Clarissans, assisted by Cardinal Colonna, made substantial transformations to the conventual complex to reconcile the church with their liturgical needs, while opening it to the local population at the same time.[302] Padre Andrea states that the original church was reduced to a single nave. One of the lateral aisles was transformed into the chapel inside the sacristy and the chaplain's house, while the other was converted into the parlour as well as other spaces serving the nuns.[303] On that occasion, for the first time, the division appeared between the inner and the outer church

---

299. Cohn, "Renaissance Attachment to Things", p. 984.

300. Rome, Archivio Storico Capitolino, busta 756 bis: "profexis dicti monasterii, congregatis ad sonum campanelle in loco capitulari, videlicet ante gratas ferreas existentes ante altare maius dicti monasterii unanimi".

301. Andrea da Rocca di Papa, *Memorie storiche della chiesa*, p. 12.

302. *Ibid.*

303. *Ibid.*: "Il certo è la chiesa constava di tre navate; sapendosi della storia che il cardinal Colonna la ridusse a una sola navata, e di una laterale fece fare la cappella interna, la presente sagrestia, e, più in dietro, l'abitazione pel Cappellano; dell'altra poi il parlatorio ed altre officine per le Monache. Fece inoltre dividere per metà la navata grande di mezzo, lasciando la parte esteriore per i fedeli e l'interiore per coro delle Religiose". Also Fallica, "Sviluppo e trasformazione", p. 127: "Secondo il religioso, sin dal primo momento del loro insediamento le Clarisse, assistite dal cardinale Colonna, apportarono sostanziali trasformazioni alla chiesa conventuale, per conciliare la clausura, con le necessità liturgiche e con l'apertura alla popolazione locale. Essa fu ridotta ad una sola navata, mentre una di quelle laterali fu trasformata nella cappella interna, nella sagrestia e nell'abitazione del cappellano, e l'altra nel parlatorio e in altri locali a servizio delle monache".

that would characterize the sixteenth-century reconstruction in the future. The intervention allowed the nuns to attend liturgical ceremonies not only without being seen by the lay population but also, hidden from the clergy and ministers of the sacraments. We shall examine this possibility in the plan we have tentatively reconstructed for the complex.

During the sixteenth century, the Clarissans of San Lorenzo in Panisperna were reformed by Abbess Violante Savelli from the convent of Santi Cosma e Damiano in Mica Aurea. Abbess Violante, along with thirteen sisters from her original community, was transferred to San Lorenzo in Panisperna in 1517.[304] During the sack of Rome in 1527, the chronicles from the nunnery of Santi Cosma e Damiano in Mica Aurea testify that seventy nuns left Trastevere and joined the community at San Lorenzo in Panisperna.[305] Throughout the course of the century, both the community of nuns and their patrons started an ambitious building enterprise which resulted in the loss of almost all the convent's original medieval fabric. Between 1566 and 1577 the complex was completely rebuilt including the church from its foundations. This was possible due to the generous donations of Pius V and Gregory XIII but in great part also thanks to the contributions of the community itself.[306] A document from the Archivio Storico Generale dell'Ordine dei Frati Minori dated 1598 states:

> These holy founding nuns began to build and restore the nunnery, the ancient church of San Lorenzo and the old church inside the convent a portion of which was used as a liturgical station [...] the church inside the nunnery was planned with three naves terminating in three altars composed of four columns with beautiful cibori like the ones we find in ancient Roman altars; the choir was in the middle of the church and was built in mosaic and marble [...] they made a beautiful choir in another church, and built a room next to the choir which they call chapel where they can hear mass and sermons.[307]

Although in terms of the original medieval fabric, very little survives at San Lorenzo in Panisperna, this case study offers an invaluable insight into the multifaceted role of nunneries in medieval Rome. Three main factors come into play, namely, its foundation by Giacomo Colonna, its role as recruitment centre

---

304. AGOFM, D/4-53; Fallica, "Sviluppo e trasformazione", p. 137; Andrea da Rocca di Papa, *Memorie storiche della chiesa*, pp. 14-15.
305. Formicini, *Liber monialum*.
306. Fallica, "Sviluppo e trasformazione", p. 136; Andrea da Rocca di Papa, *Memorie storiche della chiesa*, p. 14.
307. "Queste sante Monache fondatrici cominciarono a fabbricare et assettare il monasterio, la Chiesa antica di S. Lorenzo che havev.o dentro, fuora havevano un poco di Chiesa vecchia per la stattione [...] fabbricarono la Chiesa ch'havev.o dentro a tre navi co' delle colonne; in capo delle navi c'erano tre belli altari, a ogni nave c'era il suo altare, con belli cibori j sostenati da Quattro colonne per altare, come s'usa a Roma nelli altari antichi; il coro era in mezzo della Chiesa ed era di Marmoro lavorato a Musaico [...] fabbricarono un belliss.o coro con un'altra Chiesa, acanto il coro che la chiamano capella, dov'odono la messa le prediche i sermoni": AGOFM, D/4-53 (post 1598); Fallica, "Sviluppo e trasformazione", p. 126.

for Roman noblewomen and its real estate portfolio. This identifies San Lorenzo in Panisperna as pivotal in the expansionistic aims of the Colonna family. More broadly, it underscores the role of nunneries as centres of power and territorial control both in the city and in Latium. This comprehensive interdisciplinary survey of the nunnery has pushed its enquiry beyond medieval art history and architecture, of which very little survive to date, into a broader historical and social context. This methodology has attempted to offer a tentative reconstruction of the convent's dynamic role during the Middle Ages. Archival records at the Archivio Storico Generale dell'Ordine dei Frati Minori, the Archivio Storico Capitolino, and Padre Andrea's testimony have contributed to create a provisional attempt to sketch a hypothetical plan of the medieval church. The AutoCAD drawings are based on textual evidence and only offer a suggestive appearance of the conventual building. Without proper archaeological investigations, this reconstruction is only speculative and by no means represents a definitive layout of the internal disposition of the church. With the objective of translating literary primary sources into physical areas, this investigation reasoned around the role of space in relation to norms of ideals of chastity and seclusion. As we have seen in other nunneries, *clausura* acted as a *fil rouge* in planning churches destined to women, attempting to separate them both from the officiating clergy and the laymen. Although these separations were likely more permeable than what we imagine them to be, it is difficult to trace a standard building practice when so little of the original architectural fabric has survived, San Lorenzo in Panisperna as a case in point. Finally, the nunnery also testifies to the popularity of the Mendicant orders in late medieval Rome, especially in so far as religious women are concerned. This appears to be the case for the Clarissans in particular; a trend which we shall also witness in Latium. It is hoped that this case study has tentatively connected the dots by potentially conceiving of nunneries in the context of medieval social, political and economic networks.

6. *Comparing Roman Conventual Communities in Context: A Few Considerations*

The settlement of female communities in pre-existing complexes, the loss of a significant number of convents and the perishable nature of the construction materials used, has too often impaired the study of female monastic architecture. For these reasons, when it comes to religious women, fixed architectural schemes cannot be traced on the basis of surviving elements. The shared need for enclosure acted as a thematic thread in the planning of these nunneries, especially after the *Periculoso*. Through an interdisciplinary and multifaceted approach, I assembled a portfolio of case studies in order to address the patronage question, showcase the diverse solutions adopted to observe *clausura*, further the contextualisation of artworks in their original space, witness their artistic output in the pre- and post-Avignon years and draw several hypotheses of choir placement inside conventual churches. If we choose to validate the hypothesis of a choir inside the *matroneum* at Sant'Agnese fuori le Mura, this church presents a very original architectural solution in response to *clausura*. While the position of the choir at San Sisto Vecchio was harder to determine, its location was reasoned around the arrangement of the Icon, crucifix, fresco cycle, testimonies from Sister Cecilia, and surviving evidence at the lost nunnery of Sant'Aurea. While for the Clarissan settlements, I believe that the influence exerted by the disposition of the choir at San Damiano at Assisi was extremely significant. As the first Clarissan house, this conventual complex likely acted as the ideal model to replicate. This possibly explains the position of the choir either behind or above the apse in San Silvestro in Capite and San Cosimato. As far as San Lorenzo in Panisperna was considered, it was impossible to determine the position of the choir inside the church with absolute certainty on the basis of surviving evidence.

I have tentatively sought to reconstruct the medieval *facies* of these churches by combining new and established tools of scholarly enquiry. These include but are not limited to: archival research, empirical display of extant objects, and the meticulous study of building structures with drawings on AutoCAD. Indeed, the plans acted as a visual map to combine and to a certain extent reinterpret the different primary evidence present in these complexes. With this objective in mind, Roman convents were selected according to the existence of solid archival, documentary, artistic or architectonic evidence. This was especially true for Sant'Agnese fuori le Mura and San Sisto Vecchio, where by contextualising artefacts I hypothesised on the internal disposition of the church. The role of Marian icons in the planning of these complexes, for San Sisto Vecchio and San Cosimato in particular, was another theme that emerged from this investigation. I aimed to contextualise these artefacts inside the church space, trying to understand how their presence influenced the architectural makeup and pictorial program of these churches. Nevertheless, as far as San Silvestro in Capite and San Lorenzo in Panisperna were considered, the evidence was mostly documentary, and archival records proved indispensable to retrace their medieval history.

In the attempt to understand religious architecture's liturgical and social function, themes of patronage, gaze, gender, and nunnery art were addressed. Determining whether the artwork commissioned inside conventual spaces was financed by the community, by members of the clergy or by lay men and women is challenging and usually only remains hypothetical. Questions of patronage are therefore shifted towards the significance of these artworks in spaces destined for women. The monumental cross at San Sisto Vecchio, and its extraordinary iconography, seemingly testified to the equality of men and women in front of Christ's sacrifice, or alternatively to the cohesive front put forward by the Church of Rome. In the patronage context, I advanced the hypothesis that the importance of these commissions derived from the notion that women could guarantee, as testified at Sant'Agnese fuori le Mura, that their private apartments were decorated by leading painters in the latest style. While at San Cosimato, a significant operation of artistic and architectonic renewal was carried out by a woman, namely Abbess Iacopa Cenci as testified in the chronicle written by

Orsola Formicini. This led me to hypothesise whether abbesses in other conventual communities were also responsible for leading large-scale renovations of their complexes. Out of the five selected case studies, three were Clarissan, bearing witness to the rise of the Mendicants in Rome during this period. This was at least partially due to the papal support enjoyed by the Franciscans in curial circles and baronial families. This was undoubtedly also the case for San Silvestro in Capite. Here, documentary evidence attested to its extensive land holdings both in Rome and in Latium; while illustrating how the Isabelline rule was used to guarantee that the Colonna family could extend its influence over these territories. Overall, the collected evidence demonstrates that female conventual realities in Rome were active players in the community. They operated both as promoters or recipients of artistic and architectonic commissions, and as playmakers in the power balance between the baronial clans and curial circles. As we shall witness, several of these trends and observations are also valid for conventual communities in Latium.

Fig. 1. Rome, Sant'Agnese fuori le Mura, bird's eye view: 1. Mausoleum of Santa Costanza; 2. Remains of Constantinian Basilica; 3. Present-day Basilica; 4. Entrance to Monastery; 5. Medieval Wing; 6. Staircase connecting Monastery to Basilica; 7. Private Cloister; 8. Public Cloister.

Fig. 2. Rome, Sant'Agnese fuori le mura, 3D model, interior of the basilica.
Fig. 3. Rome, Sant'Agnese fuori le mura, 3D model, axonometric view.

Fig. 4. Rome, Sant'Agnese fuori le Mura, *Last Supper*, *Crucifixion*, *Washing of the Feet*, frescoes, first quarter of the 14th century.
Fig. 5. Rome, Sant'Agnese fuori le Mura, *Enthroned Christ*, fresco, 1295-first quarter of the 14th century.

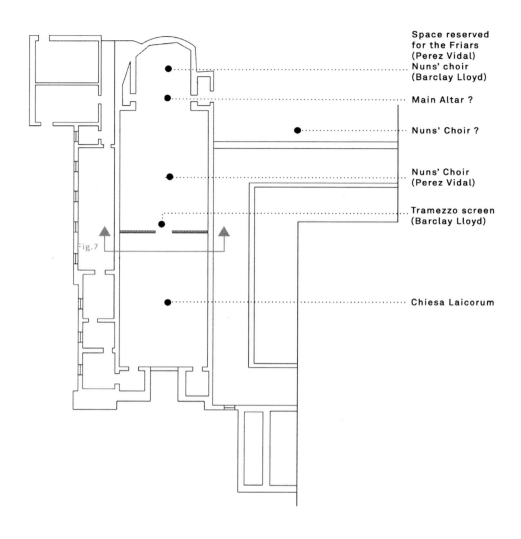

Fig. 6. Reconstruction of San Sisto ground floor plan in San Sisto Vecchio based on Barclay Lloyd, *The Architectural Planning*, M. Perez Vidal, *Estavan todas no coro e ben cantand' e Leendo. Tipologie e funzioni dei cori nei monasteri delle Domenicane con particolare riferimento alla Castiglia dal XIII al XVI secolo*, in advance of publication (2022) and Vitali, "Gli affreschi medievali di S. Sisto Vecchio in Roma".

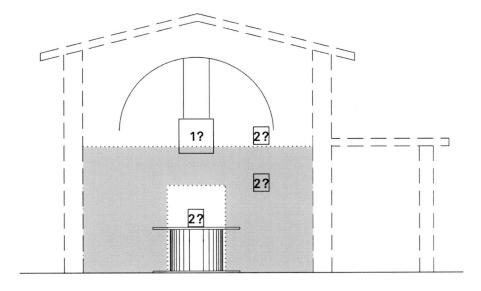

Fig. 7. Rome, San Sisto Vecchio, elevation with repositioning of monumental Cross and *Icona Tempuli*.
Fig. 8. Rome, Santi Domenico e Sisto, Painted Cross, tempera on wood, ca. 1260, 127x89 cm, from Romano, *Il Duecento e la cultura gotica*.
Fig. 9. Rome, Santa Maria del Rosario, *Madonna Advocata*, tempera on wood, 8th century, 71,5x42,5 cm (Ph. Wikimedia Commons).

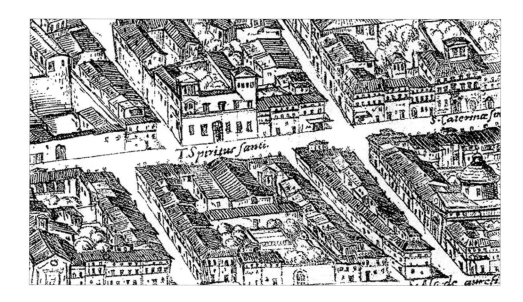

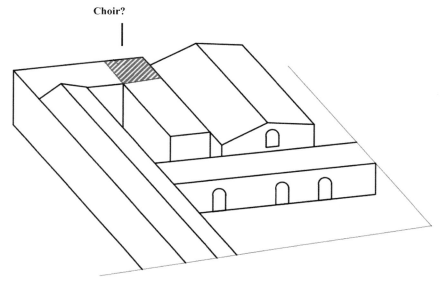

Fig. 10. Antonio Tempesta, *Plan of the City of Rome*, 1593, detail, New York, The Metropolitan Museum of Art.
Fig. 11. Reconstruction of exterior and church plan of Sant'Aurea, Rome, based on Antonio Tempesta's map.

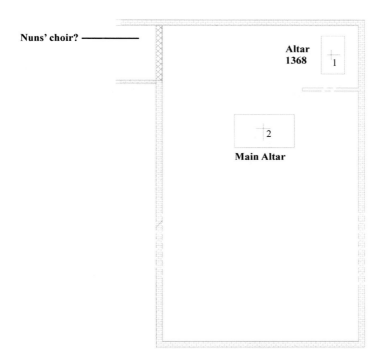

Fig. 12. Rome, Sant'Aurea, Ground floor plan based on textual evidence from Archivio della Curia Generalizia dei Padri Predicatori a S. Sabina in Roma, 1368 April 10, M4. Hypothesis of repositioning of art works.
Fig. 13. Lippo Vanni, *Reliquary with Madonna and Child with Saints*, Rome, Santi Domenico e Sisto, tempera and gold leaf on wood, ca.1350s, 49,37x45,4x6,19 cm, now Baltimore, Walters Art Museum.
Fig. 14. Lippo Vanni, *Sant'Aurea Triptych*, Rome, Santi Domenico e Sisto, tempera on wood, 1358, 172x208 cm, 85x51 cm, from B. Cerulli, "Lippo Vanni. Il Trittico di Santa Aurea", in *Apogeo e fine del Medioevo*.

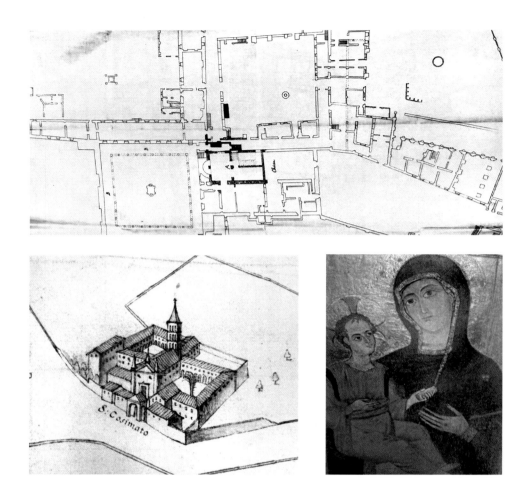

Fig. 15. Rome, San Cosimato, Floor plan, 1892 (Rome, Archivio Centrale dello Stato, AABBAA, II, II, busta 402, All.B13), with tentative repositioning of the icon inside the medieval church during the Clarissan occupation.
Fig. 16. San Cosimato bird's eye view, 1656, Biblioteca Apostolica Vaticana, ms. Chigi P. VII, 10 f. 123.
Fig. 17. *Madonna del Coro*, 13th century ca., Rome, Istituto Centrale per il Restauro.

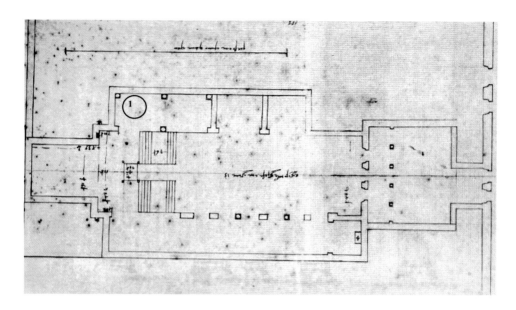

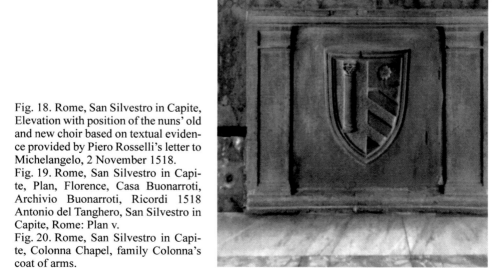

Fig. 18. Rome, San Silvestro in Capite, Elevation with position of the nuns' old and new choir based on textual evidence provided by Piero Rosselli's letter to Michelangelo, 2 November 1518.

Fig. 19. Rome, San Silvestro in Capite, Plan, Florence, Casa Buonarroti, Archivio Buonarroti, Ricordi 1518 Antonio del Tanghero, San Silvestro in Capite, Rome: Plan v.

Fig. 20. Rome, San Silvestro in Capite, Colonna Chapel, family Colonna's coat of arms.

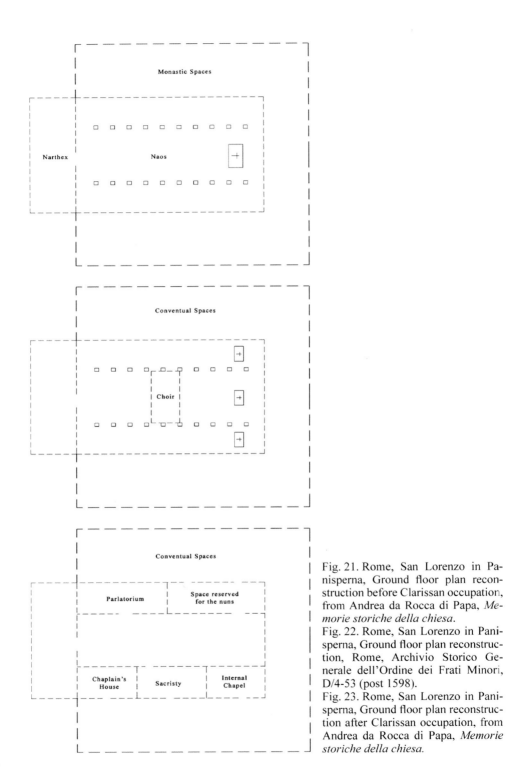

Fig. 21. Rome, San Lorenzo in Panisperna, Ground floor plan reconstruction before Clarissan occupation, from Andrea da Rocca di Papa, *Memorie storiche della chiesa*.
Fig. 22. Rome, San Lorenzo in Panisperna, Ground floor plan reconstruction, Rome, Archivio Storico Generale dell'Ordine dei Frati Minori, D/4-53 (post 1598).
Fig. 23. Rome, San Lorenzo in Panisperna, Ground floor plan reconstruction after Clarissan occupation, from Andrea da Rocca di Papa, *Memorie storiche della chiesa*.

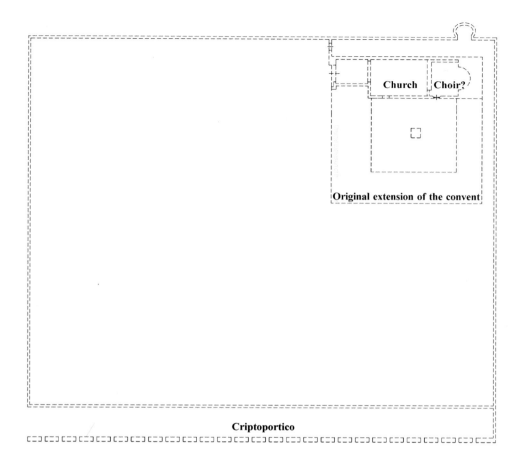

Fig. 24. Castrocielo, Santa Maria del Monacato, Ground floor plan, from Bertani, *La Chiesa del 'Monacato' in Castrocielo*.

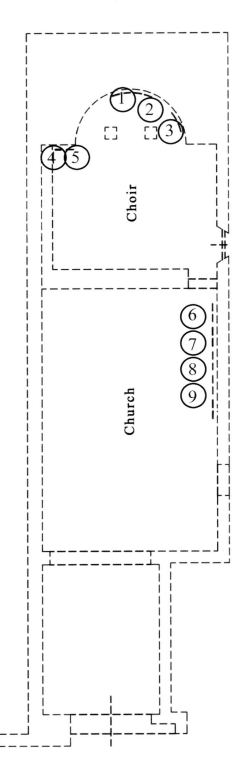

Fig. 25. Schematic diagram of the detached frescoes currently in the church of San Rocco, Castrocielo, in their original location inside the church of Santa Maria del Monacato, Castrocielo: 1. *Ascension*; 2. *Group of Saints*; 3. *Group of Saints*; 4. *St John the Evangelist*; 5. *Unidentified Bearded Saint*; 6. *Enthroned Virgin with St Benedict*; 7. *Madonna and Child with the Baptist*; 8. *Crucifixion between Mary and St John*; 9. *Crucifixion between St Benedict and St John.*

Fig. 26. Guarcino, San Luca, Conventual complex, exterior.
Fig. 27. Guarcino, San Luca, Conventual complex, exterior.
Fig. 28. Guarcino, San Luca, Church, interior.

Fig. 29. Guarcino, San Luca, interior pre-restorations counter façade, 1950s ca. (Ph. Anon repository at the Opera del Divino Amore).
Fig. 30. Guarcino, San Luca, interior pre-restorations counter façade, 1950s ca. (Ph. Anon repository at the Opera del Divino Amore).

Fig. 31. Benedetto Buglioni, *Virgin and Child between Saint Benedict and Saint Bibiana,* glazed terracotta, ca. first quarter of 16th century, Montefiascone, Santa Margherita.

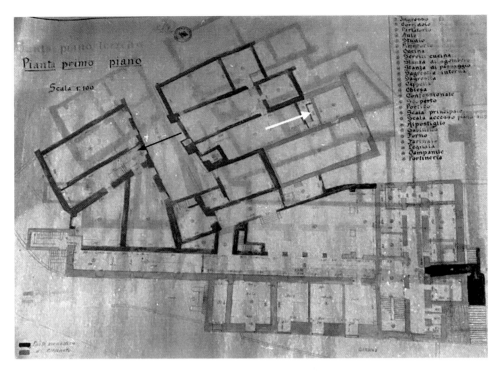

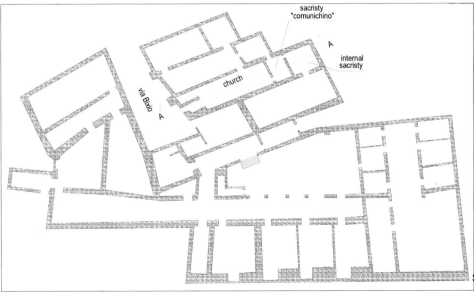

Fig. 32. Map of the nunnery of San Pietro at Montefiascone, 1934, pen on paper; arrow indicates wall of the choir where the Buglioni altarpiece was originally found. Archivio delle Benedettine di Montefiascone.

Fig. 33. Reconstruction of San Pietro's ground floor plan based on unpublished plans.

Fig. 34. Montefiascone, San Pietro, choir, *Trinity*, fresco, 1350-1375.

Fig. 35. Montefiascone, San Pietro, choir, *Adoration of the Magi*, fresco, 1350-1375.

Fig. 36. Orsano, Sant'Angelo, church exterior.

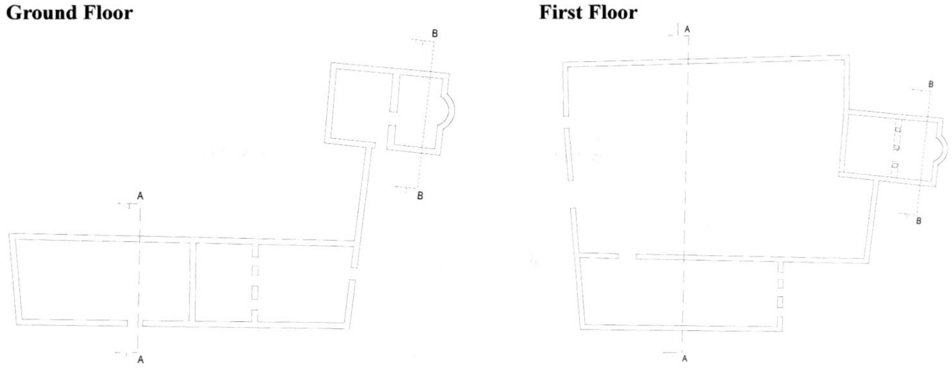

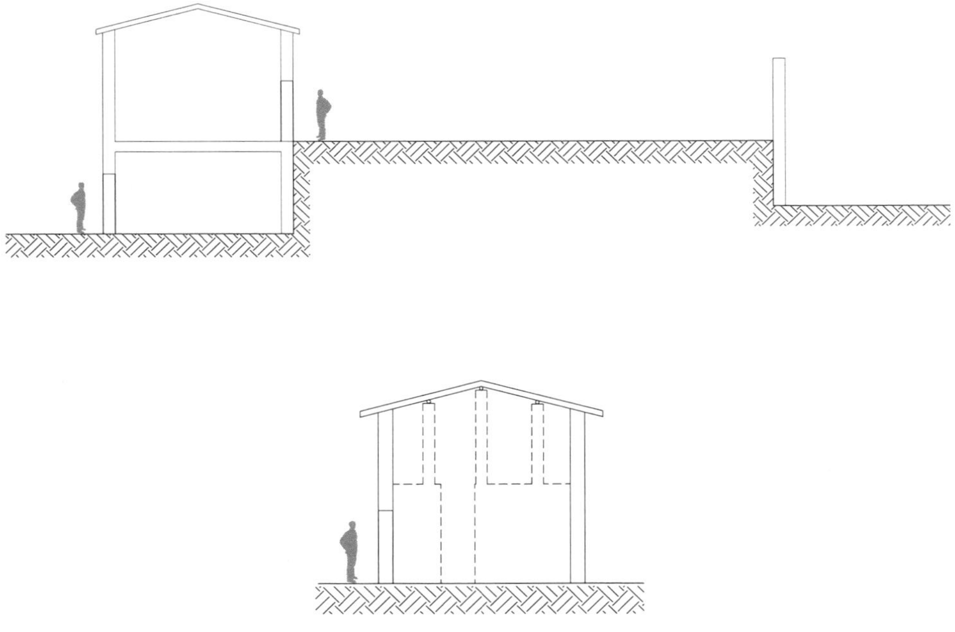

Ground Floor **First Floor**

Fig. 37. Orsano, Sant'Angelo conventual complex, Reconstruction of ground and first floor plan, from Fasolo, "Presentazione di rilievi di studenti della Facoltà di Architettura".
Fig. 38. Orsano, Sant'Angelo conventual complex, Reconstruction of sections of the convent, from Fasolo, "Presentazione di rilievi di studenti della Facoltà di Architettura".

Fig. 39. Alatri, San Sebastiano, General view.

Fig. 40. Wooden Crucifix, wood, 130x125cm, 13th century, Rome, deposit at Segreteria del Collegio Romano, from *Museo Nazionale di Palazzo Venezia. Sculture in legno.*

Fig. 41. Amaseno, San Michele Arcangelo.
Fig. 42. Amaseno, San Michele Arcangelo, Ruins of the conventual complex.

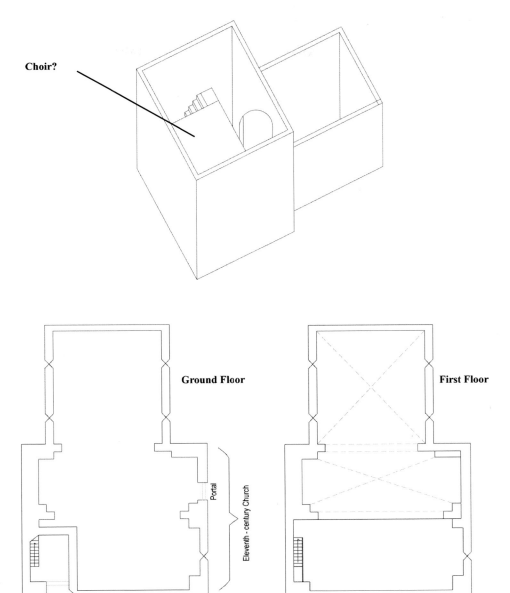

Fig. 43. Amaseno, San Michele Arcangelo, Axonometric view with reconstruction of choir enclosure, from Fasolo, "Presentazione di rilievi di studenti della Facoltà di Architettura".
Fig. 44. Amaseno, San Michele Arcangelo, Ground floor and first floor plan.

Fig. 45. Amaseno, San Michele Arcangelo, Niche (Ph. Fabio Marzi).
Fig. 46. Amaseno, San Michele Arcangelo, Fresco, 1491 (Ph. Fabio Marzi).

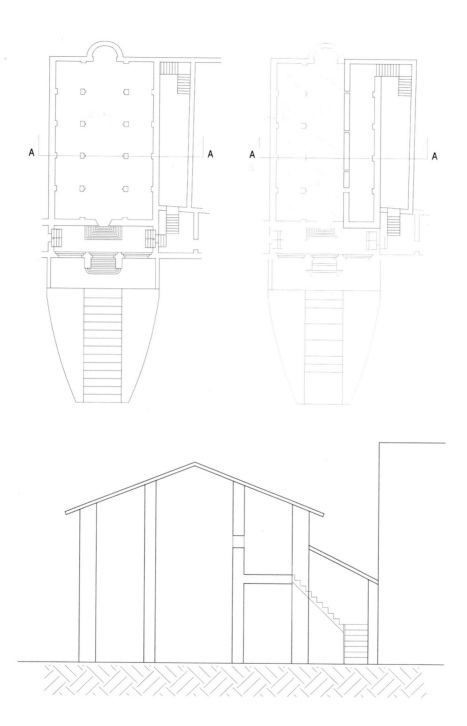

Fig. 47. Anagni, San Pietro in Vineis, Ground floor plan (left) and first floor plan (right).
Fig. 48. Anagni, San Pietro in Vineis, Section.

Fig. 49. Anagni, San Pietro in Vineis, *Last Judgement*, fresco, post 1255.

Next page:
Fig. 50. Anagni, San Pietro in Vineis, *Stigmatization of Saint Francis*, fresco, post 1255.

Fig. 51. Borgo San Pietro, Monastero di Santa Filippa Mareri, View from the Lake Salto, 1930s, Borgo San Pietro, Archivio di Santa Filippa Mareri.
Fig. 52. Borgo San Pietro, Monastero di Santa Filippa Mareri, South-east view, 1930s, Borgo San Pietro, Archivio di Santa Filippa Mareri.

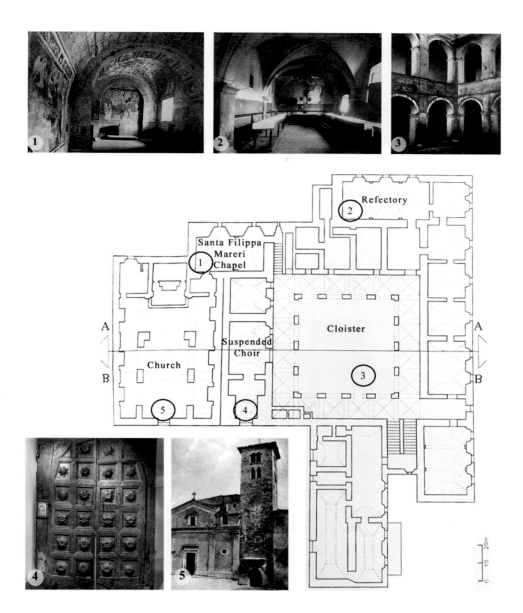

Fig. 53. Borgo San Pietro, Nunnery of Santa Filippa Mareri, Floor plan, from De Angelis, "Il monastero di Borgo San Pietro": 1. View of chapel dedicated to Santa Filippa Mareri, 1930s; 2. Refectory, 1930s; 3. View to the left of the medieval cloister, 1930s; 4. Portal with geometrical motifs, wood and metal, 15th century; 5. Church and bell tower, 1930s.

Fig. 54. Borgo San Pietro di Petrella Salto, Nunnery of Santa Filippa Mareri, Santa Filippa Chapel, right wall, *Coronation*, *Saints*, *Monks*, 14th century.
Fig. 55. Borgo San Pietro di Petrella Salto, Nunnery of Santa Filippa Mareri, Santa Filippa Chapel, *Christus Triumphans*, fresco, 16th century.

Fig. 56. Borgo San Pietro di Petrella Salto, Nunnery of Santa Filippa Mareri, Museo del Monastero di Santa Filippa Mareri, Grilled window, iron.

Fig. 57. Borgo San Pietro di Petrella Salto, Monastero di Borgo San Pietro, Museo del Monastero di Santa Filippa Mareri, Portal with geometrical motifs, wood and metal, 15th century.

3. The Benedictines in Latium

1. *Forlorn Latium: Medieval Nunneries in the Region*

Although the past two decades have witnessed a substantial rise in the study of religious women, in-depth studies devoted to Latium's convents have yet to make their appearance. The study of the region's late medieval convents still lacks a thorough historiography; a surprising deficit if we consider that, between the thirteenth and the fourteenth centuries, the area was densely populated by religious women and their nunneries. Reassessments of female religious experiences are still lacking a thorough survey that often results in the devaluation of women's place and space. Though the limited evidence for conventual communities has been associated with women's sparse economic and cultural resources, our knowledge is still largely impressionistic hindering any generalisation on the subject. As previously stated, convents have been selected in accordance to the presence of solid artistic, architectural, or documentary data. This results in a chronological fluctuation of the examined complexes, which have been arranged in alphabetical order for the purpose of this book.

In the *Monasticon Italiae*, 1, Filippo Caraffa provides a detailed list of Benedictine settlements in Rome and Latium.[1] At first glance their distribution appears to be evenly spread across the region. Nevertheless, a careful examination reveals that convents with a significant cultural presence were concentrated in the area between Rome and Naples commonly referred to as Ciociaria. Earlier foundation dates of nunneries in the province of Viterbo and Rieti compared to those in the province of Frosinone may account for this. Another possibility could be that these settlements were inhabited with a greater continuity due to their proximity to major Benedictine abbeys – such as Montecassino and Subiaco. This trend was also reinforced by the male Cistercian houses established in the area, which included: Fossanova (Santa Maria consecrated in 1208) and Casamari (Santa Maria Assunta consecrated in 1217).[2] These large rural monastic

---

1. *Monasticon Italiae*, 1, Tav. VII.
2. According to recent studies, Santa Maria Maggiore in Ferentino was not a Cistercian house like Fossanova and Casamari: E. Gallotta, "L'architettura come spazio per la liturgia: l'interno di

complexes undoubtedly maintained a significant influence over the region both from a religious and a cultural standpoint. The proliferation of nunneries likely came as a result of female mysticism and the region's proximity to Rome. The traditional coenobitic framework was also imposed on the hermit experience, which gained popularity south of Rome during the eleventh century.[3] Saint Chelidonia's (1077-1152) life is exemplary of this. A popular hermit during the eleventh century, she retired to the cave of Mora Ferogna in the Aniene valley around 1090. At her death, a nunnery was founded on the hermitage in 1152.[4] The Roman Curia attempted to normalize these types of religious experiences according to the more common canons of coenobitism, ultimately exercising palpable control over female hermits.[5] By this time, all major urban settlements in the province had a nunnery close to their perimeter, the inclusion, or otherwise, close proximity to villages was justified as a necessary measure for an effective defence of these settlements against potential external danger. Following the Council of Trent (1545-1563), there were some precise dispositions entrusted to bishops to transfer all nunneries within city walls.[6] According to Annibale Ilari, the transmigration of nuns from one nunnery to another, which began in the mid-thirteenth century and continued unabated, was a consequence of changes to the economy in which monasticism had originally prospered.[7] Its causes are identified in: the crushing of the feudal economy, the collapse of the manorial system, and the decline in production and trade from which monasticism had drawn.[8] In turn, a decentralization of their patrimonies, which created many small and increasingly passive administrations, gradually led to the dismemberment and alienation of a certain monastic ideal. But what was the rhetorical value of reform?[9] It is very possible that this was a strategy to undermine territorial hegemony by convents.

An analysis of data collected to date indicates that nunneries north of Rome – in the area defined as Tuscia – were generally founded at an earlier date. This is both true for the nunnery of San Biagio in Nepi founded in 921 and that of

Santa Maria Maggiore a Ferentino alla fine del Duecento", *Quaderni dell'Istituto di Storia dell'Architettura*, 71 (2019), pp. 5-22: 7.

3. F. Caraffa, "L'eremitismo nella valle dell'alto Aniene dalle origini al secolo XIX", *Miscellanea Antonio Piolanti*, 2 vols., Rome, Facultas Theologiae Pontificiae Universitatis Lateranensis, 1963-1964, II, pp. 226-232.

4. G.G. Meersseman, "Eremitismo e predicazione itinerante", in *L'eremitismo in Occidente nei secoli XI e XII*, Acts of the conference (Mendola, 1962), Milan, Vita e Pensiero, 1965, pp. 164-179; S. Boesch Gajano, *Chelidonia. Storia di un'eremita medievale*, Rome, Viella, 2010, p. 54.

5. Meersseman, "Eremitismo e predicazione itinerante", pp. 166-167.

6. A. Ilari, "Il monachesimo femminile in Ciociaria", in *Il monachesimo benedettino femminile in Ciociaria. Atti del convegno di studi per il 25° della beatificazione di suor Maria Fortunata Viti*, ed. by Giuseppe D'Onorio, Acts of the conference (Veroli, 1992), Veroli, Monastero di Santa Maria, 1994, pp. 17-51: 17.

7. *Ibid.*, p. 50; A.M. Piazzoni, *Guglielmo di Saint-Thierry. Il declinio dell'ideale monastico nel secolo XII*, Rome, Carocci, 1988.

8. Ilari, "Il monachesimo femminile", p. 50.

9. J. Van Engen, "The 'Crisis of Cenobitism' Reconsidered: Benedictine Monasticism in the Years 1050-1150", *Speculum*, 61, 2 (1986), pp. 269-304.

San Giovanele in Orte, ca. 537-555.[10] The area around Rieti was also the chosen location for early female monastic foundations such as the nunneries of San Giorgio – sold by the Dukes of Spoleto to the abbey of Farfa in 751 – and Santa Maria in Sectuno, confirmed as part of the abbey's possessions by Otto I in 967.[11] In the area to the south of Rome, referred to as Ciociaria, a series of conventual settlements stem across the length of the ridge of the Ernici-Simbruini Mountains – an important element of the Subappenino mountain range. The centres of Alatri, Veroli, Ferentino, Paliano, Anagni, Arpino, Guarcino, Trevi nel Lazio, Torre Caietani, Sgurgola, and Sora are located along the slopes of this area.[12] The nunneries in these centres were all roughly founded between the eleventh and the twelfth centuries.[13] The oldest monastery in Anagni is that of Santa Reparata in which the relics of the Saints Aurelia and Neomisia were transferred before the pontificate of Leo IX.[14] At Ferentino, a ninth-century seal depicts an abbess with the wording on the edge, ABBATISSE ST BENEDICT CIVITATIS FERENTINI. It is followed by that of Sant'Angelo in Ceccano founded by Bishop Rodolfo of Ferentino (1161-1191).[15] Moreover, Saint Dominic of Sora founded a nunnery dedicated to San Nicola in the vicinity of the charterhouse of Trisulti in the first decade of the eleventh century.[16] Lastly, Agostino, abbot of Casamari (1088-1106), installed a convent in Veroli next to the church of San Ippolito from which it took its name.[17]

Another factor was the political instability that characterized the area south of Rome during the thirteenth and fourteenth centuries, which ironically contributed

---

10. *Monasticon Italiae*, 1, p. 103; L. Cavazzi, *La diaconia di S. Maria in Via Lata e il monastero di S. Ciriaco. Memorie storiche*, Rome, Pustet, 1908.

11. W. Van Heteren, "Due monasteri benedettini più volte secolari (Rieti)", *Bollettino della Regia Deputazione di Storia Patria per l'Umbria*, 12 (1906), pp. 51-55.

12. R. di Cola, "Topografia e geografia dei monasteri femminili nel basso Lazio", in *Il monachesimo benedettino*, p. 87.

13. *Ibid.*, p. 88.

14. *Acta Sanctorum Septembris*, t. VII, Antverpiae, apud Bernardum Alb. vander Plassche, 1760, De ss. Aurelia et Neomisia vv., p. 137; V. Fenicchia, "Aurelia e Neomisia", in *Bibliotheca Sanctorum*, 2, Rome, Istituto Giovanni XXIII nella Pontificia Università Lateranense, 1962, col. 601; C. Mengarelli, "La presenza monastica ad Anagni nell'alto Medioevo (sec. IX-XII)", *Rivista cistercense*, 31 (2014), p. 221; P. Zappasodi, *Anagni attraverso i secoli*, Veroli, Tip. Reali, 1908.

15. Ilari, "Il monachesimo femminile", p. 19; *Monasticon Italiae*, 1, p. 103.

16. V. Danesi, "San Nicola di Trisulti: un insediamento certosino femminile?", *Arte medievale*, 4 (2015), pp. 153-164; Valeria Danesi, who has studied the complex of San Nicola extensively, advances the hypothesis that this is the first female Carthusian settlement in Central Italy. She draws these conclusions by comparing San Nicola's architectonic layout with surviving Clarissan settlements in the area (San Pietro in Vineis, Anagni, San Sebastiano, Alatri) together with the celebrated example of San Damiano. Although the proximity to the Charterhouse of Trisulti is a strong point towards the identification of this nunnery as a female Carthusian convent, architectural analogies with surviving Clarissan settlements also point towards a Mendicant occupation; B. Fornari, "I monasteri di San Bartolomeo e San Nicola presso Trisulti", *Terra Nostra*, 22 (1983), pp. 17-19.

17. G. D'Onorio, G. Trulli, *Veroli. Un percorso di storia e di arte*, Veroli, Arti grafiche Pasquarelli, 2011.

to establish an economic continuity in settlements across this region.[18] Carocci maintains that strong ties between the Roman baronial aristocracy and this specific geographical area gave rise to its feudal structure.[19] Indeed, in contrast to northern Latium, where the provinces of Viterbo and Rieti were bordered by the Duchies of Tuscany and Spoleto and by cities eager to establish their independence, southern and eastern Latium was contested by the leading Roman baronial families.[20] These are likely to have also exercised their control over the territory through monastic and conventual foundations. An emblematic case is Santa Maria in Viano in Sgurgola, which is extremely significant in this regard.[21] The nunnery, located in a Conti fief and endowed by the powerful cleric Stefano di Anagni, canonic to the cathedral of Anagni and chaplain to Pope Gregory IX, Innocent IV and Alexander IV,[22] was placed under the authority of Abbess Gemma, daughter of Corrado I Conti.[23] The convent through Gemma's familial ties, inherited considerable authority over the town and fief of Sgurgola. In 1300, Pietro Caetani bought lands from the nuns, who were dissatisfied by the administration of these land holdings by Gemma's relatives. It seems that the Caetani influence was already in place given that a certain "Maria soror domini Raynaldi de Supino" is found in this agreement of sale.[24] Maria had been previously married to Francesco Caetani, who had divorced her in 1295 in order to become a cardinal.[25] Ironically, the transaction – which marked the definitive supremacy of the Caetani over the Conti in the area of the Monti Lepini – was the sales settlement between Pietro II and the nunnery of Santa Maria in Viano in the person of Abbess Mabilia.[26]

Overall, we may assume that multiple motivations underpinned the establishment of these convents. They were both the product of an intensely female religious experience and acted as a stable residence for unmarried daughters or widows. However, as with their male counterparts, nunneries also acted as bastions of effective control over territories north and south of Rome for the region's leading families. In contrast to other aristocracies, the Roman baronial class was exceptionally bound to the Holy See.[27] Indeed, in the thirteenth

18. Carocci, *Baroni di Roma*, p. 1.
19. *Ibid.*, p. 2.
20. "Le mostre del Lazio meridionale e di Celestino V nel Palazzo di Bonifacio VIII in Anagni", ed. by Istituto di Storia e di Arte del Lazio meridionale, *Bollettino dell'Istituto di Storia dell'Arte Meridionale*, 6 (1969-1970).
21. F. Caraffa, "I monasteri medievali nella parte Nord-orientale dei Monti Lepini", *Bollettino dell'Istituto di Storia dell'Arte Meridionale*, 11 (1979-1982), pp. 45-57. Forthcoming Federici in *Mediaevalia*.
22. *Ibid.*, p. 87; F. Caraffa, "Il testamento di Stefano di Anagni", *Archivio della Società romana di storia patria* (1981), p. 110; Zappasodi, *Anagni attraverso i secoli*, 1, pp. 313-316.
23. G. Caetani, *Regesta chartarum. Regesto delle pergamene dell'Archivio Caetani*, 1, Perugia, Stab. tip. F. lli Stianti, 1922, p. 126.
24. *Ibid.*, p. 126.
25. *Ibid.*
26. Subiaco, Archivio Colonna, prg. LIV. N. 91.
27. Carocci, *Baroni di Roma*, p. 17; Toubert, *Les structures du Latium médiéval*, p. 1038.

century, the succession of popes was always tied to one of the leading families: the Savelli, the Orsini, the Frangipane, the Conti, the Colonna or the Caetani.[28] Enjoying the periodic and sometimes frequent support of the papacy allowed families to safeguard certain territories and slowly incorporate them into their personal dominions.[29] This differs significantly from other regions, which had less fractured territories and longer reigns.[30] In Latium, these families extended their influence and privileges (both political and economic) to female monastic institutions, where daughters, widows and female members of their clan resided and whose land possessions were frequently part of their fiefs. Their ties to the Holy See (the Conti in Sgurgola and Alatri; the Colonna in Palestrina; the Caetani in Anagni)[31] made it only natural for them to endow these convents with economic and political prestige while they held office in curial circles.

During the second half of the thirteenth century, the Caetani imposed their political and territorial authority on neighbouring fiefs, which had been under the authority of the Conti, the Segni and most importantly the Colonna.[32] The Caetani were eager to consolidate their power south of Rome and broaden their domain from Anagni. They replaced the earlier Counts of Tuscolo, the Frangipane and the Annibaldi from Torre Astura and Terracina in the Agro Pontino area along the Tyrrhenian coast towards the Via Appia.[33] From Anagni, they spread into the Sacco Valley along the Via Latina and into the Aniene Valley, threatening the lordships of the Counts of Segni, the Colonna, and the Conti di Ceccano. Indeed, the Caetani further secured their position by occupying several strongholds such as the castles at Sgurgola, Trivigliano, Torre in the Sacco Valley, Trevi, Vallepietra and Filettino.[34] They had thus seized control of the three valleys adjacent to the Tiber and the three major arterial roads: the Appia, the Latina-Valeria and the Tiburtina. The Caetani's hegemony over local convents is evident throughout this period.[35] This was heightened by Pope Boniface VIII's frequent residencies in Anagni. The latter became an influential stronghold in Ciociaria and attracted major personalities from clerical circles that gravitated around the Roman Curia, replacing Viterbo as the principal base for the Apostolic See outside of Rome.[36] This was particularly relevant at the dawn of the first Jubilee in 1300 when Boniface had to secure a territorial buffer south of Rome.

---

28. "Le mostre del Lazio Meridionale", pp. 115-116.
29. P. Partner, *The Lands of St Peter*, London, Eyre Metheun, 1972, pp. 138-228; E. Petrucci, *Ecclesiologia e politica. Momenti di storia del papato medievale*, Rome, Carocci, 2001.
30. G. Marchetti Longhi, "Il Lazio Meridionale triplice via di espansione della Civiltà Latina", *Bollettino dell'Istituto di Storia e di Arte del Lazio Meridionale*, 4 (1966), p. 201.
31. *Ibid.*
32. G. Carpaneto, *Le famiglie nobili romane*, Rome, Rendina, 2001, pp. 103-114.
33. Marchetti Longhi, "Il Lazio Meridionale triplice via", p. 203.
34. Carpaneto, *Le famiglie nobili romane*, p. 104.
35. *Monasticon Italiae*, 1, pp. 107-108; "Le mostre del Lazio Meridionale".
36. M. Andaloro, *Bonifacio VIII*, Rome, Istituto Storico Italiano per il Medioevo, 2006, p. 59.

As previously stated, during the Avignon period and the power vacuum that followed, southern Latium essentially came to resemble a feudal state.[37] In fact, by the fourteenth century the area between Rome and Naples was divided between eight feudal lordships, five papal territories, three monastic dominions, and four free communes.[38] As stated by Romanini in the introduction to Romano's *Eclissi di Roma. Pittura murale a Roma e nel Lazio da Bonifacio VIII a Martino V (1295-1431)*, the art historical historiography for Rome during the Avignonese papacy "corresponds to a sort of black hole that extends far beyond the reacquisition of the papal seat, and that negates all types of artistic production, and as a consequence, every possibility of cognitive research".[39] However, the existence of an uninterrupted artistic production in Rome and Latium in general, contradicts this desolate scenario.[40] While Rome undoubtedly lost some its brightness as a result of the Avignonese exile, this absence left space for other agencies which may be evaluated in the context of female religious patronage in greater Latium.

Few artworks survive from Latium's medieval nunneries, it is, however, safe to assume that conventual spaces were embellished with some form of artistic presence. Apart from the fresco cycle in the Benedictine convent of Santa Maria in Palazzolo at Castrocielo (in the province of Frosinone), pictorial evidence is in fact scanty. We usually only have the outer shells of these complexes, as is the case for Sant'Angelo Orsano. It is worth noting that the most complete fresco cycles outside of Rome survive in two Clarissan convents, namely San Pietro in Vineis at Anagni and San Sebastiano at Alatri. This should not be dismissed as mere chance, as the Clarissan order enjoyed strong support across the Curia throughout the thirteenth and fourteenth centuries. This may have shifted major patronal activities to new Clarissan foundations settlements at the expenses of their older Benedictine rivals.

In Latium, the proliferation of nunneries came as a result of female mysticism and the region's proximity to Rome. Local sources in the form of papal bulls and apostolic letters abound in the greater regional area between the thirteenth and the fifteenth centuries, with quite an impressive archival record.[41] Unfortunately, documents have been spread across various locations, which makes an overarching study somewhat challenging. As previously mentioned, a comprehensive guide to the *archivi* is lacking. Nevertheless, the amount of source material is quite surprising if we account for the fact that during the thirteenth century, in contrast to the bordering regions of Umbria and Tuscany, Latium did not witness the birth of any new major monastic movement.[42] This trend likely explains the success of the Cistercian order in the region.

37. Marchetti Longhi, "Il Lazio Meridionale triplice via", p. 201.
38. *Ibid.*
39. Romanini, "Introduzione", in Romano, *Eclissi di Roma*, p. 7: "Corrisponde ad una sorta di buco nero che si estende ben oltre la riacquisizione del soglio pontificio romano, e che vanifica ogni sorta di produzione artistica, e di conseguenza ogni possibilità di indagine conoscitiva".
40. *Ibid.*
41. Ilari, "Il monachesimo femminile", pp. 17-18.
42. *Monasticon Italiae*, 1, p. 102.

2. Women's Place and Space: Introducing Benedictine Art and Architecture

Although less researched than its male counterpart, female monastic architecture created and disseminated similar structures for its organisational needs.[43] These complexes included Chapter houses, cloisters, dormitories and choirs in the proximity to the congregation's church.[44] Even though there has been an unquestionable surge in publications on this subject from the 1990s onwards, there is an objective difficulty in the study of these complexes which is tied to their physical vulnerability.[45] As far as Rome and Latium are concerned, I am not aware of any overview study on female monastic architecture during the medieval period. The reasons behind this are manifold. Little has survived, and what has is often fragmentary or much rebuilt. Indeed, this is the case for numerous convents such as Sant'Angelo in Orsano or Santa Maria in Viano. Additionally, women often inherited complexes from male orders like Santa Maria del Monacato in Castrocielo. It is also true that religious women had considerably fewer financial means. Consequently, their complexes often had a private and domestic quality to them, which resulted in a less formalized spatial division made of perishable materials.[46] This was in turn challenged by the need to separate the officiating clergy and the laity from the nuns. These divisions were especially prescribed after the promulgation of the *Periculoso* decree by Boniface VIII in 1300 and later reinforced by the Council of Trent.[47] It is fair to say that we do not know the degree of enforcement of these measures in provincial areas.

It is challenging to reconstruct the original divisions imposed by *clausura* schemes inside churches. This difficulty is exacerbated by the fact that such divisions were often crafted in perishable materials such as wood, linens or even mud. As Bruzelius rightly points out, "these types of structures can only be retrieved by archaeology, and then only at foundation level. The picture that we are now able to reconstruct of women's monasticism may, therefore, be biased in favour of those with more permanent, stone structures".[48] From this research, it would appear that Benedictine nunneries usually had choirs positioned at ground level, either adjacent to, or behind the altar. The form and scale were usually in

---

43. See also Chapter 1 of this book.
44. Lirosi, *I monasteri femminili*; Stein-Kecks, "Claustrum and capitulum"; Thomas, *Art and Piety*.
45. See Chapter 1 for bibliography.
46. Bruzelius, "Hearing is Believing", pp. 83-84; Hamburger, *The Visual and the Visionary*.
47. According to Zappasodi, *Sorores*, p. 10: "Le nuove disposizioni rendevano ora gli spazi claustrali impenetrabili, tanto alle monache che non potevano piu abbandonarli, quanto agli esterni a cui venne interdetto l'accesso senza speciale licenza. I passaggi furono chiusi, le finestre ferrate, la sola porta di accesso serrata perennemente con due differenti serrature. […] Le conseguenze della Periculoso furono notevoli. Le religiose a indirizzo eremitico furono costrette ad abbandonare i propri romitori per trasferirsi all'interno della cerchia ubica e si rese necessaria e vincolante un'architettura monastica che permettesse una vita comunitaria nel pieno rispetto della clausura rigorosa".
48. C. Bruzelius, "Architecture monastic", in *Women and Gender in Medieval Europe. An Encyclopedia*, ed. by M. Schaus, New York, Routledge, 2006, p. 32.

keeping with the simplicity of the church.[49] There was often no cloister, but simply a square court with one covered passageway. Moreover, the most secluded part of the convent was usually the dormitory. The spaces in which contact was permitted with the clergy in particular, and perhaps the laity too, were closer to the church alongside the apse. Smaller congregations lack a real planimetric consistency and Chapter halls or an internal visitation room were not necessarily present.[50]

Given the dire state in which most of these female monastic complexes survive, a comparable architectural survey of the region's civil and religious buildings is crucial to facilitate an overall understanding of Latium's late medieval architecture. The most comprehensive publication on the subject is by the architectural historian Donatella Fiorani.[51] In her view, the period between the thirteenth and the beginning of the fourteenth century represents the "golden age" of architecture in Latium.[52] This is exemplified by the great Cistercian abbeys of Fossanova and Casamari, but also by the cathedral at Anagni, the *palazzi* of local nobles in the towns of Guarcino (Palazzo Patrasso, Palazzo Tomassi) and Alatri (Palazzo Gottifredo, Palazzo Patrasso-Grappelli), and the *castra* at Sermoneta (Caetani family) and Colleferro (Castello Vecchio, Conti family).[53] The existence of a somewhat standardized architectural style during this period is attributed (especially by Italian historiography) to the birth of Cistercian "cantieri-scuola", literally "construction-site schools" inside the great abbeys of Fossanova and Casamari.[54] Specialized workers were trained on these building sites and were subsequently employed by lay or religious patrons. This is evident both in the stratigraphic analysis of building materials, which mostly employed limestone blocks joined by hydraulic lime mortar with dressed quoins, and in the adoption of repeated modules and vaulted arches on square bays (the so-called *ad quadratum* technique). The study of conventual churches across a comparative architectural context allows us to further our understanding of these complexes of which so little has survived. Having said this, although there was certainly a tendency to standardize building forms and

49. *Ibid.*, pp. 31-34.
50. *Ibid.*
51. D. Fiorani, *Tecniche costruttive murarie medievali. Il Lazio meridionale*, Rome, L'Erma di Bretschneider, 1996.
52. *Ibid.*, p. 30.
53. For architectural surveys of these towns, please refer to: *Lazio medievale. Ricerca topografica su 33 abitati delle antiche diocesi di Alatri, Anagni, Ferentino, Veroli*, ed. by C. Carbonetti Vendittelli, Rome, Multigrafica, 1980; P. Delogu, "Castelli e palazzi. La nobiltà ducentesca del territorio laziale", in *Roma anno 1300*, pp. 705-713; *Sermoneta e i Caetani. Dinamiche politiche, sociali e culturali di un territorio tra medioevo ed età moderna*, ed. by L. Fiorani, Rome, L'Erma di Bretschneider, 1999; G. Floridi, *Storia di Guarcino*, Guarcino, Comune di Guarcino, 1971; G.M. Longhi, "Un insigne monumento da redimere. Il Palazzo dei Cavalieri Gaudenti in Ferentino", *Bollettino di Storia dell'Arte del Lazio Meridionale*, 1 (1963), pp. 127-140.
54. For introductory bibliography, see: V.F. Pardo, "Architettura cistercense e architettura degli ordini mendicanti", in *Il monachesimo cistercense nella Marittima medievale. Storia e arte*, ed. by R. Cataldi, Casamari, Ed. Casamari, 2002, pp. 251-297; A. Cadei, "Scultura architettonica cistercense e cantieri monastici", in *I Cistercensi e il Lazio*, Rome, Multigrafica Editrice, 1978, pp. 157-162.

techniques, stratigraphic analysis of surviving nunneries highlights a variety of masonry wall types. These were characterized by a coarser cutting and laying of stone blocks, linked to the degree of sophistication of the hired labor, which was possibly tied to the economic resources available to religious women.

As far as artistic decoration is considered, a great deal has been lost or destroyed. Indeed, these nunneries were frequently abandoned because their community dwindled or were altogether transferred. In any case, the churches of these congregations were most likely frescoed with mural cycles or devotional paintings (as is the case for Santa Maria del Monacato). Unfortunately, apart from a few well-known examples little has survived in terms of artistic resonance, and the fragments we have are almost entirely anonymous. This is due to the nature of the craft itself which is primarily still tied to local *botteghe* and expresses the collaboration of several artists. Qualitative leaps derive from the different degrees of reception and re-processing of artistic influences. This was also imparted from the commission itself and the subject matter. The social extraction of local patronage varied considerably and so did the knowledge around specific iconographies.[55] This is apparent at Santa Maria di Palazzolo in Castrocielo, which we will examine later on. At the same time, the diversification of the commissions – influenced by the availability of economic means – acted both on the technical levels and the subject matter of these painterly cycles. They vary from the Byzantine prototypes expressed in the artefacts at the time of Abbot Desiderius to the painterly traditions of regional schools.[56] These were the expression of an intense exchange between Rome and Naples and reflect the complex aesthetic relations between centre and periphery. Another element which requires special attention is the occupation of sacred spaces by votive images. This was a result of the spontaneity of commissions, which frequently resulted in additions and overlays of sacred figures. In fact, these were often doubled or tripled to reiterate a very individual link between the saint and patron.[57] In contrast to the female conventual settlements of larger urban congregations, these provincial realities had less formalised iconographic programmes. This paradoxically allows us to delve into the intentions and motivations of our patrons more deeply. As stated by Giulia Orofino, the vitality of the artistic culture expressed in Latium necessitates an overreaching historiographical analysis.[58] The precarious conditions in which these convents survive have left us almost nothing of the original extent of these cycles. Nevertheless, through reconstructions on AutoCAD and documentary evidence we may still attempt to reconstruct their medieval appearance and draw comparisons with better known case studies in Rome, hopefully producing an integrated holistic study of conventual enclosures.

55. *Affreschi in Val Comino e nel Cassinate*, ed. by G. Orofino, Cassino, Università di Cassino, 2000, p. 11.
56. *Ibid.*, p. 10.
57. V. Pace, "Per un percorso nella pittura murale nella Val Comino e nel Cassinate", in *Affreschi in Val Comino*, p. 15.
58. *Affreschi in Val Comino*, p. 4.

3. *Between Rome and Naples: Artistic Presence at Santa Maria del Monacato, Castrocielo*

The Benedictine convent of Santa Maria in Castrocielo, otherwise known as Il Monacato, is situated outside the small town of Castrocielo at Palazzolo, not far from the abbey of Montecassino in the province of Frosinone. As testified by the extensive fresco decoration, the convent underwent a period of great prosperity between the twelfth and the fourteenth centuries.[59] The perimeter of the nunnery roughly covers the area of an ancient Roman *domus* – the Villa Euchelia. The latter was constructed under the rule of Sulla (ca.138 BC-78 BC) and donated to Saint Benedict on the 14 July 529 by Gordiano, father of Saint Gregory.[60] Although we do not know when the nuns installed themselves on site, the oldest surviving document relating to the convent is dated 1134.[61] Currently preserved in the archive at Montecassino, it outlines the donation of a piece of land to the nunnery, in the person of Abbess Cecilia, by a group of citizens from Aquino.[62] As demonstrated by a series of bequests and trading records, the nunnery benefited from a period of stability (1130s-1170s), which was favoured by the protection offered from the jurisdiction of Montecassino.[63] Indeed, the inscriptions on the eleventh-century bronze doors of the abbey church list Castrocielo as part of its possessions.[64] Despite officially being under the diocese of Aquino, Montecassino exercised a palpable influence on the church's domains and it was eventually annexed to the abbey in 1465.[65]

Furthermore, archival documents at Montecassino highlight the nunnery's growing donations and patrimony, indicated through a series of legal disputes.[66] These parchments list several abbesses: Beatrice, Mendola, Maria Aquino, Aloara, Aluguara, Rogata, Giovanna, Marotta, Gemma from Gallinaro who became abbess of Santa Maria de Ripa in Pontecorvo in 1363; Maria from San Germano, and finally Rita.[67] This documentation is crucial. Indeed, it does not solely provide a detailed list of names but also underscores the nunnery's autonomy in managing

---

59. B. Bertani, "La Chiesa del 'Monacato' in Castrocielo", *Benedictina*, 21 (1974), pp. 301-307; B. Bertani, "Sulle antiche chiese di Castrocielo", *Benedictina*, 30 (1983), pp. 109-127; B.H. Bloch, *Monte Cassino in the Middle Ages*, 3 vols., Cambridge, Harvard University Press, 1986; L. Fabiani, *La Terra di S. Benedetto. Fine del dominio temporale dell'Abbazia di Montecassino*, Montecassino, Badia di Montecassino, 1981, pp. 162-163; *Abbazia di Montecassino. I regesti dell'archivio*, 9, ed. by F. Avagliano and T. Leccisotti, Rome, Ministero dell'Interno - Archivi di Stato, 1974; F. Simonelli, "Chiesa di San Rocco (dalla chiesa di Santa Maria del Monacato). La storia", in *Affreschi in Val Comino*, pp. 105-106; A. Nicosia, "Le monache di S. Maria di Palazzolo", *Benedictina*, 23 (1976), pp. 173-178; E. Parlato, S. Romano, *Roma e il Lazio*, Milan, Jaca Book, 1992; S. Romano, "Affreschi da S. Maria del Monacato a Castrocielo (e un'aggiunta da Roccasecca)", *Arte medievale*, 2 (1989), pp. 155-166.
60. Bloch, *Monte Cassino*, III, p. 777.
61. *Abbazia di Montecassino*, 9, n. 3422, pp. 368-369.
62. *Ibid.*; Simonelli, "Chiesa di San Rocco", p. 105.
63. *Abbazia di Montecassino*, 9, pp. 368-473; Simonelli, "Chiesa di San Rocco", p. 105.
64. Bloch, *Monte Cassino*, III, p. 777.
65. *Abbazia di Montecassino*, 9, n. 3483, p. 398.
66. *Ibid.*, pp. 368-473.
67. *Ibid.*

its economic affairs and electing spiritual leaders. Thus, Abbess Rita is appointed *oeconomus* of the nunnery in 1400 by Pope Boniface IX,[68] an office usually reserved for priests. After the transfer of Gemma from Gallinaro to the nunnery of Santa Maria de Ripa in Pontecorvo in 1366, the convent unanimously elected Rita as her successor.[69] This information is also significant as it demonstrates a certain degree of mobility granted to and enjoyed by nuns, while we generally tend to perceive religious women as being static and fixed.[70]

The complex is encircled by a wall in *opus reticulatum*, which surrounds its perimeter over a surface area measuring 61,60x70 m (Fig. 24).[71] Two *cryptoportici*, which respectively extend by 60 m and 78 m in length, can be found on its northern and southern sides.[72] Villa Euchelia covered an area of 5,000 square metres and the nunnery was constructed on a portion of this land.[73] Like most Benedictine convents it extended around a square courtyard, which was originally accessed through three entrances. The church occupied the northern portion while the remaining sides likely functioned as refectory, dormitory and Chapter house. The stone masonry suggests that these were constructed at different periods from the eleventh to the sixteenth centuries.[74]

Although the remaining parts of the convent have been heavily restored, at present the church is the best-preserved portion of the complex. Unfortunately, the nunnery was severely damaged by Allied bombing in World War II. After the war the church was roofless, its stone floor lost and replaced by grass and waste for almost four decades. Originally, it was characterized by a single nave, without a transept, terminating in a semi-circular apse, preceded by an arch over pilasters. This plan was particularly common in Benedictine complexes and we may trace it to other nunneries such as Sant'Angelo Orsano.

The church's rectangular plan measured 14,75x6,75 m, while the semi-circular apse is 4 m wide and roughly 2 m deep.[75] The apse is surmounted by a pointed arch like the one present at the entrance on the counter-façade but is markedly higher. The apse was separated from the remaining body of the church at an uncertain date. However, this probably occurred before the installation of the Baroque altar that was built in front of it. The two spaces had separate means of entry, with the apse now accessible through a door which opened directly onto the courtyard of the complex. This double entrance was extremely common in Benedictine convents and may also be viewed in San Luca in Guarcino. It is

68. *Ibid.*, n. 3468, p. 391.
69. *Ibid.*, n. 3466, p. 390.
70. I believe that this mobility was crucial also for maintaining a certain degree of control over remote areas, which were unguarded or abandoned. As demonstrated by this book female monastic realities guaranteed a capillary control over strategic outposts. The Benedictines took advantage of this creating a dense network of strong and lasting ties within local contexts.
71. Bertani, "La chiesa del 'Monacato'", p. 305.
72. Bertani, "Sulle antiche chiese", p. 110.
73. Nicosia, "Le monache di S. Maria", p. 175.
74. Simonelli, "Chiesa di San Rocco", p. 106.
75. Bertani, "Sulle antiche chiese", p. 111.

likely that the religious congregation entered from the cloister and that the space inside the apse functioned as a choir.[76] An example of this may still be seen in the Benedictine church of San Pietro in Montefiascone. On the opposite side, towards the western end, a bell tower survives over the entrance hall preceding the church. The southern side is characterised by the presence of three square windows and a rectangular opening. This is surmounted by an arch which likely functioned as an entrance to the courtyard.

The surviving fresco decoration was originally located on the southern wall and in the apse but has now been detached. The paintings originally found in the nave developed on two registers framed by cornices. They can be dated between the fourteenth and the fifteenth centuries. The ones located in the apse followed an analogous disposition but date to the twelfth century. The latter were discovered in 1978 during the restorations carried out by the Soprintendenza per i Beni Storico, Artistici ed Etnoantropologici del Lazio. The wall that closed off an apse from the church was demolished and the frescoes were transferred onto wooden panels. The renovations were directed by Augusta Monferini Calvesi and carried out by Dominique Queloz-Agnes and Livio Jacuitti. The fresco cycles were detached and are currently displayed on panels measuring approximately 2x2 m in the church of San Rocco at Castrociclo. According to Bernardo Bertani only one third of the original painted surface within the church was preserved.[77] This corresponds to the paintings on the lower register of the nave and the ones located in the apse. There is an evident stylistic jigsaw, which testifies to the complex and varied artistic *milieu* that existed south of Rome between the thirteenth and the fourteenth centuries and to which this monument bears witness.

The paintings will be examined in chronological order starting with the ones originally located in the apse of the church (Fig. 25). The cycle is characterised by an ambitious iconographic programme. This included an Ascension, of which very little survives, bordered by a row of saints below. The composition is flanked at its sides by Saint John the Evangelist and likely, although nothing remains, either by the Virgin Mary, or, Saint John the Baptist. Documentary sources indicate that this iconographic prototype was also present in the apse of the church of Montecassino during the reign of Abbot Desiderius.[78]

---

76. Retro-choirs have been studied by Zappasodi, *Sorores*, in the context of Clarissan nunneries. Although I am not aware of this trend in Benedictine nunneries in Rome, I am fairly certain that they were more common than expected. This is testified by San Pietro at Montefiascone and San Luca in Guarcino. Castrociclo may offer further proof of this.

77. Bertani, "Sulle antiche chiese", p. 111. The frescoes were published by Bertani in 1974, then by Romano, "Affreschi da S. Maria", and lastly by Orofino in *Affreschi in Val Comino*.

78. The source for this is Leone Marsicano or Hostiense and Pietro Diacono, *Cronaca Monastero Cassinese*, introduction and translation by F. Gigante, Cassino, F. Ciolfi, 2016, book 3, chaps. 26-34; N. Acocella, *La decorazione pittorica di Montecassino dalle didascalie di Alfano I (sec. XI)*, Salerno, Di Giacomo, 1966; Bloch, *Monte Cassino*, I, p. 43; Romano, "Affreschi da Santa Maria", p. 158; p. 165 citing Leo from Ostia ("in absidea vero hic inde sub pedibus sanctorum baptistae et evangelistae Johannis"); P. Mathis, "Chiesa di San Rocco (dalla chiesa di Santa Maria del Monacato). Gli affreschi", in *Affreschi in Val Comino*, pp. 106-114: 107.

Originally located on the left side of the arch preceding the apse, Saint John the Evangelist currently survives on a rectangular wooden panel measuring 1,90 m.[79] The full-length apostle is encircled by two bands of red and ochre and is painted over a blue-green background. He is dressed in a brown pallium marked by red brushstrokes and a white vest. He is depicted raising one hand towards the Ascension scene and holding a scroll, which reads the *incipit* of his Gospel in the other: IN PRINCIPIO ERAT VERBVM ET VERBVM ERAT A[PUD] DEVM ET DEVS ERAT VERBVM, the saint's expression is conveyed through a forceful use of line that marks its contours and gives him an expressionistic quality. The tones that prevail are various shades of browns and green. Overall, his physiognomy may be traced back to Byzantine models.[80] Analogous stylistic elements may be viewed in the church of Sant'Angelo in Asprano and in the crypt of the church of Santa Maria del Piano in Ausonia. Dense colours and sharp brush strokes build up the figure of the apostle, which emerges as an enclosed and tense ensemble culminating in the perfect oval of the head and the hand raised to indicate the apse.[81] Although there is not a marked naturalism in its expression and its forms, there is an attempt to give a sense of adherence to space through its three-quarter pose. Before restorations carried out in the 1970s, a bearded saint occupied the area directly beneath Saint John.[82] Today the figure is not identifiable and only the head and the upper portion of the torso survive. He is depicted in a full-frontal pose over a blue background and encircled by a red and ochre band. Although the same workshop likely headed the composition it is distinctively less dynamic. Its pose and expression undoubtedly contribute to this sense of immobility.

The panels that follow the original display in the church depict a group of saints that occupied the space directly beneath the image of the Ascension (which survives in a fragmentary state at present) inside the apse. According to Paola Mathis, this iconographic disposition is very rare in the area, and apart from the Grotta delle Fornelle in Calvi, other examples of this type do not survive in southern Latium.[83] We may assume that the height of the apse allowed for the inclusion of the standing saints. The composition is characterised by the presence of five male saints and two pairs of female martyrs at the sides.[84] The figures emerge from a blue-green background standing on an ochre-coloured ground. Regrettably, the frescoes have suffered a great deal of damage. This leaves very little space for any stylistic consideration. While the central male saints are almost invisible, the female figures are better preserved. Their vests are embellished by a *loros* and they are represented with one hand raised in blessing, and the other holding a cloth upon which a crown rests, the customary symbol for martyrdom. Originally, they were identified via the

79. *Ibid.*, p. 106; Romano, "Affreschi da S. Maria", pp. 155-156.
80. Mathis, "Chiesa di San Rocco", p. 106; Romano, "Affreschi da S. Maria", pp. 155-156.
81. Mathis, "Chiesa di San Rocco", p. 106.
82. *Ibid.*; Romano, "Affreschi da S. Maria", p. 157.
83. Mathis, "Chiesa di San Rocco", p. 106; A. Carotti, *Gli affreschi della Grotta delle Fornelle a Calvi Vecchia*, Rome, De Luca, 1974.
84. Simonelli, "Chiesa di San Rocco", p. 106.

use of inscriptions which are almost illegible today.[85] From the remaining fragments it would appear that each saint is represented holding his or her own attribute. One of the figures depicted with a beard and a hood could possibly represent Saint Benedict. This is very plausible given that the nunnery was under the jurisdiction of the abbey of Montecassino. This composition is fragmentary and apart from a few details it is almost illegible. In all likelihood it followed canonic iconographic schemes. However, once again very few considerations may be made on the basis of the surviving portions of the fresco.

The cycle inside the apse and over the arch preceding it is very significant from a stylistic standpoint. Indeed, the figures reflect a discontinuous pictorial performance which alternates different stylistic patterns and points to several artistic personalities working within the same workshop. The first, already seen in *Saint John* and in the bearded *Saint* beneath him, builds physiognomic details with energetic lines and dark brushstrokes, creating perfectly oval and geometric faces with big eyes, long straight noses and red cheeks. Interesting and analogous stylistic similarities emerge from the comparison with the figures of the Ascension in the nearby cave of Sant'Angelo in Asprano.[86] This is particularly true of Saint John, who shares certain features with the figures in the Asprano fresco. These include the elongation of the body and the small but energetic oval face with a low forehead, large eyes and long nose; the same kind of half-moon shadows on the neck and mottled purple tones.

Other stylistic analogies find resonance in the Byzantine *milieu* of Montecassino during Abbot Desiderius's reign in the eleventh century. Although the fresco decoration has been lost, its echoes may be found in the mural scheme at Sant'Angelo in Formis.[87] Both Montecassino and Sant'Angelo in Formis undoubtedly acted as models deeply influencing the area that extended between Rome and Naples. Though the cycles present in Latium at Ausonia in Santa Maria del Piano and those in Campania at Calvi Vecchia in the Grotta delle Fornelle embody a more cursive quality but essentially derive from the same artistic *koine*.[88] According to Romano other influences would appear to stream in from northern Latium and Rome.[89] She traces these models to the churches of Santa Maria in Ninfa, San Pietro in Tuscania and San Bartolomeo all'Isola in Rome.[90]

Based on purely stylistic grounds, the Castrociclo paintings likely originate in the first half of the twelfth century.[91] These observations derive from the

---

85. *Ibid.*; Romano, "Affreschi da S. Maria", p. 158.

86. R. Fernardo, "La chiesa rupestre di Sant'Angelo in Asprano", *Lazio ieri e oggi*, 33 (1997), pp. 248-249; P. Mathis, "Chiesa di Sant'Angelo (San Michele) in Asprano", in *Affreschi in Val Comino*, pp. 78-82; Parlato, Romano, *Roma e il Lazio*, p. 460.

87. F. Corvese, *Desiderio di Montecassino e le Abbazie di Terra di Lavoro*, Caserta, L'Aperia, 1999; G. Di Sotto, *Gli affreschi medievali dell'antica contea di Aquino: Aquino, Castrocielo, Caprile, Roccasecca*, Rome, Edizioni Grafiche Reggiori, 2007, p. 218.

88. Mathis, "Chiesa di Sant'Angelo (San Michele) in Asprano", pp. 48-54.

89. Romano, "Affreschi da S. Maria", pp. 160-166.

90. *Ibid.*

91. Mathis, *Affreschi in Val Comino*, pp. 106-109; Romano, "Affreschi da S. Maria", p. 155.

marked influence of Byzantine prototypes as developed and modified through the artistic matrix of Montecassino at the time of Abbot Desiderius. Orofino maintains that Montecassino may be considered the new Sinai of the eleventh century.[92] It established its own iconographic law and stylistic vocabulary which was widely spread across the region. The two hypotheses regarding its original apse decoration, either an *Ascension* or a *Traditio Legis*, are both supported by several replicas in the area including Santa Maria del Monacato in Castrocielo.[93]

The second part of the frescoes develops on the right side of the nave. In terms of chronology, they are considerably later than the frescoes present in the apse. The paintings unfold on two registers. While the scenes on the upper register have been completely lost, compositions from the lower level survive. They were transferred to panels currently preserved in the church of San Rocco during the restorations carried out by the Soprintendenza.[94] Starting from the presbytery, the scenes which are still discernible are the Enthroned Madonna with Saint Benedict; the Madonna and Child with Saint John the Baptist; the Crucifixion between the Virgin of Mercy and Saint John the Evangelist; the Crucifixion between Saint Benedict and Saint John the Evangelist; and the Archangel Michael. These paintings were likely devotional in character and their style testifies to a local-provincial execution. Nevertheless, they offer valuable insights into the patronship of female convents during the fourteenth century. Indeed, as we shall see, the presence of three nuns in one of the compositions appears to suggest the convent's direct involvement in this commission.

The Enthroned Madonna with Saint Benedict fresco is the work of a painter with a basic and essential stylistic language.[95] Mary is portrayed in a three-quarter pose turning her gaze towards the viewer with the Christ Child in her lap. Even the latter, not represented frontally but in profile with a disproportionate adult-like head, testifies to the executor's inexperience. On the contrary, Saint Benedict is depicted in a full-frontal position with a brown tunic and a blue mantle, holding the Rule with his left hand. Moving to the section below in the double arch we may discern the *Madonna and Child with Saint John the Baptist*. The Madonna sits on a stone throne draped in a cloth with floral motifs, which have almost entirely vanished. Saint John the Baptist is represented in a purple tunic and the customary camel hair holding a scroll. Although the text on the scroll is illegible it likely read, ECCE AGNUS DEI. Here, the tenderness and the humanity characteristic of Gothic models is possibly derived from fourteenth-century compositions by the Roman and Senese schools in Naples.[96]

---

92. *Affreschi in Val Comino*, p. 15.
93. Leone Marsicano or Hostiense and Pietro Diacono, *Cronaca Monastero Cassinese*, book 3, chaps. 26-34; Bloch, *Monte Cassino*, I, p. 43; Romano, "Affreschi da S. Maria", p. 158; Mathis, "Chiesa di San Rocco", p. 107.
94. Di Sotto, *Gli affreschi medievali*, p. 219.
95. Mathis, "Chiesa di San Rocco", p. 108.
96. *Ibid.*

In the second crucifixion, Christ shares similar features to the figures in the previous panel; however, they are modelled with greater precision and attention to detail. To the left we may witness the *Madonna of Mercy*, a widespread iconographic model amongst monastic orders during the fourteenth century. She is depicted with a purple *maphorion* while the inner hem of her mantle is embellished with a white and blue diamond pattern.[97] The Virgin is shown standing with her arms outstretched to keep her large cloak open wide like a tent, thus offering protection to devotees. It is not uncommon for the patron to appear among these figures. Here, a group of three nuns are represented in consistent black habits and white veils. This indicates that they are wearing religious garb. Behind them laywomen, and even further back, laymen can be seen. On the other side of the crucifix, the faded figure of a youthful and beardless saint, who points to the Saviour with his right hand and seems to be holding a scroll, should be identified as John the Evangelist.

The Crucifixion between Saint Benedict and Saint John the Evangelist scene is dominated by the figure of a lifeless Christ.[98] The latter is depicted hanging from the cross with his side fatally pierced. His closed eyes are characteristic of the *Christus patiens* iconography. His head is gently tilted to the left and is circumscribed by a cruciform halo with the inscription INSR on the right arm of the cross. The panel is framed by three bands of white, ochre and green while the background is rendered in blue and ochre. Christ is flanked by Saint Benedict and Saint John the Evangelist. The former is depicted wearing a monk's habit and holding the rule in his left hand. On the contrary, the Evangelist wears a tunic and a *pallium* and is also represented with his Gospel. There is both an attempt to individualise the physiognomic typologies and to render the forms with greater naturalism.

A small panel on the opposite side of the nave preserves a fragmentary fresco depicting the bust of the Archangel Michael. He appears in Byzantine military clothing with a spear in his hand. His head is gently tilted to the right and he is represented with a pensive absorbed gaze. The presence of the frame on two sides of the panel would suggest that, in this case too, the figure should be identified as an autonomous devotional panel and not a more extensive cycle. As we have seen, these frescoes are not the product of a particularly sophisticated artist and they appear to stem from local workshops. Yet, although executed in a markedly provincial language, characteristic of this area during the fourteenth century, the paintings demonstrate an awareness of the impact of Giotto and the Sienese in Naples. In contrast to the composition present in the apse, the private devotional character of these scenes suggests that they were likely commissioned by members of the religious community. This claim is reinforced by the presence of three nuns in the *Lady of Mercy* panel. Moreover, they testify to the problem of the sacred

---

97. The theme of Maria – mediator between God and men – was incredibly popular during the thirteenth and fifteenth centuries. This was due to the intervention of Mendicant orders, secular fraternities but also individual donors: Mathis, "Chiesa di San Rocco", p. 108.

98. *Ibid.*

space being newly occupied by votive images on walls and pillars.[99] This came as a consequence of the spontaneity of these commissions, which frequently resulted in additions and overlays of sacred figures. In fact, as mentioned before, these were often doubled or tripled to reiterate a very individual link between the saint and the patron.[100]

The qualitative leaps depend on the reception and re-processing of courtly models and stylistic trends to varying degrees. The range extends from Byzantine accents during the reign of Abbot Desiderius to Gothic forms streaming in from the work of Cavallini, Giotto, and Martini between Rome and Naples.[101] These models were transformed into local dialects by provincial artists. While they reflect the complex relationships between centre and periphery, the latter characterised by a limited technique, they equally attest to the vitality and dynamism of artistic culture in southern Latium. As a result, the framework of plots and stylistic contributions undoubtedly emerges as being more complex and less mechanical than previously thought.[102] Indeed, what was originally viewed as a simple chain reaction from upstream to downstream was perhaps less binding and stylistic/iconographic choices were also prescribed by local patrons.[103]

If we proceed to analyse the disposition of the frescoes inside the church, certain conclusions regarding the positioning of the scenes within this space may be suggested. As previously stated, a wall was constructed to separate the apse and part of the nave from the rest of the building. This part of the church could be accessed directly from the conventual space through an opening to the right of the apse. It is possible that the apse and the space in front were delimited as a choir for the community, while a second altar in front of this wall served for the officiating priest to perform mass in front of the laity. A solution similar to the one adopted in San Pietro at Montefiascone might have been in use here. Retro-choirs have been studied by Zappasodi in the context of Clarissan nunneries.[104] In Latium, they survive at San Pietro at Montefiascone and San Luca in Guarcino, which will be discussed further on in this study.[105] This would also explain why the frescoes in the recessed area are stylistically cohesive, possibly executed in a single campaign before the construction of the divisory wall; while the ones in the rectangular room preceding the apse developed over the course of the centuries. These also have a more private and domestic nature. It is likely that both the community and the laity who attended mass in the church commissioned the fresco cycles.

99. Pace, "Per un percorso", pp. 13-16.
100. *Ibid.*, p. 15.
101. G. Orofino, "Affreschi in Val Comino e nel Cassinate: un'iniziativa per la valorizzazione e il recupero", in *Affreschi in Val Comino*, pp. 9-12.
102. Pace, "Per un percorso, pp. 13-16.
103. Di Sotto, *Gli affreschi medievali*, pp. 218-220; *Affreschi in Val Comino*, pp. 15-17; Parlato, Romano, *Roma e il Lazio*, pp. 459-460; Romano, "Affreschi da S. Maria", pp. 158-160. Stylistic trends were not only transferred via Rome and Naples; we may assert that there was a local painterly tradition conditioned by patrons.
104. Zappasodi, *Sorores*, pp. 21-24.
105. *Ibid.*

Overall, Castrocielo furthers our understanding of female conventual communities in Latium from an artistic, architectonic and documentary perspective. The survival of these frescoes significantly advances our knowledge of the painterly tradition in Latium of which so little has survived for the period under examination. Moreover, these bear witness to the cultural permeability of the area south of Rome and to the artistic influences which migrated between Rome and Naples and were reprocessed at Montecassino. I was not able to determine whether the female community was responsible for the patronage of the paintings. Research for this book has demonstrated that in the absence of documentary evidence, it is problematic to determine the extent of the community's involvement in patronal activities. Ultimately, what can be securely identified as female religious patronage? Women paying for religious things, or men and women paying for women's religious things? Santa Maria gives us the possibility of introducing new strategies to analyse patronage as a category of art historical enquiry. Ones which evade economic transactions and rely on iconographic investigations. Indeed, while certain panels maintain a significantly devotional quality, possibly testifying to their private use by members of the congregation (like the *Archangel Michael*); others testify to a more public and formal display of the community to the lay men and women attending mass (like the *Madonna of Mercy*).

In conclusion, although we may not identify the patrons of the frescoes with certainty, the original display of these paintings allows a certain degree of speculation as to how the medieval church was internally divided. Moreover, the social extraction of local patronage varied considerably, as did the knowledge around specific iconographies. In contrast to female conventual spaces of larger urban congregations, these provincial realities had less formalised iconographic programmes, which allow us to further our understanding of church decoration in conventual complexes. For Santa Maria, I would suggest the possibility of a retro-choir, which as we shall see for other nunneries was particularly favoured amongst Benedictine communities in Latium. The combined study of art and architecture *in situ* broadens our overall knowledge on these somewhat overlooked provincial realities. On a final note, although sparse, surviving documentary evidence conceivably contributes to demonstrate that female communities played a minor but significant role in medieval social mobility.

4. *Rediscovering Forgotten Identities: San Luca, Guarcino*

Guarcino is a small town in the province of Frosinone above the Cosa river, on the route between Subiaco and Montecassino off the *via Benedicti*. The nunnery of San Luca is found outside the city walls next to the spring of the river Filette (Figs. 26-28). A steep path from Via dei Pignatari rises into the mountains and leads to the conventual complex. While an exact foundation date cannot be pinpointed, local sources claim that it was founded by Saint Benedict on his journey from Santa Scolastica to Montecassino.[106] We do know that during the sixth century the area was inhabited by a number of male anchorites, whom Saint Benedict gathered into organised communities.[107] Unfortunately, the monastery was restructured and rebuilt over the centuries. It is, therefore, perhaps tentative to attempt a comparison between its masonry structure and other complexes, such as San Sebastiano at Alatri, originally inhabited by Benedictine monks, whose foundation can be securely ascribed to the sixth century. We do know, however, that the monastery was inhabited by monks until the thirteenth century and that by the 1250s it had descended into a state of semi-abandonment.[108] The oldest document is a papal bull signed by Pope Alexander III in 1175.[109]

After the monastery was abandoned by the religious community in 1256, the Benedictine nuns of San Pietro in Alatri issued a request to Bishop Giovanni to obtain the monastery of San Luca.[110] In two bulls dated 19 January and 9 February 1257, Pope Alexander IV confirmed the nuns' acquisition of San Luca and all its dominions.[111] This came as a disappointment to the inhabitants of Guarcino who had been hoping to inherit the monastery's territories.[112] From 1294 onwards (a date that coincides with Boniface's papacy), the nunnery commenced its glorious ascent housing members of both the local and Roman nobility, such as the Caetani, Patrassi (Boniface VIII's mother, Emilia Patrassi, was a native of Guarcino), Tomassi, Colonna, Frangipane, Orsini, Celani, Milani Raimondi, Gigli and the Spada.[113] The convent's acquisition and purchase agreements are documented in the 52 parchments collected at the Archivio di Stato di Roma and by thirty notarial acts preserved in the nunnery's archive currently in Frosinone.[114] Unfortunately, these parchments are for the most part dated to the sixteenth century and therefore offer little insight into the proceedings of the nuns during the previous centuries. In addition, they are combined with those of the male Benedictine monastery of San Luca and so the documentation specifically pertaining to the nunnery is more meagre than the numbers might indicate. They do, however, confirm the status and the prestige of the community.

---

106. M. Creti, *Cenni storici della Chiesa e del Monastero di San Luca a Guarcino*, Rome, Ind. Tip. Imperia, 1948; G. Floridi, *Le pergamene di San Luca e Sant'Agnello di Guarcino*, Guarcino, Comune di Guarcino, 1967; G. Floridi, "L'abbazia di San Luca di Guarcino", *Lunario romano* (1988), pp. 145-171.

107. A. Lubin, *Abbatiarum Italiae brevis notitia*, Rome, Typis J.J. Komarek Boemi, 1693.

108. Creti, *Cenni storici*, p. 24.

109. Floridi, *Le pergamene*, p. 62.

110. *Monasticon Italiae*, 1, p. 127.

111. Floridi, *Le pergamene*, p. 321.

112. *Ibid.*, p. 101; G. Floridi, *Storia di Guarcino*, pp. 223, 459; Floridi, "L'abbazia di San Luca", p. 149.

113. Creti, *Cenni storici*, p. 23; list of abbesses from the nunnery which commences in the thirteenth century and documents from the fourteenth century onwards. Archivio di Stato di Frosinone, Fondo Monastero di San Luca, Guarcino, busta 2, filza VII.

114. Archivio di Stato di Frosinone, Fondo Monastero di San Luca, Guarcino, busta 2; ASR, Fondo Monastero di San Luca, cassetta 178.

This is especially true if we consider the lease agreements between the female community and local land owners. For example, on 22 May 1333 the nobleman Benedetto from Guarcino conceded a piece of farmland to the nuns.[115] The nuns did, however, incur the jealousy of the local community and in 1339 an edict was published by the papacy to protect their territorial assets.[116] These were being pillaged by locals, such as Clemente from Veroli, who was banned from Guarcino by Fiorello, judge of the province of Campagna and Marittima.[117] Moreover, in 1455, an inventory of the community's possessions was filed by Bishop Giovanni of Alatri.[118] This parchment provides a detailed list of the nuns' landholdings in the area. This did not deter illegal selling agreements at the expense of the nuns, and Bishop Giovanni had to intervene a year later to excommunicate those deemed responsible.[119] The acts that follow describe a series of lettings and selling agreements between the nuns and the lay community. However, the congregation did not officially elect a procurator, in the person of Nasimbene da Ferrara, to administer their purchases until the year 1536.[120] This did not hinder Abbess Antima Caetani from becoming the sole fiduciary named in the sale agreement for a piece of land valued at 18 golden florins from Giovanni Tomassi in 1541.[121] As testified by the numerous land purchases finalised by the community, under the rule of Abbess Caetani, the nunnery must have enjoyed a period of relative wealth and stability.

The nunnery's church and its conventual spaces are still extant. The latter have been heavily restored and are currently part of the Opera della Madonna del Divino Amore. In 1857, Giacinto Santesarti wrote a report on the state of the monastery which is currently preserved at the Archivio Apostolico Vaticano.[122]

115. ASR, Pergamene dal fondo dei monasteri di San Luca a Guarcino, 178/6; Floridi, *Le pergamene*.

116. ASR, Pergamene dal fondo dei monasteri di San Luca a Guarcino, 178/6; Floridi, *Le pergamene*.

117. ASR, Pergamene dal fondo dei monasteri di San Luca a Guarcino, 178/12; Floridi, *Le pergamene*.

118. ASR, Pergamene dal fondo dei monasteri di San Luca a Guarcino, 178/16; Floridi, *Le pergamene*.

119. ASR, Pergamene dal fondo dei monasteri di San Luca a Guarcino, 178/27; Floridi, *Le pergamene*.

120. ASR, Pergamene dal fondo dei monasteri di San Luca a Guarcino, 178/35; Floridi, *Le pergamene*.

121. ASR, Pergamene dal fondo dei monasteri di San Luca a Guarcino, 178/34; Floridi, *Le pergamene*.

122. Archivio Apostolico Vaticano, Congregazione dei vescovi regolari, n. 20996, 1857, G. Santesarti: "Si tratta di un fabbricato a picco sul fiume, con ampio piazzale retrostante, cinto da un claustro scoperto, con sorgente in mezzo ed un cortile che gira intorno al convento. A sinistra dopo l'ingresso vi è un ambiente per la foresteria e la camera per il garzone con il suo caminetto; dopo il granaio e due vastissime cucine, indi il refettorio. Al secondo piano sedici ambienti per dormitorio. Adiacenti alla chiesa lunga oltre 35 metri e larga 15, vi è il coro, la sacrestia, la camera per guardiani e poi le stalle, mola da macina, valca ed altri accessori nei sotterranei. In complesso si tratta di tutti vani molto ampi e con muri spessi e solidissimi. Normalmente vi abitano non meno di 30 monache, oltre numerose converse ed educande"; Creti, *Cenni storici*, pp. 34-35.

The report states that the convent developed on the mountain over the river with buildings rising around an open *claustrum* over two floors. At ground level, he describes a guesthouse, a room for the guardian, a granary, two large kitchens and the refectory. Sixteen large cells for the religious community were located on the first floor. The choir, sacristy, a room for the convent's guard, stables, millstone and other utensils could be found adjacent to the church (35x15 m). At present, the convent has been completely refurbished and restored. In fact, only the perimeter walls surrounding the cloister appear to be coeval with the thirteenth-century medieval construction. Furthermore, this is only the case up to the first floor of the conventual block.

It is not clear when the church was erected, local tradition dates the complex between the eleventh and the thirteenth century.[123] Yet, by analysing its external structure and peripheral walls it would appear that it was constructed in the tenth century and likely refurbished during the female occupation of the settlement. The masonry in *pietra viva*, characterised by uneven limestone blocks with a substantial use of mortar to fill and seal the irregular edges, is consistent with this dating. The edifice was restored by the Soprintendenza between 1978 and 1980. The roof, which had completely collapsed leaving the church exposed and overgrown, was replaced by a vaulted ceiling and a pointed arch to separate the nave from the presbytery. The new roof attempted to recreate the original vaulting by retracing the ribs of the covering which were still extant when the reconstructions took place. The gabled façade is characterized by the presence of a single slit window, which covers the uppermost portion of the triangular pediment. This opening is axially aligned to the entrance, encircled by a cornice of three rectangular lintels, and crowned by an arched lunette. The latter was likely decorated with frescoes or stucco. The single nave church occupies a total surface area of 200 square meters, and terminates in a simple square apse. Three entrances can be found on the side adjacent to the cloister. The first two, on the left, are characterized by an arched lunette similar to the one in the façade. A cross decorates the arch above the central opening. This motif is present in several churches in the area and has been linked by local scholars to a Templar presence in Latium.[124] Finally, the entrance on the right has a slightly thicker pointed arch and was possibly executed at a later date. It is quite rare to find three portals on the same side of a church especially given its modest dimensions. We may assume that one was used by the nuns (possibly the entrance closest to the apse), while the central one was reserved for the officiating clergy. Two lancet windows are also positioned on this side. The apse itself is decorated by three pointed windows, which most probably represented the trinity. The walls of this edifice are extremely robust and are constructed in *pietra viva* in the technique of uneven ashlar masonry blocks bedded with lime mortar and calcareous aggregates. This technique was fairly common during the second part of the thirteenth century in Southern Latium's civil and religious architecture. The pavement was

123. Floridi, "L'abbazia di San Luca", p. 147.
124. A. Vacca, "La chiesa di San Domenico di Trisulti", *Rivista cistercense*, 8 (1991), p. 10.

completely rebuilt during the restorations as were the steps leading into the apse. An examination of unpublished pre-restoration photographs reveals large portions of plaster. This likely indicates that the church was embellished with a fresco cycle, as was the case with other nunneries, such as Santa Maria di Palazzolo in Castrocielo. Indeed, one may still discern fragments of the original pictorial decoration in the lancet window of the counter-façade. The photographs preserved in albums at the nuns' document repository at the Opera del Divino Amore possibly date to the 1950s (Figs. 29-30). They represent the church and the monastic complex in a state of ruin and abandonment before the restorations carried out by the Soprintendenza during the 1980s. These photographs are especially useful in so much as they document the refurbishments of the vaulted ceiling and the extent of the perimeter covered by the conventual complex. The new roofing appears to be in accordance with the original ribbed vaulting that may still be discerned in the photographs of the interior of the church towards the apse.

Through architectonic and documentary evidence, the church of San Luca in Guarcino furthers our knowledge of female Benedictine architecture between the thirteenth and the fourteenth centuries. The three entrances on the side of the church possibly point towards a tripartite internal division of the internal space during the Middle Ages. Conceivably the nuns used the entrance closest to the convent, leading directly to the apse; the clergy, the central opening; and the laity, the door next to the counter-façade. This disposition, and the likelihood of the existence of a retro-choir, is furthered by the evidence provided in the apostolic visit. While the presence of a pictorial decoration inside the church is possibly testified by the fragments in the lancet window documented in the pre-restoration photographs. The documentary evidence demonstrated that women from local baronial families namely the Caetani, Frangipane and Patrassi were part of the congregation. As witnessed in Rome, nunneries were divided according to territorial divisions of familial power; a trend that extended to convents in Latium. Although San Luca lends itself to a broader understanding of female conventual realities in the region, it also testifies to moderate cultural level of these religious women and to their sparse economic resources. Guarcino also points towards the objective loss and fragmentation of primary evidence and the challenges facing the study of regional nunneries. Hopefully, this loss does not devalue the study of peripheral realities altogether.

5. *Hidden Gems: San Pietro, Montefiascone*

The town of Montefiascone rises over the highest peak of the Volsini mountains, dominating the Tuscia region – the northern portion of Latium – in the province of Viterbo.[125] Almost a century ago, Allan Marquand (1853-1924)[126]

---

125. G. Breccola, *Montefiascone. Guida alla scoperta*, Viterbo, Annulli, 2006; M.E. Piferi, *Montefiascone. Città e territorio*, Viterbo, Betagamma editrice, 1996.

126. He was the founder of the Department of Art and Archaeology at Princeton University and inventor of the "logic machine", a precursor of the modern computer.

published a remarkable picture of a terracotta altarpiece from the cathedral of Montefiascone in the *Art Studies* journal (Fig. 31).[127] Here, Marquand, an eminent authority on the production of Renaissance glazed terracotta, rectified the attribution of the altarpiece on stylistic grounds. He suggested that it was not in fact created by Andrea della Robbia (1435-1525) but, rather, by Benedetto Buglioni (1459-1521).[128] Indeed, the altarpiece's location was solely questioned by the scholar in terms of its chronology. Given that the cathedral was approximately finished in 1519, a 1520s dating was put forward for the Buglioni piece.[129] Marquand therefore disqualified a four century-old attribution but fell short of rigorously addressing another pressing issue: its provenance.

While the altarpiece's attribution is most certainly correct, a closer look at the artwork's iconography should have shed reasonable doubt on its location. The Buglioni terracotta measures approximately 2,5x2,5 m and is framed by a sumptuous Baroque niche inside the cathedral's chapel of the Holy Sacrament. It depicts an enthroned Madonna and Child flanked by two saints, angels holding a crown and flying cherubs. The standing male saint donning a monk's habit is clearly Saint Benedict. He is characteristically depicted carrying his rule and a tied bundle of rods. On the contrary, the identification of the female saint martyr is more problematic due to the absence of specific attributes. The obvious choice – as Marquand points out – might have been Saint Margaret, the titular saint of the cathedral. However, in absence of her identifying symbols, he puts forward the hypothesis (based on the analogy with two paintings by Perugino in Rome and Perugia) that the figure be identified as Saint Flavia.[130] Given that the predella scenes at the bottom of the altarpiece do not corroborate this, the identification of the female martyr remained ambiguous for the American scholar.[131]

The five predella scenes represent: the Annunciation and the Nativity at opposite ends, the central panel depicts scenes from the life of Saint Joachim and Anna, which is flanked by two miracles by Saint Benedict, namely, the Healing of the paralytic woman and the Resurrection of the peasant's son. Finally, given that the altarpiece is found in a private chapel, what appears to be missing is a coat of arms or an identifying symbol tied either to a lay patron, or, a religious confraternity. This absence along with the dubious identity of the female martyr, and the subject matter of the predella scenes, raises significant questions about the artwork's presumed *in situ* location within the cathedral.

127. A. Marquand, "An Altarpiece by Benedetto Buglioni at Montefiascone", *Art Studies*, 1 (1923), pp. 3-6.
128. *Ibid.*, p. 3. His monograph on Benedetto and Santi Buglioni (1494-1576) had been published only two years previously, and this artwork was a precious addition to the artists' *oeuvre*. A. Marquand, *Benedetto and Santi Buglioni*, Princeton, Princeton University Press, 1921.
129. Marquand, "An Altarpiece", p. 5.
130. *Ibid.*, p. 3.
131. *Ibid.*, p. 4.

An analysis of primary sources inside the archive of the nunnery of San Pietro at Montefiascone confirms doubts raised in the artwork's iconography. In fact, these documents revealed that the Buglioni terracotta was *not* actually designed for the cathedral but for the choir of the Benedictine *moniales* of the convent.[132] Indeed, its function inside the oratory may finally be contextualised through pastoral visits and chronicles. This testifies to the high quality of objects commissioned for religious women, thus helping us to reshape the role of nuns as key players in the production of art and architecture. It is impossible to determine the extent to which the female community acted as a catalyst for the renovations in the complex; however, it is evident that the sisters were able to ensure that their own private conventual spaces were decorated by leading painters, and in the latest style. This underscores the methodological implications of studying provenance as a key element of agency. Given that the choir space was only accessible to the female community of nuns, can we safely ascribe the patronage act to the congregation? This is one of the major challenges faced by studies focusing on nunnery art and female agency. Ultimately, however, the significance of these commissions lies not so much in who paid for what but, rather, in women's access to specific artworks and their iconographic programs. Therefore, while patronage encompasses fundamental criteria of creativity exposing practices tied to the conception, funding, and fabrication of an artwork, or, an architectural ensemble; the analysis of documentary and iconographic sources will shift the focus to the study of art in spaces destined exclusively for women.

Based in New Jersey, Marquand could not have known that the precious altarpiece had been removed from the choir of San Pietro against the nuns' will only fifteen years earlier. The convent's chronicle refers to this matter as follows:

> On July 22, the feast of Saint Magdalene, the community suffered a very serious loss, and an artistic treasure that had been preserved for several centuries in the nunnery: a terracotta by Andrea della Robbia (fifteenth century) representing the Madonna and Child between Saint Benedict and Saint Bibiana with rich decorations, previously marred by Napoleonic bayonets. It was fixed in the niche behind the main altar of the choir [*comunichino*] of the church, where an ancient painting of the *Trinity* was discovered when the della Robbia terracotta was removed. […] The precious terracotta initially destined for a museum, or a monument; was given to the Cathedral of Santa Margherita in Montefiascone.[133]

This testimony provides three crucial details: the identification of the female saint, the original location of the terracotta, and the discovery of "un'antica pittura" of the Trinity.

---

132. *Monasticon Italiae*, 1, p. 98; R. Cordovani, *Il monastero delle monache benedettine di San Pietro a Montefiascone*, Viterbo, Centro di Iniziative Culturali Montefiascone, 1994, p. 16; G. Breccola, "Storia breve del monastero di San Pietro", in *M. Cecilia Baij e le altre*, ed. by N. Togni and M. Valli, Acts of the conference (Montefiascone, 2016), Montefiascone, Centro Storico Benedettino Italiano, 2018, pp. 87-104: 92.

133. Archivio delle Benedettine di Montefiascone, Armadio 5, ripiano 2, fasc. 95, *Diario Monastico*, 1 (1919-1929); Breccola, "Storia breve del monastero di San Pietro", p. 102.

This is not the first time that Saint Bibiana, the female saint identified in the nunnery's chronicle, is mentioned in conventual documents. In a 1363 will, preserved in the archive of the cathedral of Montefiascone, Tuzio de Rubeis, known as il Femminella, endowed the convent of Santa Bibiana with "40 soldi paparini". While Girolamo de Angelis and Vincenzo Macchi identify this as the lost convent in via della Porticella next to the cathedral; Rinaldo Cordovani, Filippo Caraffa and Giancarlo Breccola opt for our nunnery.[134] They argue that the change in dedication took place when the Benedictine monastery of San Pietro on Lake Bolsena was destroyed in the second half of the ninth century. In addition to the existence of this altarpiece, a dedication to Saint Bibiana would have been extremely fitting for a community of religious women in Montefiascone. Bibiana was, in fact, the daughter of Saint Flaviano, the titular saint of the town's majestic double basilica, which preserves his relics.

Before the seventeenth-century restoration of the Roman church of Santa Bibiana by Gian Lorenzo Bernini (1598-1680), who also produced a sculpture of the female saint for the main altar, there is no clear indication regarding the Saint's iconography prior to the Baroque period.[135] However, in *La vita di S. Bibiana vergine, e martire romana* (1627), Canon Domenico Fedini describes part of the basilica's fifteenth-century decorative program before Bernini and Pietro da Cortona's (1596-1669) large scale restoration. The original paintings in the central nave displayed a fresco representing the nuns distributing a miraculous thaumaturgical plant which was thought to grow around the saint's house.[136] He also describes "una pittura" that "non può avere meno di duecento anni" opposite the main altar. Here, the saint is represented standing with a branch of the miraculous plant.[137] It should be noted that the cult of Saint Bibiana was frequently associated with Asclepius and Minerva Medica. This link is therefore very significant given that the convent of San Pietro (originally dedicated to Saint Bibiana) in Montefiascone housed a renowned pharmacy.[138] Moreover, it is no coincidence that Saint Benedict is represented as a healer in the predella scenes of the Buglioni altarpiece. Indeed, this underscores the thaumaturgical powers associated both to him, and hence, to the female saint by proximity.

Addressing the issue of provenance also raises questions about the chronology put forward by Marquand for the altarpiece. The scholar proposes a 1520s

---

134. Archivio Capitolare di Montefiascone, parch. n. 13; G. de Angelis, V. Macchi, *Commentario storico-critico su l'origine e le vicende della città e chiesa cattedrale di Montefiascone*, Montefiascone, Tipografia del Seminario, 1841, p. 159; *Monasticon Italiae*, 1, p. 98; Cordovani, *Il monastero delle monache*, p. 16; Breccola, *Montefiascone*, p. 92.

135. S. Novelli, "L'iconografia di Santa Bibiana nel Seicento", *Iconographica* (2002), pp. 107-123; D. Fedini, *La vita di Santa Bibiana vergine e martire romana*, Rome, F. Corbelletti, 1627.

136. *Ibid.*, p. 63.

137. *Ibid.*

138. M. Selene Sconci, D. Luzi, *La spezieria di San Benedetto a Montefiascone. Dalle collezioni di Palazzo Venezia in Rome*, Rome, Berliguardo, 1994; in particular the essay by M. Luzi and B. Mancini, "Il monastero delle benedettine in Montefiascone e la sua spezieria: storia e documenti", *ibid.*, pp. 45-64.

dating, however, we know that Cardinal Giovanni de Medici (future Pope Leo X) financed the restorations works carried out at the Collegiata di Santa Cristina in the neighbouring town of Bolsena, where Buglioni executed the lunettes on the façade, the ciborium and the main altar (1503-1512).[139] Given the proximity to Montefiascone, we may assume that the San Pietro altarpiece was executed sometime between 1503-1512 when the artist was working in Bolsena, or in the immediate aftermath of the Collegiata commission.

The nunnery's twentieth-century chronicle clearly states that the terracotta was removed from the choir in 1907. Sixteenth-century visitation records provide further proof that this was its original location. On 1st and 2nd of May 1583 Giuseppe Mascardo, papal legate of Pope Gregory XIII, visited the church and the nunnery of San Pietro.[140] In contrast to the pastoral visitation of 1487 (the oldest to have survived), he provides a detailed analysis of the internal lay-out of the convent. Mascardo initially inspected the external church or the "parochialis ecclesia Sancti Petri contigua monasterio monialium ordinis Sancti Benedicti" and the following day, the "ecclesiam interiorem monasterij". He describes the church as being differently oriented compared to the original and displaying a rectangular plan. The laymen accessed the church through a portal in the centre of the main façade, opposite the main altar, originally adorned with paintings already blackened by the sixteenth century. Above it a small, oblong grated window allowed the nuns to view the elevation of the Holy Host from the internalchurch and attend to the sacred functions from their conventual spaces. Broken stone seats were positioned around the walls of the altar. The church comprised two additional altars, one dedicated to Our Lady of the Snow, and the other to Saint Blaise. These did not include statues but were adorned with frescoes. The former housed images of the Madonna and Child, Saint Augustine and Saint Michael the Archangel, while the latter included images of Saint Blaise, Saint Gilles and Saint Lucy. As previously stated, Mascardo also entered the nunnery's interior. He described the kitchen, the wine cells, the granary, the dormitories on the upper floor and the *ecclesiam interiorem*. Thus, it follows that this was either a small church inside the nunnery, or, a choir. According to Sister Angela Pigni, the convent's archivist until 1982, the *comunichino* (as described in the chronicle) referred to the choir and the passageway through which the convent's students could enter the church directly from the conventual apartments.[141] Mascardo's report claimed that

> the church inside the convent houses an altar with an icon adorned with sacred images in stucco, brass candlesticks, tablecloths, silk blankets and cushions. So far, mass has been said when the nuns take on the veil. In the wall that divides this

---

139. Marquand, *Benedetto and Santi Buglioni*.
140. Archivio Vescovile di Montefiascone, *Visite apostoliche 1583*, II, fols. 38-40; Cordovani, *Il monastero delle monache*, p. 26.
141. Archivio delle Benedettine di Montefiascone, 3.5.C *Cartella delle Religiose Defunte* (1907-1998), *Angela Pigni: 1908-1982*; Cordovani, *Il monastero delle monache*, p. 91.

church from the inside, there is a window with an iron grille through which the nuns witness the elevation of the sacred host.[142]

The room described in the apostolic visit appears to be the one which housed the Buglioni altarpiece – described by Mascardo as an altar in stucco with saints – before its transfer to the cathedral in 1907, which led to the discovery of the Trinity fresco (Figs. 32-33).[143] Pigni states that after "rediscovering" «l'antica pittura», older nuns used to claim that "if you peel off these walls, who knows what will come out!".[144] Indeed, during restoration works carried out in 1972 to level flooring between the choir-*comunichino* and the church, an impressive fresco cycle was discovered. The paintings restored by the Soprintendenza per i Beni Archeologici del Lazio make up a rather impressive decorative scheme, which has virtually gone unstudied. These frescoes unfold on the eastern wall of the nuns' current lower choir. Although the original function of this space is unclear, the disposition of the scenes combined with documentary evidence indicate that it was an oratory where the nuns received communion.

The representation of the Trinity is found inside a niche on the eastern portion of the room (Figs. 34-35). It is surrounded by a white and red rosette pattern framed by a yellow cornice on three sides. Here, God the Father is portrayed against a dark blue and pastel green background. A long faded red, white and green mantle slides down to his feet. He is represented seated on a throne, decorated with light vegetal motifs, holding the crucified Christ. The latter is represented in the *patiens* mode: his side fatally wounded and a transparent loin-cloth tied to his lower abdomen. His halo is pierced by the Holy Spirit, which is represented as a dove. The two figures of the Angel and Mary are positioned on the sidewalls of the niche representing the Trinity. The angel appears with a white garment featuring red geometric patterns and a golden collar. His tunic is embellished by two gold/yellow rectangles adorned with a diamond motif. He is represented in the act of blessing whilst holding lilies in his left hand. His face is rendered through precise brushstrokes and is encircled by a rayed halo. On the opposite side of the niche, the Virgin is also dressed in a white tunic with red geometric patterns. She is depicted holding a prayer book in her left hand with her right arm raised above her chest in the act of receiving the Holy Spirit. Her lineaments are rendered with a fair line and her head is also encircled by a rayed halo. Her white and brown dress is adorned with small dark geometrical motifs.

The wall to the right of the niche features a representation of the Adoration of the Magi. Here, the Christ child is represented standing on the Virgin's lap receiving a gift from the first king. Though his representation has not survived, he was likely shown kneeling before the Virgin and Child. He is followed by the other two kings who are respectively dressed in a light green tunic with shades of

---

142. Archivio Vescovile di Montefiascone, *Visite apostoliche 1583*, II, fols. 46-48.
143. V. Carrelli, "Pregevoli affreschi scoperti nel Monastero delle Benedettine", *La Voce*, December 1973, p. 4.
144. Cordovani, *Il monastero delle monache*, p. 91.

pale blue, and a red vest adorned with a gold spiralling geometric motif around the collar. The fourth figure, a shepherd, is represented more modestly with a light brown tunic and burgundy braies. There is an attempt to individualise the figures although certain physiognomic traits such as, the elongated brow and eyes, the full upper and thin lower lip appear in all the figures.

The upper fresco on the same wall survives in an extremely fragmentary state. Nevertheless, it is possible to identify the subject of the Virgin of Mercy and fragments of the heads of Saint Peter and Saint Paul. Unfortunately, the figures below her cloak have been lost, so we do not have the clear indications of patronage that we do, for example, have in the nunnery of Santa Maria del Monacato at Castrocielo in the province of Frosinone. The upper portion of her head is depicted surrounded by a rayed halo. A piece of her mantle, lined with a pattern of blue and white ovals, is characteristically held open. Her hands share an identical physiognomy with the ones of the Virgin in the Adoration fresco. This confirms the paternity of the whole cycle to the same artist. The background simulates a curtain backdrop encircled by a frame of rosettes. From the surviving fragment, we may still discern stylistic similarities to other parts of the cycle, thus allowing us to reaffirm the same authorship as the other paintings. Moreover, what can be seen of the embellishment inside the cloak is enough to evoke the *Madonna of Mercy* by Lippo Memmi in Orvieto.[145] This permits us to trace the unknown artist at Montefiascone to an Umbrian-Tuscan *milieu*. In the report undertaken by the Soprintendenza dated 1984, the frescoes are dated to the end of fourteenth century and described as having a Sienese influence.[146] This painter may have been influenced by Lippo Memmi (1291-1356) and therefore familiar with the Sienese tradition, which gravitated in his artistic circles in the nearby town of Orvieto. The frescoes' chronology should therefore be brought forward to the third quarter of the fourteenth century. Indeed, the elongated brow, the courtly figures and the elegant proportions appear to be a synthesis – and a rather simplistic one – of Tuscan and Umbrian traditions stemming from the Assisi experience.

The fresco, which is still visible on the adjacent wall, should be dated to the last quarter of the fifteenth century. The Madonna and Child are seated to the far left of the scene while Saint Catherine kneels at their feet in the mystical marriage with the Christ child. The Archangel Michael is also represented treading the demon with his feet. He is wearing a coat of arms and holding a sword and balance. The figures are all haloed displaying a courtly grace one may associate to Perugino with decorative accents that may be linked to Pinturicchio (1454-1513).[147] The artist is clearly from Viterbo, or, its surroundings, and familiar with the style of painting popular at the Vatican. This is not surprising, as the popes resided in the Tuscia region bringing the styles and fashions of Rome with them.

145. Archivio delle Benedettine di Montefiascone, A.5, r. 2, cont. 3: Scheda OA Soprintendenza ai monumenti di Roma e del Lazio, "San Pietro a Montefiascone. Dipinti nel cosiddetto Comunichino delle Monache", 1984.
146. *Ibid.*
147. *Ibid.*

Three other depictions can be found in the direction of the wall leading to the church. The majestic pontiff and a female saint should be identified as Saint Peter and Mary Magdalen and are dated to the second half of the sixteenth century while the third figure, Saint Scholastic, is dated to the seventeenth century.[148] No other fresco survives in the convent's space making these paintings quite exceptional both in terms of quality and of location. Indeed, apart from the basement level, which currently houses the canteens and acts as storage for the community's wine and oil production, very little of the structure's medieval fabric has survived.

It is very significant that the Buglioni ceramic was located inside the choir, as opposed to the main church. This undoubtedly testifies to the prestige of this space, which was not only embellished by frescoes but also by this majestic altar. Can the female agency of these works be secured on the exclusive basis of their position inside choirs? Probably not. Nevertheless, it is still important to acknowledge the nuns' role as the recipients of ambitious decorative programs. This is particularly true for Montefiascone whereby the patron/s went to impressive lengths to ensure that these spaces were arrayed by leading painters in the latest styles. The altar inside the choir created a sort of church within the church with its own set of rules and prescriptions, which ultimately reassessed the nuns' visual access towards the elevation of the host. In this light, this case study furthers the supposition that the function of the choir space was not only manifold, but likely enjoyed regulations that were distinct, separate and independent from the main church. This influenced it profoundly, both in its arrangement and decorative choices. As we have seen, these choices were thematised around the subject of Christ, the Virgin and the Eucharist. Ultimately, the rediscovery of female agency through the study of provenance of art in spaces destined for women, reinforces the notion that female patronage cannot be treated as an exception.

6. *Off the Beaten Tracks: Sant'Angelo di Orsano, Trevi nel Lazio*

The nunnery of Sant'Angelo di Orsano is found outside Trevi nel Lazio between the Simbruini and the Ernici mountains in the Aniene valley, on one of the sides of mount Piaggio (Fig. 36). Orsano's name, a toponym, originates from the barley plantations that once covered the area.[149] Historically, Trevi nel Lazio was incorporated into the Conti family estate through the Jenne branch.[150] It was donated by Pope Alexander IV to his nephew, Rinaldo Rubeis, on 21 November 1257.[151] Rinaldo was then excommunicated by Urban IV for being a Ghibelline

---

148. *Ibid.*
149. D. Zinanni, *Trevi nel Lazio nella storia dell'arte e nelle tradizioni*, Trevi nel Lazio, Edizioni Pro Loco, 1972, p. 167.
150. F. Caraffa, *Trevi nel Lazio dalle origini alla fine del secolo XIX*, 1, Rome, Facultas Theologica Pontificiae Universitatis Lateranensis, 1976, p. 72.
151. *Les registres d'Alexandre IV. Recueil des bulles de ce pape, publiées et analysées d'après les manuscrits originaux des Archives du Vatican*, 3 vols., ed. by C. Bourel de La Roncière and J.

and was able to regain possession of the family estate through a concession made by Clement IV in 1265.[152] However, the Caetani had assumed full ownership by the end of 1297, when Boniface VIII authorized the bishop and the Chapter of Anagni to permanently grant the feudal estate to the family.[153] Pietro, Boniface VIII's favourite nephew, came into possession of the hamlet in 1299, that same year, the pope resided in Trevi for the month of September.[154] The Caetani subsequently retained control of the territory for almost two centuries.[155] This in no way benefited its inhabitants, who were severely affected by the disgrace into which the family fell at the death of the pope. When the Caetani were forced to leave Trevi in 1471, the town was placed under the temporal dominion of the abbey of Subiaco and Cardinal Rodrigo Borgia, future Pope Alexander VI (1492-1503).[156]

Given its proximity to Subiaco, both male and female monasteries varying in both size and importance dotted the territories around Trevi. Sant'Angelo di Orsano is, in fact, one of the best preserved in the area. The *Chronicon Sublacense* (Chronicle from the monastery of Subiaco) offers early insights into the nunnery's history. The earliest one was written by Guglielmo Capisacchi from Narni (1508-1571), and the second by Cherubino Murtz (1632), commonly referred to as Mirzio.[157] Another important source was published by Domenico Antonio Pierantoni (1727), whose work, *Aniene illustrato*, substantially draws from Mirzio's chronicle.[158] At the beginning of the 1900s, Vincenzo Federici indexed the entire documentary corpus of Santa Scolastica in Subiaco, which holds the *fondo* pertaining to the nunnery of Sant'Angelo after its annexation by Pope Sixtus IV in the year 1478.[159] Federici's work provides the opportunity to study the surviving 59 documents. These are dated between 1280-1478, and their significance is such that they allow us to reconstruct the nunnery's history for two whole centuries. The documents were transcribed and published by Angelo Amati in 1982, which

de Loye, Paris, Coulon, 1895-1959, II, p. 727, n. 2352; *Codex diplomaticus dominii temporalis s. sedis. Receuil de documents pour servir à l'histoire du gouvernement temporel des états du Saint-Siège extraits des archives du Vatican*, 3 vols., ed. by A. Theiner, Rome, Imprimerie du Vatican, 1861-1862, I, pp. 136-137, n. 259.

152. *Codex diplomaticus dominii temporalis s. sedis*, I, p. 166, n. 312.
153. G. Falco, *Albori d'Europa*, Rome, Le Edizioni del Lavoro, 1947, pp. 335-343.
154. Caraffa, *Trevi nel Lazio*, p. 131.
155. Caetani, *Regestum*, pp. 125-128.
156. G. Tomassetti, *La campagna romana antica medievale e moderna*, 2, Rome, Loescher, 1910, p. 150.
157. G. Capisacchi, *Chronicon Sacri monasterii Sublaci anno 1573*, ed. by L. Branciani, Subiaco-Monastero Santa Scolastica, Tipografia Editrice Santa Scolastica, 2005; Cherubino Mirzio da Treviri, *Chronicon Sublacense (1628-1630). Co-redattore Pietro Clavarini detto Romano*, ed. by L. Branciani Branciani, Subiaco-Monastero Santa Scolastica, Tipografia Editrice Santa Scolastica, 2014, pp. 520-522: "Ut autem aliquid posteris de fundatione monasterii S. Angeli de Ursano scriptis tradam, paucaquae hinc inde sparsa e archive nostri istrumentis cum labore college praetaxatis annectere volui".
158. D.A. Pierantoni, *Aniene illustrato*, Rome, Istituto di storia e di arte del Lazio meridionale, 2005, p. 428.
159. V. Federici, *I monasteri di Subiaco*, 2, Rome, Ministero della Pubblica Istruzione, 1904.

proved instrumental to further our understanding of the complex.[160] Additionally, the convent is mentioned in a series of guides dedicated to the town of Trevi nel Lazio, of which only Filippo Caraffa's publication attempts an historically objective analysis as opposed to the other, more connoisseurial surveys of the area.[161] Although a rich documentary corpus survives, and the nunnery's ruins and church are still standing today, no overreaching study exists. This is surprising if we acknowledge that Sant'Angelo is the only female Benedictine foundation in the high valley of the Aniene and that the lives of the nuns of Sant'Angelo di Orsano likely mirror those of other female Benedictine nunneries. Indeed, as testified by the numerous notarial acts, a life in reclusion certainly did not hinder contact with the external world nor with the local community.

The origins of Sant'Angelo di Orsano remain for the most part unknown due to a lack of sources pertaining to its foundation. According to a local legend it was founded by Saint Benedict himself, though this is unlikely given that the saint only founded male branches of the order.[162] The oldest surviving document is a parchment dated 1280 which testifies to the donation of land as part of Liuto de Theobaldi's daughter Pace dowry to enter the nunnery.[163] The convent was originally characterised by the presence of a wall that extended over its entire perimeter. Several rooms destined to the nuns and a church dedicated to the Archangel Michael were arranged along the edges of an internal court. The church is typified by the presence of an apse and a free-standing altar, possibly an *iconostasis*, and two additional altars, one in front of the entrance and another to the left of the apse.[164] A water cistern was placed between the church and the internal courtyard. This feature is quite characterising given its remote location outside the city walls. After being abandoned during the seventeenth century and used by local hermits, the church has today been transformed into a sheepfold.

Documents confirm that the nuns came from the local noble and baronial class.[165] As in other female Benedictine houses, the nuns communally elected an abbess and were expected to carry out various duties for their community. From surviving testimonies, we learn that the nunnery's administration was originally held by a nun and that it subsequently passed to a fiduciary elected by the congregation. The convent's patrimony did not solely depend on the nuns' dowries but also drew on lay bequests. As mentioned above, its oldest parchment – dated 1280 – is a donation by Liuto *domini* Theobaldi di Trevi. He granted two pieces of land to the nunnery; one in Vineali and the other in Valle Competa, as a dowry for his daughter Pace, who was joining the convent

---

160. A. Amati, *Il monastero di S. Angelo di Orsano in Trevi nel Lazio: contributo per il codice diplomatico*, Casamari, Terra Nostra, 1982.
161. Caraffa, *Trevi nel Lazio*, pp. 213-233.
162. *Ibid.*, p. 213.
163. Subiaco, Archivio di Santa Scolastica, XXXI, 2; Caraffa, *Trevi nel Lazio*, p. 215.
164. The church is extremely isolated and during the site visit pictures were taken quickly.
165. Federici, *I monasteri di Subiaco*, p. 72.

as an oblate.[166] The lands were conceded to Sister Bona, who acted as the legal representative of the nunnery. The document reads: "sorore Bona moniali ipsius monasterii recipiente pro ipso monasterio", which suggests that she acted as a legal intercessor for the community. At the time, Liuto *domini* Theobaldi was one of the most influential personalities in Trevi. He was responsible for stipulating the contractual agreement between the town of Trevi and Rinaldo de Rubeis, nephew of Pope Alexander IV. Therefore, his daughter's entry into the community at Orsano would appear to testify to the prestige and authority the nunnery reached during the thirteenth century. This is noteworthy considering the relatively modest remains that survive today.

A letter dated 1289 and signed by Nicholas IV, conceding an indulgence of one year and forty days to those who visited the nunnery on the feast days of Archangel Michael and the Virgin Mary, has also survived.[167] The fame of the nunnery was growing. Indeed, in 1294, Maria, known as Santa – widow of Trasmondo di Santo and a member of Anagni's baronial class – joined the community at Orsano in front of Agnese, the first abbess of the convent whose name has come down to us.[168] The nunnery's landholdings continuously expanded beyond Trevi into the neighbouring towns throughout the 1290s. In addition, forty days of indulgences were granted to those who visited the convent by bishops from the towns of Molfetta, Recanati, Fano, Epiro, Palestrina and Anagni, especially during the prescribed festivities of Saint Mary Magdalene and Saint Catherine of Alexandria in whose honour an altar was constructed *ex novo*.[169] These twelve bishops, all of whom we know by name, were present in Anagni alongside Boniface VIII in the year 1295.[170] The document, which was signed by them all, was presented to the pope by Pietro bishop of Anagni.[171] By 1359, for security reasons, the community was transferred inside the city of Trevi and was soon forced to abandon the settlement altogether.[172] The sisters pressed the bishop of Anagni for permission to rebuild the convent, which he granted in 1366.[173] Under his prescriptions, the nuns were to stay in Trevi and restore the nunnery as soon as they had enough funds. He granted forty days of indulgences to those who contributed to the reconstructions and temporarily suspended the celebration of mass inside the church.[174] Benedetto Caetani and his wife, Aquina di Valeriani,

166. Caraffa, *Trevi nel Lazio*, p. 198.
167. *Ibid.*, p. 218.
168. Federici, *I monasteri di Subiaco*, p. 72.
169. *Ibid.*, pp. 75-76; Caraffa, *Trevi nel Lazio*, p. 218.
170. Federici, *I monasteri di Subiaco*, p. 75.
171. They are: Ruggero archbishop of Santa Severina (1273-1296), Paolo bishop of Molfetta (1295-1344), Salvo from Recanati (1289-1301), Francesco from Fano (1289-1295), Romano from Croja (1286-1298), Uberto from Feltre, Francesco from Avellino (1285-1310), Pietro from Cajazzo (1308), Giacomo from Trivento (1290-1334), Andrea from Lidda (Palestrina), Aimardo from Lucera (1295-1302) and Pietro from Larino (1284-1309); Federici, *I monasteri di Subiaco*, p. 89; Caraffa, *Trevi nel Lazio*, p. 219.
172. Federici, *I monasteri di Subiaco*, p. 98.
173. Amati, *Il monastero di Sant'Angelo*, p. 27.
174. *Ibid.*

donated a farmhouse in the proximity of Sant'Angelo to Abbess Cecca in 1371.[175] Through these donations, oblations, selling agreements and acquisitions, we may grasp the vibrant atmosphere that characterised the community. This points towards a great dynamism which starkly contrasts the rigid perception we tend to have of these enclosed communities. By 1372, surviving documents denote that the nunnery had an *oeconomus* in the person of Antonio di Ienne.[176] Antonio is not mentioned in the sale agreement of three land holdings just a year later. This agreement was in fact made in the presence of Benedetto Caetani, his wife Aquina de Valerianis and Abbess Cecca. Indeed, the nuns only elected an administrator, Biagio di Nicola from Acuto, in 1420.[177]

Perhaps the most noteworthy event during the fifteenth century was the reconstruction of the church of the nunnery of Sant'Angelo di Orsano on its original site (Fig. 37-38). The resulting space had a larger perimeter and a semi-circular apse. The church was consecrated on 14 May 1441, and in 1448, Pope Nicholas V granted new indulgences to those who visited the nunnery during the feast of Saint Michael.[178] Yet, the convent was abandoned once again by the end of the fifteenth century, when Abbess Letizia presented Pope Sixtus IV with a request to leave the nunnery, as the community had extinguished.[179] Pope Sixtus IV therefore annexed Sant'Angelo di Orsano to the monastery of Santa Scolastica in Subiaco in 1478.The nunnery was subsequently used as a granary, while the church was active in keeping with religious functions.[180] In the pastoral visit of 28 June 1826, Cardinal Francesco Vici, acting in the name of Cardinal Galeffi, went to Orsano and was shocked by the dire state into which the church had fallen. As a result, he ordered that the badly deteriorated paintings be restored, the roof of the church rebuilt and the altars protected by a cloth while windows and doors were repaired.[181] The current construction has a *terminus ante quem* of 1441, the date of its official inauguration. We are not sure whether this followed the perimeter of the original thirteenth-century building or if it was in any way modified or enlarged. The church comprises two rectangular rooms which respectively measure 4,80x5,50 m and 3,50x5,50 m.[182] The former has two entrances, one on the southern side pointing towards the exterior of the nunnery, and the other (likely opened at a later date) to the west facing the internal court. This room communicates with the eastern portion of the church through the opening of an *iconostasis*-type screen, which separates the two rooms almost entirely. The second opening terminates in a semi-circular apse, with a diameter of 2 m and three slit windows on its northern, southern and eastern sides. As

---

175. Federici, *I monasteri di Subiaco*, p. 163; Caraffa, *Trevi nel Lazio*, p. 224.
176. Amati, *Il monastero di Sant'Angelo*, p. 38.
177. Federici, *I monasteri di Subiaco*, p. 226; Caraffa, *Trevi nel Lazio*, p. 226.
178. Federici, *I monasteri di Subiaco*, p. 246; Caraffa, *Trevi nel Lazio*, p. 227.
179. Federici, *I monasteri di Subiaco*, p. 273.
180. Caraffa, *Trevi nel Lazio*, p. 231.
181. *Ibid.*, p. 175.
182. *Ibid.*, p. 216.

previously stated, the church has been converted into a stable, as a consequence, there are no remains of the original pictorial decoration, which likely existed. This is confirmed by the above-mentioned pastoral visitation describing severely damaged paintings and pieces of mortar on the walls of the building in need of urgent restoration. The western portion of the church is enclosed by a perimeter wall forming a quadrilateral court and bordering the nun's living quarters on the southern side. These rooms all have a width of 6,30 m but varying lengths, which respectively measure 7,50 m, 4,50 m and 14,30 m.[183] This most probably indicates that they were used for different purposes. One could have been a Chapter house or a refectory, another a dormitory and a third, a reception hall or a storage area. From the surviving remains it would appear that the central room developed on two stories and opened onto the cloistered portion of the nunnery. Additionally, the north-western portion of the court was also possibly covered. Indeed, this hypothesis appears to be confirmed by the presence of a window, which suggests that a building was most likely adjacent to the enclosing wall. The entire surface of the complex measures approximately 845 square metres; its walls constructed in *pietra viva* using local limestone and mortar with uneven layering measuring 25x17 cm.

Sant'Angelo di Orsano underscored the objective difficulties in reconstructing and reassessing the role of female patronage, and more generally that of female conventual realities in Latium. The combination of the moderate cultural level of these religious women, their sparse economic resources and ultimately the suppression of their convents significantly challenge the study of these complexes. Through surviving documentation, I attempted to outline the general history of the complex in broad terms. However, I could not draw clear cut conclusions on the real decision-making power of this community. Members of the local nobility did join the convent, possibly highlighting the significance of rural foundations as outposts for baronial territorial claims. However, as far as Sant'Angelo is considered this claim is only based on a sparse number of documents and therefore must be advanced with caution. The fact that these findings are partial and only offer a snapshot of the convent's history should be kept in mind. I also attempted to reconstruct the late medieval architectural remains of the church, while acknowledging the possibility that they were heavily reworked over the centuries. Indeed, the hypothesis advanced for the church's internal distribution, must account for the fact that it was abandoned for several centuries and transformed into a sheepfold. The *iconostasis* screen-like structure is problematic both in terms of dating and of structural interpretation, it may have been a later addition. Overall, determining whether these changes were implemented by the nuns, the church, or lay patrons is extremely problematic. Hopefully, this case study has furthered an integrated methodology to contextualise peripheral nunneries within a social, political and historical framework. At the same time, it acknowledges the objective limitations that result from the study of peripheral rural outposts in late medieval Latium.

183. *Ibid.*

7. Comparing Benedictine Conventual Communities: A Few Considerations

By conducting a gazetteer on surviving conventual complexes pertaining to the Benedictine order, I selected and performed an in-depth analysis of the nunneries which had the most promising collection of archival, artistic and architectural remains. The relationship of these convents to secondary literature is uneven; while some convents have been published, others remain largely unknown. Indeed Guarcino and Orsano are off the beaten track, while Montefiascone and Castrocielo have a meagre, although relevant bibliography. This was also the case for archival sources, which turned out to be either immensely valuable, or sparse and scattered; therefore offering no effective history on the convent, but only a snapshot of certain years. For example, convents such as San Pietro at Montefiascone have a rich documentary corpus both pertaining to their congregation and to the medieval socio-political setting; others like Sant'Angelo in Orsano only grant us a bird's eye view of the settlement's (fragmentary) history. Documents at Guarcino emphasised the high status of its members who came from the Patrassi and Caetani clans. Archival evidence at Santa Maria in Viano (presented in the introduction to this section) offers further proof of convents as effective bastions of power for baronial families in the region. While we had already certified this in Rome, for example at San Silvestro in Capite, it was crucial to offer further proof of this trend outside the city as well. Ultimately, the objective was to select those case studies that would further our understanding of female conventual communities in a regional peripheral context, largely proving the significance of rural foundations in the earlier period, as outposts for baronial territorial claims.

The selection, though limited, nevertheless uncovered patterns and furthered hypotheses which would have gone undetected. Through the integrated study of art and architecture I theorised a retro-choir for the church at ground level plan both at Castrocielo and Montefiascone. I also put forward the hypothesis for this arrangement for San Luca at Guarcino through pastoral visits and the three surviving entrances on the side wall of the church. The altar inside the choir created a sort of church within the church with its own set of rules and prescriptions, ultimately reassessing the visual access of nuns towards the elevation of the Host. Thus, these case studies furthered the supposition that the use of the choir space was not only manifold, but likely had distinguished, separate and independent regulations from the main church. This influenced it profoundly both in its arrangement and in the decorative choices, thematised as we witnessed at Castrocielo and Montefiascone around the subject of Christ, the Virgin and the Eucharist.

Surviving conventual complexes at Santa Maria del Monacato, San Luca at Guarcino indicate an inheritance from the Benedictine tradition of arranging spaces around the square of the cloister. However, we must acknowledge that most of these convents survived in a dire state for several centuries and were refurbished (San Luca at Guarcino, Santa Maria del Monacato) and adapted

(Sant'Angelo at Orsano) to fulfil other needs. These nunneries suffered profound alterations to their medieval fabric. Therefore, while the AutoCAD reconstructions attempt to advance reasoning around conventual spaces, we must acknowledge that these drawings are in no way definitive, but hopefully shed new light on these nunneries and unveiled patterns which were not immediately detectable. When present, surviving artistic testimonies were put into context in the attempt to frame them both *in situ* and in a wider stylistic analysis. I attested that few artworks survive from Latium's Benedictine nunneries; it is, however, safe to assume that conventual spaces were embellished with some form of artistic presence. Apart from the fresco cycle in the Benedictine convent of Santa Maria in Palazzolo at Castrocielo, pictorial evidence was in fact scanty. We usually only have access to the outer shells of these convents, as witnessed at Sant'Angelo Orsano. Especially in so far as Castrocielo was considered, I acknowledged the stylistic influences that travelled between Rome and Naples ranging from Byzantine models to Gothic forms.[184] The qualitative leaps were caused by the reception and re-processing of courtly models and stylistic trends to varying degrees transformed into local dialects by provincial artists. This was the case at Castrocielo and also at Montefiascone where another medieval pictorial cycle was analysed. While they reflect the complex relationships between centre and periphery, the latter characterised by a limited technique, they equally attest to the vitality and dynamism of artistic culture in Latium. As a result, the framework of plots and stylistic contributions undoubtedly emerges as being more complex and less mechanical than previously thought.[185] The survival of the Buglioni altarpiece at Montefiascone also testified to the high level of these commissions inside spaces exclusively reserved for the nuns. Additionally, the fresco program and the Buglioni terracotta not only underscore the high-quality decoration, but also testify to the recurring Marian and Christological subjects we encounter inside choir spaces. Whether the nuns commissioned these artworks is yet impossible to determine on the basis of surviving evidence. However, the patron/s responsible for these commissions ensured that the choir space was richly adorned. This undoubtedly underscores the importance and the prestige of this devotional space. Through a multidisciplinary study of conventual realities in Latium, we may attempt to extend our knowledge on the female religious experience during the medieval period, by thinking of these nunneries organically from a social, political and economic standpoints. Even within the strict limits of the cloister, women were guaranteed social protection and belonging. Ultimately these offered a comparative perspective for Roman nunneries. In contrast to Rome, I did not encounter the names of exceptional abbesses. We did, however, investigate architectural palimpsests which had not been as heavily reworked nor were as stratified as convents in Rome. These furthered and secured hypotheses on the

---

184. *Affreschi in Val Comino*, p. 108.
185. Pace, "Per un percorso nella pittura murale", pp. 13-16.

consistent arrangement of choir spaces and on the iconographic themes inside choirs. Moreover, Latium offered additional insight into the use of convents by baronial families to secure their territorial presence. These case studies will hopefully shed new light on a period that has generally been dismissed by mainstream historiography as being architecturally and artistically insignificant.

4. The Mendicants in Latium

1. *Game Changers and Puzzling Absences: The Ascent of the Clarissans in Latium*

By the end of the thirteenth century, the popularity of the Order of the Poor Clares had transformed it into something of a mass movement. This phenomenon was not limited to Central Italy, but was spread across the entire peninsula.[1] These new female religious experiences were overseen by the Church within the project designed by Cardinal Ugolino under the prescriptions of Pope Honorius III, characterized by the imposition of a rigid *clausura* scheme.[2] *Clausura* allowed these women to live communally in controlled circumstances and, ultimately, to differentiate them from their male counterparts.[3] Although there has been an undeniable rise in research devoted to the Clarissan order, a broader statistical analysis has largely been neglected. While in the last twenty years a number of monographs on single case studies have made their appearance, the first in-depth survey was conducted by Riccardo Pratesi in 1953 during the seminar series organised for the seventh centenary of the death of Saint Clare.[4] The author largely centred his survey on single reports sent from Franciscan provinces in

---

1. M. Bartoli, "Francescanesimo e mondo femminile nel XIII secolo", in *Francesco, il francescanesimo*, pp. 167-180; Casimiro da Roma, *Memorie istoriche delle chiese e dei conventi dei frati minori della Provincia romana*, Rome, Pietro Rosati, 1774; M. D'Alatri, "Gli insediamenti francescani del Duecento nella Custodia di Campagna", *Collectanea Franciscana*, 47 (1977), pp. 297-315; R. Manselli, "La donna nella vita della Chiesa tra Duecento e Trecento", in *Il movimento religioso femminile in Umbria nei secoli XIII-XIV*, ed. by R. Rusconi, Acts of the conference (Città di Castello, 27-29 October 1982), Florence, La Nuova Italia, 1984, pp. 241-255; Marini, "Le fondazioni francescane femminili", pp. 71-96; A. Cignoni Pecorini, "Fondazioni francescane femminili nella Provincia Tusciae del XIII secolo", *Collectanea Franciscana*, 80 (2010), pp. 181-206; B. Roest, *Order and Disorder. The Poor Clares between Foundation and Reform*, Leiden, Brill, 2013.

2. G. Adenna, *Convengno di Studi in occasione del VII centenario della nascita di Santa Chiara*, Acts of the conference (Manduria, 14-15 December, 1994), Galatina, Congedo, 1998, p. 234.

3. G. Paolin, *Lo spazio del silenzio. Monacazioni forzate, clausura e proposte di vita religiosa femminile nell'età moderna*, Rome, Biblioteca dell'immagine, 1998, p. 12.

4. R. Pratesi, "Le Clarisse in Italia", in *Santa Chiara d'Assisi. Studi e cronaca del VII centenario, 1253-1953*, Assisi, Comitato centrale per il VII centenario della morte S. Chiara, 1954, pp. 339-377.

Italy based on their archival records. Although Father Pratesi was well aware of the approximate nature of the research, his analysis undoubtedly provided a preliminary base for future research in the field. His work was followed by *Medieval Franciscan Houses*, written by John Moorman, which incorporated lists of Clarissan foundations (essentially compiled around the *Bullarium Franciscanum*), and by the census curated by Anna Benvenuti in 1992.[5] As far as the greater Latium area is concerned, the article by Alfonso Marini in the *Archivio della Società romana di storia patria* may be safely considered a milestone for female religious studies.[6] By combining previous data with archival research from the papal registry, Marini provides an accurate picture of Clarissan convents in Latium throughout the thirteenth century. This survey is based on the use of papal bulls and critically engages with the work done by Pratesi, Moorman, and the *Bullarium Franciscanum*.[7]

While an attempt has been made to census the female Franciscan monastic communities in the region during the late medieval period, according to Giovanni Carbonara a comprehensive art-historical survey is lacking.[8] No extensive overview exists and single case studies are the result of interdisciplinary approaches, which lack both an effective order and a systematic historiographic perspective. In the thirteenth century, this is further complicated by the Clarissan custom of settling in pre-existing buildings.[9] It was only later (possibly out of necessity) that female communities oversaw the construction of their own conventual spaces through bequests and donations.[10] This likely determined the structural differences that may be observed between early settlements. In keeping with the rigid *clausura* imposed upon the order, Clarissan churches tend to be separated into two distinct bodies. This structural division was devised to separate the laity and the officiating body from the female community. As Bruzelius rightly affirms in her oft-cited article "Hearing is Believing", this allowed the nuns to experience the service on an aural rather than visual level.[11]

The spontaneity that characterized the first settlements of the order was explicit in the frequent re-use of existing structures, and in the slow definition of the spiritual and liturgical practice. This, together with the need to maintain

---

5. A. Benvenuti, "La fortuna del movimento damianita in Italia (XIII secolo)", in *Chiara d'Assisi. Atti del XX Convegno Internazionale*, Acts of the conference (Assisi, 15-17 October, 1992), Spoleto, Centro di Studi sull'Alto Medioevo, 1993; J.R.H. Moorman, *Medieval Franciscan Houses*, New York, Franciscan Institute Publication, 1983.

6. Marini, "Monasteri femminili".

7. *Bullarium Franciscanum*, ed. by G.G. Sbaralea, 4 vols., Rome, typis Sacrae Congregationis de Propaganda Fide, 1759-1768.

8. G. Carbonara, "Gli insediamenti degli ordini mendicanti in Sabina", in *Lo spazio dell'umiltà. Atti del convegno di studi sull'edilizia dell'Ordine dei Minori*, Acts of the conference (Fara Sabina, 3-6 November 1982), Fara Sabina, Centro Francescano Santa Maria in Castello, 1984, pp. 125-126.

9. C. Frugoni, *Chiara d'Assisi. Una solitudine abitata*, Rome-Bari, Laterza, 2006, p. 238.

10. For example, Santa Maria Donnaregina in Naples; Bruzelius, *Stones of Naples*.

11. Bruzelius, "Hearing is Believing", pp. 83-91.

a rigid enclosure and the expression of an essentially meditative dimension, contributed to determine the architecture of the Poor Clares.[12] Indeed, the need to create differentiated spaces from those accessible to the lay community resulted in a different development of settlements. Thus, unlike those of their male counterparts, and with rare exceptions, female communities never achieved a remarkable growth in size, or complex spatial articulation, even in their church buildings.[13] The process of spatial reduction, which unites the Clarissan experience with that achieved for the female branches of other orders (the Cistercians, for example) determined the creation of structures that merge the criteria of poverty, of simplicity and mimicry with local building traditions.[14] Recent studies have demonstrated the widely generalized preference for single-nave churches of modest size and spatial articulation, which abandoned the transept and the chapels flanking the altar. This solution did not pose a serious problem to the implementation of small-scale spaces such as oratories.[15] Different types of screens – required to separate the monastic cloistered communities from the outside world – sometimes suffered radical changes over time. This was due to the growing reverence for the Eucharist in the fourteenth century, which required the community to have a direct view of the Holy Host and altar.[16]

Excluding unrepresentative complexes such as Santa Chiara in Assisi or Santa Maria Donnaregina in Naples which are unusual and do not reflect normative Clarissan practice, surviving monasteries indicate a modest development. This was generally organized around the quadrangle of the cloister with the church, mostly located on the north side and fully inserted within the other architectural blocks in plan and elevation.[17] In Italy, the capillary/territorial spread of the order started in the second decade of the thirteenth century. In most cases, this initially involved the settlement of existing rural chapels and only later the development of the first modest, purpose-built structures. Very little monumental or material evidence has survived from this formative period. Generally located outside city walls, they were subsequently abandoned by their communities, which moved into more comfortable and more secure locations inside towns, and were sometimes converted into fortifications due to their proximity to city gates and important roads (a pattern which can be seen at San Sebastiano, Alatri, and San Pietro in Vineis, Anagni).

12. *Ibid.*, p. 88.
13. A.M. Romanini, "Architettura degli ordini mendicanti", *Storia della città*, 9 (1978), pp. 5-15: 10.
14. *Ibid.*, p. 15.
15. C. Bozzoni, "Centoventi anni di studi sull'architettura degli ordini mendicanti", in *Arnolfo di Cambio e la sua epoca*, ed. by V.F. Pardo, Rome, Viella, 2007, p. 50.
16. Bruzelius, "Hearing is Believing", p. 89.
17. A. Cadei, "Si può scrivere una storia dell'architettura mendicante? Appunti per l'area padano-veneta", in *Tommaso da Modena e il suo tempo. Atti del convegno internazionale di studi*, Acts of the conference (Treviso, 1979), Treviso, Stamperia di Venezia, 1980, pp. 337-362.

In contrast to the sparse architectural analysis provided by the study of the first foundations, the church of San Damiano in Assisi retains the complexity of the aspects that characterized the origins of the order.[18] It is in fact an existing church, restored by Francis in two successive stages. The first intervention seems limited to the rebuilding of the barrel vault lancet arches on the longitudinal body of the church, while the second which included the construction of the dormitory, made the settlement of Chiara and her companions possible. The former resulted in the construction of the dormitory, a simple rectangular room with a wooden roof built above the vault of the longitudinal body of the church. According to Mary Angelina Filipiak this solution shows clear links with structural and formal elements of secular buildings.[19] Only later would they switch to the simple structure consisting of two floors, a semi-circular termination to the choir and overlying chapel, built in a single block. Although the conventual complex of San Damiano is well outside Latium, it acts as an ideal model for Clarissan settlements in this area. As previously stated, it bears witness to the order's custom of settling in pre-existing buildings. Through the analysis of surviving Clarissan houses in this region, I noticed a consistent pattern of choir arrangements possibly derived from the oratory at San Damiano. This was found in the area directly above the presbytery and communicated with it through a narrow slit and auditory canal.[20] The solution of a suspended room over an area of the church appears in almost every Clarissan settlement I examined. Localization in Latium highlights the different dynamics of settlement between female and male branches of the order: Franciscans are widely distributed throughout the Latium area, settling in all urban centres. In contrast, Poor Clares are primarily concentrated in four areas: the Valle Reatina, where there are six monasteries (four in Rieti, plus Borgo San Pietro and Magliano Sabina); in the Roman area (three in Rome, one each in Tivoli, Palestrina, Valmontone and Velletri); in Campagna (Anagni, Alatri, Ferentino, Fiuggi, Frosinone); and in the Tuscia region (Viterbo, Tuscania, and Civita Castellana). The control exercised by the popes and the Curia on women's monasteries is highlighted by their distribution in areas where papal presence was stronger. Indeed, in addition to Rome, Viterbo and Anagni were strongholds for the papal court, and housed its residence at different periods during the thirteenth century.

18. Bruzelius, "Hearing is Believing", p. 86; Cadei, "Si può scrivere", p. 341; M.A. Filipiak, *The Plans of the Poor Clares Convents in Central Italy. From the Thirteenth through the Fifteenth Century*, PhD dissertation, University of Michigan, 1957; M. Righetti Tosti-Croce, "La chiesa di Santa Chiara in Assisi: architettura", in *Santa Chiara in Assisi*, ed. by P. Tomei, Cinisello Balsamo, Silvana, 2002, pp. 23-28; L. Ermini Pani, M.G. Fichera, M.L. Mancinelli, *Indagini archeologiche nella chiesa di San Damiano in Assisi*, Assisi, Porziuncola, 2005; Zappasodi, *Sorores*, pp. 24-26.

19. Filipiak's dissertation is of extreme utility because it provides a general overview of Clarissan architecture in Central Italy during the late medieval period. It demonstrates an established pattern of construction derived from the church of San Damiano in Assisi. To a certain extent her work provides the basis for almost every investigation on Clarissan art and architecture.

20. Zappasodi, *Sorores*, p. 26.

2. Female Patronage or Baronial Intervention? San Sebastiano, Alatri

The abbey of San Sebastiano is prominently sited at the foot of Mount Pizzuto, across the Cosa river valley from the town of Alatri in the province of Frosinone (Fig. 39). Set amidst a densely packed landscape of olive groves, the site maintains a secluded dimension. Over the years the convent has attracted a good deal of interest from both local scholars and international academics. This is likely due to the stratification within the building complex, which can be traced from the fifth century up to the twentieth-century restorations undertaken by Romolo Giralico. The first systematic study of the convent was carried out by the local historian Camillo Scaccia-Scarafoni in 1916.[21] Scaccia-Scarafoni's meticulous archival research, conducted between the Archivio Apostolico Vaticano, the Archivio Doria Pamphilj and the archives in Subiaco and Trisulti, established the basis for all subsequent studies. While his findings have been integrated and revised over the last century, the scholar's work is representative of a particularly brilliant phase of Italian erudition within the Ministry of Culture of which Scaccia-Scarafoni was part. Following his publication in the *Archivio della Società romana di storia patria*, the conventual complex was mainly the subject of articles by local scholars in the monthly periodical *Terra Nostra* and in bulletins of the Ministry of Culture.[22] The articles range from brief informative entries to complaints on the state of abandonment of the monastery and its possible reuse and transformation. In the 1953 edition of the *Bollettino d'Arte*, Yvonne Batard published an article on the frescoes mentioning their common stylistic matrix to the Lower Basilica of Assisi and a possible connection to the work of Giunta Pisano.[23] On the contrary, in his 1971 article on medieval Tuscan painting, Eric Prehn linked the frescoes to the work of Coppo di Marcovaldo dating them to the third quarter of the thirteenth century.[24] Furthermore, thanks to the contribution by Tiziana Iazeolla in her article *Gli affreschi di San Sebastiano ad Alatri* on the surviving frescoes in the church, the nunnery was exposed to a larger academic circle.[25] As we shall examine, the paintings appear to suggest an effective synthesis of a workshop with artists from very different stylistic backgrounds working side by side, furthering our knowledge on the art of Umbria and Latium during the thirteenth century.

21. Scaccia-Scarafoni, "Memorie storiche".
22. W. Pocino, "Due Santi nell'Abbazia di Alatri", *Lazio ieri e oggi*, 10, 7 (1974), p. 157; G. Scalisi, "L'abbazia di San Sebastiano nel territorio di Alatri", *Lazio ieri e oggi*, 9, 12 (1973), pp. 282-233; G. Floridi, "Nozze Floridi-Pogson Doria Pamphilj e la badia di San Sebastiano di Alatri", *Terra Nostra*, 32, 3-4 (1993), pp. 7-8; "La quarta conferenza sul riuso dei castelli. La badia di San Sebastiano in Alatri, un gioiello d'arte in rovina", *Data News. Notiziario dei Beni Culturali e Ambientali*, 3, 7 (1994), p. 10; "Promemoria per i detentori e per gli acquirenti di edifici soggetti a vincolo monumentale", *Data News. Notiziario dei Beni Culturali e Ambientali*, 5, 9 (1996), p. 20.
23. Y. Batard, "Notes sur des fresques récemment découvertes entre Veroli et Alatri", *Bollettino d'arte*, 4, 43 (1958), pp. 177-180.
24. E.T. Prehn, "Una decorazione murale del duecento toscano in un monastero laziale", *Antichità viva*, 10 (1971), pp. 3-11.
25. Iazeolla, "Gli affreschi di San Sebastiano ad Alatri", pp. 467-475.

According to Iazeolla these paintings' marked difference from other religious commissions in the town of Alatri seem to suggest a *scelta di gusto* on behalf of the nuns to decorate their convent's church. Although this cannot be proven with absolute certainty, and frequently the commission itself was paid by a third party, the possibility remains a tantalizing one. Whatever the case, the resonance of Iazeolla's claim attracted further contributions to the field. In a 1990 collection of studies on mural painting in the town of Alatri, Achille Donò dedicated a chapter to the frescoes in the *badia* and largely confirms the hypothesis advanced by Iazeolla.[26] The site continued to attract interest, but the majority of publications were primarily based on the work conducted by Scaccia-Scarafoni offering very little by way of new insights on the building. Finally in 2005, after a visit led by the then director of the American Academy in Rome, Bruzelius, in 1999, a group of fellows published, in the words of the project's director Elizabeth Fentress, "the first systematic and synthetic archaeological and architectural investigations of the building and the surrounding territory with the results of newly discovered archival sources to further the work begun by Scaccia-Scarafoni nearly a century ago".[27] This publication's approach is quite distinctive integrating archaeology, architectural analysis, history and art history resulting in a comprehensive interdisciplinary analysis of the complex.

The abbey has a long and intricate history seemingly rooted in the initial stages of the first Benedictine settlements. Indeed, scholars have referred to San Sebastiano as a *proto-cenobio*. As noted in previous publications thanks to the testimony offered by Gregory the Great in his *Dialogues*, we know that the monastery was founded by the patrician Liberius under the spiritual guide of the deacon Servandus.[28] This is corroborated by a twelfth-century inscription located in the church.[29] The single most important piece of evidence regarding San Sebastiano is preserved in the *Rerum Italicarum Scriptores*. It records a visit made by Saint Benedict to the abbey on his way to Montecassino in 529.[30]

Gregory the Great testifies to a special friendship that existed between Servandus and Saint Benedict and reveals that the deacon was present during

---

26. A. Donò, *Storia dell'affresco in Alatri*, Rome, Istituto Poligrafico della Zecca dello Stato 1990.

27. E. Fentress, "Documenting the Building", in *Walls and Memory*, pp. 18-31: 22.

28. Scaccia-Scarafoni, "Memorie storiche", p. 8; Gregory the Great, *Dialogues*, ed. by A. de Vogué, Paris, Éditions du Cerf, 1979 (SC, 260), 2.35: "Servandus diaconus et abbas eius monasterii, quod in Campaniae partibus a Liberio quondam Patricio fuerat constructum".

29. HOC OPUS ALTARIS SPLENDET DE MARMORE FACTUM / MONACUS ECCLESIAE THOMAS QVOD FECERAT ATVM / COLLOCET HUNC DOMINVS POST MORTEM SEDE SVPERNA / MARTIRIS ET SANCTI SERVANDI PRECE BENIGNA BEATI; C. Bruzelius, C.J. Goodson, "The Buildings", in *Walls and Memory*, pp. 72-113: 96-97.

30. The *Vita Placidi* states that: "(huic monasterio) Servandus praeerat et S.P. Benedictum illac transeuntem, cum Sublaco Casinum pergeret (ea siquidem via ducit), hospitio suscepit" (*Rerum. Italicarum. Scriptores*, ed. L. Muratori and F. Angelati, Milan, Ex typografia Societatis Palatinae, 1721-1738, IV, p. 229, from E. Fentress, "The Sixth-Century Abbey", in *Walls and Memory*, pp. 32-71: 37).

one of the saint's miracles.[31] After the death of Servandus, we do not have a clear account of the abbey's historical development. Nevertheless, one may identify the different building phases through a study of the surviving structures.[32] It appears that the monks extended the rectangular plan of the *badia* with heterogeneous additions, which reflected the community's needs. For Bruzelius and Caroline Goodson, the original plan of the church was maintained up to the thirteenth century. The abbey was then granted by Pope Gregory IX to the newly established Order of the Poor Clares under the patronage of the cardinal of Santa Maria in Trastevere, Stefano Conti dei Segni.[33] In order to favour the pope's decision, Bishop Giovanni of Alatri annexed the church of San Benedetto de Plagis and its lands to the abbey in 1233. The document's text is very clear in stating that the concession made by the bishop was explicitly arranged to please Cardinal Stefano Conti.[34] This decision was reiterated by a papal bull written by Gregory IX from Perugia in 1233. These documents reflect "the bishop's insistence of substantial property for the new Clarissan community was intended to be a guarantee of financial stability. As such, the community of San Sebastiano played a part in the debate over the ownership of property that positioned Saint Clare against the Minister Generals".[35] Indeed, in contrast to their male counterparts these communities were not self-sufficient and had to rely on benefactions, donations, and dowries bestowed either by patrons or members of their own community. The Clarissan community resided in the abbey until 1442 when the last four nuns were expelled for misconduct.[36] On 23 February of that year the *badia* lost its monastic status and was placed under the jurisdiction of the Chapter of Alatri. The abbey underwent a period of steep decline and was eventually transformed into a farm. Finally, in 1653 Innocent X (1644-1655) annexed San Sebastiano and its properties to the church of Sant'Agnese in Agone in Rome and to the Doria Pamphilj family.[37] This explains why most of the surviving documentary evidence is currently held at the Archivio Pamphilj in Rome.

The stratigraphic study of the remaining structures corroborates important changes implemented by the different inhabitants of the *badia*. After the first building campaign that characterised the *proto-cenobio*, it is likely that the Benedictines made some fundamental adjustments. These were subsequently adapted to the needs of the Clarissan community. This practice was quite frequent given that in the early years of its foundation, the Poor Clares were regularly installed into pre-existing buildings and, in Bruzelius' and Goodson's words, "the architectural arrangements put in place for the new female community at San Sebastiano reflect the type of *ad hoc* solutions often found in Clarissan

31. J.J. Odonnel, "Liberius the Patrician", *Traditio*, 37 (1981), pp. 31-72.
32. Fentress, "The Sixth-Century Abbey", p. 35.
33. Bruzelius, Goodson, "The Buildings", p. 107.
34. Scaccia-Scarafoni, "Memorie storiche", p. 12.
35. Bruzelius, Goodson, "The Buildings", p. 110.
36. Scaccia-Scarafoni, "Memorie storiche", p. 15.
37. *Ibid.*, p. 18.

convents".[38] Given the strict *clausura* observed by the nuns, the main concern was to separate the laity from the religious community. The changes present in the church and in the adjacent Benedictine monastery exhibit this primary concern for segregation. Furthermore, although the solid brick structure is all that remains, there were likely additions in wood and other more perishable materials, which have now been lost.[39] Indeed, according to Scaccia-Scarafoni, the western cloister was largely built out of wood.[40] Stratigraphic analysis of the standing walls demonstrate that the oldest part of the abbey is certainly Benedictine and should therefore be dated before 1233.[41] The Clarissan occupation (1233-1241) marks another major building phase. All secondary additions must be ascribed to a relatively modern fifteenth-century construction when ownership of the nunnery passed to Giovanni Tortelli (ca. 1400s-1466). In fact, given that the abbey was left in a state of semi-abandonment from the fifteenth century onwards this prevented major structural changes.

Overall, we can safely affirm that the complex maintains a distinctly medieval character. The original core of the sixth-century monastery was thoroughly transformed. The monks added a Chapter room, a refectory, an auditorium, new dormitories, and a cloister to the rectangular plan of the complex, originally characterized by the church, living quarters and a cistern. While, according to Scaccia-Scarafoni, the enlargement of the cloister, the pictorial decoration of the church and the choir/oratory can be attributed to the work of the nuns.[42] In addition, the nuns were most certainly responsible for building the choir adjacent to the church in one of the suspended rooms. This structure allowed them to participate in the liturgical services at least on an auditory level without being seen by the laity. Additionally, this provided a direct architectural reference to the church-choir-dormitory scheme present at San Damiano. As one of the first Clarissan settlements outside Assisi, such ties to the mother church would have been fundamental in bolstering the spiritual and institutional links between different convents of the newly founded order.

The complex, which preserved a very elongated rectangular plan, can be divided into two bodies. The first, closer to the entrance, is composed of the churchyard and the parts of the *badia* open to the laity. The second part consists of the cloister around which areas reserved for members of the religious community who had to observe a rigid *clausura*, are grouped. Scaccia-Scarafoni maintains that this work was undertaken by local masonry workers.[43] These conclusions are derived from comparative evidence in the territory of Alatri, which not only confirms the use of the same limestone, but also of its building

38. Bruzelius, Goodson, "The Buildings", pp. 110-111.
39. *Ibid.*, p. 73. As Bruzelius and Goodson rightly point out, we should view the transformations that took place in San Sebastiano as fluid in nature.
40. Scaccia-Scarafoni, "Memorie storiche", p. 15.
41. E. Fentress, "Documenting the Building", in *Walls and Memory*, pp. 18-31: 25-26.
42. Scaccia-Scarafoni, "Memorie storiche", p. 16.
43. *Ibid.*; Donò, "Storia degli affreschi", p. 34.

techniques. Additionally, the surviving portions of the monastery preserves an extremely rustic quality. This reinforces the intensely isolated state of the *badia* and the likely intervention of local masons which followed. Indeed, as far as the Clarissan period is concerned, we only know of one external patron by name: Stefano Conti. Is it possible that his involvement in the instalment of the Poor Clares may be justified by his need to secure political authority in the territories of Alatri, which were part of his *castrum*? Although this remains a viable possibility, these claims must be advanced with caution due to the lack of archival documents. Our hypothesis is largely based on other case studies in Latium.

Despite not knowing of any female patron involved in the architectural refurbishment of the church, the portraits of two nuns present in the frescoes inside may bear witness to their involvement in the adaptation of the existing architectural remains. Convents such as San Cosimato substantiate the role played by abbesses in extensive refurbishment projects of pre-existing structures. Indeed, we may not exclude the possibility of the female community intervening personally in the reconstruction plans of the nunnery. As we shall examine in the paintings, especially the later fourteenth-century votive panels, women were active and participating patrons.

The frescoes at San Sebastiano constitute one of the first examples of a comprehensive narrative cycle designed for a Clarissan community. The small church is divided into two adjoining bays by an arched vault and richly adorned by an elaborate decorative program. Although the *sorores* were installed inside the convent in 1233, a stylistic analysis suggests a later chronology for our paintings. These were likely executed in two distinct phases. While the main cycle in the two bays of the church may be dated to the last quarter of the thirteenth century, the votive panels present in the presbytery and the choir/oratory are a clear product of a local fourteenth-century workshop. Undoubtedly, the most surprising element of these paintings is the complete absence of the figures of Saint Francis and Saint Clare or of episodes tied to the history of the order. This is unlikely to be because of San Sebastiano's peripheral location. Saint Clare was canonized in the cathedral of Anagni, only twenty kilometres from the *badia*, in 1255. In addition to a cycle devoted to episodes of the Passion, frescoes in the surviving nunnery of San Pietro in Vineis outside the city walls of Anagni – transferred to the Order of the Poor Clares by Pope Alexander IV in 1256 – represent both Saint Francis and Saint Clare. The latest studies on this convent conducted by Bianchi and Romano date these frescoes to the third quarter of the thirteenth century.[44] Thus, we may assume that the absence of the order's titular saints in the convent of San Sebastiano may have been intentional given that the decorative scheme appears to be relatively complete. Iazeolla argues that the paintings are an iconographic commentary on the *Apocrypha*, and more specifically on the *Meditationes Vitae*

---

44. A. Bianchi, "Affreschi duecenteschi nel S. Pietro in Vineis in Anagni", in *Roma anno 1300*, pp. 379-392.

Christi defined by the scholar as the equivalent of a Franciscan gospel.[45] In her opinion, the paintings give voice to the text and express the community's desire to adhere both to a humanized vision of the Christ and to the first ideals of the Franciscan movement.[46] This claim is refuted by Romano who suggests – even though the date of the *Meditationes Vitae Christi* is still largely debated – that the frescoes present at Alatri likely predate the text.[47] Although the nuns were installed in a Benedictine abbey and followed the *formae vitae* of Saint Benedict, which might lead us to believe that this tradition superseded the order's figurative agenda; other iconographic programs, such as the one in San Pietro in Vineis, oblige us to refute this claim entirely. In order to shed some light on this matter let us directly turn to the iconographic programme of the first phase present in the church.

If we proceed from the western portion of the church, we may witness the figure of Saint Sebastian with the bishop of Alatri John V and the pendant Saint Benedict and Cardinal Stefano Conti. These four figures are identified by inscriptions. Although these two historical characters were responsible for the transfer of the abbey to the Poor Clares in 1233, given the later chronology of the paintings it is unlikely that they were directly responsible for commissioning the frescoes. Both saints are represented in niches and the prototypes for Sebastian are rooted in a tenth-century tradition, which depicts the saint as a bearded old man. Their position at the entrance of the church and their assertive frontality strongly attest to their role as patrons of the abbey. Again, given the dedicatory nature of this panel, the absence of Saint Clare and Saint Francis is somewhat striking. These votive frescoes are followed by the Martyrdom of Saint Sebastian, the *Dormitio Virginis* and the Assumption.

While the martyrdom is practically illegible, both the *Dormitio* and the *Assumption* are extremely well preserved. Iazeolla traces stylistic matrices for these images in Roman thirteenth-century prototypes (mosaics of Santa Maria Maggiore or Santa Maria in Trastevere), while Romano states that as demonstrated by Gandolfo, "these characteristics already formed part of the older formal inheritance of the *cultura soziesca* [by this she refers to the painter Alberto Sozio from Spoleto] in Umbrian painting during the second half of the century, particularly in Spoleto".[48] Donò also vouches in favour of this Umbrian connection, but traces the physiognomic types of the apostles to scenes of the Lower Basilica of Assisi attributed to the Maestro di San Francesco.[49] This Roman-Umbrian dispute will be addressed later in our attempt to trace stylistic origins of these paintings.

---

45. Iazeolla, "Gli affreschi di San Sebastiano ad Alatri", p. 470.
46. *Ibid.*
47. S. Romano, "The Frescoes of the Church and Oratory", in *Walls and Memory*, pp. 114-141.
48. Iazeolla, "Gli affreschi di San Sebastiano ad Alatri", p. 470; Matthiae, *Pittura romana*, II, p. 352.
49. Donò, *Storia dell'affresco*, p. 45.

Moving on to the eastern portion, or presbytery, a small almost illegible fragment of a Flagellation followed by a Disrobing of Christ, a Crucifixion and Christ between two angels can be identified. Indeed, Christ stripped of its garments and the Crucifixion are two subjects which were very dear to the Mendicant order and may be witnessed in the first bay of the Lower Church of Assisi. As Donò rightly observes, this scene is also present in the altarpiece by the Master of Farneto from the Pinacoteca in Perugia thought to be derived from the Lower Church frescoes.[50] This *mise-en-scène* is also characteristic of Coppo di Marcovaldo, whose work and influence has been linked to the frescoes by Prehn.[51] The scholar also suggests that the scene's iconography is derived from the Gospel of Nicodemus introduced in the work of Coppo for the first time in the lateral scene of the San Gimignano crucifix dated ca. 1255.[52] Though he also recognizes the presence of this scene in Assisi, he claims that no stylistic analogy may be drawn between the two.[53]

As far as the Crucifixion is concerned, Christ is depicted in the *patiens* formula, surrounded by the three Marys on one side and Saint John and a group of Roman soldiers on the other. Prehn associates this with a sinopia from San Domenico in Pistoia, attributed by Baldini to Coppo.[54] Romano agrees that Christ's physiognomy is reminiscent of the work attributed to the Tuscan master.[55] It may be that someone from Coppo's *entourage* or at least familiar with his style could have worked inside the *badia*. Batard adds that the Crucifixion is overall a direct replica of the signed cross by Giunta Pisano in Santa Maria degli Angeli at Assisi. Like Prehn, Batard seems to vouch for a Tuscan influence rather than an Umbrian or Roman one.[56] Nevertheless, this Crucifixion maintains a vivid connection to the one present at San Saba in Rome and dated to the 1280s.

In the last panel, we have the *Noli me tangere*, a view of a city and the Christ in Limbo. According to Scaccia-Scarafoni the latter has been heavily repainted.[57] Close observation of the folds on Christ and Adam's tunic demonstrates that they are characterized by the use of *chiaroscuro*. This is markedly out of tune with the surrounding thirteenth-century paintings, which are defined by a decisive and marked use of the line. Moreover, while Mary Magdalene is the protagonist of the *Noli me tangere* directly beneath the panel depicting Christ in Limbo, her presence is not, as Romano rightly points out, sufficient proof for its inclusion in response to a female commission.[58] Christ is depicted in almost the same fashion as above, but unfortunately his clothing has been completely lost in both renditions.

50. *Ibid.*, p. 46.
51. Prehn, "Una decorazione murale", p. 8.
52. *Ibid.*, p. 10.
53. *Ibid.*; Derbes, *Picturing the Passion*, pp. 8-9.
54. Prehn, "Una decorazione murale", p. 10.
55. Romano, "The Frescoes of the Church and Oratory", p. 124.
56. Batard, "Notes sur des fresques", p. 181.
57. Scaccia-Scarafoni, "Memorie storiche", p. 18.
58. Romano, "The Frescoes of the Church and Oratory", p. 125.

The view of the city on the wall has been identified by Romano as Christ's sepulchre.[59] The architectonic rendering is unclear: it may equally be interpreted as one single building or as the perspective of a city. I am inclined to believe that either a representation of Jerusalem, or possibly that of the town of Alatri, or, indeed Anagni might have been attempted. Another possibility is that the convent is being represented as seen from one of the church's sides. Finally, on the vault of this room one may view the *Agnus Dei* and the symbols of the four evangelists. The *Tetramorph* was popular in Christian iconography and is found across the Italian peninsula in different mediums throughout the centuries. The execution presents itself without any particular stylistic mark. According to Iazeolla, the iconography would point towards a Roman context as evidenced, for instance, in the Sancta Sanctorum at the Lateran.[60]

With regard to the workshop responsible for the material execution of the paintings, it is likely that a commission produced through a network of artists from different regional schools presents a more plausible scenario. This challenges Iazeolla's hypothesis of two separate workshops from a respective Roman and Umbrian context.[61] Had it been the work of a single workshop, it is unlikely that the style would have remained isolated in this one production. The frescoes at San Sebastiano are extremely significant because they testify to an on-going stylistic dialogue between central Italian regions before the rise of masters such as Torriti, Giotto, or Cavallini. In my opinion, it is therefore very limiting to view the Alatri production as a work influenced by one specific regional school. As far as secondary commissions are considered, it is more realistic to view this work as a product of a network of artists likely working for the Franciscan movement.

For obvious chronological reasons, the fourteenth-century votive paintings located in the lower register of the presbytery and in the choir/oratory point to a completely different painterly tradition. The possibility that the frescoes found in the church were executed after the earthquake of 1350 remains a viable option.[62] As for the paintings located in the choir/oratory, I believe it is more likely for these to have been independently commissioned to embellish the walls of this space. The nuns' role in the commissioning of the panels is unquestionable. Although we do not have any documentary proof for this claim, the presence of two portraits of members of the community in the church and in the oratory above confirms their involvement. Indeed, donor portraits of abbesses or nuns were quite frequent in nunneries especially in the fourteenth century and we find a number of examples both in Rome and in Latium. In contrast to the thirteenth-century Marian/Christological program, these frescoes have received very little scholarly attention.[63] This is probably due to their execution by a local workshop

59. *Ibid.*
60. Iazeolla, "Gli affreschi di San Sebastiano ad Alatri", p. 470.
61. *Ibid.*
62. Donò, *Storia dell'affresco*, p. 45.
63. C.J. Goodson, "The Abbey in the Middle Ages. The Devotional Paintings", in *Walls and Memory*, pp. 142-151: 142.

of artists working in the town of Alatri. Surviving visual evidence in the churches of Alatri supports this claim.[64] As with the structural modification that occurred thanks to the intervention of local masons, it is therefore plausible that something similar occurred for the fourteenth-century decoration of the sacred spaces.

The fresco in the presbytery on the eastern side of the church behind the altar, positioned at eye level for a standing viewer, represents Saints Crescentia, Vitus and Modestus. A Gothic capitalized script identifies the saints by name and their haloes are rendered in plaster which might have originally been gilded. The almost life-size figures are depicted frontally. Directly below Modestus' feet, one may view a small representation of a nun with her hands joined in a gesture of prayer. Donò, Goodson and Scaccia-Scarafoni have suggested a date between the fourteenth and the fifteenth centuries.[65] What is evident is that a certain courtly culture, especially apparent in the clothing, has clearly influenced this overtly Gothic rendition. Another votive panel representing a saint survives inside the presbytery. This figure has been identified as Saint Anthony Abbot through the characteristic symbol of a pig. The painting is extremely damaged and cannot offer a ground for further stylistic comparisons.

The nuns' choir/oratory, located in a suspended room overlooking the church, is itself divided into two rooms. Unfortunately, the complete decorative program has been lost and what remains are a series of votive paintings and ornamental motifs consisting of crosses providing a fictive decorative pattern. In addition to these decorations, we may view an Enthroned Christ, Saint John the Baptist, Saint Christopher, and two groups of three and two saints respectively. Fragments of what was likely a Dormition are still visible. The Enthroned Christ is still very legible. It sits directly above the modern altar in the choir/oratory which possibly substituted the one dated to the Clarissan occupation.[66] Stylistically, it recalls the votive panel depicting Crescentia, Vitus and Modestus. These analogies are reinforced by the presence, also in this painting, of a nun in a Clarissan habit who was likely the patron of the fresco. These panels have been linked to the Maestro di San Leonardo who worked in the Church of the Dodici Marie and in San Silvestro at Alatri during that period.[67] Here, there is an obvious courtly influence, which recalls and is possibly influenced by the work of artists who adhered to the International Gothic culture. Christ is depicted with an ample tunic with deep folds. He is shown blessing with one hand, while holding an open book with the words EGO SVM VIA VERITAS ET VITA written in Gothic characters, with the other. His expression is both peaceful and severe, and characterized by regular brushstrokes and the use of *chiaroscuro*. The scene is enclosed in a Cosmatesque frame.

---

64. As exemplified by other frescoes in the churches of the Dodici Marie and of San Silvestro, Donò, *Storia dell'affresco*.
65. Goodson, "The Abbey in the Middle Ages", pp. 142-152.
66. Zappasodi, *Sorores*, p. 32.
67. Donò, *Storia dell'affresco*, p. 34.

The other painting, which is worth examining in some detail, is the *Saint Christopher* opposite the enthroned Christ. Due to both its calligraphic use of the line and frontal rendering, this painting may also be attributed to the Maestro di San Leonardo. Goodson makes a convincing argument about the positioning of the Saint opposite the altar. She claims that if we assume that the choir/oratory faced east, Saint Christopher would have been located on the counter-façade, like in other examples of chapels in Italy, as the last thing seen by the faithful upon exiting the room.[68] Unfortunately, the other panels have suffered great damage and do not offer any further insight into question of form and style. A striking difference between these paintings and the larger thirteenth-century cycle present in the lower church is their marked devotional and private character. It is probable that they were commissioned in moments of intense spiritual devotion by the female community of Clarissan nuns, or perhaps by a single member of the congregation. They encourage a precise form of intercession between the patron and the saint, which renders an overall intimate atmosphere.

Documentary evidence preserved between the archives at Subiaco and Trisulti and the Archivio Doria Pamphilj in Rome does not offer any further insight into the patronage of these paintings; however, an eighteenth-century inventory lists a series of religious goods present in the church including a painting of Saint Sebastian and a wooden crucifix. The inventory preserved at the Doria Pamphilj archive is dated May 1719 and entitled *Stato della Badia d'Alatri fatta nel mese di maggio 1719 et Inventario delle robbe, e suppelletti di sacre di d.a Abbazia*.[69] Although I was not able to trace the painting of Saint Sebastian, the 2011 catalogue of the Palazzo Venezia collection states that the crucifix was initially transferred to the Museo di Castel Sant'Angelo, then to the Museo Nazionale di Palazzo Venezia, and finally to one of the secretarial offices of the Ministry of Culture at the Collegio Romano (Fig. 40).[70] Unfortunately, the Ministry was unable to tell me in which secretarial office the crucifix is currently located.[71] From the only surviving picture that I was able to find, the crucifix appears to be dated to the thirteenth century. This would place it within the period in which the church was occupied by the Clarissan community. The small black and white photograph does not really allow for any further comment in terms of style or technique and we may assert that it likely belongs to a Roman-Umbrian context. Its dimensions (130x125 cm) suggest that it hanged from the wall or/and that it rested on a beam. It is unlikely that a niche of this size could enclose it as has been hypothesized for other convents such as San Pietro in Vineis.

---

68. Goodson mentions the San Vittore del Lazio and Priverno frescoes: Goodson, "The Abbey in the Middle Ages", p. 148.

69. Rome, Archivio Doria Pamphilj, 95,34.8.4; this document is published in *Walls and Memory*, p. 326.

70. *Museo Nazionale di Palazzo Venezia. Sculture in legno*, ed. by G.M. Fachechi, Rome, Gangemi, 2011, p. 177.

71. Private email communication, 03/10/2016.

The complex of San Sebastiano at Alatri testifies to the role of nunneries in a significant operation of artistic renewal outside of Rome.[72] Overall, the data assembled to date is significant due to its great variety, which spans crucifixes to frescoes; bells to liturgical apparatuses. Moreover, at Alatri we can determine the position of choir and the dormitory with absolute certainty. The convent's disposition was possibly influenced by San Damiano, the first Clarissan settlement and the ideal model to replicate. Therefore, although the nunnery was established on the outskirts of a provincial city in Latium, this did not deter its large-scale refurbishment. To a certain extent, the significant artistic and architectonic vestiges provide further proof of the role of nunneries as strategic social, political and economic outposts in peripheral suburban areas. What is also particularly striking about San Sebastiano compared to other provincial centres in Latium is the degree of preservation of the fresco cycles. Along with Santa Maria in Castrocielo and San Pietro in Vineis at Anagni this is one of the few instances where we have an uncompromised pictorial intervention. The recurring challenge in determining the patron was likewise encountered at Alatri. While the presence of a nun provides the necessary evidence towards her involvement in votive panels, this is not clear in the church cycle overall. The chronological gap between the stylistic analysis of the fresco and the life span of Stefano Conti makes it difficult to identify him as the sole patron of the paintings. Although information is extremely sparse and I was not able to find any definitive documentary evidence, it is possible that the nunnery of San Sebastiano was founded to consolidate the Conti family's sphere of influence in the territorial region of Alatri. This would account for the donation on the part of Stefano Conti. By establishing the Poor Clares – who were protected and particularly favoured by Pope Gregory IX – is it possible that Cardinal Stefano made this politically strategic donation to extend his own position and influence within the circles of the Curia? Or should we ascribe the large-scale renovation, as was the case for other Clarissan convents like San Cosimato, as the initiative of a particularly entrepreneurial community?

3. *Shedding New Light on Neglected Sites: San Michele Arcangelo, Amaseno*

The nunnery of San Michele Arcangelo or Sant'Angelo fuori le Mura is sited on the road linking the town of Amaseno (originally San Lorenzo), three kilometres south of Frosinone, to Fontanelle di San Marco on Mount Sant'Angelo.[73] Though

---

72. I have not included in this discussion the church bell currently preserved at the convent of the SS. Annunziata becase I was unable to view it. It lacks an inscription or anything which can secure a dating to the Clarissan occupation. Bruzelius and Goodson opt for a stylistic analogy with other church bells such as the one preserved at San Cosimato by Bartholomeus Pisanus in 1238. Bruzelius, Goodson, "The Abbey", pp. 104-105.
73. G. Fasolo, "Presentazione di rilievi di studenti della Facoltà di Architettura di Roma relativi alla villa romana di lago S. Puoto, i monasteri di S. Spirito di Zannone in Gaeta, di S. Michele Arcangelo di Amaseno e del Palazzo Zaccaleoni in Priverno", *Bollettino dell'Istituto di storia e di*

it currently survives in a state of semi-ruin and abandonment, its architectonical vestiges testify to its wealth and prestige during the late medieval period (Figs. 41-42). The religious order to which the inhabitants of the first settlement complied to is unclear. Stylistic analogies with other Cistercian monastic complexes, namely Fossanova and Casamari – the most celebrated examples in Latium – suggest an adherence to this rule. Analogous building techniques shared with these two complexes shall be examined in an architectonic overview executed through on-site visits and early photographs. However, what remains to be clarified is whether the nunnery was inhabited by Clarissan nuns from the onset or whether it belonged to a male monastic community – possibly the Cistercian order. Pratesi, Moorman and the *Bullarium Franciscanum* make no mention of this settlement, which has only been studied by local historians.

Documentary evidence pertaining to the nunnery is extremely meagre. A total of four thirteenth-century parchments are known. Of these, one has been lost but is cited in the work of historian Giuseppe Tomassetti in 1899.[74] The nunnery is named in the breviary of Alexander IV dated 5 February 1260. Here, we learn that the convent was inhabited by *monialium inclusarum* who were granted the privilege of owning property by the pope. Although the apostolic breviary does not specifically identify the rule followed by these nuns, Tomassetti identified it as Clarissan through the other surviving documents.[75] The first one is a parchment signed by Clement IV (1265), which lists the privileges offered to the community by Alexander IV (*in sede vacante*); the nuns are expressively identified as members of the *Ordinis S. Damiani*.[76] Finally, the nuns were left 10 golden florins in the will executed by Berardo Count of Ceccano, son of Annibaldo, on 31 July 1299.[77]

The Ceccano family was extremely influential in the area and dominated extensive portions of Ciociaria from their feud based in Ceccano for almost five centuries. The counts had close ties to the papacy and we know that Berardo was an exceptionally pious man. Indeed, this donation to Sant'Angelo may be interpreted in a number of ways. It is likely that a member of the family had joined the convent, or that Berardo was diversifying his control over Monte Sant'Angelo by securing financial ties with this nunnery. Subsequent references

---

arte del Lazio meridionale, 4 (1966), pp. 63-77; E. Giannetta, *Le chiese di Amaseno*, Frosinone, Tipografia Tecnostampa, 1987; L. Zaccheo, *Amaseno*, Amaseno, Amministrazione comunale, 1979; G. Tomassetti, *Amaseno*, Rome, Unione Coperativa, 1899.

74. *Ibid.*, p. 29.

75. *Ibid.*, p. 31; Marini, "Le fondazioni francescane femminili".

76. Tomassetti, *Amaseno*, p. 31; Marini, "Le fondazioni francescane femminili". This parchment survives in the Archivio Storico della Diocesi di Frosinone currently under restoration.

77. Tomassetti, *Amaseno*, p. 138; the author transcribes and offers only a translation in Italian of the document which is part of the Archive in Guarcino today inaccessible because it is being transferred to Frosinone: 1299, "31 luglio Berardo di Ceccano, figlio di Annibaldo, fa testamento, nel quale lascia un legato di 10 fiorini d'oro alle monache di Sant'Angelo, in San Lorenzo. Lascia eredi i figli Annibaldo, Nicola Tommaso e Giacomo, e le figlie Jocobela e Francesca fra i testimoni: Alberto di Pietro di Alberto canonico della basilica dei XII Apostoli, e Giovanni di Assisi medico. Atto rogato in Giuliano dal notaio Nicola Luce, di Guarcino Archivio Colonna, III BB. LIV. N. 4".

to Sant'Angelo are made in relation to the cathedral of Santa Maria in Amaseno in 1533 and 1717 with a view to establish the convent's territorial boundaries.

The church consists of various architectural layers, which testify to its existence prior to the Clarissan occupation during the thirteenth century. It likely dates to the Romanesque period with subsequent Cistercian additions, notably the rib vaults and pointed arches. It has a single nave with a rectangular plan measuring 16x6 m and built from regular square blocks of local limestone (Figs. 43-44). As in Sant'Angelo in Orsano, the façade of the church is tangential to the conventual complex. This allowed the nuns to access the church directly from the choir, which is positioned on a suspended level in the nave facing the altar. By contrast, the officiating clergy and laymen most likely entered through the door on the southern side. This portal comprises two splined shafts, which support two modillions and a lintel. Originally, there was a fresco in the archivolt directly above the lintel which has not survived. Five windows can be found on the southern and northern aisles: two slit windows in the upper storey and three rectangular openings with arched tops on the lower side. A double lancet window surmounted by a quatrefoil rosette dominates the eastern side of the apse.

In addition, the interior of the church consists of two distinct architectural bodies. The one towards the convent likely predates the second, which was most likely built during the Clarissan occupation in order to enlarge the church's pre-existing body. This western portion communicates with the eastern part through a vaulted arch resting on solid pilasters. The former is divided into two bays by a vaulted arch and covered by two sets of cross barrel vaults. In the interstitial space between the roof and the barrel-vaulted cover, the choir was accessed through a set of stairs that led directly into the conventual complex.

The small chapel on the northern portion was probably built at a later date. It is 2 m high, 2 m wide and 2.40 m long and is characterised by a vaulted ceiling with an arched lunette (Figs. 45-46). Fabio Marzi, editor at the online newspaper *Amaseno News*, claims that it formerly housed a fresco of a Madonna and Child identified by a photograph of the mural taken by him in the 1970s.[78] This picture has not been published and regrettably today the fresco is almost illegible. The painting measures 1.80x1.60 m and used to have an inscription in its lower portion which stated DM.MCCCCLXXXXI.MSE MAI ("In the year of our Lord 1491 in the month of May"). Moreover, Fabio Marzi claims that a group of nuns was originally portrayed in the lower left portion of the fresco. These figures can be faintly discerned in the surviving photograph and their presence would testify to the commission on the part of the congregation of this chapel. The remaining portions of the painting appear to be more readable. The Christ Child is portrayed

---

78. This photograph was given to me by Fabio Marzi. I was unable to establish whether this fresco was originally found in the apse of this lunette, as claimed by the photographer. The vaulted shape of the ceiling in this photograph raises doubts as to where it was originally located. The site is now on private property and is very difficult to access. At the time of publication I am waiting on the owners to grant me access to re-visit the nunnery. In the meantime, I am unable to provide a detailed photo of the surviving pictorial fragments to support Marzi's claim.

on the Virgin's left knee. The Madonna is wearing a red vest and a blue tunic with a gold rim while the throne is characterised by a geometrical motif.

From this first Romanesque ensemble we move into the next bay through a pointed arch, its pavement slightly raised and thus joined by three steps. This hall is covered by a gabled roof and the space beneath the quatrefoil rosette window originally housed the altar. The latter is currently found in the cathedral of Santa Maria in Amaseno. This part of the church appears to have been built by local masons inspired by the great abbeys of Casamari and Fossanova. Indeed, both the coarse stone work and the irregularities present on the perimeter walls support this claim. A pointed arch, likely functioning as a niche, lies on the northern side. Traces of red paint may still be discerned and it is probable that the niche housed a devotional painting of some sort with a smaller altar also present on the southern side. Vestiges of the conventual complex still survive in the area around the church. These include the outer walls, a cistern, the courtyard, and parts of the living quarters. The entire complex occupied a total area of 1,000 square metres, a large site which significantly underscores the importance and relevance of the settlement. The entire complex survives in a state of semi-ruin today; according to the parish priest of Santa Maria in Amaseno, this is partly due to the complex being scavenged for building materials after the Second World War. This came about in order to reconstruct the façade and the roof of the cathedral of Amaseno, which had been severely damaged by shelling.

In conclusion, San Michele Arcangelo fuori le Mura provides an invaluable testimony towards the study of the first Clarissan settlements in Central Italy. By looking at the more complex and neglected sites, we can shed new light on the other well-studied nunneries and place them in a broader and more comprehensive art historical context. However, a site like Amaseno also attests to the dire state in which most of these provincial settlements survive, testifying to the objective difficulties in studying provincial communities. Today, the convent rests on private property and is not readily accessible for study. These difficulties are further exacerbated by the sparse documentary and artistic evidence. Indeed, parchments have either been lost or are under restoration, while on-site paintings have been severely damaged. Overall, these considerations partially justify the general lack of secondary literature, and are not limited to Amaseno but to provincial realities more generally. Nevertheless, architectural remains and reconstructions on AutoCAD allow us to consider the articulation of sacred space, especially in the context of *clausura*. The choir space at Amaseno communicated directly with the conventual complex. This disposition is traceable to several Clarissan settlements in Central Italy. It would appear that in Clarissan communities there was a pattern in choir arrangements that entailed a room overlooking the church; and although connected to a later chronology, a complex like Santa Maria Donnaregina in Naples and its suspended choir overlooking the altar springs to mind. By all means I exclude direct contact between these two settlements, which nonetheless share analogous articulations of space in response to the shared need for enclosure. In particular, this solution provided nuns access to the church and the liturgical service in compliance to the promulgation of their rule and the *Periculoso*. As previously stated, the study of greater Latium and of peripheral convents furthers our understanding of conventual complexes in Rome and in Central Italy in general.

4. *A New Manifesto for the Mendicant Order: San Pietro in Vineis, Anagni*

The town of Anagni, south of Rome in the modern province of Frosinone, underwent a period of great prosperity between the pontificates of Gregory IX and Boniface VIII.[79] Both popes were natives of the town and frequently resided there. This inevitably gave rise to an influx of cardinals, bishops, and civil dignitaries from the Roman Curia. During the thirteenth century, Anagni flourished as one of the most vibrant religious, political and economic centres in Latium, rivalling and then replacing Viterbo as the principal base of the Apostolic See outside of Rome.[80] Several factors contributed to the town's growing popularity. By the second quarter of the thirteenth century, Viterbo had become a hostile battleground between the Roman baronial class and the local population. The former was eager to consolidate a state of political supremacy over this geographically strategic standpoint. This prompted Frederick II (1194-1250) to finance the independence of Viterbo, thus securing an imperial stronghold in northern Latium, in the Tuscia region.[81] During the schism between the Emperor and Gregory IX, the latter was forced to flee from Viterbo and seek refuge in his hometown.[82]

Due to its proximity to Subiaco and Montecassino, the Benedictine influence on Anagni was consistently strong.[83] However, a Franciscan community was also on site by 1219.[84] This is corroborated by a bequest dated 25 October 1219, made by Ugolino cardinal of Ostia (future Pope Gregory IX) in favour of his nephew, and witnessed by five Franciscan friars in Anagni.[85] Rinaldo bishop of Ostia and Velletri, nephew of Gregory IX, and future Pope Alexander IV (1254-1261), was

---

79. Caraffa, "Visite pastorali nel Lazio Meridionale", pp. 245-248; F. Caraffa, *Il monastero di S. Chiara in Anagni dalle origini alla fine dell'Ottocento*, Anagni, Istituto di Storia e di Arte del Lazio Meridionale - Centro di Anagni, 1985, p. 29; V. Fiocchi Nicolai, *Anagni cristiana e il suo territorio*, Tivoli, Tored, 2014; A. De Magistris, *Istoria della città e S. Basilica cattedrale d'Anagni*, Rome, nella stamperia di San Michele, 1749, p. 101; A. Panza, "Anagni nel XIII secolo. Iniziative edilizie e politica pontificia", *Storia della città*, 6 (1981), p. 62.

80. *Bonifacio VIII. Ideologia e azione politica. Atti del convegno organizzato nell'ambito delle celebrazioni per il VII centenario della morte*, ed. by M. Andaloro, Acts of the conference (Vatican City, 26-28 April 2004), Rome, Istituto Storico Italiano per il Medioevo, 2006, p. 59.

81. T.C. van Cleve, *The Emperor Frederick II of Hohenstaufen. Immutator Mundi*, Oxford, Oxford University Press, 1972, pp. 541-598.

82. O. Capitani, "Gregorio IX", in *Enciclopedia dei Papi*, 2, Rome, Istituto della Enciclopedia Italiana, 2000, pp. 379-391.

83. Caraffa, *Il monastero di S. Chiara*, p. 56.

84. C. Mengarelli, "La presenza monastica ad Anagni", *Rivista cistercense*, 31 (2014), p. 247.

85. D'Alatri, "Gli insediamenti francescani del Duecento", pp. 290-316.

closely tied both to Anagni and its Franciscan community.[86] It is no coincidence that on 26 September 1255, only two years after Saint Clare's death, he solemnly canonized her in the cathedral of Anagni.[87] Moreover, during his pontificate Alexander IV retained the title of protector of the Franciscans. His actions were primarily directed towards strengthening ties between the Friars and the Clarissans.

The nunnery of San Pietro in Vineis was founded during the pontificate of Alexander IV, during or immediately after the insertion of Clare into the catalogue of saints in 1255. Although Father Pratesi dates its foundation to the year 1253, he offers no documentary evidence to support this claim.[88] It is therefore more likely that the nunnery was erected in honour of the saint's canonization (in 1255 or 1256).[89] Even before the sanctification of Clare, the Clarissans were established in the church of San Biagio at Anagni, they subsequently transferred to San Cesareo and finally settled in San Pietro just outside Porta Cerere by 1256.[90] The Clarissan nunnery in Anagni is the second oldest female Franciscan house in Latium (Alatri being the oldest, founded ca. 1233-1244). It remains unclear whether a Benedictine monastery preceded the Clarissan occupation; however, despite not providing any solid bibliographical evidence, Alessandro Bianchi supports this claim.[91] Citing eighteenth-century sources, he asserts that before becoming a Clarissan convent, San Pietro in Vineis was actually a male Benedictine monastery,[92] while Romano and Caraffa refute this possibility.[93] San Pietro in Vineis is mentioned for the first time in a bequest dated 1193, in which Rogerius prior of the church of San Pietro received an endowment from Giovanni, archbishop of Palestrina, and native of Alatri.[94] Rogerius is identified with the title *priorem*, but given the lack of documentation confirming the presence of a male monastic community, this is not sufficient proof to support Bianchi's claim. It does nevertheless testify to the Clarissan habit of settling in pre-existing buildings.[95] Following the tradition of San Damiano, this trend in Latium was quite frequent as is testified by numerous settlements, such as San Sebastiano at Alatri and Sant'Angelo at Amaseno.

86. S. Sibilia, *Alessandro IV (1254-1261)*, Anagni, La Cassa Rurale, 1961, p. 53.
87. Sibilia, *Bonifacio VIII*, p. 53.
88. Pratesi, "Le Clarisse in Italia", pp. 339-377.
89. Zappasodi, *Sorores*, p. 26; S. Romano, "Gli affreschi di San Pietro in Vineis", in *Il Collegio Principe di Piemonte e la chiesa di San Pietro in Vineis in Anagni*, ed. by M. Rak, Anagni, Indap, 1997, p. 101.
90. Rak, "Vedere, ricordare, raccontare", p. 21; Federici, "I francescani in Anagni", pp. 442-443; A papal bull by Alexander IV dated 12th January 1256 grants privileges to the nuns of San Pietro; this has been lost and transcribed in copy dated 1377, *Bullarium Franciscanum*, IV, p. 585, n.1472, cited in Zappasodi, *Sorores*, p. 26.
91. Romano, "Gli affreschi", p. 101.
92. A. Bianchi, "Affreschi duecenteschi nel S. Pietro in Vineis in Anagni", in *Roma anno 1300*, p. 379.
93. Caraffa, *Il monastero di S. Chiara*, p. 49; Romano, "Gli affreschi", p. 101.
94. Caraffa, "Visite pastorali nel Lazio Meridionale", p. 49; Romano, "Gli affreschi", p. 101.
95. Romano, "Gli affreschi", p. 101: "bisogna probabilmente pensare che qui priore avesse valore di 'rettore'; ruoli e funzioni potevano essere, all'epoca, più complessi e sfuggenti di quanto noi oggi ci aspettiamo e siamo abituati a vedere".

The *sorores* resided in the nunnery from the second half of the thirteenth century until 1556 when the building was used as an artillery post in the war between the Caraffa family and Philip II (1527-1598).[96] As a result, the community was relocated to the convent of Santa Chiara inside the city walls[97] and San Pietro in Vineis was annexed to the Capuchins in 1575.[98] The simple architectonic plan of the church, which consists of three naves composed of five bays with barrel vaults sustained by pilasters and terminating in a single apse, appears to indicate a twelfth-century construction. Overall, the edifice has stylistic links with other buildings in the Latium region, such as Casamari or the cathedral of Priverno, respectively dated to the second half of the twelfth century and 1205. Both are preceded by a three-arched portico crowned by a triangular pediment testifying to the influence of Cistercian architecture in southern Latium. The arched portico is reached through a steep staircase, built during the restorations carried out by Alberto Calza Bini in the 1930s. Radical refurbishments during the Fascist Era transformed the nunnery into the Collegio Principe di Piemonte and destroyed much of the medieval fabric. In addition to the church, the only surviving portion is the two-story addition adjacent and surmounting the right nave which opens onto a modern cloister today.

It is likely that the nuns adapted the existing church to the needs prescribed by their rule. The imposition of a rigid *clausura* implied a staunch separation between the religious community, the laity and the officiating clerics. This was especially important during the celebration of the liturgy. Although a large portion of the convent's medieval fabric was lost during the 1930s restorations, when placed in context with other Clarissan settlements in southern Latium, Anagni offers a valuable comparative example of female monastic architecture during the thirteenth century. The church itself, and the adjacent extension on the right, are the only surviving portions of the medieval nunnery today (Figs. 47-48). This part of the convent consists of two floors. Today, there is a corridor at ground level, which extends for the length of the church's exterior nave and opens into one of the arms of the modern cloister. The walls are decorated with devotional paintings, which span from the thirteenth to the fifteenth centuries. These frescoes represent two images of the Madonna and Child accompanied by saints, an image of Saint Peter with a donor in one case, and the Stigmatization of Saint Francis in the other. Votive panels were extremely common in conventual complexes. The image of the two donors, a laywoman with the Madonna and Child and a nun, likely a member of the congregation, attests to the role of women in commissioning art works. What is particularly striking is not so much the artistic quality, which is unsophisticated and not particularly innovative, but the presence of women depicted alone without a male counterpart. This is rather impressive at this juncture. Another interesting detail of these frescoes is the fictive ashlar

96. Caraffa, "Visite pastorali nel Lazio Meridionale", p. 55.
97. *Ibid.*
98. Rak, "Vedere, ricordare, raccontare", p. 13.

masonry wall in the upper band of the Madonna and Child panels. This same pattern may be viewed in the nuns' choir (found in the room directly above) and is also visible in the choir/oratory at San Sebastiano at Alatri. This design is suggestive of an enclosed space and is not particularly appropriate for the wall of a cloister. I am tempted to agree with Bruzelius that, as at San Damiano, there was a succession of ancillary rooms "as choirs reflecting the arrangements found in churches to which the cells of recluses were attached [...] these often took the form of small rooms open to a church through grated windows".[99]

A recessed room, directly above the right nave and measuring approximately 17x4 m, is found on the upper floor to the left of this corridor. This space features an impressive fresco depicting a Passion cycle and a recessing niche likely used to display a monstrance for the consecrated Eucharist.[100] From an architectonic standpoint San Pietro in Vineis reflects a number of trends which recur in Clarissan conventual complexes throughout Latium. From the surviving evidence collected at San Sebastiano at Alatri, Sant'Angelo at Amaseno, the Santuario di Borgo San Pietro at Petrella Salto and San Pietro at Tuscania, we may assert that, as far as Latium is considered, Clarissan choir spaces were almost always positioned in a suspended room overlooking the church. The only surviving instance which I know of in Latium, where the choir of a Clarissan community is positioned at ground level alongside the church, is Santa Rosa at Viterbo. This is consistent with San Damiano and Santa Chiara at Assisi, both of which have choirs on the same level as the church. Nevertheless, San Damiano had a suspended oratory over the apse which connected to it directly through ventilation canals. To the best of my knowledge, the only other conventual complex in Latium with a suspended choir which cannot be securely identified as a Clarissan house is San Nicola di Trisulti. The lack of documentation may indeed suggest that this was not a female Cartusian settlement, as Danesi has suggested, but a Clarissan one.[101] As we have seen, the Benedictine house of Sant'Angelo in Orsano possessed an iconostasis but from the church's remains it is unclear whether there was also a suspended choir. Outside of Latium, the most celebrated example of a suspended choir which has survived with its pictorial decoration intact is of course Santa Maria Donnaregina in Naples. As in Anagni, the fresco cycle in Naples includes a Passion cycle and a Last Judgment. Given that the nuns could not view the mass, these were deemed appropriate subjects for the congregations in order to meditate on the sufferings of Christ. What is particularly significant for San Pietro is the survival of the pictorial programme, which gives us a glimpse into the decorative ambition of these communities. In contrast to other choirs in Latium's Clarissan

---

99. Bruzelius, "Hearing is Believing", p. 85.
100. Zappasodi, *Sorores*, p. 27; C. Jäggi, U. Lobbedey, "Church and Cloister: The Architecture of Female Monasticism in the Middle Ages", in *Crown and Veil*, pp. 109-131.
101. Danesi, "San Nicola di Trisulti", pp. 157-159. Indeed, Danesi herself highlights the architectural resemblances between the San Nicola and San Sebastiano at Alatri, ultimately deriving these analogies from the shared model of San Damiano at Assisi.

settlements where we usually find a patchwork of votive images (Borgo San Pietro, San Sebastiano at Alatri), the cycle here is intact.

San Pietro in Vineis and its ambitious decorative programme reflects a visual rendition of the Clarissan dogma: *clausura*, prayer and poverty. The frescoes were first presented by Bianchi in 1983 at the International Conference on Medieval Studies at the Università degli Studi di Roma La Sapienza. They were subsequently discussed more extensively in Margret Boehm's doctoral thesis (awarded in 1995, published 1999), published by Romano in 1997 after restorations promoted by the Banca di Anagni and again by Zappasodi in 2018.[102] While the paintings in the church predate the Clarissan occupation, the presence of a haloed Saint Clare in the frescoes in the room above the modern cloister, which represent a Passion cycle, the Stigmatization of Saint Francis and Three Saints, fix the post quem date to 1255, the year she was canonized by Alexander IV via the papal bull *Clara Claris praeclara* in the cathedral of Anagni. By considering both the subject matter of the paintings and their location, an attempt will be made to hypothesise the original function of this space.[103] What is apparent at first glance is that this environment, which was originally just a loft space over the church, was adapted to satisfy the immediate needs of the new community. As stated, these were primarily geared towards separating them from the laity and maintaining a rigid *clausura*. Although this room was at first identified as the nunnery's refectory, it is more likely that it functioned as the community's choir.[104] This is evident both from the space itself and the decorative program on its walls. As in other Clarissan nunneries, the choir is suspended over the church and "communicates" with it through small slit windows.

The Passion cycle is composed of ten scenes (with a total area of 12x1 m). It does not end with the Last Judgment but with a panel depicting Three Saints. The scenes are bordered by a red, white and blue band. The tones that prevail are blue, red ochre and brown with a predominance of earthy tones. The cycle begins with the Entry into Jerusalem, which despite being badly damaged is still legible.[105] The city, represented by its walls, arched gate and towers is clearly identified by the inscription HIERVSALEM. One of the four standing characters holds a scroll, which reads OSSAN FILOP DAVID (Mathew, 21, 9).[106] Christ is seated on a donkey followed by two apostles and preceded by Peter and John. Two children solemnly lay out

---

102. Refer to footnotes above for Bianchi, "Affreschi duecenteschi nel S. Pietro in Vineis in Anagni", and Romano, "Gli affreschi"; M. Boehm, *Wandmalerei des 13. Jahrhunderts im Klarissenkloster S. Pietro in Vineis zu Anagni Bilder fur die Andacht*, Munster, Lit, 1999; Zappasodi, *Sorores*, pp. 26-31.

103. Others have already said this including Bruzelius, "Hearing is Believing", p. 86; Romano, "Gli affreschi", p. 106; Zappasodi, *Sorores*, p. 27; all these authors suggest it was used as a choir.

104. Romano, "Gli affreschi", p. 106: Romano states that local sources without giving further specifications identified this space as a refectory, however, all scholars who have published the frescoes including Romano herself, Bianchi and Boehm identify this room as a choir.

105. The scene before this is completely illegible but most likely represented the *Dinner in Bethany*, Romano "Gli affreschi", p. 108; Zappasodi, *Sorores*, p. 26.

106. Mathew, 21, 9: "Turbae autem, quae praecedebant eum et quae sequebantur, clamabant dicentes: Hosanna filio David! Benedictus, qui venit in nomine Domini! Hosanna in altissimis!".

their coats on the road to pave the way for Christ. The Entry is followed by the Last Supper, portraying the moment in which Christ announces his betrayal by one of the apostles (John, 13, 26-27). The scene takes place beneath a detailed architectural complex. This is constituted by a tower-like construction flanked by two lodges, sustained by arches over columns. Excluding Judas, all the apostles are represented on the far side of the table. A clear attempt has been made to individualise the poses and physiognomies of each character. The white cloth over the table creates a dramatic contrast separating it from the rest of the scene, which is characterized by the use of darker tones.

This scene is followed by a representation of the Washing of the Feet (John, 13, 9). The latter unravels beneath an extremely elaborate architectural backdrop composed of Solomonic columns, arches and towers. Christ is depicted washing Peter's feet. As Peter watches him, he touches his head in a gesture of dismay. The Washing of the Feet is followed by the Arrest of Jesus. Here, the scene is dominated by the kiss of Judas, while Peter and Malchus are represented on the left. This painting is highly evocative and dramatic. The Jews are identified through the use of caricature types. Without any apparent sequential continuity, the Flagellation of Christ and Christ in front of Pilate follow.[107] The latter is portrayed like a thirteenth-century magistrate. In the former, Jesus is tied to a column with a Corinthian capital, his body marked by wounds. It is quite curious that this scene, which depicts two different episodes in the trial of Jesus, does not have an architectural backdrop.

From Christ's Judgment, we move directly to the Deposition. The absence of the Crucifixion, pivotal to all Passion cycles, may be attributed to the original presence of a wooden cross inside the nuns' choir.[108] Although we have no tangible proof of this, it remains a very viable hypothesis. Like the Franciscans, the Poor Clares had a special devotion towards the Crucifixion as testified by the miraculous crucifix at San Damiano moved into the chapel of San Giorgio in Santa Chiara at Assisi. At Anagni, a Crucifixion may be found in the choir but it was painted after the Passion cycle in a separate cornice with a fake wall background.[109] We must

---

107. Although surely there is a broad narrative sequence of Gospels being observed in this cycle.

108. Bianchi, "Affreschi duecenteschi nel S. Pietro in Vineis in Anagni", p. 383; Romano, "Gli affreschi", p. 110. Further proof of this is given by Zappasodi, *Sorores*, pp. 92-93, who states: "per la sua importanza eccezionale, la Croce di San Damiano esercitò un fascino significativo su diversi insediamenti femminili, imponendosi rapidamente come un modello da seguire. Si spiega così la fortuna perdurante incontrata in contesti simili dall'iconografia arcaizzante del *Christus triumphans*, cui si attennero anche pittori dalla sintassi tutt'altro che attardata. [...] Con la croce di San Damiano il Tabernacolo dei Crociati costituiva un *ensemble* autorevole, presto replicato in altri monasteri femminili. Lo stesso Rainaldetto licenziò per le Clarisse di Matelica – il più antico insediamento femminile francescano delle Marche – una tavola gemella [...] in *pendant* con una croce dipinta consapevolmente esemplata sul crocefisso di San Damiano". In 1253 when Saint Clare died her body was transferred from San Damiano to San Giorgio. Her community followed her relics the same year and the miraculous crucifix likely followed: Zappasodi, "Intus Dictum", p. 134.

109. Bianchi, "Affreschi duecenteschi nel S. Pietro in Vineis in Anagni", p. 383; Romano, "Gli affreschi", p. 110.

presume that a painted panel crucifix, possibly a portable image, which was lost alongside other mobile liturgical apparatuses used during the celebration of mass, was present.[110] Indeed, it would have been quite unusual for the culminating point of this narrative sequence to be discarded without a proper alternative. Alternatively, as suggested above, the painter condensed the iconography of the Crucifixion with that of the Last Judgement by substituting John the Baptist with John the Evangelist. The Deposition scene is overly dramatic and takes place in front of a cross with diagonal arms. Christ's dead body lies inside a sarcophagus. Joseph of Arimathea, Nicodemus, and John the Evangelist can be seen on the left. Meanwhile the right features the three Marys and a fourth woman who crosses over into the next scene, the Descent into Limbo. Christ is depicted with a banner while taking Adam – positioned in front of Eve and Saint John the Baptist – by the arm. The two crowned figures on the right are David and Solomon. Christ's figure is extraordinarily dynamic: while grabbing Adam's arm he also steps over the broken sepulchres under which a diabolical figure lies.

This is followed by the *Noli Me Tangere* in which Mary Magdalene speaks to Christ identifying him as RABONI, or master, while Jesus is represented with a scroll bearing the legend MARIA NOLI ME TA[N]GE[RE] (John, 20, 17). The scene of the Mission of the Apostles is a curious iconographic mix of the Ascension and the Pentecost. Christ is depicted behind an altar holding an open book where the phrase EGO SU VIA can be read. He is surrounded by the apostles and an articulate architectural backdrop. The latter is composed by arches, columns, towers and windows, which are clustered together to emphasize Christ's cruciform halo. The cycle terminates with the Last Judgment. An enthroned Christ is depicted between two encircled half-length portraits of Mary and Saint John the Evangelist (the presence of the former recalls the traditional iconography of the Crucifixion, indeed by substituting the Baptist with the Evangelist this might possibly explain the absence of a Crucifixion scene altogether in the Passion cycle), and two angels holding trumpets. The fact that the Virgin and John are depicted in roundels is also significant. This places them on a different plane separated from the rest of the scene, almost bearing the status of icons. On the left, the blessed are depicted like a group of ecclesiastics, while on the right, the damned are engulfed in flames. The judged souls are represented directly alongside the open sepulchres. The abbess of the nunnery and the bishop of Anagni – either Pandolfo (1237-1257) or Giovanni Comparte (1257) – are shown kneeling beside Christ's throne with their hands joined in prayer.

While Bianchi and Romano confidently identify the kneeling figure as the bishop of Anagni, in her PhD dissertation Margaret Boehm reads this figure as a portrait of Pope Alexander IV.[111] She affirms that the abbess of the convent should be rightly identified as the pope's sister Agnes.[112] These assumptions are largely

---

110. Bianchi, "Affreschi duecenteschi nel S. Pietro in Vineis in Anagni", p. 383; Romano, "Gli affreschi", p. 110.
111. Boehm, *Wandmalerei des 13*, p. 211.
112. *Ibid.*

based on Alexander IV's relation with the Poor Clares and the headpiece worn by the donor in the Last Judgment panel, described by Boehm as a double pointed mitre (also depicted in the crowd of the blessed). However, by 1150 the use of the mitre had also spread to bishops throughout the Latin church.[113] Although fascinating, her claim remains somewhat hypothetical. Next to the abbess, a small portrait of a friar – possibly in charge of confessing the community and performing the liturgical service – can be identified. It is worth noticing that the abbess is portrayed to the right of the Enthroned Christ in a position of honour and directly below the Virgin. Although her role as the patron of the fresco cannot be determined on the basis of surviving documents, her position and her identical dimensions to the bishop of Anagni suggest that she had a degree of authority in the commissioning of the painting.

Two scenes which have no direct link to the Passion cycle follow the Last Judgment. One is the Stigmatization of Saint Francis, the other is a panel depicting Three Saints (Figs. 49-50). Given the cycle's early chronology, the 1250s, in strictly iconographic terms the former is particularly advanced. The fresco depicts Saint Francis receiving the stigmata from a flying seraph during his prayer on mount La Verna. Francis is surrounded by a group of friars. The first one directly behind him can be identified as Saint Anthony through an inscription. Although the painting has suffered some damage one can still identify a halo. As a pendant for Saint Francis, we may view Saint Clare followed by two nuns. In the lower register a friar and possibly the abbess of San Pietro in Vineis can be seen. This panel is extraordinarily significant and may almost be viewed as a manifesto for the order.

Indeed, in contrast to a historiographic perspective, which views religious women as being segregated and enclosed, this painting would appear to demonstrate a very different scenario. Here, men and women coexist in a peaceful setting under the canons of the same rule. If we attribute it to the third quarter of the thirteenth century, this idyllic scenario of coexistence between male and female religious experience is quite exceptional. As far as Franciscan and Clarissan art is considered, I am not aware of any other representation of this kind. Under the Franciscan and Clarissan habit, men and women are equal with no hierarchical supremacy present. In a context where segregation is continuously marked and underlined by architecture, this position of equality between the genders is noteworthy. Does this ultimately further our knowledge of medieval religious art towards a more neutral and unbiased reading of primary sources? Another important factor to underline is the dual presence of the abbess of the community who appears twice in this cycle. This may indicate that she had some sort of role in the commissioning of the paintings. Moreover, given that this space has been identified as a choir we know for a fact that its viewers were exclusively the nuns of San Pietro (possibly including the confessors and priests who administered

---

113. V. D'Avino, *Cenni storici sulle chiese arcivescovili, vescovili e prelatizie (nullius) del Regno delle Due Sicilie*, Naples, Ranucci, 1848, p. 331.

communion). This spectatorship reinforces the message of unison between the Friars and the Poor Clares, which in turn confirms the political measures taken by Pope Alexander IV. This idyllic view was very far from reality, male members of the order were often quite hesitant in accepting roles as confessors or spiritual leaders of female communities.[114] Indeed, Alexander IV actively promoted contact between the male and female branch of the order. This concept appears to be reinforced in the last panel which depicts *Saint Benedict, Saint Scolastica and Saint Aurelia* (the last a local saint), with three adoring figurines at their feet – namely a laywoman, a nun and a friar.

The cycle has been stylistically linked to the work of the Terzo Maestro di Anagni and to the frescoes in the basilica of San Nilo in Grottaferrata. In his article on the crypt of the Duomo of Anagni, Pietro Toesca was among the first to make a stylistic analogy between the Terzo Maestro and the paintings at San Pietro.[115] During the restoration at the *badia* of Grottaferrata, Carlo Bertelli identified a painter from the *entourage* of the Terzo Maestro as being responsible for both the execution of these panels and those in the passage connecting the crypt of the Duomo di Anagni to the chapel of Saint Thomas Becket.[116] Conversely, Miklòs Boskovits refuted the connection between the San Pietro and the Terzo Maestro claiming that the former accentuated archaic forms and gestures and therefore predated the frescoes in the cathedral.[117] Bertelli's claim is supported by Bianchi, Francesco Gandolfo[118] and Romano, in her latest monograph on the convent. They argue that this artistic personality was likely formed inside the workshop of the Terzo Maestro of Anagni but was a distinct painter nonetheless. His work is traceable at Grottaferrata, in the Duomo of Anagni, and in San Pietro in Vineis. As far as chronology is considered, the presence of Saint Clare with a distinctively drawn halo should fix a *post quem* date to 1255, the year of her canonization by Alexander IV in the cathedral of Anagni. In relation to the fresco depicting Saint Francis receiving the stigmata, Romano fixes a *terminus ante quem* to 1263, when the *Legenda Maior* was presented.[119] Bonaventure's text describes how the Seraphim revealed himself to Saint Francis as a manifestation of the Crucified Christ. Given Anagni's ties to Rome and Assisi, this episode would have been noted by the patron responsible for the execution of the frescoes who would have likely altered the present iconography. Zappasodi refutes this claim stating that iconographical prototypes of the *Legenda Maior* were only established after Giotto's codification of the text in painting in the Upper Church at Assisi.[120] The fact that the monumental

114. Hamburger, "Art, Enclosure and the *Cura Monialium*", pp. 108-134.
115. P. Toesca, *Gli affreschi della Cattedrale di Anagni*, Subiaco, Iter, 1994, p. 116.
116. C. Bertelli, "La mostra degli affreschi di Grottaferrata", *Paragone*, 21, 249 (1970), p. 93.
117. M. Boskovits, "Gli affreschi del duomo di Anagni: un capitolo di pittura romana", *Paragone*, 30, 357 (1979), p. 6.
118. Matthiae, *Pittura romana*, II, p. 128.
119. Romano, "Gli affreschi", p. 110.
120. Zappasodi, *Sorores*, p. 29.

fresco cycle by the Maestro di San Francesco in the Lower Church of Assisi was painted in 1260 (possibly between 1263/1264-1266/1267), and likely constituted a model for Francis-Christ analogy, reinforces the claim that the cycle has a later dating and not necessarily an earlier chronology, around the 1250s, brought forward by Romano.[121]

Addressing the viewer's gaze in the deconstruction of artistic content is not new to scholarship on female conventual spaces in Italy.[122] However, as far as San Pietro in Vineis is concerned, it offers greater insight into the patron's (possibly the abbess of the community?) decision-making. This is one of the few instances in which we can safely assume that an artwork's location does not solely determine its *raison d'être*, but also constructs a visual lexicon for its spectator. These paintings were indeed designed *ad hoc* for nuns. Therefore, the survival of an extensive decorative program at San Pietro in Vineis allows us to further our understanding of the use of images inside spaces reserved for religious women. Indeed, this is the only example of a fairly complete decorative cycle inside a Clarissan choir in Latium. These images served a specific purpose, namely fostering the Clarissan spiritual connection with liturgical services celebrated in the main church. Additionally, the fresco program not only underscores the high-quality decoration, but also testifies to the recurring Christological subjects we encounter inside choir spaces. The Passion cycle made them empathise with the figure of the suffering Christ, while the Stigmatization likely acted as a manifesto for their newly founded order as envisioned by Pope Alexander IV. Thus, they had the twofold function of spiritually engaging the nuns during mass and expressing a precise political message. This is particularly significant when we consider that these frescoes were housed inside a space made of architectural and decorative (fictive ashlar masonry) prescriptions that reinforced precise physical reminders of women's segregation. Additionally, the position of the oratory at Anagni furthers the pattern of Clarissan choirs placed in a room overlooking the main church. As in previous examples, this might have been a recurring theme that originated from the position of the oratory in a suspended room above the apse at San Damiano. As we have witnessed for other settlements, this nunnery acted as an ideal model emphasising the importance of architectural norms at Assisi in the iconography of Clarissan convents in Latium. Therefore, it would appear that although these women were placed in existing settlements, these were coherently and systematically adjusted to address enclosure.

121. J. Cannon, "Redating the Frescoes by the Maestro di S. Francesco at Assisi", in *Survivals, revivals, rinascenze. Studi in onore di Serena Romano*, ed. by N. Bock, I. Foletti and M. Tomasi, Rome, Viella, 2017, pp. 445-446; Romano "Gli affreschi", p. 111 states: "Per mio conto su base stilistica, ma sopra tutto perché credo che la decorazione del locale sia stato un fatto immediatamente legate all'ingresso delle suore nel monastero e alla santificazione di Chiara, l'anno 1256 è ben indicativo della datazione più plausibile, e andrà superato, semmai, di pochissimo".

122. Bruzelius, "Nuns in Space", pp. 53-74.

5. *Treasures under Water: The Nunnery of Santa Filippa Mareri, Borgo San Pietro*

The nunnery of Borgo San Pietro founded by Saint Filippa Mareri, a disciple of Saint Clare, was originally found in the province of Rieti in Borgo San Pietro.[123] This is a hamlet of the municipality of Petrella Salto, on the right bank of the Salto Lake, right in the heart of the region kown as Cicolano. Like the rest of the village of Borgo San Pietro, the building currently housing the religious community was rebuilt on a different site during the second half of the twentieth century. This massive reconstruction came about as a result of the planning of the hydroelectric dam built during the Fascist period. Apart from the nunnery of Acquaviva, Borgo San Pietro is considered to be the oldest Clarissan settlement in Latium. It was established between 1228 and 1230 by Filippa Mareri who died in 1236.[124] Filippa was the daughter of Filippo Mareri and Imperatrice from the town of Montanea, sister of Ruggero of Montanea. She had three siblings: Tommaso, Gentile and a sister who joined her community at San Pietro.[125] Through a bequest by her brothers, Filippa inherited the existing monastery of San Pietro de Molito and Villa Casardita, a village in the valley of Vallebona castle, which bordered the nunnery.[126] Filippa is acknowledged in secondary sources as a *Francescana Feudataria* because of her land holdings.[127] This granted her a tangible income to provide sustenance to her community of followers.[128] In accepting this allowance, she renounced the *privilegium pauperitas*, which was so dear to Saint Clare to whom she was often

---

123. G. Passarelli, "Filippa Mareri, il culto e il suo processo", in *Santa Filippa Mareri. Atti del II Convegno Storico*, ed. by A. Cacciotti and M. Melli, Acts of the conference (Greccio, 2003), Rome, Editrici Francescane, 2007, pp. 1-56, at p. 13: "Filippa Mareri seguace di san Francesco, fondatrice del monastero di Borgo San Pietro (Rieti), pur avendo goduto di un culto *ab immemorabile* e del titolo di "santa" per secoli, è definita oggi ufficialmente 'beata, sancta nuncupata'". For the purpose of this case study we will use the title "saint".

124. P.E. Cerafogli, *La Baronessa Santa Filippa Mareri*, Vatican City, Libreria Editrice Vaticana, 1979; *Le più antiche pergamene del monastero di Santa Filippa: i Mareri, Borgo San Pietro e il Cicolano fra 12° e 14° secolo*, ed. by T. Leggio and R. Marinelli, L'Aquila, Edizione Libreria Colacchi, 2016; M. De Angelis, "Il monastero di Borgo San Pietro di Filippa Mareri. Ricostruzione storico-architettonica", in *Santa Filippa Mareri*, pp. 93-142; Marini, "Le fondazioni francescane femminili"; *Santa Filippa Mareri e il Monastero di Borgo S. Pietro nella storia del Cicolano*: atti del Convegno di studi, ed. by R. Marinelli, Acts of the conference (Petrella Salto, Borgo San Pietro, 1986), Rieti, Istituto Suore Clarisse di Santa Filippa Mareri, 1989; R. Scotti, "Il monastero di borgo S. Pietro e la storia della beata Filippa Mareri", *Lazio ieri e oggi*, 8 (2004), pp. 89-101.

125. T. Leggio, "I Mareri dalle origini alla prima metà del 14° secolo", in *Le più antiche pergamene del monastero*, p. 3.

126. *Ibid.*, p. 4.

127. "After a period as a religious recluse Filippa was convinced by her brother Tommaso to settle in the church of San Pietro di Molito accepting the title of *mater et domina* like the abbess of a traditional nunnery with its possessions and its precise political position on the territory. The Mareri were feudal lords in the Cicolano territory and Filippa had to take a religious role that was as dignified as her social rank": A. Marini, "Filippa Mareri Francescana", in *Santa Filippa Mareri*, pp. 77-92.

128. *Ibid.*

compared especially by contemporary hagiographers. The endowment of San Pietro de Molito by Tommaso and Gentile Mareri to their sister Filippa, regardless of the circumstances, was a precise strategy to transform the monastic complex into a familial reality and ultimately exercise veritable control over the dioceses of Rieti.[129] Its authority relied on the dependence of several small churches and chapels in the area, such as Sant'Andrea, San Rufizio and San Giovanni di Mareri. We are aware of these connections through a census compiled by the bishop of Rieti between 1252 and 1253.[130] This scenario seems to preclude a possible parallel between the experience of Filippa and that of Clare, to which Filippa's anonymous biographer was clearly inspired.[131] Rather, it confirms the disordered nature of the Clarissan movement during its early years. Indeed, facilitating the insertion of the two sisters into a conventual environment demonstrates Tommaso's determination to keep the baronial structure intact. Moreover, it promoted and maintained cohesion through direct familial control over the church of San Pietro de Molito and the dependent chapels, no longer mediated through the *jus patronatus*. The aristocratic character of the nunnery of San Pietro appears to be confirmed by the recruitment of *moniales* and abbesses who came from the Mareri clan.[132] According to a proposed reading, the Mareri were able to exploit strategic possibilities offered by a border region, such as the Cicolano.[133] Thus, through the restoration of ecclesiastical structures in this central Apennine basin they controlled various routes to neighbouring territories.

Following a similar pattern to the bishops of Rieti, who consolidated their power through the great Benedictine abbeys in the region; members of the Mareri family likewise maintained territorial control over their lands through San Pietro and its dependent chapels. From the outset, and in addition to the Mareri endowments, the nunnery also received the support and favour of the Apostolic See.[134] The convent suffered mixed fortunes mainly due to a lack of livelihoods, which proved insufficient to support a large community. Nevertheless, in July 1231, Gregory IX formally received the community under the authority of the Holy See, thus certifying its independence from any other ecclesiastic or lay protection.[135]

---

129. R. Brentano, "S. Filippa nel movimento religioso del XIII secolo", in *Santa Filippa Mareri e il Monastero*, pp. 27-44: 30.

130. Leggio, "I Mareri dalle origini alla prima metà del 14° secolo", p. 5.

131. The main source for Saint Filippa Mareri and her Legend comes from the liturgical office in her honor. These are nine readings taken from a *Life* probably written a few years after her death in 1236 in view of the canonization of which no manuscripts have been preserved but only the editions that today constitutes the nine readings of the *Officium Beate Philippae Mareria virginis Ciculanea* known in print from a first edition in Rome 1545 and a second in Naples in 1668: Leggio, "I Mareri dalle origini alla prima metà del 14° secolo", p. 5.

132. R. Cosma, "I documenti", in *Le più antiche pergamene del monastero*, p. 89. Cosma also provides an indexed transcription of the documents inside the convent's archive (hereafter ASFM).

133. Leggio "I Mareri dalle origini alla prima metà del 14. secolo", p. 21.

134. H. Romanin, "La scelta di Filippa Mareri nella politica equicola del suo tempo", in *Santa Filippa Mareri e il Monastero*, pp. 89-99: 86.

135. De Angelis, "Il monastero di Borgo San Pietro", pp. 95-114: 101; *Bullarium Franciscanum*, I, nos. 140-141, 147.

Therefore, one may hypothesise that the nunnery was officially structured in three years.[136] In a letter addressed to the nuns, Gregory IX refers to Filippa as *priorissa* and to the community as *sorores ecclesie Sancti Petri de Marerio ordinis pauperarum inclusarum*.[137] The nunnery's church was consecrated on 23 November 1231 by the bishop Rinaldo of Rieti.[138] In 1234, the pope intervened once again in order to establish that the convent could not exceed twelve members and certifying that it was officially part of the *Ordinis Sancti Damiani*.[139] At the death of Filippa in 1236, twenty days of indulgences were granted to those who visited the convent.[140] The founder's death inevitably initiated a series of jurisdictional conflicts with local dioceses. This was due to the fact that the nunnery's authority over specific chapels, which were on the Mareri estates, also fell under the jurisdiction of the bishop of Rieti.[141] Consequently, the expansion of the nunnery's holdings was received with suspicion by the local clergy.[142]

Moreover, one cannot underestimate the hostility, or to say the least, the general distrust caused by the affirmation of a nunnery linked to a family that had not always enjoyed good papal relations. Indeed between 1268/69 and the beginning of the *Trecento*, due to the aid lent to the Swabians by Filippo and Giovanni, sons of Tommaso, the Mareri had been deprived of their lands by Charles I of Anjou.[143] The new vassals, now owners of the castles of the original Mareri fiefs, tried to eliminate the interference of San Pietro de Molito over local churches. This was also spurred on by the attempt of local baronial families, such as the Boccamazza, to exert their privileges through the fief of Vallebona which had come in their possession to ultimately extend their dominion over Casardita, which was part of the nunnery's holdings.[144] In a parchment dated 1338, Abbess Perna Mareri together with the Franciscan friar Francesco from the church of Santa Rufina enlisted an attorney to represent the community in the legal suit regarding the Chapel of San Giovanni di Terminara.[145] This document contains a complete list of the conventual community, which comprised twenty-eight nuns whose place of origin or family name is duly cited: Philippa de Marerio, Lippa Francisci de Marerio, Cecha Francisci de Marerio, Clara *domini* Philippi de Marerio, Butia Brancaleonis, Catharina Conradi, Paulutia de Castro Veteri, Butia *domini* Branche, Catharina Andree de Branaleone, Vanna Andree de Brancaleone, Catharina de Podio Victiani, Vanna de Podio Victiani, Cecha Allevi, Bartholomutia de Burgo Sancti Petri, Andreutia de Rocha

---

136. Cosma, "I documenti", p. 97.
137. ASFM, doc. 6 (1231); Cosma, "I documenti", p. 118.
138. ASFM, doc. 7 (1231); Cosma, "I documenti", p. 118.
139. ASFM, doc. 10 (1234); Cosma, "I documenti", p. 118.
140. ASFM, doc. 12 (1236); Cosma, "I documenti", p. 120.
141. *Ibid.*, p. 90.
142. Leggio, "I Mareri dalle origini alla prima metà del 14° secolo", p. 5.
143. A. Iaconelli, "Il monastero di San Pietro de Molito", in *Le più antiche pergamene del monastero*, p. 82.
144. *Ibid.*, pp. 81-82.
145. ASFM, doc. 67 (1338); Cosma, "I documenti", p. 175.

de Saltu, Illuminata de Pennencia, Laurentai de Castro Veteri, Philippa de Rasino, Thomassutia de Vallebona, Margaritutia de Rocca Siniballi, Iola *domini* Oddonis Buccamatiis, Micarella *domini* Oddonis de Buccamatiis, Mutia Antonii de Rasino, Butia de Malialando, Pernutia Iohannis Brancaleonis, and Philippa Angeloni de Rasino.[146] This list allows us to draw some observations regarding the breadth of the territory where ties with the nunnery appear to have been consolidated. The Salto Valley is represented by six communities that were distributed on both sides of the river (Borgo San Pietro, Vallebona, Mareri, Pendenza, Poggio Vittiano, and Rocca del Salto). In addition to the Mareri, other illustrious names such as the Boccamazza and the Brancaleoni are also present. As noted above, the places mentioned on the list are largely in the territory that remained under the control of the Mareri at the beginning of the fourteenth century. Women from the Brancaleoni and Boccamazza clans also testify to the prestige the nunnery enjoyed with other families of the local and Roman nobility. While the presence of twenty-eight nuns – in contrast to the original prescription of twelve – underlines the wealth of the community, which underwent a period of great prosperity during the fourteenth century.

Before disappearing under water, the nunnery was an imposing building on the southern side of the hill dominating the village of Borgo San Pietro. It was equipped with a large perimeter wall that occupied the entire hillside sloping down the valley (Fig. 51-52). From the surviving photographs, we may deduce that the space between the wall and the nunnery was used as an orchard, while the living quarters were all concentrated on the hill summit. Moreover, the monastic complex built around the cloister expanded over time with the addition of new buildings. What is above all apparent from the pre-reconstruction photographic material is that it had significantly grown in height, dominating the environment facing the central space of the claustral wall. This development gave the monastery the appearance of a fortress, which may be read as a defensive tactic, given its location in a fairly isolated and peripheral area. The mighty bell tower and the compact mass of the tall perimeter walls appear predominant in relation to the volume of the church lying on the northern side of the building complex, which was also partially concealed by several architectonic additions.

Given that the nunnery no longer survives, it was challenging to carry out an in-depth architectural analysis of the building complex. Accessible archival material essentially consists of the survey by the Genio Civile before the flooding of the valley (Fig. 53).[147] This material, together with historical photographs, constitutes the essential data for studying the convent. It is thus possible, on the basis of this documentation, to hypothesise the various building phases for the nunnery. These may be summarized as follows: 1) adaptation of the existing

---

146. ASFM, doc. 67 (1338); Iaconelli, "Il monastero di San Pietro de Molito", p. 81.

147. ASFM, *Stato di Consistenza del Vecchio Monastero Redatto dal Genio Civile di Rieti nel 1937*; *Stato di Consistenza della Chiesa Parrocchiale di Borgo S. Pietro Eseguito dall'Ufficio del Genio Civile di Rieti 27 luglio 1940*, cartella 21, titolo III, *Edilizia e Beni immobili sez. 1 Affari generali*: cited and partially transcribed by De Angelis, "Il monastero di Borgo San Pietro".

structures of the *pievana* church of San Pietro de Molito and adjacent buildings (i.e. Villa Casardita) during the first half of the thirteenth century; 2) enlargement and reconstruction of the monastery from the fourteenth to the fifteenth centuries; 3) transformations and additions in the fifteenth and sixteenth centuries; 4) eighteenth-century refurbishments and reconstruction; 5) additions and functional transformations in the nineteenth and twentieth centuries.[148]

The first phase may be linked to the donation of San Pietro de Molito and Villa Casardita to Filippa by her brothers. Considering that the bequest took place in 1228, and that the nunnery's church was consecrated in 1231, we may assume that only minor changes took place during this time. It is likely that certain spaces were adapted to suit the needs of the community while others were built anew. In the following decades, the convent was likely refashioned following a standard Benedictine plan. This presumably came about with the formal adoption of the Clarissan rule and the protection of the Holy See. This remodelling comprised the development of conventual spaces around the perimeter of the cloister. The medieval layout of the nunnery had a north-west/south-east orientation, which applied both to the church and the conventual spaces. The Chapter hall and the refectory were found around the square cloister on the south-eastern side, the kitchens and the deposits on the south-western portion, while a fortified entrance which opened across the bell tower was placed on the north-eastern perimeter. The entrance portal was accessed through an ogival arch and an elaborately decorated wooden gate, which opened out into a room with an altar that subsequently led to the cloister. Archival photographs indicate that the cloister had an austere appearance and was characterized by low barrel-vaulted arches sustained by heavy square pilasters. Another vaulted loggia supported by smaller pilasters was located on the first floor. The nuns' cells were on the south-eastern and south-western sides, while the side adjacent to the church was occupied by an eighteenth-century choir. In fact, it is possible that a choir was here from the onset. This would not be the first example of a Clarissan nunnery in Latium with a choir overlooking the church from the cloister. Indeed, other examples such as San Pietro in Vineis at Anagni testify to this custom. Some important additions were made during the fifteenth century, such as the construction of a new refectory and a rectangular chapel (9.70x5 m) dedicated to Saint Filippa Mareri. The latter is composed of two bays and covered by a vaulted ceiling on pilasters in the first area, and a cross vault in the space adjacent to the church. This chapel was found in a liminal space on the eastern side of the complex between the ground floor and the first floor, and it communicated with the choir and the church through small grated windows. As far as the sixteenth and seventeenth centuries are concerned, no major reconstruction campaigns can be identified on the basis of surviving elements.

148. *Ibid.*, p. 107: "1) adattamento delle strutture preesistenti della chiesa pievana di San Pietro di Molito e delle costruzioni adiacenti, prima metà del secolo XIII, 2) ampliamento/ricostruzione del monastero, secoli XIII-XIV, 3) trasformazioni e aggiunte, secoli XV-XVI, 4) sopraelevazioni e rifacimenti, secolo XVIII, 5) aggiunte e trasformazioni funzionali, secoli XIX-XX".

However, the complex underwent major reconstructions and refurbishments during the eighteenth century. These affected both the nunnery and the church, which was completely refashioned and redecorated. The description by the Genio Civile also provides insights into the church's layout.[149] This originally consisted of three naves and a transept. The side naves were covered by barrel vaults and comprised two chapels one in each bay and at the crossing of the transept. It was illuminated by two windows, which opened onto the façade and inside the church. Finally, a large edifice was built on the northern side to house the school administered by the convent in the nineteenth century. The chapel of Saint Filippa Mareri was dismantled and moved to the new convent site after the flooding of the valley (Figs. 54-55). This consists of two small rooms with a barrel-vaulted ceiling on two different levels, separated by a round arch on masonry pillars. It is largely covered by wall paintings superimposed upon one another as juxtaposed panels: a practice similar to an *ex voto*, a devotional custom which was popular from the fourteenth to the sixteenth centuries. Unfortunately, documents relating to the conventual complex of Borgo San Pietro do not discuss the paintings in great detail, and tend to exclusively focus on a few elements. Thus, for example, the correspondence of Father Angelo Benedetto of Rome in 1706-1710, confessor of the community (who also engaged in the recognition of the saint's body) only describes one of the votive frescoes of the chapel in reference to the iconography of Saint Filippa.[150] The testimony provided by Father Antonio Chiappini in 1922, together with archival photographs taken before the demolition of the chapel, become invaluable sources to decode the alcove's decorative program.[151] Through Chiappini's affirmations, we know that the burial of Saint Filippa was originally found in the first span of the chapel on the left wall. Some paintings are completely ignored in the descriptions of 1922 because they were not visible at that date. Restoration work carried out on the seventh centenary of the death of the saint by the Soprintendenza of L'Aquila in 1936 uncovered a series of paintings that had been concealed by overlapping architecture.[152] In particular, the frescoes on the left wall of the first bay were finally revealed. These represented Saint Francis, Saint Catherine of Alexandria, and a cluster of nuns adoring the Virgin, a Last Supper and a Nativity scene, originally in front of the burial of the saint. Unfortunately, when the frescoes were detached in 1940, Saint Catherine and the Madonna and Child were lost. Moreover, from archival photographs, we may note that the second bay of the chapel was adorned with an image of a Crucifixion, another depiction of Saint Catherine and one of Saint Lucy.

149. De Angelis, "Il monastero di Borgo San Pietro".
150. R. Cantone, "Il ciclo pittorico della Cappella di Santa Filippa", in *Santa Filippa Mareri e il Monastero*, pp. 257-275: 257.
151. *Ibid.*
152. C. Ceschi, "Restauro dei monumenti nel Lazio (1951-1961)", *Atti dell'Accademia Nazionale di San Luca*, n.s., 1 (2010) (www.sa-Lazio.beniculturali.it/getFile.php?id=497, last accessed 03/07/2018).

The left wall of the first bay is occupied by votive images executed in various stages by different artists. The oldest frescoes are those representing the Death of the Virgin and her Coronation. Despite the absence of an architectural backdrop, the fresco is spatially effective. This is especially evident from the thrust of the throne, which is conveyed in a realistically rendered space within the composition. There is a "Giottesque" influence, which is the result of a local painterly tradition originating in Latium, Umbria and Tuscany due to the works of anonymous itinerant painters.[153] No objective element has been found to determine a precise dating for the work. The possible chronology generally spans from the *Trecento* to the first half of the fifteenth century. The only element that could be taken as the *post quem* term is the Mareri coats of arms with three pyramids crowned by roses on a vermillion backdrop.[154] The family seal originally had the heraldic element of pyramids in the red field. Here, however, it already appears with the addition of the rose, symbol granted to the Mareri by the Norman kings. This coat of arms was already in use at the beginning of the fourteenth century.[155] Surviving documentation indicates that at the beginning of the *Trecento*, a certain Caterina Mareri was abbess of the convent, and that three miracles tied to Filippa's close family members also took place during this period, which might indicate a commission on their part.[156]

Another interesting panel in terms of iconography and chronology is the one representing three saints: two Franciscans and a Clarissan. In 1706, Father Angelo Benedetto explicitly discusses the panel and mentions a badly preserved inscription, which has unfortunately since gone missing.[157] He identified the words, "Saint Filippa" under the Clarissan nun, a date deciphered as 1450, recognised the saint to the left as Saint Bernardino from Siena, and revealed certain attributes of Franciscan friars in the description of the central figure beside him.[158] However, in another letter dated 1707, the same source partially modifies the description of the previous year and adds that the Franciscan priest is holding a chalice in his hands. While we may identify the female saint as Saint Filippa Mareri, it is likely that the two male figures represented are Saint Bernardino from Siena and possibly Saint Anthony from Padua. These were probably executed around the 1450s given that Bernardino is haloed making this an effective *terminus post quem*. The votive box with Saint Francis and Saint Catherine of Alexandria with a group of Clarissan nuns is perhaps slightly later in terms of chronology but still traceable to the second half of the fifteenth century. This includes the patron on the left side of the chapel's presbytery area. Domenico Santarelli, who was

---

153. Cerafolgi, *La Baronessa*, pp. 117-121; Cantone, "Il ciclo pittorico della Cappella di Santa Filippa", p. 260.
154. Cerafogli, *La Baronessa*, pp. 117-121; Cantone, "Il ciclo pittorico della Cappella di Santa Filippa", p. 257.
155. *Ibid.*, p. 262.
156. Ceschi, (1951-1961)"; Cantone, "Il ciclo pittorico della Cappella di Santa Filippa", pp. 262-264.
157. *Ibid.*, p. 260.
158. *Ibid.*

responsible for the restorations of 1934-1936, describes the group in adoration in front of a Madonna and Child.[159]

Six episodes of Saint Filippa's life are portrayed in the arch of the division arc between the two bays of the chapel itself. Finally, a Christ in Glory is depicted in the vault. The artist Panfilo Carnassai was identified as its author and dated around 1585.[160] The medallions with the Franciscan proto-martyrs, the glory of Saint Francis and the saints belonging to the Second Franciscan order may be attributed to the same artist. A new popularity of the cult of the saint re-emerged in conjunction with the Counter-Reformation.[161] The first edition of the rhythmic office in Rome with the liturgical legend of Saint Filippa was published in 1545. A new, complete and homogeneous decorative cycle was carried out in accordance with the reform.[162] This was done to fulfil an explicit didactic prescription and functioned as a clear glorification of the founding Clarissan of the Salto Valley community.

Although the original convent of San Pietro is no longer accessible, sufficient documentary evidence survives and provides an invaluable testimony for the study of female nunneries during the late medieval period. As a *Francescana Feudataria*, Filippa was forced to abandon her *privilegium pauperitas*, which was so dear to Saint Clare. As we have witnessed in Roman convents, who adopted the Isabelline rule, this was a ploy on the part of baronial clans to use nunneries as feudal hamlets to secure strategic lands. The importance of this ancient Clarissan house is further testified by the survival of documentary, pictorial as well as architectural elements. The museum dedicated to Saint Filippa Mareri, inside the reconstructed conventual complex, which houses a variety of artefacts from the primitive settlement, is of particular significance (Figs. 56-57). These include objects which were part of the liturgical furniture and of the nuns' everyday life. Amongst them the iron grill of the nuns' choir is particularly striking. This is modelled with a spiralling motif of interconnected S shaped geometries, while the central square opening was probably used by the officiating priests to administer the sacrament of the Holy Communion to the congregation. Another object which survived the flooding is the fifteenth-century wooden door at the entrance of the convent. This was decorated with geometrical motifs placed in square cornices. Finally, the processional cross, probably dating to the seventeenth century, testifies to the high quality of objects commissioned for religious women; thus helping us reshape the role of nuns as key players in the production of art and architecture. Borgo San Pietro offers a comparative context for other nunneries, which survive in a less fortunate state, especially in so far as objects from the community's daily activities are concerned. This is true also for Roman settlements which have been thoroughly transformed over centuries, causing the loss of a great deal of medieval material. Indeed, it is ironic that a convent that was purposefully destroyed and flooded would ultimately be the keeper of several medieval vestiges.

159. *Ibid.*, p. 261.
160. *Ibid.*
161. *Ibid.*, p. 263.
162. *Ibid.*, p. 270.

6. *Comparing Clarissan Conventual Communities: A Few Considerations*

As with the section pertaining to Benedictine convents, I conducted a gazetteer on Clarissan nunneries in Latium, progressing with an in-depth analysis of settlements that had the most significant architectural, artistic or archival data. These four case studies represent the best attested female settlements relating to the Mendicant order in the region during the period covered by this research. The relationship of these convents to secondary literature is uneven; while some nunneries have been thoroughly published, others remain largely unknown. Indeed, while convents at Borgo San Pietro and Amaseno are off the beaten track, Alatri and Anagni have been comprehensively analysed by secondary literature. Archival sources were particularly decisive for the study of Borgo San Pietro, highlighting the crucial relationship between convents and baronial clans in the claim for territorial expansion of feudal hamlets. While the presence of artworks, inside choirs at Alatri and Anagni, encouraged discussions tied to patronage, gender, gaze and nunnery art. From this limited survey, it would appear that conventual patronage was attested in the form of devotional portraits, either by single members of the congregation, or, by the entire community. Indeed, I verified the presence of this genre at Alatri, Anagni and Borgo San Pietro. Overall, however, there was an objective difficulty in determining the real decisional power of women in the patronage context. I was able, through surviving architectural elements, to detect a *fil rouge* between these settlements and the first Clarissan house at Assisi. Analogies with San Damiano became evident by reasoning around proposed reconstructions on AutoCAD created through existing plans and on-site investigations. From the selected case studies pertaining to Clarissan settlements in Latium, I have detected a consistent pattern of choir arrangements. As far as these four nunneries are concerned, the choir or oratory was originally found in a suspended room adjacent to the main body of the church. Was this architectural trend, determined by the position of the oratory in San Damiano over the presbytery, reserved for the adoration of the Holy Host? We cannot determine this with certainty, and although the selection of case studies was limited, this possibility seems a viable one. On the other hand, when we encountered suspended choirs on counter-façades in remote outposts like Amaseno, other celebrated examples of Clarissan architecture such as Santa Maria Donnaregina in Naples came to mind.

As previously mentioned, two of the selected convents, namely Alatri and Anagni, have extensive surviving fresco cycles. This is particularly striking especially when we consider that these settlements were found in peripheral centres. Indeed, Roman Clarissan convents have preserved almost nothing of their original decoration underlying the importance of examining regional settlements in the context of religious women. Moreover, the extent and quality of the surviving pictorial decorations offer further proof of the role of nunneries as strategic social, political and economic outposts in suburban areas. This is particularly evident in two frescoes, namely the Stigmatization of Saint Francis at Anagni and in the donor portraits of Bishop John V and Cardinal Stefano Conti at Alatri. Especially at Anagni, what is really quite exceptional, is the portrayal of what would appear to be a manifesto of the order as envisioned by Alexander IV. We are aware that in reality Franciscan monks were rather reticent when it came to spiritually/materially assisting Clarissan nuns. To my knowledge, this is an original isolated iconographic formula in the region and rather extraordinary in this respect.

As demonstrated by Borgo San Pietro and Amaseno, it is not only the well-preserved convents that further our understanding of the female religious experience. Documentary evidence in the convent of the Beata Filippa Mareri was crucial to reiterate our initial hypothesis that nunneries acted as effective outposts to secure territorial claims on the part of baronial families. While Amaseno unveiled a rather original architectural solution to the problem of *clausura*, suggesting that regional convents were not as peripheral as their dire state would seem to indicate. Indeed, they contribute to further our understanding of the Clarissan order particularly in so much as the Roman convents have been completely refashioned and maintain almost nothing of their original medieval *facies*. Both architectonically and artistically, the lesser-known nunneries turn out to be strategic in retracing the first phases of the female Franciscan experience. Nevertheless, there were undeniable objective difficulties in the study of convents in this regional context. For the most part, these settlements have sparse documentary evidence which is scattered in local archives and is frequently lost, destroyed or inaccessible. In addition they are privately owned today, which makes direct access even more challenging. Finally, the moderate cultural level of these religious women has not made them the obvious recipients of patronal activities. For these reasons, Clarissan communities in Latium need to be studied in a multidisciplinary framework that allows us to examine them in a broader comparative context.

Epilogue

Can We Really Speak about Nunnery Art? Some Thoughts for Future Research

Tucked away in the heart of Rione Monti, the nunnery of San Lorenzo in Panisperna houses a tiny community of nuns to this day, namely Sister Benedetta and her two loyal attendants. These women live on the edge of poverty, their sustenance guaranteed through alimonies and a meticulously tended vegetable garden. Most of the backyard is characterized by significant portions of medieval masonry. This is not infrequent in a city like Rome, which has preserved a great deal of its historic past; nevertheless the nuns' seclusion at San Lorenzo in Panisperna leaves its visitors with the uncanny feeling of bearing witness to the promulgations of Boniface's *Periculoso*. In recent years, the analysis of female monasteries has experienced a renewed interest. However, aside from single case studies, little attention has been paid to Rome and Latium. This research has a larger scope, namely to join the ongoing debate on the role of convents within a broader social, political, urban, and artistic fabric of medieval society. At the same time, this selection of case studies has rationalised the artistic and architectonic response to the stricter need for enclosure imposed by the Curia. It has also attested the difficulty in determining the real decisional capacity of women in the patronage context. Especially in so far as religious women in Latium are considered, what is identifiable as female patronage? Is it women paying for religious things (matronage), or, men and women paying for religious things? Out of the thirteen case studies selected for this book, I identified only a few instances in which women had a direct involvement in the artistic and architectonic renewal of their own conventual complexes. This scenario is rather different when we examine female lay patrons, who are usually identified through an inscription, or a patronymic under their portrait. The anonymity behind female religious patronage suggests a different attitude towards the donation/patronage act. This is derived from our impressionistic understanding of religious women and the intrinsic need of presenting the congregation as a unified whole. Therefore, while most nunneries undertook radical refurbishments during their occupation in the Middle Ages, as far as Rome and Latium are considered we lack the necessary evidence to safely ascribe these initiatives to female agency. For example, while at

Sant'Agnese fuori le Mura the survival of an inscription and the refurbishment of private quarters testified to the community's prestige; it did not necessarily reflect its direct involvement in the thirteenth-century restoration campaigns. In fact, the extent to which the female community acted as a catalyst for the renovations of the complex was impossible to determine. It was, however, evident that the sisters could ensure that their own private conventual spaces were decorated by leading painters and in the latest style. At San Cosimato, the circumstances were slightly different: the large-scale refurbishments promoted by Abbess Cenci were recorded in the 1558 chronicle of the convent by Orsola Formicini. Having said this, we did not encounter any other evidence substantiating Formicini's claim. While the Eustachio coats of arms in the fresco preserved at San Sisto Vecchio pushed forward the hypothesis of a commission on the part of Andrea, or, Sopphia. The latter were both members of the Dominican community during the execution of the paintings. Further proof of this may be read in the depiction of a nun in the frescoed panel under the family coats of arms. In convents outside of Rome, I was able to identify devotional portraits either of single members or of the entire religious congregation (Alatri, Anagni, Castrocielo); and exceptional artworks (Anagni, Alatri, Borgo San Pietro, Montefiascone) for the community's use, but no direct evidence of patronage *per se*. For peripheral settlements, rather than detect remarkable instances of patronage, I retraced the role of conventual communities as instrumental players in the feudal rivalries between baronial clans. This was particularly true for Santa Maria in Viano in the Caetani-Conti contention, and in Borgo San Pietro in its pivotal use by the Mareri clan to assert supremacy over the dioceses of Rieti.

Although I was unable to securely identify artistic and architectonic commissions tied to the female agency of single congregations, I examined the most complete pictorial cycles in peripheral convents, namely Santa Maria del Monacato, San Sebastiano, San Pietro in Vineis and San Pietro at Montefiascone, in great detail. While this book attempted to advance existing scholarship on the female religious experience, this research was also faced with objective limitations of scarcity. As a result, several questions remain unanswered. What was the decisional power of religious women towards decorative choices inside conventual spaces? To what degree did men influence iconographic choices inside nunneries? In other words, is it acceptable to speak of female autonomy in the years of forced enclosure? Is it more accurate to think of expectations and prerogatives imposed on women by men as intermediaries, rather than initiatives promoted from within the cloister?

Is it Possible to Speak about Nunnery Art?

Undoubtedly, the loss of iconographic and documentary evidence has a crucial role in our limited understanding of the female religious experiences. Ultimately, however, the significance of these commissions lies not so much in who payed for what, but rather in women's access to specific iconographic programs. This is possibly one of the values in contextualising art in space as a vehicle to assert specific social or religious meanings.

While research on convents like Alatri and Anagni draws on the findings of pre-existing literature; the study of Castrocielo or Amaseno, for example, analysed scarcely published foundations. Indeed, there is an uneven relationship towards secondary literature. Overall, it appears that Roman convents have frequently been refurbished maintaining a smaller portion of their original medieval *facies*; while in Latium conservation of nunneries experienced mixed fortunes. Convents like San Sebastiano have preserved a great deal of their original features, while others, for instance Sant'Angelo in Orsano, survive in a dismal state. This survey also attested the relative absence of Dominican female communities outside of Rome. As Joanna Cannon rightly points out, there is an objective lack of documentation as far as these female foundations are considered.[1] Indeed, if we exclude the frescoed cycle at San Sisto Vecchio and the Lippo Vanni triptych at Sant'Aurea, there is no significant artistic output within these geographical limits pertaining to the Second order.

Nevertheless, through the study of art, architecture and written testimonies it has been possible to recover the role of female monasticism in a broader historical setting. This study has hopefully furthered the understanding of religious space especially with regard to the church and the orientation of the choir. As the liturgical heart of the convent, the choir held a particular significance inside female religious communities. This was especially the case after *Periculoso* exacerbated the consequences of forced enclosure. The effects of Boniface's promulgations must have been extreme. Women had to be *dead to the world*, forcing the female experience, be it communal or single, to adhere to more accepted norms of religious life. In these fascinating thirteen case studies we have witnessed the promulgations of *Periculoso* and its long standing impact on sacred architecture. In particular, this research focused on the liturgical use of space by female communities, the relationship between enclosure and painted images, and the organization/orientation of monastic choirs.

The study of these convents highlighted the use of architecture and its effective capacity to convey leading principles of *clausura*, namely chastity, obedience and seclusion. Through an interdisciplinary multifaceted approach, the case studies showcased the variety of solutions built to observe *clausura*. The shared need for enclosure acted as a thematic thread in the planning of these nunneries. The process of drawing and designing plans on AutoCAD forced the analysis of *clausura* both on a symbolic and spatial level. Reasoning around physical space unveiled complex patterns of female religious architecture that were not immediately apparent, ultimately producing new original findings. Given that our knowledge is still largely imprecise when it comes to women during the medieval period, reconstructions fostered a closer engagement with primary

---

1. Cannon, *Religious Poverty, Visual Riches*, pp. 9-16.

sources and uncovered designs that were not immediately detectable. Their aim was to reveal and reconstruct the internal dispositions of conventual churches which are either lost or remain inaccessible. There has been an attempt to refute excessively ideological standings and historiographies in order to maintain an empirical methodology throughout this enquiry.

To a certain extent, the deconstruction of the use of space, particularly in so far as the church was considered, followed the considerations brought forward by Gilchrist. The scholar conceives the convent as a social space where "power" is negotiated. Women had to undergo two layers of separation, first from the officiating clergy, then from the laymen attending mass. I observed a variety of solutions in response to the need for *clausura*, ranging from matroneums to iconostasis screens, identifying a consistent pattern of choir arrangements in Clarissan houses in Latium. In these settlements, choirs tend to be located in a suspended room overlooking the church. This can also be ascertained for San Silvestro in Rome where the nuns' medieval choir was most likely found in a room above the apse. Was this architectonic trend determined by the position of the oratory over the presbytery reserved for the adoration of the Holy Host at San Damiano? This cannot be determined with certainty, nevertheless, the possibility remains a fascinating one. On the other hand, when we encountered suspended choirs on counter-façades in remote outposts like Amaseno, other celebrated examples of Clarissan architecture such as Santa Maria Donnaregina in Naples came to mind. In Benedictine foundations, the choir was frequently positioned at ground level, either behind the apse by means of a *comunichino,* or, directly in front of it. Sant'Agnese fuori le Mura appears to defy this trend opting instead for a *matroneum* to house its female community. As far as the Dominican order is considered, I have engaged with a number of viable possibilities especially in so far as the single case study of San Sisto Vecchio was concerned. Even if we choose to refute Barclay Lloyd's *tramezzo* solution, it is distinctly possible that the choir was positioned on the same level as the church. This is also likely for the chosen architectural scheme at Sant'Aurea.

Can we trace a consistent architectonic relationship between these three orders and their convents? From the case studies collected in this book, the extent of the influence exercised by the Benedictines over the Clarissan and the Dominicans is not clear. Indeed, if we exclude the church space (choir), it was not always possible to reconstruct the conventual remains of these settlements. This seems to suggest that there were no fixed architectural schemes when it came to religious women. As Bruzelius rightly affirms, this trend was likely derived from the instalment of female communities in existing structures, the loss of a significant number of convents and the perishable nature of the materials used.[2] This study substantiates and offers further proof towards the scholar's claim. What we can determine with a relative degree of certainty is that the new orders adopted the rectangular space of the cloister as an organisational unit for their convents from the Benedictines. But this in itself is not surprising and it equally

---

2. Bruzelius, "Hearing is Believing", p. 54; Zappasodi, *Sorores*, p. 11.

applies to male orders. The division of the liturgical space inside the church was instead addressed by employing a number of different and profoundly original solutions.

Both in Latium (Anagni, Alatri, Montefiascone) and Rome (Sant'Agnese fuori le Mura, San Silvestro in Capite, San Sisto Vecchio) the presence of artworks inside choirs encouraged discussions tied to patronage, gender, gaze and "nunnery art". We also determined the frequent presence of Marian icons/cycles, Crucifixions (either painted or sculpted), and Christological scenes inside these spaces. As previously stated, the real agency of the patron was impossible to determine on the basis of surviving elements. We may, however, hypothesise that these iconographic prototypes were selected as a visual lexicon for the audience to follow the celebration of the religious service, or, as a means for the female community to identify with Christ and the Virgin Mary. Is it possible to secure female agency of these works based exclusively on their position inside choirs? Probably not.[3] Nevertheless, it is still important to acknowledge their role as recipients of ambitious decorative programs. This is particularly true for Anagni and Montefiascone whereby the patron/s went to impressive lengths to ensure that these spaces were embellished by leading painters in the latest styles. At Anagni, the Passion cycle made nuns empathise with the figure of the suffering Christ, while the Stigmatization possibly acted as a manifesto for their newly founded order as envisioned by Pope Alexander IV; thus, embodying the twofold function of spiritually engaging the nuns during mass and expressing a precise political message. At San Pietro in Montefiascone, the survival of the Buglioni terracotta and the fresco cycle by an artist stylistically close to Lippo Memmi was extremely noteworthy. Furthermore, I noted the presence of male and female members of the same order represented as equals under the sign of the cross: the aforementioned Stigmatization and the *Painted Cross* from San Sisto Vecchio. Both depict male and female individuals of their respective orders in a seemingly iconographic indistinctness in front of Christ. Within the strict observance of *clausura*, the presence of these artefacts is quite extraordinary.

This research has also underscored a remarkable popularity of the female branches of the Mendicant orders, especially the Clarissan. Moreover, as noted by Giulia Barone, "the success of the Mendicants seems to have been earlier as regards the female monasteries: but this is not surprising if we keep in mind that the Clarissan and the Dominicans did not differ much in their lifestyle and in the strict enclosure from the more traditional Benedictine communities, from which only a form of more 'modern' spirituality separated them".[4] As far as Rome is considered, we may ascribe their popularity to their foundation by influential members of the Curial circles. San Silvestro in Capite and San Lorenzo in Panisperna were promoted by the political activity of Giacomo Colonna; the

3. J. Gardner, "Nuns and altarpieces agendas for research", *Römisches Jahrbuch der Bibliotheca Hertziana*, 30 (1995), pp. 27-57.
4. Barone, "Margherita Colonna", p. 800.

driving force behind their foundation and their initial prosperity. Whereas San Cosimato was founded by Pope Gregory IX, a renowned supporter of the female branch of the Mendicants. The Clarissan popularity, both in Rome and in Latium in general, possibly resulted from the election of Franciscan popes first and foremost Nicholas IV. The fact that, as far as Latium is concerned, the best-preserved fresco cycles survive inside Clarissan nunneries should not be dismissed as mere chance. This would appear to highlight a special attention on part of ecclesiastical circles that gravitated around the Curia towards the endowment of Clarissan convents.

I would also like to address the significance of rural foundations in the earlier period, largely as outposts for baronial territorial claims. We have witnessed this for example in the introduction to Benedictine convents through the documentary corpus of Santa Maria in Viano. The land contestation between the Conti and the Caetani was indeed centred around the possessions of this nunnery. Something similar also occurred with the Mareri family in Rieti, who reclaimed part of the territories from the bishopry through Filippa's foundation of the convent. This is further corroborated by the level of mobility and, to a certain extent, autonomy that characterised these female communities. This changed during the fourteenth century, as testified by the frequent abandonment of rural convents in the later medieval period, due to stricter imposition of *clausura* and the desire for increased security. But what was the rhetorical value of reform? Can we ascribe this to a strategy on behalf of convents to undermine territorial hegemony? Was this the case at Sant'Angelo in Orsano which was abandoned, reconstructed and finally extinguished? San Sebastiano at Alatri suffered a similar faith ultimately passing into the hands of Giovanni Tortelli. On the contrary, is it possible that these convents were abandoned or suppressed by the municipality on false pretexts to secure territories? Was the nuns' misconduct used as an excuse by the clergy to reclaim conventual spaces?[5] I believe all of these to be viable hypotheses, however, as far as this research is considered, I have not found sufficient evidence to support these claims. Future investigations will hopefully shed new light on these problematic controversies.

For the period in question we have recounted how baronial families protected territorial hamlets by ensuring that female members of their clans joined these communities, thus indirectly accessing the convent's wealth. This is surprising if we acknowledge that remote outposts like San Luca in Guarcino housed members from the Caetani family even after Boniface's reign. In this respect, the real estate portfolios were particularly striking. In particular, San Silvestro in Capite testified to the authority exercised by the Colonna to expand their sphere of influence, through the convent, over neighbouring areas inside the city. Not only was there a wish to assert supremacy over the Orsini, but also ensure access to strategic commercial roads. This of course was also the case for the Mareri

---

5. J. Van Engen, "The 'Crisis of Cenobitism' Reconsidered: Benedictine Monasticism in the Years 1050-1150", *Speculum*, 61, 2 (1986), pp. 269-304.

clan and the establishment of Filippa's nunnery to supersede the dioceses of Rieti. Convents were effective batteries of power and prestige, something that has only been partially investigated as regards Rome and Latium. Yet, their capillary spread on strategic routes, both in and out of the city, has made this network seemingly clear. Indeed, the political authority of conventual institutions, further corroborates this.

Women's place and space during the late medieval period was undoubtedly one of profound suppression and segregation; nevertheless, this study will hopefully contribute to a fairer portrayal of their position in Rome and Latium during the Middle Ages, as limited yet active players in its society. Through the lens of patronage, accumulated evidence in this book has testified to the role of conventual realities in Latium and Rome, as culturally defining agents. I stand by the belief that female patronage cannot be treated as an exception. This claim does not solely rest on the role of extraordinary abbesses like Lucia at Sant'Agnese or Iacopa at Cosimato but rather on the variety of commissions, written testimonies and the tangible political weight testified by these convents. By contextualising nunneries in a political, social and historical framework, this pattern has become apparent. Even within the strict limits of the cloister, women were guaranteed protection and social belonging. This apparent segregation was in reality a means by which women enjoyed greater liberties in medieval society – as key players in shaping cultural and political stability during periods of profound social upheaval and change.

Appendix

Benedictine Convents in Latium (ca. 1200-1400)

ALATRI, SAN PIETRO[1]
According to a local legend, the nunnery of San Pietro, which is located in the historical city centre of Alatri, was founded by Saint Benedict himself. The oldest document concerning the nunnery is a bequest, dated 1256, in the testament of Stefano Conti. In the year 1300, Boniface VIII allowed the nuns of Santa Maria in Paliano to join the nunnery of San Pietro. It was annexed to the convent of San Luca in Guarcino between 1328 and 1329, suppressed in 1515 and reconstituted as Santissima Annunziata in 1561.

AMATRICE, SANTA CATERINA DI SCAI[2]
The nunnery of Santa Caterina was likely founded in the fourteenth century despite the fact that almost nothing of its original medieval fabric has survived. The sole documentary evidence for this period is a testamentary bequest in favor of the nunnery by Bartolomuccia di Pietro di Tommaso in 1357.

ANAGNI, SANTA CECILIA[3]
Abandoned by the fourteenth century, one of the few documents which mentions this convent in the Anagni archives is entitled, *Deputatio abbatissae monasterii S. Ceciliae ord. S. Benedicti in Monte Anagnino facta per episcopum anagninum.*

ANAGNI, SANTA MARGHERITA AL FUSANO[4]
Nothing remains of the convent of Santa Margherita al Fusano. We know of its existence through a series of papal documents dating to the pontificate of Boniface VIII. These confirm the arbitration over a piece of land between the abbess and the convent of San Benedetto in Roiate, which was settled by Pietro, the bishop of Anagni.

ANAGNI, SANTA REPARATA[5]
Very little is known about this nunnery. Although its exact location is uncertain, local historians such as De Magistris claim that it was originally found on the road that led out of town towards Ferentino. The oldest testimony is the *Acta SS. Aurelia e Neomisia*. The

---

1. Alatri, Archivio Molella I. Danti, Storia del monastero di S. Pietro, ms. sixteenth century; G. Floridi, *Storia di Guarcino*, Guarcino, Comune di Guarcino, 1971; M. Ritarossi, *Alatri*, Alatri, Arti Grafiche Tofani, 1996.

2. Several documents survive at the Archivio Vescovile in Rieti, the first visitation is dated 1549, *Visitatio Columnae* 1549, c. 92v; *Monasticon Italiae*, 1, p. 119.

3. Archivio Capitolare di Anagni, fasc. 4, n. 177; Zappasodi, *Anagni attraverso i secoli*, 1, p. 215.

4. *Ibid.*, pp. 212, 215, 334, 413; *Monasticon Italiae*, 1, p. 121.

5. *Acta passionis atque translationume S. Magni episcopi tranensis et martyris notis illustrata ab uno ex eiusdem ecclesiae canonicis*, Iesi, typis Joannis Baptistae de Juliis publici impressoris, & episcopalis, 1743, p. 164; De Magistris, *Istoria della città e S. Basilica Cattedrale di Anagni*, p. 103; Zappasodi, *Anagni attraverso i secoli*, p. 108.

latter was composed at the turn of the twelfth century, and states that the relics of these two female saints were transferred into the nunnery at *Civitates Anagniae in Monasterio Monialium S. Reparatae Virginis*; unfortunately the *Acta* do not provide an exact date.

AQUINO, SANTA MARIA DELLE MONACHE[6]
The existence of this foundation, found on the road between Aquino and Pontecorvo, is attested to by a document dated 1063 recording the donation of a windmill to the nunnery by a certain Gerardo.

ARICCIA, SAN NICCOLÒ[7]
The nunnery lies in close proximity to Ariccia's city walls, as was the case with many convents in the region. A document dated 1251 confirms that the foundation had been placed under the jurisdiction of the Roman monastery of SS. Ciriaco e Niccolò since 1030.

ARPINO, SANT'ANDREA AL COLLE[8]
Reference is first made to this nunnery in 1084. This date is also referred to in the Registry of the Archival *fondo* compiled by Tommaso Leccisotti. The abbey at Montecassino holds a *fondo* with all the documentation pertaining to the Arpino convent (a total of 87 parchments, the oldest dating to 1249). From an artistic standpoint, a thirteenth-century crucifix was found beneath a seventeenth century oil painting and restored in 1994. The crucifix originally came from a male monastery in the nearby town of Montenero. The nunnery's original medieval fabric has been largely replaced by the seventeenth-century refurbishments of the convent.

BAGNOREGIO, SAN CIPRIANO[9]
Very little is known about this nunnery and a precise foundation date is lacking. The oldest document is a papal bull by Innocent IV dated 1243, which asks the bishop of Orvieto to defend the nuns from the convent of Santa Trinità, as this community was being pestered by the one of San Cipriano. It was supressed in 1368 by Urban V, who ordered its reconstruction inside Viterbo. However, this project never took place.

CASTROCIELO, SANTA MARIA IN PALAZZOLO[10]
This nunnery is situated over the ruins of a Roman *domus*, the Villa Euchelia, in the town of Castrocielo. Although we do not know when the nuns installed themselves on site, the oldest surviving document relating to the nunnery is dated 1134. Currently preserved in the archive at Montecassino, it outlines the donation of a piece of land to the convent – represented by its Abbess Cecilia – by a group of citizens from Aquino.

6. *Abbazia di Montecassino. I regesti*, 9, 390, n. 3467; *Monasticon Italiae*, 1, p. 124.
7. E. Lucidi, *Memorie storiche dell'antichissimo municipio ora terra dell'Ariccia*, 1, Rome, Lazzarini, 1976, pp. 375-385; Cavazzi, *La diaconia di Santa Maria in via Lata*, pp. 318-321.
8. U. Caperna, "Il monastero di S. Andrea Apostolo in Arpino", in *Il monachesimo benedettino femminile in Ciociaria*, pp. 412-448; U. Caperna, *Il monastero di S. Andrea Apostolo di Arpino*, Rome, Gruppo Culturale di Roma e del Lazio, 1993; L. Ippoliti, *Il monastero delle benedettine di S. Andrea al Colle in Arpino: descrizione storico-artistica illustrata*, Arpino, Società Tipografica Macioce e Pisani, 1931; M.T. Valeri, "Il crocifisso del monastero di S. Andrea al Colle in Arpino", in *Il monachesimo benedettino femminile in Ciociaria*, pp. 449-464.
9. M. Mercurio, "La dimora estiva in Italia di Urbano V", *Archivio della Società romana di storia patria*, 65 (1942), pp. 153-161: 161; F. Macchioni, *Storia civile e religiosa di Bagnoregio dai tempi antichi sino all'anno 1503*, Viterbo, Agnesotti, 1956.
10. For complete bibliography refer to main text.

Ceccano, Sant'Angelo[11]
Originally Benedictine, this nunnery was transferred to the Poor Clares by Gregory IX. This community was joined to the order's house in Ferentino by Bishop Ruggero in 1370.

Cittaducale, Santa Caterina[12]
The nunnery of Santa Caterina di Alessandria was built in 1327, a few years after the foundation of Cittaducale in 1311. It is a complex structure that includes a church, choir, museum, library, refectory, cells, and a vegetable garden. The sixteenth-century cloister is rectangular with arches resting on round columns with simple capitals, both on the ground and upper floors replaced the original medieval structure. Santa Caterina is still a functioning nunnery and houses about twenty nuns.

Collepardo, San Nicola[13]
There is no clear documentary evidence, nevertheless according to a local tradition Saint Dominic of Sora founded the nunnery of San Nicola. In a recent publication on the convent, Valeria Danesi claims that this could be the first and only female Carthusian settlement in Central Italy.

Ferentino, San Benedetto[14]
This nunnery is first mentioned in a papal bull dated 5 March 1289. Here, Pope Nicholas IV granted indulgences for visitors to the church on certain prescribed festivities to the *abbatissae et conventui monasterii Sancti Benedicti Ferentinatis*. In 1300, Boniface VIII agreed that the nuns from San Pietro in Paliano should be transferred to San Benedetto. The convent was transferred to the Clarissans by the second half of the fourteenth century.

Ferentino, San Matteo[15]
Surviving documentary evidence on this nunnery, which was likely abandoned in the fifteenth century, is very scarce. A letter from Pope Boniface VIII to Cardinal Robert of Santa Pudenziana in Rome dated 1300, authorized the transfer of a group of nuns from the nunnery of San Pietro in Paliano to San Matteo and San Benedetto in Ferentino.

Guarcino, San Luca and Sant'Angelo[16]
The nunnery's twelfth- or thirteenth-century church is still extant. The earliest documentary evidence consists in a papal bull by Pope Lucius III dated 1182. Both the Archivio di Stato di Roma (52 parchments) and the Archivio di Stato di Frosinone (the *fondo* monastero di San Luca holding the remaining documentation dated 1571-1885) have *fondi* on the nunnery. Giuliano Floridi has published and transcribed the parchments from the ASR.

---

11. M. Sindici, *Ceccano. L'antica "Fabrateria". Studi storici con documenti inediti*, Rome, Befani, 1893, pp. 81-83; Zappasodi, *Anagni attraverso i secoli*, 1, p. 313.

12. Van Heteren, "Due monasteri benedettini", pp. 66-73; *Annuario delle religiose d'Italia*, Grottaferrata, Paoline, 1959, p. 8; *Monasticon Italiae*, 1, p. 136.

13. G. Sanità, *Collepardo nella sua storia e nelle sue memorie*, Rome, Alfapress, 1972, p. 11; Danesi, "Un monastero certosino", pp. 153-164.

14. B. Catracchia, "Memorie benedettine a Ferentino", *Il Sacro Speco*, 77 (1974), pp. 152-153; G. Battelli, "Il comune di Ferentino e i Francescani nei secoli XIII e XIV", Acts of the conference, *Archivio della Società romana di storia patria*, 67 (1944), pp. 361-369.

15. G. Battelli, "Le fonti per la storia di Ferentino nel Medioevo", *Storia della Città*, 15-16 (1980), pp. 9-16; *Monasticon Italiae*, 1, p. 142.

16. For complete bibliography refer to main text.

Marta, Santa Maria Maddalena[17]

The nunnery is found on the island of Marta on Lake Bolsena. The convent was built over the shrine where Gerardo count of Burgundy left St Mary Magdalene's relics in 741. At the turn of the thirteenth century, a group of nuns from the convent of Montefiascone installed themselves on the site. Apart from the indulgences granted by Pope Nicholas IV, and the transfer of nuns from San Pietro in Paliano authorized by Boniface VIII, very little is known about this settlement. It was transferred to the male branch of the Augustinians in the fifteenth century.

Montefiascone, San Pietro[18]

Although the oldest surviving document is Tuzio de Rubeis' will of 1363 – preserved in the cathedral archive at Montefiascone – the nunnery is thought to have been founded in the seventh century. The convent holds an archive with a series of chronicles redacted by nuns, including the seventeenth-century history of Santa Bibiana by Sister Cecilia Baij.

Nepi, SS. Maria e Biagio[19]

Located inside the city centre, this nunnery is first recorded in a lease agreement signed by the abbess in 921. In 996, Gregory V instructed Guinzio from Nepi and Sichifredo to resolve the disputes between Abbess Teodora and a group of local laymen regarding the ownership of a piece of land. The convent was later placed under the jurisdiction of the monastery of Santi Ciriaco and Nicola in Rome, which holds a *fondo* with the nunnery's documents.

Orte, Sant'Antonio Abate o Santa Maria delle Grazie[20]

Very little is known about the nunnery before the sixteenth century apart from the fact that two women decided to install a small community in the house left to them by a pious man in 1387. Bishop Giovanni from Foligno granted them the privilege to erect a small sanctuary in honour of Saint Anthony Abbott.

Paliano, San Pietro[21]

The nunnery was established between 1230-1240 by Cardinal Giacomo de Pecoraria, bishop of Palestrina and former abbot of the Abbazia delle Tre Fontane. The nuns

---

17. Orvieto, Archivio dell'Opera del Duomo, 1411-1417, 188; Cattedrale di Montefiascone, Archivio Vescovile, Visite pastorali, vol. XVI, fols. 269-270; G. Fazzini, "Amalasunta regina dei Goti e il tetro scoglio dell'isola Martana", *Lazio ieri e oggi*, 51 (2015), pp. 22-24; G. Montanucci, "L'isola Martana nel Medioevo", *Studi vetrallesi*, 9 (2002), pp. 30-32; A. Tarquini, *L'isola di Amalasunta: escursione geologica e storica al comprensorio del Lago di Bolsena*, Rome, Alma Roma, 1976.

18. For complete bibliography refer to main text.

19. Rome, Archivio del Capitolo di Santa Maria in via Lata transferred in part to the Vatican Library, documents edited by L. Hartmann, *Ecclesiae S. Mariae in Via Lata Tabularium*, 2 vols., Vienna, Gerold, 1895-1901; Cavazzi, *La diaconia di S. Maria in Via Lata*, pp. 312-318.

20. D. Gioacchini, *Curiosità ortane*, Orte, Museo Diocesano di Arte Sacra, 1961; Viterbo, Archivio di Stato, Documenti della Delegazione Apostolica di Viterbo, b. 54, c. 224r; *Monasticon Italiae*, 1, p. 153.

21. Archivio Apostolico Vaticano, Schedario Garampi, 94 (Indice 357); Rome, Archivio della Basilica Vaticana, cart. XLIX, 73; *Monasticon Italiae*, 1, pp. 154-15; Tomassetti, *La campagna romana*, III, p. 546; G. Navone, "Paliano. Appunti Storici", *Archivio della Societa Romana di Storia Patria*, 43 (1920), pp. 356-358; Zappasodi, *Anagni attraverso i secoli*, 1, p. 313.

followed the Cistercian Rule. Following the abbess's request, Pope Innocent IV granted the nunnery an annual visit by the abbot of Casamari in 1243. In 1256, the powerful Cardinal Stefano Conti of Santa Maria in Tratevere bequeathed money to the convent in his will (approximately thirty *denari provisini*). Pope Boniface VIII eventually transferred the nuns to other convents and the nunnery complex was transferred to Cistercian monks in 1300.

POGGIO NATIVO, SAN PAOLO[22]
The construction of the nunnery dates back to the mid thirteenth century. This is demonstrated by an inscription dated 1261 carved in the church's lintel.[23] The Abbey of Farfa promoted its rights to secure land holdings in the area through bequests to the nuns of San Paolo. As testified by the pastoral visit to the diocese of Sabina, the nunnery was dependent on the monastery of San Salvatore di Scandriglia. Between the end of the fourteenth century and the beginning of the fifteenth century the convent passed to the male Augustinians. However, it was suppressed by Pope Paul II in 1463 due to the community's misconduct, *collapsum quodammodo ut accepimus, et regulari observantia destitutum*.

RIETI, SAN BENEDETTO[24]
The nunnery of San Benedetto was erected over the foundations of the church of Sant'Agata. The latter was under the domain of the Abbey of Farfa in 761. In a document dated 1308, the bishop of Rieti, Giovanni Muto de Papazzurri, granted forty days of indulgences to all those who assisted in constructing the convent. In the early fourteenth century the nuns obtained permission from the *comune* to extend a path along Vicolo il Cántaro to facilitate the passage of travellers visiting the church. The church was radically restructured in the early sixteenth century and completely refurbished during the eighteenth, when it received its Baroque shell. Confiscated and assigned to the town of Rieti after Italian unification, the nunnery currently functions as a school building.

RIETI, SAN GIORGIO[25]
This nunnery, one of the oldest in Lazio, was likely founded in the first half of the eighth century. This may be deduced from the survival of a parchment recording a trade agreement between the convent and the abbot of Farfa in 744. The community lived here from 751 until at least 1118, after which we lose track of its records.

RIETI, SAN TOMMASO[26]
Initially a male Benedictine monastery, Pope Nicholas IV wrote to the *abatissae et conventui Sancti Thomae reatini Cisterciensis ordinis* in 1293 confirming that the monastery had turned into a female Cistercian house. This change was promoted by the

---

22. BAV, Cod. Barberini Lat. 2509; I. Schuster, "Il monastero di S. Salvatore. Gli antichi possedimenti farfensi nella Massa Torana", *Archivio della Società romana di storia patria*, 41 (1919), pp. 5-58: 46.
23. AD PORTV (M) VI (TA) AND QVI Q / FERT VENIT TER (R) AM / CALCANTES SVRSVM PIA (M) / ROPE (M) LEVANTES / ARCHIPR. ODO HOC OP (VS) / ANN (O) DMNI MCCLXI.
24. *Monasticon Italiae*, 1, p. 160; Van Heteren, "Due monasteri benedettini", pp. 58-61.
25. *Monasticon Italiae*, 1, p. 161.
26. *Il Chronicon Farfense di Gregorio da Catino. Precedono la* Constructio Farfensis *e gli scritti di Ugo da Farfa*, ed. by U. Balzani, 2 vols., Rome, Forzani & C. Tipografi del Senato, 1903, I, pp. 248, 316; *Monasticon Italiae*, 1, p. 162.

powerful Cistercian Cardinal Giovanni da Toledo who had done the same for Santa Maria del Paradiso in Viterbo. A few other documents survive for San Tommaso. These date to Boniface VIII's pontificate and to the fifteenth century, after which traces of the convent are lost. Nevertheless, we do know that it was located inside the city walls.

Rieti, Santa Margherita[27]
Nothing about this nunnery is known from its foundation period. The oldest surviving document is dated 1359 and relates how the bishop of Rieti came to the aid of the nuns, who were living in a perilous state of poverty.

Rieti, Santa Scolastica[28]
The nunnery of Santa Scolastica was established in 1334 along with the other female Benedictine foundation of San Benedetto, which is also in Rieti. The nuns joined the convent of Santa Margherita in 1453, and subsequently Sant'Andrea in 1498. We do not have other documentary information for the foundation during the medieval period.

Roiate, San Benedetto[29]
Today, only the church survives and it holds the celebrated relic of St Benedict's footprint. The nunnery is mentioned in papal bulls from the time of Boniface VIII. These relate to the arbitration between the nunnery and the abbess of the convent of Santa Margherita al Fusano in Anagni.

Segni, San Gregorio[30]
Apart from its tax returns in 1328-1329 and 1333-1335 nothing else is known about this nunnery.

Sezze Romano, Santa Lucia[31]
Very little is known about this nunnery, which was located outside Sezze's city walls. Nothing survives besides a letter by Pope Nicholas IV, which confirms indulgences to those who visited the convent on certain feast days. These privileges were again confirmed by Clement V in 1313.

Sgurgola, Santa Maria in Viano[32]
Although the church still exists and a twelfth-century fresco survives inside, there is very little information on this nunnery. In this case, the oldest surviving document takes the form of Stefano Conti's will of 1256 in which he offers bequests to the nunnery. A list of abbesses also survives, testifying to the status of the convent. Moreover, a document

---

27. *Ibid.*, p. 161; Van Heteren, "Due monasteri benedettini", pp. 51-55.
28. *Ibid.*
29. B. Bovi, *Roiate: ambiente, tradizioni, folklore, religione, storia, dialetto*, Palestrina, s.n., 1979; Zappasodi, *Anagni attraverso i secoli*, I (1908), p. 212.
30. C. Jonta, *Storia di Segni*, Gavignano, Tipografia Francescana, 1928, pp. 338-340.
31. *Monasticon Italiae*, 1, p. 169.
32. M. Morgia, *Sgurgola e la sua Badia*, Rome, Gavignano, 1962; G. Caetani, *Domus Caietana. Il Medioevo*, 1, San Casciano Val di Pesa, Stab. tip. F. lli Stianti, 1927, p. 126; *Monasticon Italiae*, 1, p. 87; F. Caraffa, "Il testamento di Stefano di Anagni", *Archivio della Società romana di storia patria* (1981), p. 110; Zappasodi, *Anagni attraverso i secoli*, pp. 313-316; *Restauro della facciata e del nartece della Badia della Madonna di Viano*, ed. by A. Ferrazzano, P. Iecco and N. Temperilli, Sgurgola, Comune di Sgurgola, 2004.

containing a list of 28 nuns dated 1300 mentions the names of "Scolastica filia domina Raynaldi Rubei" (a daughter of Pope Alexander IV's nephew), and "Maria soror domini Raynaldi de Supino" (the ex-wife of Francesco Caetani who had divorced her in 1295 to become cardinal). The nunnery was the theater of the fierce territorial dispute between Pietro Caetani and Gualgano and Pietro Conti.

SONNINO, SANTA MARIA DELLE CANNE[33]
The nunnery is first mentioned in a papal document signed by Pope Honorius IV and dated 1286. In 1291, Pope Nicholas IV granted an indulgence to the "abbatissae et conventus monasterii de Sonnino, ordinis S. Benedicti". In the year 1300, Boniface VIII allowed the nuns from the convent of San Pietro in Paliano to be transferred to Santa Maria delle Canne. Documentary evidence does not indicate when the nuns adopted the Cistercian rule.

SORA, SANTA MARIA[34]
Located five kilometers from Sora, the nunnery was founded by Pietro Ranieri in the first two decades of the eleventh century. Following advice from St. Dominic of Sora the nuns were suspended for misconduct in the eleventh century. The nunnery was converted to a male monastery and St. Dominic became its first abbot.

SUBIACO, SANTA CHELIDONIA[35]
The nunnery was founded next to the cave where Saint Chelidonia (1077-1152) had spent her years as a hermit. Given the number of followers she had gained during her lifetime, the Roman Curia attempted to regulate the community by establishing a nunnery. The convent located in Morraferogna – three kilometers from Subiaco – was abandoned for security reasons during the fifteenth century.

TARQUINIA, SAN GIOVANNI IN ISOLA[36]
Located inside the city of Tarquinia, this nunnery has not been securely identified as Benedictine. This is due to the fact that it is only mentioned in the registry of Lanfranco di Scano (1291) in which a monastic order is not specified: "Requisite abbatissa et conventus non solverunt in triennio per eas acceptato et ideo excommunicate".

TIVOLI, SANT'AGNESE[37]
From the sixteenth century, the little church of Sant'Agnese, once called "dei Reali", was part of a female monastic community. The church is currently deconsecrated and abandoned. However, the inscription *Passions Martyrion* is still legible in the portal.

---

33. Tomassetti, *Amaseno*, p. 58; A. Cardosi, *L'antico statuto di Sonnino (sec. XIII)*, Rome, Edizioni Sidera, 1965, pp. 68-69; A. de Sanctis, "Toponimi e cognomi di Sonnino cinque secoli fa", *Lazio ieri e oggi*, 11 (1975), p. 123.

34. M. Cassoni, *Sguardo storico sull'abbazia di S. Domenico di Sora*, Sora, Tip. lit. V. D'Amico, 1910, p. 15; G. Pierleoni, "Per la storia della badia di S. Domenico di Sora", in *Per Cesare Baronio. Scritti vari nel terzo centenario della sua morte*, ed. by V. Simoncelli, Rome, Athenaeum, 1911, pp. 661-663; A. Carbone, "Il monastero di S. Domenico di Sora", *Lazio ieri e oggi*, 3 (1967), pp. 29-30.

35. Boesch Gajano, *Chelidonia*; Caraffa, "L'eremitismo nella valle dell'Alto Aniene", pp. 228-229; B. Cignitti, "S. Chelidonia, Patrona di Subiaco", *Lunario Romano* (1978), pp. 180-181.

36. *Le 'Liber Censum' de l'Eglise Romaine*, 2 vols., ed. by P. Fabre and L. Duchesne, Paris, Ernest Thorin, 1902, I, p. 56; II, p. 110; P. Cicerchia, *Tarquinia. Borgo medievale*, Rome, Istituto Poligrafico e Zecca dello Stato, 1990.

37. G.M. Zappi, *Annali e memorie di Tivoli (ms. 1572-1590 c.)*, ed. by V. Pacifici, Tivoli, Società Tiburtina di Storia e d'Arte, 1920; *Monasticon Italiae*, 1, p. 180.

By examining the documents from Sant'Agnese in Rome – held at the Archivio di San Pietro in Vincoli – we can determine that the Roman nunnery comprised a number of land holdings in the city and in the area around Tivoli and Monte Soratte. It is possible that this little church was actually annexed to the one in Rome.

TORRE CAIETANI, SAN BENEDETTO[38]
Likewise, no information survives besides tax records for 1331-1333 and 1334-1335.

TREVI NEL LAZIO, SANT'ANGELO ORSANO[39]
The nunnery of Sant'Angelo di Orsano is found outside Trevi nel Lazio between the Simbruini and the Ernici mountains in the Aniene valley, on one of the sides of mount Piaggio. Historically, Trevi nel Lazio was incorporated into the Conti family estate through the Jenne branch. However, the Caetani had assumed full ownership by the end of 1297, when Boniface VIII authorized the bishop and the Chapter of Anagni to permanently grant the feudal estate to the family. Although a rich documentary corpus survives, and the nunnery's ruins and church are still standing today, no overreaching study exists. This is surprising if we acknowledge that Sant'Angelo is the only female Benedictine foundation in the high valley of the Aniene and that the lives of the nuns of likely mirror those of other female Benedictine nunneries.

VALMONTONE, SANTA MARIA IN SELCI[40]
Originally Benedictine, it was transferred to the Clarissan order during the second half of the thirteenth century. The oldest relevant document dated 1182 states that its possessions were under the jurisdiction of the cathedral of Segni.

VELLETRI, SANTA MARIA DELL'ORTO[41]
A papal bull granting protection to the nuns, which was issued by Alexander IV in 1256, is the oldest document relating to the nunnery. The pope conceded three years of indulgences to all those who helped to restore the convent in 1257. Then, in 1351, Pope Clement VI united its possessions to the nunnery of Santa Martina. Finally, its six remaining nuns were transferred inside the city walls for security reasons at the start of the fifteenth century.

VELLETRI, SANTA MARTINA[42]
Despite not having a foundation date we know that the nunnery was located two kilometers from the town of Velletri. During the first half of the fourteenth century, the nuns were forced to abandon its premises for security reasons. Subsequently, Pope Clement VI united its possessions to that of Santa Maria dell'Orto in 1351.

VEROLI, SAN MARTINO[43]
The convent of San Martino in Veroli was initially a Cistercian monastery under the control of the abbey of Casamari. It was transferred to Benedictine nuns by 1289 when

---

38. I. Schuster, *Storia di San Benedetto e dei suoi tempi*, S. Giuliano milanese, Abbazia di Viboldone, 1965; *Monasticon Italiae*, 1, p. 185.

39. For complete bibliography refer to main text.

40. *Monasticon Italiae*, 1, p. 188; not cited in Marini, *Fondazione francescane*.

41. F. Lazzari, *Velletri nel Medioevo*, Viterbo, Centro Studio Antonio Mancinelli, 2015; M. Nocca, *Velletri. Guida alla città*, Rome, Palombi, 2002.

42. B. Teoli, *Teatro istorico di Velletri*, 2, Velletri, Bertini, 1885, pp. 319-320.

43. A. Sarra, *Potenza e carità di Dio*, Casamari, Tipografia dell'Abbazia, 1972.

Pope Nicholas IV granted indulgences to those who visited the nunnery. It was closed in 1449 and subsequently occupied by a group of Franciscan friars. Today it survives but underwent a dramatic restoration during the eighteenth century.

VEROLI, SANT'IPPOLITO[44]

The nunnery was founded by Agostino, abbot of Casamari, between 1088 and 1106. It was built next to the church of Sant'Ippolito inside the city walls. By the thirteenth century, the nunnery was transformed into a collegiate church and subsequently into a male Cistercian house.

VITERBO, SAN FORTUNATO[45]

A female Cistercian house, it was first annexed to Santa Maria in Grado and subsequently to Santa Maria del Paradiso. The Cistercian nuns inhabited the convent from 1369. Consequently, numerous notarial acts survive from 1372-1420.

VITERBO, SANTA MARIA DEL PARADISO[46]

The church of Santa Maria del Paradiso was originally a male Benedictine monastery. However, it was transferred to Cistercian nuns in 1270 by Giovanni da Toledo, cardinal bishop of Porto and Santa Rufina. Finally, due to the nuns' misconduct in 1439, Cardinal Giovanni Vitelleschi assigned the church to the Franciscan order. Presently, the only medieval trace that survives is the thirteenth-century cloister. Unfortunately, the absence of documentary sources makes it very difficult to ascribe its construction to either the Cistercian nuns or the Benedictine monks. However, there is a clear architectonic reliance on the Loggia dei Papi in Viterbo which is the expression of an exquisitely *rayonnant* style. This is likely to have reached the city in the second half of the thirteenth century and as a result the new Cistercian foundation may have spurred the construction of this cloister.

VITERBO, SANTA MARIA DELLA PALOMBA[47]

The nunnery, which has almost completely vanished due to its incorporation into the city walls of Viterbo, can be found towards Porta di Valle. Indeed, one may still notice the semicircular apse of the church, which extends outwards from the city walls. It is referred to as a convent by 1341. However, by analyzing its masonry structure, Cesare Pinzi claims that it was likely constructed during the eleventh century. Documentary evidence from the fifteenth century suggests that there was a curious overlap of authorities. A certain Bartolomeo is mentioned as dean of the church, while we simultaneously know that one of the abbesses, Anna Teutonica, headed the congregation. The nuns inhabited its premises until the fifteenth century when they were replaced by the Jesuit friars.

---

44. *Monasticon Italiae*, 1, pp. 189-190; C. Scaccia-Scarafoni, *La chiesa di San Leucio nella rocca di Veroli*, Veroli, E. Calzone, 1953.

45. F. Cristofori, *Le tombe dei papi in Viterbo e le chiese di S. Maria in Gradi, di S. Francesco, e di S. Lorenzo. Memorie e documenti sulla storia medievale viterbese*, Siena, San Bernardino, 1887, p. 426, n. 65.

46. F. Bartoloni, "Suppliche pontificie", *Bullettino dell'Istituto Storico Italiano per il Medio Evo*, 67 (1995); M.G. Gimma, *Il centro storico di Viterbo*, Viterbo, Betagamma editrice, 2001, p. 236; P.G. Zucconi, *S. Maria del Paradiso in Viterbo*, Rome, Tipografia Artigiana Grafica Commerciale, 1971.

47. P. Egidi, "L'Archivio della Cattedrale di Viterbo", *Bollettino dell'Istituto Storico Italiano* (1906), pp. 38-39; C. Pinzi, *Storia della città di Viterbo nel medioevo*, 1, Rome, Palombo, 1887, p. 80.

VITERBO, SANTA MARIA IN VALVERDE[48]
Other than testamentary bequest (1281) in favour of the convent, very little is known of its foundation history. During the reign of Boniface VIII, the nuns were transferred to the convent of Santa Maria della Ginestra and the nunnery was occupied by Abbot Angelo of Sassovio and his male Benedictine congregation.

VITERBO, SANTA MARIA IN VOLTURNA[49]
Located outside the city walls, the oldest surviving document is a letter authorizing the bishop of Viterbo to seize the convent from the nuns due to unspecified misconduct. The nunnery eventually passed to the female branch of the Cistercians, who abandoned it during the fourteenth century for safety reasons.

Clarissan Convents in Latium (ca. 1200-1400)

ACQUAPENDENTE, SANTA CHIARA[50]
Santa Chiara in Acquapendente is still in existence and was consecrated in 1333. The Franciscans had established themselves here when Francis was still alive and were granted the church of Santa Maria del Borgo in 1255. The Ministral Provincial, Father Tommaso da Acquapendente, founded the nunnery of Santa Chiara with the contribution of local citizens in the year 1333. The concession to the nuns is dated 6 June 1333 and is signed by John of San Teodoro, apostolic legate of Pope John XXII. The first community of Clarissans was formed by nuns from the convents of Orvieto and Bagnoregio. During the Napoleonic suppression, the convent's archive was burnt and its altarpiece dismembered. The nuns were allowed to return to its premises in 1815.

ACQUAVIVA, SANTA MARIA[51]
The nunnery of Acquaviva was already in existence by 1228. This is corroborated by a letter written by Cardinal Rainaldo, which mentions 24 convents and announces the replacement of Friar Pacifico by Friar Rainaldo as their general supervisor. Moreover, the convent is acknowledged in a papal bull dated 1236. In the mid-eighteenth century, the town was originally found in the district of Civita Castellana. A church dedicated to the Blessed Virgin currently stands on the original site of the nunnery.

ALATRI, SAN SEBASTIANO[52]
According to a papal bull we know that on 25 October 1234 Gregory IX ratified the concession by the cathedral Chapter of Alatri of the church of San Benedetto de Plagis to the monastery of San Sebastiano. Its foundation date should therefore be ascribed to 1233. Eventually entitled to Sant'Agnese in Agone in Rome, it was abandoned in 1442.

---

48. *Monasticon Italiae*, 1, p. 194.

49. I. Ciampi, *Cronache e statute della città di Viterbo*, Florence, Cellini, 1872; C. Pinzi, *Storia della città di Viterbo*, Bologna, Forni, 1974; F. Bussi, *Istoria della città di Viterbo*, Viterbo, Nella stamperia di Bernabò e Lazzarini, 1742.

50. L. Oliger, "De origine regularum ordinis santae Clarae", *Archivium Franciscanum Historicum*, 5 (1912), pp. 207, 444. Pratesi, "Le Clarisse in Italia", p. 350.

51. Oliger, "De origine regularum", pp. 207 and 444; Marini, "Le fondazioni francescane femminili", p. 77; *Bullarium Franciscanum*, I, p. 204.

52. For complete bibliography refer to main text

AMASENO, SAN MICHELE ARCANGELO[53]
The nunnery of San Michele Arcangelo or Sant'Angelo of Amaseno is known through local studies. Mentioned by Alexander IV for the first time in a document dated 5 February 1260, the nunnery was granted the rural church of San Benedetto and the surrounding lands. This occurred via an *instrumentum* between the bishop of Ferentino and the abbess Francesca the following year.

ANAGNI, SAN PIETRO IN VINEIS[54]
1253 is also the foundation date for the nunnery of Santa Chiara at Anagni, for which Pratesi does not provide any additional information. Similarly, the *Bullarium Franciscanum* makes no mention of it. This is due to the fact that the nunnery was originally called San Biagio and later San Pietro in Vineis or de Vineis. As testified by the bull, *Praesentium auctoritate*, the convent was active by 1261. Here, Urban IV orders the abbess and the nuns of the convent to follow the prescription of the bishop of Anagni. The nunnery, currently transferred to the Collegio Principe, preserves the original church and a fresco cycle in the nave and the choir dated to the thirteenth century.

BORGO SAN PIETRO, SANTA FILIPPA MARERI[55]
The nunnery of Borgo San Pietro was founded by the Blessed Filippa Mareri (1190-1236) between 1228 and 1230. Filippa, beatified in 1247 by Innocent IV, was a disciple of Saint Claire and a member of the local nobility. A bull in the *Bullarium Franciscanum*, dated 27 June 1248, states that Innocent IV will grant forty days of indulgences to whoever will visit the church during the feasts of SS. Peter and Paul, Philip, James apostle, and Blessed Filippa (Mareri?). Although Filippa died in 1236, we know other thirteenth-century abbesses: Illuminata (1252), Giovanna (1259) and Caterina (1295). The convent was submerged during the Fascist era with the construction of the artificial Salto lake.

FERENTINO, SAN BENEDETTO[56]
This nunnery is first mentioned in a papal bull dated 5 March 1289. Here, Pope Nicholas IV granted indulgences to the *abbatissae et conventui monasterii Sancti Benedicti Ferentinatis* for visitors to the church on certain prescribed feasts. In 1300, Boniface VIII agreed that the nuns from San Pietro in Paliano be transferred to San Benedetto. The convent was transferred to the Clarissans by the second half of the fourteenth century.

FERENTINO, SAN MATTEO[57]
The nunnery of San Matteo was founded in Ferentino around 1260, according to Pratesi. This is the only information provided by Pratesi, the *Bullarium Franciscanum* makes no mention of it.

FROSINONE, SANT'AURENZIO[58]
The monastery of Sant'Aurenzio or Orenzio in Frosinone was first mentioned in 1260 through the papal bull, *Devotionis augmentum*, in which Pope Alexander IV conceded

---

53. For complete bibliography refer to main text.
54. For complete bibliography refer to main text.
55. For complete bibliography refer to main text.
56. Caetani, *Regesta*, 1, p. 242; Battelli, "Il comune di Ferentino", pp. 361-369.
57. Moorman, *Medieval Franciscan Houses*, p. 585; Pratesi, "Le Clarisse in Italia", p. 351.
58. *Bullarium Franciscanum*, II, p. 395; Moorman, *Medieval Franciscan Houses*, p. 585; Pratesi, "Le Clarisse in Italia", p. 350.

two pounds of wax to the nuns. This allowance was confirmed by Pope Boniface VIII in the *Lecta nobilis* of 1295.

MAGLIANO SABINA, SANTA CROCE[59]
According to Pratesi, the nunnery of Santa Croce in Magliano Sabina was founded in 1230. Pratesi also states that the convent incorporated the other nunnery in Magliano, that of the Perpetuo Soccorso. By the seventeenth century, it had been abandoned by the nuns.

PALESTRINA, CASTEL SAN PIETRO[60]
Castel San Pietro near Palestrina is linked to the story of Margherita Colonna. It is a nunnery *sui generis* because Margherita lived in the house of her brother Giovanni on Monte Prenestino, commonly referred to as Castel San Pietro (Romano). Between 1273 and 1274 Margherita adhered to Clare's *formae vitae*. Upon her death in 1280, her followers remained on Monte Prenestino until 1284 when they moved to the nunnery of San Silvestro in Capite under the rule of Abbess Erminia.

RIETI, SAN FLAVIANO/FLABIANO[61]
A third monastery in Rieti, San Flaviano or San Fabiano, is recorded in 1289. This convent is neither mentioned by Pratesi nor by Moorman, yet its existence is confirmed by the papal bull *Splendor paternae gloriae*. This bull dated 13 September of that year, grants indulgences to its visitors during the feasts of the Virgin Mary, and Saint Flavianus and Saint Clare.

RIETI, SAN FRANCESCO DE MACHILONE[62]
San Francesco de Machilone (sometimes Machialone), in the diocese of Rieti, is the last nunnery with documents pertaining to the thirteenth century. In the papal bull, *Vitae perennis Gloria*, Pope Nicholas IV grants a year and forty days of indulgences to those visiting the convent during its major festivities namely those of the Virgin Mary, St Francis, St Clare and St Anthony. On the 7 of May 1291 Nicholas IV conceded a plenary indulgence to those who visited the monastery of San Francesco in the town of Posta and the convent of San Francesco of Machilone. Therefore, we may assume that the latter was originally located near this town. The convent was probably found near the town of Posta.

RIETI, SANTA LUCIA IN COLLE ALTO[63]
Santa Lucia in Colle Alto is the first Clarissan convent established in Rieti. Pratesi argues that it was originally planned in 1236 and eventually founded in 1253 – the year of Saint Clare's death. However, this occurred before Clare died on 11 of August, that same year given she sent two sisters from San Damiano, Beatrice and Pacifica, to Rieti in order to set up the new foundation. The nunnery was enlarged and eventually transferred to the church of San Sebastiano inside the city walls and changed its name to Santa Lucia in 1574.

---

59. Marini, "Le fondazioni francescane femminili", p. 79; Pratesi, "Le Clarisse in Italia", p. 341.
60. D'Alatri, "Gli insediamenti francescani del Duecento", pp. 299-300; Marini, "Le fondazioni francescane femminili", p. 88; Moorman, *Medieval Franciscan Houses*, p. 568.
61. *Bullarium Franciscanum*, IV, pp. 93; Marini, "Le fondazioni francescane femminili", p. 94.
62. *Bullarium Franciscanum*, IV, p. 248; De Angelis, *Il monastero di Borgo San Pietro*, p. 67. For further reference also information on the official website of the town of Posta, http://www.comunediposta.it/attrazioni/convento-di-san-francesco.html, last accessed 31/01/2021.
63. *Bullarium Franciscanum*, IV, pp. 97-98; Pratesi, "Le Clarisse in Italia", p. 345.

Tivoli, San Michele[64]

Originally dedicated to San Giovanni, the convent of San Michele in Tivoli was founded in 1262. The nuns inhabited the convent from the pontificate of Alexander IV to the year 1477. According to Casimiro da Roma, the nuns perished in 1476 "per cagioni della pestilenza, dell'aria insalubre, e di altri gravi incomodi". This was quite common among female Franciscan houses due to their position outside city walls. In 1544, the nunnery was reinstalled inside the city walls and inhabited by ten nuns and an abbess from the convent of San Lorenzo in Panisperna in Rome.

Rieti, Santa Chiara[65]

The nunnery of Santa Chiara, established in 1289, is the second Clarissan convent located in the city of Rieti. Indeed, that same year Pope Nicholas IV participated in the General Chapter of the friars held in the city. Consequently, the house of the Blessed Tancredi, companion of Saint Francis, was granted to four nuns for the purpose of communal living under the rule of the Third Order issued by Pope Nicholas IV that same year. The first female community alternated between working to assist the sick and a contemplative lifestyle. They were subsequently transferred to the church of Santo Stefano and embraced a rigid regime of *clausura* during the course of the sixteenth century.

Tuscania, Santa Maria de Gavillione[66]

Santa Maria de Gavillione in Tuscania was founded in 1258. The nunnery was transferred to the church of San Paolo as the original one had become too small in 1441.

Trevi, San Francesco[67]

The nunnery of San Francesco in Trevi is first mentioned in a papal bull dated 13 August 1289. This granted one year and forty days of indulgences for visits to the nunnery during its principal festivities namely Christmas, Easter, the four principle festivities dedicated to Mary; and during the feasts of the Saint Bartholomew, Francis and Lucy. Given that the city of Trevi (not the modern one of Trevi nel Lazio but a thirteenth century castle) was destroyed by the inhabitants of Sezze at the end of the fifteenth century and never rebuilt, very little is known of the nunnery.

Valmontone, Santa Maria in Silice[68]

The existence of the convent of Santa Maria in Silice in Valmontone is also confirmed in a papal bull. Moreover, Casimiro da Roma gathers more details on the convent's history in the following centuries. After the Clarissans abandoned the convent in 1470, the community was initially replaced by a group of Benedictine monks and subsequently by a Franciscan community.

---

64. For pestilence, unhealthy living conditions, and other grave inconveniences: Casimiro da Roma, *Memorie istoriche delle chiese e dei conventi dei frati minori della Provincia romana,* Rome, Pietro Rosati, 1774, pp. 375-376; D'Alatri, "Gli insediamenti francescani del Duecento", p. 670.

65. *Bullarium Franciscanum*, II, pp. 94-97; Benedetto Spila da Subiaco, *Memorie storiche del ven. Monastero di santa Chiara in Rieti*, Milan, Tipografia Capriolo e Massimino, 1896; Marini, "Le fondazioni francescane femminili", p. 92.

66. *Bullarium Franciscanum*, II, p. 309; Marini, "Le fondazioni francescane femminili nel Lazio nel Duecento", p. 84.

67. *Bullarium Franciscanum*, IV, p. 93; Marini, "Le fondazioni francescane femminili", p. 93.

68. *Bullarium Franciscanum*, IV, p. 107; Casimiro da Roma, *Memorie istoriche*, p. 388; D'Alatri, "Gli insediamenti francescani del Duecento", p. 300.

Velletri, Santa Chiara[69]

The monastery of Santa Chiara in Velletri dates back to 1274. Casimiro da Roma refers to it as one of the oldest monasteries of the Roman province. A notarial *instrumentum* dated 1274 registers the donation of several goods by Bruna from Anagni.

Viterbo, Santa Rosa[70]

Although the *Bullarium Franciscanum* makes no mention of the nunnery of Santa Rosa in Viterbo, Pratesi dates its foundation to the year 1235.

---

69. *Bullarium Franciscanum*, IV, p. 295; Casimiro da Roma, *Memorie istoriche*, p. 340; Marini, "Le fondazioni francescane femminili", p. 88; Pratesi, *Le Clarisse in Italia*, p. 350.

70. D'Alatri, "Gli insediamenti francescani del Duecento"; Marini, "Le fondazioni francescane femminili", p. 82.

Bibliography

Primary Sources

Abbazia di Montecassino. *I regesti dell'archivio*, 1, ed. by T. Leccisotti, Rome, Ministero dell'Interno - Archivi di Stato, 1964
Abbazia di Montecassino. *I regesti dell'archivio*, 9, ed. by F. Avagliano and T. Leccisotti, Rome, s.n., 1974
Acta passionis atque translationum S. Magni episcopi tranensis et martyris notis illustrata ab uno ex eiusdem ecclesiae canonicis, Iesi, typis Joannis Baptistae de Juliis publici impressoris, & episcopalis, 1743
Andrea da Rocca di Papa, *Memorie storiche della chiesa e monastero di San Lorenzo in Panisperna*, Rome, Tipografia Editrice Romana, 1893
Armellini M., *Le chiese di Roma*, Rome, Pasquino, 1891

Bartolini, D., *Gli atti del martirio della nobilissima vergine romana Sant'Agnese illustrati con la storia e coi monumenti*, Rome, Congregazione di Propaganda Fide, 1858
Benedetto Spila da Subiaco, *Memorie storiche del ven. Monastero di santa Chiara in Rieti*, Milan, Tipografia Capriolo e Massimino, 1896
Beverini, B., *Vita e culto di Sant'Agnese V. e M. con addizione di note*, Naples, Tipografia forense, 1856
Bosio, A., *Roma sotterranea*, Rome, appresso Guglielmo Facciotti, 1632
Bullarium Franciscanum Romanorum Pontificum. Constitutiones, Epistolas, ac Diplomata continens Tribus Ordinibus Minorum, Clarissarum et Poenitentium a Seraphico Patriarca Sancto Francisco institutis concessa ab ilorum exordio ad nostra usque tempora, 4 vols., ed. by J.H. Sbaraleae, Rome, Congregazione di Propaganda Fide, 1759-1768
Bussi, F., *Istoria della città di Viterbo*, Viterbo, Nella stamperia di Bernabò e Lazzarini, 1742

Cadderi, A., *Beata Margherita Colonna. Le due vite scritte dal fratello Giovanni, senatore di Roma e da Stefania, monaca di San Silvestro in Capite; testo critico, introduzione, traduzione italiana a fronte da un manoscritto latino del XIV secolo*, Palestrina, ITL, 2010
Caetani G., *Domus Caietana. Il Medioevo*, 1, San Casciano Val di Pesa, Stab. tip. F. lli Stianti, 1927
Caetani, G., *Regesta chartarum. Regesto delle pergamene dell'Archivio Caetani*, 1, Perugia, Stab. tip. F. lli Stianti, 1922

Capisacchi, G., *Chronicon Sacri monasterii Sublaci anno 1573*, ed. by L. Branciani, Subiaco-Monastero Santa Scolastica, Tipografia Editrice Santa Scolastica, 2005

Carletti, G., *Memorie istorico-critiche della chiesa, e monastero di S. Silvestro in Capite di Roma*, Rome, Pilucchi Cracas, 1795

Ciampi, I., *Cronache e statute della città di Viterbo*, Florence, Cellini, 1872

Coppi, A., *Memorie colonnesi*, Rome, Salviucci, 1855

Coretini, G., *Brevi notizie della citta di Viterbo*, Rome, presso Paolo Giunchi, 1774

Cristofori, F., *Le tombe dei papi in Viterbo e le chiese di S. Maria in Gradi, di S. Francesco, e di S. Lorenzo. Memorie e documenti sulla storia medievale viterbese*, Siena, San Bernardino, 1887

D'Avino, V., *Cenni storici sulle chiese arcivescovili, vescovili e prelatizie (nullius) del Regno delle Due Sicilie*, Naples, Ranucci, 1848

de Angelis G., Macchi V., *Commentario storico-critico su l'origine e le vicende della città e chiesa cattedrale di Montefiascone*, Montefiascone, Tipografia del Seminario, 1841

De Magistris, A., *Documenti anagnini*, Rome, Forzani e C., 1891

De Magistris, A., *Istoria della città e S. Basilica cattedrale d'Anagni*, Rome, Ottavio, 1749

Ecclesiae S. Mariae in Via Lata Tabularium, 2 vols., ed. by L. Hartmann, Vienna, Gerold, 1895-1901

Fabricius, G., *Roma. Antiquitatum libri duo*, Basel, Oporin, 1550

Fedele, P., "Carte del monastero di SS. Cosma e Damiano", *Archivio della Società romana di storia patria*, 21 (1898), pp. 459-534

Federici, V., "Regesto del Monastero di S. Silvestro in Capite", *Archivio della Società romana di storia patria*, 22 (1899), pp. 213-300, pp. 498-538; 23 (1900), pp. 67-128, pp. 411-439

Forcella, V., *Le iscrizioni delle chiese e d'altri edifici di Roma dal secolo XI fino ai nostri giorni*, 9, Rome, Cecchini, 1876

Formicini O., *Liber monialum sancti Cosmati de Urbe in regione Transtiberim de observantia sub regula sancte Clare [...]*, Rome, Biblioteca Nazionale Centrale di Roma, Fondi Minori, Ms. Varia, 6

Giacchetti, G., *Historia della venerabile chiesa et monastero di S. Silvestro de Capite di Roma: compilata da antichi scritti, gravi autori e apostoliche bolle*, Rome, G. Mascardi, 1629

Il Chronicon Farfense di Gregorio da Catino. Precedono la Constructio Farfensis *e gli scritti di Ugo da Farfa*, ed. by U. Balzani, 2 vols., Rome, Forzani & C. Tipografi del Senato, 1903

L'Archivio Tiburtino di S. Giovanni Evangelista, ed. by V. Pacifici, Subiaco, Tipografia dei Monasteri, 1922

"Le due vite scritte dal fratello Giovanni Colonna, senatore di Roma, e da Stefania monaca di S. Silvestro in Capite, testi inediti illustrati e pubblicati", ed. by L. Oligier, *Lateranum*, 1, 2 (1935)

Le 'Liber Censum' de l'Eglise Romaine, 2 vols., ed. by. P. Fabre and L. Duchesne, Paris, Ernest Thorin, 1902

Le Liber pontificalis. Texte, introduction et commentaire par l'abbé L. Duchesne, 2 vols., Paris, de Boccard, 1886-1892

Le Liber pontificalis. Texte, introduction et commentaire par l'abbé L. Duchesne, 3 vols., Paris, de Boccard, 1981
Leone Marsicano or Hostiense, Pietro Diacono, *Cronaca Monastero Cassinese*, introduction and translation by F. Gigante, Cassino, F. Ciolfi, 2016

Mirzio da Treviri, *Chronicon Sublacense, anno 1628 <1630>. Co-redattore P. Clavarini detto Romano*, ed. by L. Branciani, Subiaco-Monastero Santa Scolastica, Tipografia Editrice Santa Scolastica, 2014

Oliger, L., "De origine regularum ordinis santae Clarae", *Archivium Franciscanum Historicum*, 5 (1912), pp. 181-209, 413-447, 644-654

Panciroli, O., *I tesori nascosti dell'alma citta' di Roma*, Rome, per gli Heredi di A. Zanetti, 1600

Salomonia, D., *Narratione historica del monastero dei SS. Domenico e Sisto et sua origine cavata dalle Cronache di San Domenico da varie traditioni et altre scritture autentiche raccolte da sor Pulcheria Carducci et sor Domenica Salomonia monache in detto monastero, l'anno MDCXXXVIII sotto il priorato della molto R. sor Maria Tenaglini*, Rome, 1638
Salvini, U., *Raccolta di stemmi di famiglie di Ancona, Firenze, Montemignaio, Recanati, Roma, Senigallia, Tolentino*, Florence, 1954
Senis, de, T., *Sanctae Catharinae Senensis Legenda Minor*, ed. by. E. Franceschini, Milan, Bocca, 1942
Seroux d'Agincourt, J.B., *Histoire de l'art par les monumens depuis sa décadence au IVe siècle jusqu'à son renouvellement au XVIe siècle*, 2, Paris, Treuttel et Würtz, 1823

Ugonio, P., *Historia delle Stationi di Roma*, Rome, appresso Bartholomeo Bonfadino, 1588

Wadding, L., *Annales minorum seu Trium Ordinum a S. Francisco institutorum*, 6, Florence, Rochi Bernabò, 1886

Secondary Literature

Abulafia, D., *Federico II*, Turin, Einaudi, 2006
Acocella, N., *La decorazione pittorica di Montecassino dalle didascalie di Alfano I (sec. XI)*, Salerno, Di Giacomo, 1966
Affreschi in Val Comino e nel Cassinate, ed. by G. Orofino, Cassino, Università degli Studi di Cassino, 2000
Alberzoni, M.P., *Chiara e il papato*, Milan, Electa, 1995
Amati, A., *Il monastero di S. Angelo di Orsano in Trevi nel Lazio: contributo per il codice diplomatico*, Casamari, Terra Nostra, 1982
Andaloro, M., *Bonifacio VIII*, Rome, Istituto Storico Italiano per il Medioevo, 2006
Angelelli, W., L'Adorazione dei Magi e Quattro Santi, I Santi Cosma e Damiano e San Leonardo *nel convento di Sant'Agnese fuori le mura*, in Romano, *Apogeo e fine del Medioevo*, pp. 373-374
Angelelli, W., *La Madonna Lactans e la Madonna in trono col bambino e Sant'Ansano in Sant'Agnese fuori le mura*, in Romano, *Apogeo e fine del Medioevo*, pp. 409-411

Antonelli, F., "I primi monasteri di monaci orientali in Roma", *Rivista di archeologia cristiana*, 5 (1928), pp. 105-121

Antonelli, G., "L'opera di Odone di Cluny in Italia", *Benedictina*, 4 (1950), pp. 19-40

Attorno al Cavallini. Frammenti del gotico a Roma nei Musei Vaticani, Milan, Jaca Book, 2008

Bacci, A., "Scavi nel cimitero e nella basilica di S. Agnese", *Rivista di archeologia cristiana* (1902), pp. 222-297

Bacci, A., "Ulteriori osservazioni sulla basilica nomentana", *Rivista di archeologia cristiana* (1906), pp. 77-87

Ballardini, A., "*Habeas Corpus*: Agnese nella basilica di via Nomentana", in *«Di Bisanzio dirai ciò che è passato, ciò che passa e che sarà». Scritti in onore di Alessandra Guiglia*, ed. by S. Pedoni and A. Paribeni, Rome, Bardi edizioni, 2018

Barclay Lloyd, J., "Paintings for Dominican Nuns: A New Look at the Images of Saints, Scenes from the New Testament and Apocrypha, and Episodes from the Life of Saint Catherine of Siena in the Medieval Apse of San Sisto Vecchio in Rome", *Papers of the British School at Rome*, 80 (2012), pp. 189-232

Barclay Lloyd, J., *The Architectural Planning of Pope Innocent III's Nunnery of S. Sisto in Rome*, in *Innocenzo III: Urbs et Orbis*, pp. 1292-1311

Barclay Lloyd, J., "The Medieval Benedictine Monastery of SS. Cosma e Damiano in Mica Aurea in Rome, c. 936-1234", *Tjurunga. An Australian Benedictine Journal*, 34 (1988), pp. 25-35

Barclay Lloyd, J., Guerrini Ferri, G., *"San Chosm'e Damiano e 'l suo bel monasterio...": il complesso monumentale di San Cosimato ieri, oggi, domani. Un itinerario tra le memorie ed i tesori del Venerabile Monastero dei Santi Cosma e Damiano in Mica Aurea*, Rome, Testo e Senso, 2013

Barone, G., "La presenza degli ordini religiosi nella Roma di Martino V", in *Alle origini della nuova Roma. Martino V (1417-1431)*, ed. by M. Chiabò, G. D'Alessandro, P. Piacentini and C. Ranieri, Acts of the conference (Rome, 2-5 March 1992), Rome, Nuovi Studi Storici, 1992, pp. 353-365

Barone, G., "Margherita Colonna e le Clarisse di San Silvestro in Capite", in *Roma anno 1300*, pp. 799-805

Barral i Altet, X., "Strategie e specificità della committenza artistica femminile nel medioevo: ipotesi per un dibattito", in *Medioevo. I committenti*, ed. by A.C. Quintavalle, Acts of the conference (Parma, 2010), Milan, Electa, 2011, pp. 77-88

Bartoloni, F., "Suppliche pontificie", *Bullettino dell'Istituto Storico Italiano per il Medioevo*, 67 (1995), pp. 1-187

Batard, Y., "Notes sur des fresques récemment découvertes entre Veroli et Alatri", *Bollettino d'arte*, 4, 43 (1958), pp. 177-180

Battelli, G., "Il comune di Ferentino e i Francescani nei secoli XIII e XIV", *Archivio della Società romana di storia patria*, 67 (1944), pp. 361-369

Bell, S.G., "Medieval Women Book Owners: Arbiters of Lay Piety and Ambassadors of Culture", *Signs*, 4 (1982), pp. 742-768

Bellosi, L., "The Function of the Rucellai Madonna in the Church of Santa Maria Novella", in *Italian Panel Painting of the Duecento and Trecento*, ed. by V. Schmidt, Washington, National Gallery of Art, 2002, pp. 146-159

Belting, H., "Icons and Roman Society", in *Italian Church Decoration of the Middle Ages and Early Renaissance*, ed. by W. Tronzo, Bologna, Nuova Alfa Editoriale, 1989, pp. 27-41

Bergamaschi, P., *Vita della serva di Dio Donna Maria Cecilia Baij*, Viterbo, Tipografia Agnesotti, 1923
Bertani, B., "La Chiesa del 'Monacato' in Castrocielo", *Benedictina*, 21 (1974), pp. 301-307
Bertani, B., "Sulle antiche chiese di Castrocielo", *Benedictina*, 30 (1983), pp. 109-127
Bertelli, C., "La mostra degli affreschi di Grottaferrata", *Paragone*, 21, 249 (1970), pp. 91-101
Berthier, J.J., *Chroniques du monastère de San Sisto et de San Domenico e Sisto à Rome écrites par trois religieuses du même monastère et traduites par un religieux dominicain*, Levanto, Imp. de l'Immaculée, 1919-1920
Bertolini, O., "Per la storia delle diaconie romane nell'Alto Medio Evo sino alla fine del secolo VIII", *Archivio della Società romana di storia patria*, 70 (1947), pp. 1-147
Binski, P., *Westminster Abbey and the Plantagenets. Kingship and the Representation of Power, 1200-1400*, New Haven-London, Yale University Press, 1995
Bloch, B.H., *Monte Cassino in the Middle Ages*, 3 vols., Cambridge, Harvard University Press, 1986
Boehm, M., *Wandmalerei des 13. Jahrhunderts im Klarissenkloster S. Pietro in Vienis zu Anagni Bilder fur die Andacht*, Munster, Lit, 1999
Boesch Gajano, S., *Chelidonia. Storia di un'eremita medievale*, Rome, Viella, 2010
Bolgia, C., *Reclaiming the Roman Capitol: Santa Maria in Aracoeli from the Altar of Augustus to the Franciscans c. 500-1450*, London, Routledge, 2017
Borsi, F., "L'antico convento di S. Maria in Campo Marzio", in *Santa Maria in Campo Marzio*, ed. by N. Iotti, Rome, Editalia, 1987
Boskovits, M., "Insegnare per immagini: dipinti e sculture nelle sale capitolari", *Arte cristiana*, 77 (1990), pp. 123-142
Bovi, B., *Roiate: ambiente, tradizioni, folklore, religione, storia, dialetto*, Palestrina, s.n., 1979
Brandenburg, H., *Die frühchristlichen Kirchen in rom von 4. bis zum 7. Jahrhundert. der Beginn der abendländischen Kirchenbau- Kunst*, Regensburg, Schnell & Steiner, 2013
Brandenburg, H., *Le prime chiese di Roma. IV-VII secolo*, Milan, Jaca Book, 2004
Breccola, G., *Montefiascone. Guida alla scoperta*, Viterbo, Annulli Editori, 2006
Bruzelius, C., "Hearing is Believing. Clarissan Architecture, ca. 1213-1340", *Gesta*, 31, 2 (1992), pp. 83-91
Bruzelius, C., "Nuns in Space: Strict Enclosure and the Architecture of the Clarisses in the Thirteenth Century", in *Clare of Assisi. A Medieval and Modern Woman. Clarefest Selected Papers*, ed. by I. Peterson, New York, Columbia University Press, 1996, pp. 53-74
Bruzelius, C., *The Stones of Naples. Church Building in Angevin Italy, 1266-1343*, New Haven, Yale University Press, 2004
Burti, V., "I campanili di Roma e le loro decorazioni", *Emporium*, 28 (1908), pp. 123-130
Bynum, C.W., *Jesus as Mother. Studies in the Spirituality of the High Middle Ages*, Berkeley, University of California Press, 1982
Bynum, C.W., *Holy Feast, Holy Fast. The Religious Significance of Food to Medieval Women*, Berkeley, University of California Press, 1987

Cadei, A., "Scultura architettonica cistercense e cantieri monastici", in *I Cistercensi e il Lazio*, Rome, Multigrafica Editrice, 1978, pp. 157-162
Callahan, M., "Review of Crown and Veil: Female Monasticism from the Fifth to the Fifteenth Centuries", *The Burlington Magazine*, 151, 1275 (2009), pp. 400-401

Cangemi, L., Trivelli, P., *Roma. Chiesa di S. Silvestro in Capite: lo stato attuale*, Rome, International Maxpress, 1995 (Materiali per la storia e il restauro dell'architettura: scheda per le esercitazioni)

Cannon, J., *Religious Poverty, Visual Riches. Art in the Dominican Churches of Central Italy in the Thirteenth and Fourteenth Centuries*, London-New Haven, Yale University Press, 2013

Caperna U., "Il monastero di S. Andrea Apostolo in Arpino", in *Il monachesimo benedettino femminile in Ciociaria*, pp. 412-448

Caperna U., *Il monastero di S. Andrea Apostolo di Arpino*, Rome, Gruppo Culturale di Roma e del Lazio, 1993

Capitani, O., "Gregorio IX", in *Enciclopedia dei Papi*, 2, Rome, Istituto della Enciclopedia Italiana, 2000, pp. 379-391

Caraffa, F., "I monasteri medievali nella parte nord-orientale dei Monti Lepini", *Bollettino dell'Istituto di Storia dell'Arte Meridionale*, 11 (1979-1982), pp. 45-57

Caraffa, F., *Il monastero di S. Chiara in Anagni dalle origini alla fine dell'Ottocento*, Anagni, Istituto di storia e di arte del Lazio meridionale - Centro di Anagni, 1985

Caraffa, F., "L'eremitismo nella valle dell'Alto Aniene dalle origini al secolo XIX", *Lateranum*, 30 (1964), pp. 226-232

Caraffa, F., *Trevi nel Lazio dalle origini alla fine del secolo XIX*, 1, Rome, Facultas Theologica Pontificiae Universitatis Lateranensis, 1976

Caraffa, F., "Visite pastorali nel Lazio meridionale dal Concilio di Trento al secolo XIX", *Archiva Ecclesiae. Bollettino dell'Associazione Archivistica Ecclesiastica*, 22-23 (1979-1980), pp. 245-248

Carbonetti Vendittelli, C., "Il registro di entrate e uscite del convento domenicano di San Sisto degli anni 1369-1381", in *Economia e società a Roma tra Medioevo e Rinascimento. Studi dedicati a Arnold Esch*, ed. by A. Esposito and L. Palermo, Rome, Viella, 2005, pp. 96-127

Carbonetti Vendittelli, C., Carocci, S., "Le fonti per la storia locale", *Rassegna degli Archivi di Stato*, 44 (1984), pp. 68-148

Cardosi, A., *L'antico statuto di Sonnino (sec. XIII)*, Rome, Edizioni Sidera, 1965

Carli, E., "La pittura gotica in Italia", in *La pittura gotica*, ed. by E. Carli, J. Gudiol and G. Souchal, Milan, Mondadori, 1964, pp. 7-30

Carocci, S., *Baroni di Roma*, Rome, École française de Rome, 1993

Carocci, S., *Tivoli nel basso Medioevo: società cittadina ed economia agraria*, Rome, Istituto Storico Italiano per il Medioevo, 1988

Carotti, A., *Gli affreschi della Grotta delle Fornelle a Calvi Vecchia*, Rome, De Luca, 1974

Carpaneto, G., *Le famiglie nobili romane*, Rome, Rendina, 2001

Cartwright, L., Sturken, M., *Practices of Looking. An Introduction to Visual Culture*, Oxford, Oxford University Press, 2009

Casanova, E., "Le carte di Costantino Corvisieri", *Archivi Italiani*, 7 (1920), pp. 20-48

Cassoni, M., *Sguardo storico sull'abbazia di S. Domenico di Sora*, Sora, Tip. lit. V. D'Amico, 1910

Cavallaro, A., "Recensione. *Osservazioni sulla pittura a Roma sotto Martino V* di S. L'Occaso", *Archvio della Società romana di storia patria*, 125 (2005), pp. 146-148

Cavallaro, A., "Roma 1420-1431. La pittura al tempo di Martino V", in *La storia dei giubilei*, pp. 312-327

Cavazzi, L., *La diaconia di S. Maria in Via Lata e il monastero di S. Ciriaco. Memorie storiche*, Rome, Pustet, 1908

Cecchelli, C., *Sant'Agnese fuori le Mura e Santa Costanza*, Rome, Danesi, 1961
Cerafogli, P.E., *La Baronessa Santa Filippa Mareri*, Vatican City, Libreria Editrice Vaticana, 1979
Ceschi, C., "Restauro dei monumenti nel Lazio (1951-1961)", *Atti dell'Accademia Nazionale di San Luca*, n.s., 1 (2010), online
Cicerchia, P., *Tarquinia. Borgo medievale*, Rome, Istituto Poligrafico e Zecca dello Stato, 1990
Claussen, P.C., *Die Kirchen der Stadt Rom im Mitterlater, 1050-1300. A-F (Corpus Cosmatorum II, 1: Forschungen zur Kunstgeschichte und christlichen Archaologie)*, Stuttgart, Steiner, 2002
Claussen, J., *Papst Honorius III (1216-1227)*, Hildesheim, Olms, 2004
Coakley, J., *Women, Men and Spiritual Power*, New York, Columbia University Press, 2006
Cohn, S.K., *Cultures of the Plague*, Oxford, Oxford University Press, 2010
Cohn, S.K., "Renaissance Attachment to Things: Material Culture in Last Wills and Testaments", *Economic History Review*, 65 (2012), pp. 984-1004
Constable, G., *Cluny from the Tenth to the Twelfth Centuries. Further Studies*, Aldershot, Ashgate, 2000
Cooper, D., "Recovering the Lost Rood Screens of Medieval and Renaissance Italy", in *The Art and Science of the Church Screen in Medieval Europe*, ed. by S. Bucklow, R. Marks and L. Wrapson, Woodbridge, The Boydell Press, 2017, pp. 220-245
Cooper, D., Robson, J., *The Making of Assisi. The Pope, the Franciscan and the Painting of the Basilica*, New Haven-London, Yale University Press, 2013
Corbett, S., Frankl, W., Krautheimer, R., *Corpus basilicarum christianarum Romae. The Early Christian Basilicas of Rome (4.-9. cent.)*, 1, Vatican City, Pontificio Istituto di Archeologia Cristiana, 1937
Cordovani, R., *Il monastero delle monache benedettine di San Pietro a Montefiascone*, Viterbo, Centro di Iniziative Culturali Montefiascone, 1994
Corvese, F., *Desiderio di Montecassino e le Abbazie di Terra di Lavoro*, Caserta, L'Aperia, 1999
Crescenzo, P., Scaramella, A., *La chiesa di San Lorenzo in Panisperna sul Colle Viminale*, Rome, Ministero dell'Interno - Direzione generale degli Affari dei culti, 1998
Creti, M., *Cenni storici della Chiesa e del Monastero di San Luca a Guarcino*, Rome, Ind. Tip. Imperia, 1948
Crown and Veil. Female Monasticism from the Fifth to the Fifteenth Centuries, ed. by J. F. Hamburger and S. Marti, New York, Columbia University Press, 2008

Danesi, V., "S. Nicola di Trisulti: un insediamento certosino femminile?", *Arte medievale*, 4 (2015), pp. 153-164
De Angelis M., "Il monastero di Borgo San Pietro di Filippa Mareri. Ricostruzione storico-architettonica", in *Santa Filippa Mareri*, pp. 93-142
De Marchi, A., "Un cadre béant sur le monde. La révolution giottesque à travers le developpement de nouveaux types de croix et de retable monumentaux», in *Giotto e compagni*, ed. by D. Thièbaut, Exhibition catalogue (Paris, 2013), Paris, Ed. du Louvre, 2013, pp. 49-65
Deichmann, F.W., "Die Lage der konstantinischen Basilika der heiligen Agnes an der Via Nomentana", *Rivista di archeologia cristiana*, 22 (1946), pp. 213-234
Derbes, A., *Picturing the Passion in Late Medieval Italy. Narrative Painting, Franciscan Ideologies, and the Levant*, Cambridge, Cambridge University Press, 1996

Donò, A., *Storia dell'affresco in Alatri*, Rome, Istituto Poligrafico della Zecca dello Stato, 1990

D'Onorio, G., Trulli, G., *Veroli. Un percorso di storia e di arte*, Veroli, Arti grafiche Pasquarelli, 2011

Dressler, R., "Continuing the Discourse: Feminist Scholarship and the Study of Medieval Visual Culture", *Medieval Feminist Forum*, 43, 1 (2007), pp. 15-34

Dunlop, A., "Dominicans and Cloistered Women: The Convent of Sant'Aurea in Rome", *Early Modern Women*, 2 (2007), pp. 43-71

Dunn, M., "Roman Nuns, Art Patronage, and the Construction of Identity", in *Wives, Widows, Mistresses and Nuns in Early Modern Italy. Making the Invisible Visible through Art Patronage*, ed. by K.A. McIver, Farnham, Ashgate, 2012, pp. 183-224

Eckenstein, L., *Women under Monasticism*, Cambridge, Cambridge University Press, 1896

Egidi, P., "L'Archivio della Cattedrale di Viterbo", *Bollettino dell'Istituto Storico Italiano* (1906), pp. 38-39

Ekonomou, A., *Byzantine Rome and the Greek Popes*, Plymouth, Lexington Books, 2007

Ermini Pani, L., Fichera, M.G., Mancinelli, M.L., *Indagini archeologiche nella chiesa di San Damiano in Assisi*, Assisi, Porziuncola, 2005

Esposito, A., "Il mondo della religiosità femminile romana", *Archivio della Società romana di storia patria*, 132 (2009), pp. 149-172

Fabiani, L., *La Terra di S. Benedetto. Fine del dominio temporale dell'Abbazia di Montecassino*, Montcassino, Badia di Montecassino, 1981

Falco, G., *Albori d'Europa*, Rome, Le Edizioni del Lavoro, 1947

Fallica, S., "Sviluppo e trasformazione della chiesa di San Lorenzo in Panisperna a Roma", *Studi romani*, 62 (2015), pp. 117-148

Fasolo, G., "Presentazione di rilievi di studenti della Facoltà di Architettura di Roma relativi alla villa romana di lago S. Puoto, i monasteri di S. Spirito di Zannone in Gaeta, di S. Michele Arcangelo di Amaseno e del Palazzo Zaccaleoni in Priverno", *Bollettino dell'Istituto di storia e di arte del Lazio meridionale*, 4 (1966), pp. 63-77

Fazzini, G., "Amalasunta regina dei Goti e il tetro scoglio dell'Isola Martana", *Lazio ieri e oggi*, 51 (2015), pp. 22-24

Federici, V., *I monasteri di Subiaco*, 2, Rome, Ministero della Pubblica Istruzione, 1904

Fenicchia, V., "Aurelia e Neomisia", in *Bibliotheca Sanctorum*, 2, Rome, Istituto Giovanni XXIII nella Pontificia Università Lateranense, 1962, col. 601

Ferrari, G., *Early Roman Monasteries. Notes for the History of the Monasteries and Convents at Rome from the V through the X Century*, Vatican City, Pontificio Istituto di Archeologia Cristiana, 1957

Fiocchi Nicolai, V., *Anagni cristiana e il suo territorio*, Rome, Tored, 2014

Fiorani, D., *Tecniche costruttive murarie medievali. Il Lazio meridionale*, Rome, L'Erma di Bretschneider, 1996

Film Theory and Criticism. Introductory Readings, ed. by L. Braudy and M. Cohen, New York-Oxford, Oxford University Press, 1999

Floridi, G., *Le pergamene di San Luca e Sant'Agnello di Guarcino*, Guarcino, Comune di Guarcino, 1967

Floridi, G., "Nozze Floridi-Pogson Doria Pamphilj e la badia di San Sebastiano di Alatri", *Terra Nostra*, 32, 3-4 (1993), pp. 7-8

Floridi, G., *Storia di Guarcino*, Guarcino, Comune di Guarcino, 1971

Foreville, R., *Latran I, II, III et Latran IV*, Paris, Editions de L'Orante, 1965

Fornari, B., "I monasteri di San Bartolomeo e San Nicola presso Trisulti", *Terra Nostra*, 22 (1983), pp. 17-19

Francesca Romana. La santa, il monastero e la città alla fine del Medioevo, ed. by A. Bartolomei, Florence, Edizioni del Galluzzo, 2009

Francesco e la croce di San Damiano, ed. by M. Bollati, Milan, Edizioni Biblioteca Francescana, 2016

Francesco e la croce dipinta, ed. by M. Pierini, Exhibition catalogue (Perugia, 2016-2017), Milan, Silvana Editoriale, 2016

Frugoni, C., *Chiara d'Assisi. Una solitudine abitata*, Rome-Bari, Laterza, 2006

Frutaz, A.P., *Il complesso monumentale di Sant'Agnese*, Vatican City, Tipografia Poliglotta Vaticana, 1960

Frutaz, A.P., *Le piante di Roma*, 3, Vatican City, Tipografia Poliglotta Vaticana, 1962

Gaeta, M., *Giotto und die "croci dipinte" des Trecento Studien zu Typus, Genese und Rezeption; mit einem Katalog der monumentalen Tafelkreuze des Trecento (ca. 1290-ca. 1400)*, Munster, Rhema, 2013

Gallotta, E., "L'architettura come spazio per la liturgia: l'interno di Santa Maria Maggiore a Ferentino alla fine del Duecento", *Quaderni dell'Istituto di Storia dell'Architettura*, 71 (2019), pp. 5-22

Gambuti, E., "Porticus Ecclesiae Sanctae Agnetis: lo scalone di accesso alla basilica onoriana", *Quaderni dell'Istituto di Storia dell'Architettura* (2015), pp. 5-18

Gambuti, E., "Ricondurre all'ordine un'antica fabbrica: l'opera del cardinale Alessandro de Medici in Sant'Agnse fuori le mura", *Palladio. Rivista di Storia dell'Architettura*, 65-66 (2020), pp. 123-146

Gandolfo, F., "Il ritratto di committenza", in *Arte e iconografia a Roma da Costantino a Cola di Rienzo*, ed. by M. Andaloro and S. Romano, Milan, Jaca Book, 2000, pp. 175-192

Gandolfo, F., "Il ritratto nobiliare di committenza", in *La nobiltà romana nel medioevo*, ed. by S. Carocci, Rome, École française de Rome, 2006, pp. 279-290

Gardner, J., "Andrea di Bonaiuto and the Chapter House Frescoes in Santa Maria Novella", *Art History*, 2, 2 (1979), pp. 107-138

Gardner, J., "For Whom the Bell Tolls: A Franciscan Bell Founder, Franciscan Bells and a Franciscan Patrons in Late Thirteenth-Century Rome", in *Medioevo. I committenti*, ed. by A.C. Quintavalle, Acts of the conference (Parma, 2010), Milan, Electa, 2011, pp. 460-468

Gardner, J., "Nuns and altarpieces agendas for research", *Römisches Jahrbuch der Bibliotheca Hertziana*, 30 (1995), pp. 27-57

Garrison, E., "Dating the Vatican Last Judgement Panel: Monument *versus* Document", *La bibliofilia*, 70 (1970), pp. 121-160

Gaynor, J.S., Toesca, P., *San Silvestro in Capite*, Rome, Danesi, 1963

Giannetta, E., *Le chiese di Amaseno*, Frosinone, Tipografia Tecnostampa, 1987

Gilchrist, R., *Gender and Material Culture. The Archaeology of Religious Women*, London, Routledge, 1994

Gimma, M.G., *Il centro storico di Viterbo*, Viterbo, Betagamma editrice, 2001

Gioacchini D., *Curiosità ortane*, Orte, Museo Diocesano di Arte Sacra, 1961

Giovetti, P., *Brigida di Svezia. Una santa europea*, Rome, San Paolo Editore, 2002

Goodson, C.J., *The Rome of Pope Paschal I. Papal Power, Urban Renovation, Church Rebuilding and Relic Translation, 817-824*, Cambridge, Cambridge University Press, 2010

Gordini, G.D., "Origini e sviluppo del monachesimo a Roma", *Gregorianum*, 37 (1956), pp. 220-260
Graham, E.E., "Memorializing Identity: The Foundation and Reform of San Lorenzo in Panisperna", *Franciscan Studies*, 75 (2017), pp. 467-495
Guido, S., "Il monastero di San Lorenzo in Panisperna in Rione Monti a Roma", *Frate Francesco*, 81 (2015), pp. 185-195

Hall, M.B., "The Ponte in S. Maria Novella: The Problem of the Rood Screen in Italy", *Journal of the Warburg and Courtauld Institutes*, 37 (1974), pp. 157-173
Hamburger, J.F., "Art, Enclosure and the *Cura Monialium*: Prolegomena in the Guise of a Post Script", *Gesta*, 31, 2 (1992), pp. 108-134
Hamburger, J.F., *Nuns as Artists. The Visual Culture of a Medieval Convent*, Berkeley, Berkeley University Press, 1997
Hamburger, J.F., *The Visual and the Visionary. Art and Female Spirituality in Late Medieval Germany*, New York, Zone Books, 1998
Herklotz, I., *Sepulcra e monumenta del Medioevo*, Naples, Liguori, 2001
Hermanin, F., *San Marco*, Rome, Danesi, 1932
Hood, W., *Fra Angelico at San Marco*, New Haven-London, Yale University Press, 1993
Hubert, E., "Un censier des biens romains du monastère S. Silvestro in Capite (1333-1334)", *Archivio della Società romana di storia patria*, 111 (1988), pp. 93-140
Hueck, I., "Review of M. Bigaroni, H.R. Meier and E. Lunghi *La Basilica di Santa Chiara in Assisi* (Quattroemme: Perugia, 1994)", *Kunstchronik*, 50 (1997), pp. 287-292
Hugh, H., "Adoro Te Devote", in *The Catholic Encyclopedia*, 1, New York, New Advent, 1907, online
Hulsen, C., *Le chiese di Roma nel Medioevo*, Florence, Olschki, 1927

Iazeolla, T., "Gli affreschi di San Sebastiano ad Alatri", in *Roma anno 1300*, pp. 467-475
"Il Catalogo di Torino delle chiese, degli ospedali dei monasteri di Roma nel secolo XIV", ed. by G. Falco, *Archivio della Società romana di storia patria*, 32 (1909), pp. 411-433
Il Collegio Principe di Piemonte e la chiesa di San Pietro in Vineis in Anagni, ed. by M. Rak, Anagni, Indap, 1998
Il monachesimo benedettino femminile in Ciociaria, ed. by G. D'Onorio and A. Ilari, Acts of the conference (Veroli, 1992), Veroli, Monastero di Santa Maria, 1994
Il monachesimo femminile in Italia dall'alto medioevo al secolo XVII a confronto con l'oggi, ed. by G. Zarri, Verona, Il Segno dei Gabrielli editori, 1997
Il Quattrocento a Camerino, ed. by A. De Marchi and M. Giannatiempo Lopez, Milan, Motta, 2002
Il restauro della facciata e del nartece della Badia della Madonna di Viano, ed. by A. Ferrazzano, P. Iecco and N. Temperilli, Sgurgola, Comune di Sgurgola, 2004
Innocenzo III: Urbs et Orbis, ed. by A. Sommerlechner, Acts of the conference (Rome, 1998), Rome, Nuovi Studi Storici, 2003
Ippoliti L., *Il monastero delle benedettine di S. Andrea al Colle in Arpino: descrizione storico-artistica illustrata*, Arpino, Società Tipografica Macioce e Pisani, 1931

Jäggi, C., *Frauenklöster im Spätmittelater*, Petersberg, Michael Imhof Verlag, 2006
Jäggi, C., "Review of J. Elliott and C. Warr, eds., *The Church of Santa Maria Donna Regina. Art, Iconography and Patronage in Fourteenth-Century Naple*s; C. Bruzelius: *The Stones of Naples: Church Building in Angevin Italy, 1226-1343*", *Speculum*, 81 (2006), pp. 507-509

Jonta, C., *Storia di Segni*, Gavignano, Tipografia Francescana, 1928

Kaeppeli, T., "Dalle pergamene di S. Maria in Gradi di Viterbo", *Archivum Fratrum Prae-dicatorum*, 33 (1963), pp. 243-259

Kane, E., *The Church of San Silvestro in Capite in Rome*, Genoa, Marconi, 2005

King, C., *Renaissance Women as Patrons Wives and Widows in Italy, 1300-1550*, Manchester, Manchester University Press, 1998

Krautheimer, R., *Rome. Profile of a City, 312-1308*, Princeton, Princeton University Press, 1980

Krone und Schleier Kunst aus mittelalterlichen Frauenklösten: Ruhrlandmuseum: Die frühen Klöster und Stifte 500-1200. Kunst – und Ausstellungshalle der Bundesrepublik Deutschland: Die Zeit der Orden 1200-1500, ed. by J. Gerchow and F. Jutta, Munich, Hirmer, 2005

La Basilica Costantiniana di S. Agnese. Lavori archeologici e di restauro, ed. by C. Magnani Cianetti and C. Pavolini, Rome, Electa, 2004

Lacan, J., *The Seminar. Book XI. The Four Fundamental Concepts of Psychoanalysis*, London, Hogarth Press-Institute of Psycho-Analysis, 1977

Lazio medievale. Ricerca topografica su 33 abitati delle antiche diocesi di Alatri, Anagni, Ferentino, Veroli, ed. by C. Carbonetti Vendittelli, Rome, Multigrafica, 1980

Lazzari, F., *Velletri nel Medioevo*, Viterbo, Centro Studio Antonio Mancinelli, 2015

Lazzari, T., *Le donne nell'alto medioevo*, Milan, Mondadori, 2010

La storia dei giubilei, ed. by J. Le Goff, G. Fossi and C. Strinati, Rome, BNL Edizioni, 1997

Le più antiche carte del convento di San Sisto in Roma (900-1300), ed. by C. Carbonetti Vendittelli, Rome, Società romana di storia patria, 1987

Le più antiche pergamene del monastero di Santa Filippa: i Mareri di Borgo San Pietro e il Cicolano fra 12° e 14° secolo, ed. by T. Leggio and R. Marinelli, L'Aquila, Edizione Libreria Colacchi, 2016

Leone, G., *Icone di Roma e del Lazio*, Rome, L'Erma di Bretschneider, 2013

Lirosi, A., *I monasteri femminili a Roma tra XVI e XVII secolo*, Rome, Viella, 2012

L'Occaso, S., "Osservazioni sulla pittura a Roma sotto Martino V", *Archivio della Società romana di storia patria*, 125 (2002), pp. 42-51

Longhi, G.M., "Un insigne monumento da redimere: Il Palazzo dei Cavalieri Gaudenti in Ferentino", *Bollettino di Storia dell'Arte del Lazio Meridionale*, 1 (1963), pp. 127-140

Lori Sanfilippo, I., *Il monastero di Sant'Agnese sulla Via Nomentana. Storia e documenti (982-1299)*, Rome, Società romana di storia patria, 2015

Lori Sanfilippo, I., "Le più antiche carte del monastero di Sant'Agnese sulla Via Nomentana", *Bollettino dell'Archivio Paleografico Italiano*, 2-3 (1956-1957), pp. 65-97

Lovrovich, G.E., *Jacopa dei Settesoli*, Marino, Tipografia S. Lucia, 1976

Lowe, K.J.P., "Franciscan and Papal Patronage at the Clarissan Convent of San Cosimato in Trastevere 1440-1560", *Papers of the British School at Rome*, 68 (2000), pp. 217-239

Lowe, K.J.P., *Nuns' Chronicles and Convent Culture in Renaissance and Counter-Reformation Italy*, Cambridge, Cambridge University Press, 2003

Lucidi, E., *Memorie storiche dell'antichissimo municipio ora terra dell'Ariccia*, 1, Rome, Lazzarini, 1976

Macchioni, F., *Storia civile e religiosa di Bagnoregio dai tempi antichi sino all'anno 1503*, Viterbo, La Rosa, 1956

Manselli, R., "Certosini e cistercensi", in *Il monachesimo e la riforma ecclesiastica (1049-1122)*, Acts of the conference (Passo della Mendola, 1968), Milan, Vita e Pensiero, 1971, pp. 79-104

Manzi, P., *Il convento fortificato dei SS. Quattro Coronati nella storia e nell'arte*, Rome, Arma del Genio, 1968

Marchetti Longhi, G., "Il Lazio meridionale triplice via di espansione della civiltà latina", *Bollettino dell'Istituto di Storia e di Arte del Lazio meridionale*, 4 (1966), pp. 187-233

Marini A., "Le fondazioni francescane femminili", *Collectanea Franciscana*, 63 (1993), pp. 71-96

Marini, A., "Monasteri femminili a Roma nei secoli XIII-XV", *Archivio della Società romana di storia patria*, 132 (2010), pp. 81-108

Mathis, P., "Chiesa di San Rocco (dalla chiesa di Santa Maria del Monacato. Gli affreschi", in *Affreschi in Val Comino*, pp. 106-114

Matthiae, G., *Pittura romana del Medioevo, sec. XI-XIV*, ed. by F. Gandolfo, 2 vols., Rome, Palombi, 1988

McCormick, M., "The Imperial Edge: Italo-Byzantine Identity, Movement and Integration", in *Studies on the Internal Diaspora of the Byzantine Empire*, ed. by H. Ahrweiler and A. Laiou, Cambridge, Harvard University Press, 1998, pp. 17-52

Meersseman, G.G., "Eremitismo e predicazione itinerante", in *L'eremitismo in Occidente nei secoli XI e XII*, Acts of the conference (Mendola, 1962), Milan, Vita e Pensiero, 1965, pp. 164-179

Mengarelli, C., "La presenza monastica ad Anagni", *Rivista cistercense*, 31 (2014), pp. 205-248

Mercurio, M., "La dimora estiva in Italia di Urbano V", *Archivio della Società romana di storia patria*, 65 (1942), pp. 153-161

Monasticon Italiae, 1, *Roma e Lazio*, 1, ed. by F. Caraffa, Cesena, Centro Storico Benedettino Italiano, 1981

Montanucci, G., "L'isola Martana nel Medioevo", *Studi vetrallesi*, 9 (2002), pp. 30-32

Montefusco, E., "Secondo: non conservare. Per una ricostruzione dell'archivio di San Silvestro in Capite a Roma", *Archivio della Società romana di storia patria*, 135 (2013), pp. 5-29

Moorman, J.R.H., *Medieval Franciscan Houses*, New York, Franciscan Institute Publication, 1983

Morgia, M., *Sgurgola e la sua badia*, Rome, Gavignano, 1962

Mortari, L., *Il tesoro della Cattedrale di Anagni*, Rome, De Luca, 1963

Mulvey, L., "Visual Pleasure and Narrative Cinema", in *Film Theory and Criticism*, pp. 833-844

Murat, Z., Valenzano, G., "Donne dimenticate: esempi di committenza femminile nel Veneto medievale", in *Medioevo. I committenti*, ed. by A.C. Quintavalle, Acts of the conference (Parma, 2010), Milan, Electa, 2011, pp. 187-200

Museo Nazionale di Palazzo Venezia. Sculture in legno, ed. by G.M. Fachechi, Rome, Gangemi, 2011

Nardini, B., *Il complesso monumentale di S. Croce*, Florence, Nardini, 1983

Nicosia, A., "Le monache di S. Maria di Palazzolo", *Benedictina*, 23 (1976), pp. 173-178

Nocca, M., *Velletri. Guida alla città*, Rome, Palombi, 2002

Nuovi studi su San Cosimato, ed. by A.M. Velli, Rome, Graphofeel Edizioni, 2017

Oliver, J., "Review of C. Jäggi, Frauenklöster im Spätmittelater", *Speculum*, 83, 1 (2008), pp. 204-205
Odonnel, J.J., "Liberius the Patrician", *Traditio*, 37 (1981), pp. 31-72

Pagano, S., *L'archivio del convento dei SS. Domenico e Sisto di Roma. Cenni storici e inventario*, Vatican City, Archivio Vaticano, 1994
Panza, A., "Anagni nel XIII secolo. Iniziative edilizie e politica pontificia", *Storia della città*, 6 (1981), pp. 33-76
Paolin, G., *Lo spazio del silenzio. Monacazioni forzate, clausura e proposte di vita religiosa femminile nell'età moderna*, Pordenone, Biblioteca dell'Immagine, 1996
Pardo, V.F., "Architettura cistercense e architettura degli ordini mendicanti", in *Il monachesimo cistercense nella Marittima medievale. Storia e arte*, ed. by R. Cataldi, Casamari, Ed. Casamari, 2002, pp. 251-297
Parlato, E., Romano, S., *Roma e il Lazio*, Milan, Jaca Book, 1992
Partner, P., *The Lands of St Peter*, London, Eyre Metheun, 1972
Pecchiai, P., *La Chiesa dello Spirito Santo e l'antica chiesa di Sant'Aurea in via Giulia*, Rome, Ugo Pinnarò, 1953
Pesci, E., "L'Itinerario romano di Sigerico e la lista dei papi portati in Inghilterra (anno 990)", *Rivista di archeologia cristiana*, 13 (1936), pp. 43-60
Petrucci, E., *Ecclesiologia e politica. Momenti di storia del papato medievale*, Rome, Carocci, 2001
Piazzoni, A.M., *Guglielmo di Saint-Thierry. Il declinio dell'ideale monastico nel secolo XII*, Rome, Carocci, 1988
Pierantoni, D.A., *Aniene illustrato*, Rome, Istituto di storia e di arte del Lazio meridionale, 2005
Piferi, M.E., *Montefiascone. Città e territorio*, Viterbo, Betagamma editrice, 1996
Pinzi C., *Storia della città di Viterbo*, Bologna, Forni, 1974
Pinzi, C., *Storia della città di Viterbo nel medioevo*, 1, Rome, Palombo, 1887
Pocino, W., "Due Santi nell'Abbazia di Alatri", *Lazio ieri e oggi*, 10, 7 (1974), pp. 157-164
Pope, Church and City, ed. by F. Andrews, B. Brenda and C. Eggar, Leiden, Brill, 2004
Power, E., *Medieval English Nunneries c. 1275-1535*, Cambridge, Cambridge University Press, 1922
Prehn, E.T., "Una decorazione murale del Duecento toscano in un monastero laziale", *Antichità viva*, 10 (1971), pp. 3-11

Reassessing the Roles of Women as 'Makers' of Medieval Art and Architecture, ed. by T. Martin, Leiden, Brill, 2012
Rendina, C., *I papi*, Rome, Newton Compton, 1990
Righetti Tosti-Croce, M., "Architettura monastica: gli edifici. Linee per una storia architettonica", in *Dall'eremo al cenobio. La civiltà monastica in Italia dalle origini all'eta di Dante*, ed. by G.C. Alessio, Milan, Garzanti, 1987, pp. 486-575
Righetti Tosti-Croce, M., "La chiesa di Santa Chiara in Assisi: architettura", in *Santa Chiara in Assisi*, ed. by P. Tomei, Milan, Silvana Editoriale, 2002, pp. 21-57
Roma anno 1300. Atti della IV settimana di studi di storia dell'arte medievale all'Università di Roma "La Sapienza", Acts of the conference (Rome, 1980), Rome, L'Erma di Bretschneider, 1983
Roma dall'antichità al medioevo, 2, *Contesti tardoantichi e altomedioevali*, ed. by L. Paroli and L. Vendittelli, Milan, Il Bodone, 2004

Romanini, A.M., "Architettura degli ordini mendicanti", *Storia della città*, 9 (1976), pp. 5-15

Romano, S., "Affreschi da S. Maria del Monacato a Castrocielo (e un'aggiunta da Roccasecca)", *Arte medievale*, 2 (1989), pp. 155-166

Romano, S., *Eclissi di Roma. Pittura murale a Roma e nel Lazio da Bonifacio VIII a Martino V (1295-1431)*, Milan, Jaca Book, 1992

Romano, S., "I cicli a fresco di Sant'Agnese fuori le Mura", in *Fragmenta Picta. Affreschi e mosaici staccati del Medioevo romano*, ed. by M. Andaloro, A. Ghidoli, A. Iacobini, S. Romano and A. Tomei, Exhibition catalogue (Rome, 1989-1990), Rome, Electa, 1989, pp. 245-258

Romano, S., *La pittura medievale a Roma 312-1431: Corpus e Atlante*, 4, *Riforma e tradizione 1050-1198*, Milan, Jaca Book, 2006

Romano, S., *La pittura medievale a Roma 312-1431: Corpus e Atlante*, 5, *Il Duecento e la cultura gotica (1198-1280)*, Milan, Jaca Book, 2012

Romano, S., *La pittura medievale a Roma 312-1431: Corpus e Atlante*, 6, *Apogeo e fine del Medioevo (1288-1431)*, Milan, Jaca Book, 2017

Ronci, G., "Antichi affreschi a San Sisto Vecchio a Roma", *Bollettino d'Arte*, 36 (1951), pp. 15-26

Salvatori, L., "Il monastero fortificato di S. Chelidonia", *Studi vetrallesi* (2006), pp. 9-19

San Cosimato, ed. by F. Caraffa and L. Lotti, Rome, Nardini, 1971

Sandberg, E., *La croce dipinta italiana e l'iconografia della passione*, Rome, Multigraf, 1980

Sanità, G., *Collepardo nella sua storia e nelle sue memorie*, Rome, Alfapress, 1972

Sansterre, J.M., "Les moines grecs et orientaux à Rome aux époques byzantine et carolingienne (milieu du VIe-fin du IXe siécle)", *Mémoires de la classe des lettres*, 2, 661, (1983)

Santa Filippa Mareri. Atti del II convegno storico, ed. by A. Cacciotti and M. Melli, Acts of the conference (Greccio, 2003), Rome, Centro Culturale Aracoeli, 2007

Santa Filippa Mareri e il Monastero di Borgo S. Pietro nella storia del Cicolano. Atti del convegno di studi, ed. by R. Marinelli, Acts of the conference (Petrella Salto, Borgo San Pietro, 1986), Rieti, Istituto Suore Clarisse di Santa Filippa Mareri, 1989

Santità femminile nel Duecento, ed. by G. Avarucci, Acts of the conference (Cingoli, 1999), Ancona, Studia Picena, 2001

Sarra, A., *Potenza e carità di Dio*, Casamari, Tipografia dell'Abbazia, 1972

Scaccia-Scarafoni C., *La chiesa di San Leucio nella rocca di Veroli*, Veroli, E. Calzone, 1959

Scaccia-Scarafoni, C., "Memorie storiche della badia di S. Sebastiano nel territorio alatrino", *Archivio della Società romana di storia patria*, 39 (1916), pp. 5-52

Scaglia, G., "Antonio del Tanghero in Rome with Pietro Rosselli, Michelangelo Buonarroti and Antonio da Sangallo il Giovane", *Mitteilungen des Kunsthistorischen Institutes in Florenz*, 38 (1994), pp. 218-245

Scalisi, G., "L'abbazia di San Sebastiano nel territorio di Alatri", *Lazio ieri e oggi*, 9, 12 (1973), pp. 282-233

Schleif, C., "Krone und Schleier. Kunst aus mittelalterlichen Frauenklösten", *Speculum*, 82 (2007), pp. 456-457

Schmitz, P.H., "La première communautè de Vierges a Roma", *Revue bénédictine*, 38 (1926), pp. 189-195

Schuster I., "Il monastero di S. Salvatore. Gli antichi possedimenti farfensi nella Massa Torana", *Archivio della Società romana di storia patria*, 41 (1919), pp. 5-58

Schuster, I., *Storia di San Benedetto e dei suoi tempi*, S. Giuliano milanese, Abbazia di Viboldone, 1965

Scognamiglio, R., Speciale, L., "L'altra Madonna di Trastevere. La tavola della Vergine di San Cosimato", in *L'officina dello sguardo. Scritti in onore di Maria Andaloro*, ed. by G. Bordi, I. Carlettini, M.L. Fobelli, M.R. Menna and P. Pogliani, Rome, Gangemi, 2014, pp. 359-354

Scotti, R., "Il monastero di borgo S. Pietro e la storia della beata Filippa Mareri", *Lazio ieri e oggi*, 8 (2004), pp. 89-101

Sermoneta e i Caetani. Dinamiche politiche, sociali e culturali di un territorio tra medioevo ed età moderna, ed. by L. Fiorani, Rome, L'Erma di Bretschneider, 1999

Sheingorn, P., "The Medieval Feminist Art History Project", *Medieval Feminist Newsletter*, 12, 1 (1991), pp. 5-10

Sibilia, S., *Alessandro IV (1254-1261)*, Anagni, La Cassa Rurale, 1961

Sibilia, S., *Bonifacio VIII*, Anagni, La Cassa Rurale, 1949

Sicari, G., "Il monastero di SS. Cosma e Damiano in Mica Aurea: sue proprietà in Roma", *Alma Roma*, 23 (1982), pp. 30-44

Simonelli, F., "Chiesa di San Rocco (dalla chiesa di Santa Maria del Monacato. La storia", in *Affreschi in Val Comino*, pp. 1056-106

Spiazzi, R., *Cronache e fioretti del monastero di San Sisto all'Appia*, Bologna, Edizione Studio Domenicano, 1993

SS. Cosma e Damiano in Mica Aurea, ed. by J. Barclay Lloyd and K. Bull-Simonsen Einaudi, Rome, Testo Senso, 1998

Stein-Kecks, H., "Claustrum and capitulum: Some Remarks on the Façade and Interior of the Chapter House", in *Der mittelalterliche Kreuzgang*, ed. by P.K. Klein, Regensburg, Schnell & Steiner, 2004, pp. 157-189

Storia di Roma dall'antichità a oggi, 2, *Roma medievale*, ed. by A. Vauchez, Rome-Bari, Laterza, 2001

Suckale, R., "La tavola del Giudizio Universale da Santa Maria in Campo Marzio a Roma", in *Alfa e Omega*, Castel Bolognese, Itaca, 2006, pp. 99-101

Tarquini, A., *L'isola di Amalasunta: escursione geologica e storica al comprensorio del Lago di Bolsena*, Rome, Alma Roma, 1976

The Ashgate Research Companion to Women and Gender in Early Modern Europe, ed. by J. Couchman and A.M. Poska, Farnham, Ashgate, 2013

The Church of Santa Maria Donna Regina. Art, Iconography and Patronage in Fourteenth-Century Naples, ed. by J. Elliott and C. Warr, Aldershot, Ashgate, 2004

The Cultural Patronage of Medieval Women, ed. by J. Hall McCash, Athens, The University of Georgia Press, 1996

The History of Medieval Cannon Law during the Classical Period (1140-1234), ed. by W. Hartmann and K. Penninghton, New York, The Catholic University of America Press, 2008

The Pursuit of Holiness in Late Medieval and Renaissance Religion, ed. by H.A. Oberman and C. Trinkaus, Leiden, Brill, 1974

Thomas, A., *Art and Piety in the Female Religious Communities of Renaissance Italy*, Cambridge, Cambridge University Press, 2003

Toesca, P., *Storia dell'arte italiana. Il Trecento*, Turin, UTET, 1951

Toesca, P., *Gli affreschi della Cattedrale di Anagni*, Subiaco, Iter, 1994

Tomei, P., *L'architettura a Roma nel Quattrocento*, Rome, Palombi, 1942

Tomassetti, G., *Amaseno*, Rome, Unione Coperativa, 1899

Tomassetti G., *La campagna romana antica, medievale e moderna*, 2, Rome, Loescher, 1910

Tomassetti, G., *La campagna romana antica, medievale e moderna*, 3, Rome, Loescher, 1913

Tomassi, P., *Chiesa di San Lorenzo in Panisperna*, Rome, s.n., 1967

Toubert, P., *Les structures du Latium médiéval*, Rome, Ecole française de Rome, 1973

Valdez de Alamo, E., "Lament for a Lost Queen: the Sarcophagus of Doña Blanca in Nájera", *The Art Bulletin*, 78, 2 (1996), pp. 311-333

Valentini, R., Zucchetti, G., *Codice topografico della città di Roma*, 4 vols., Rome, Istituto Storico Italiano per il Medioevo, 1940

Valeri, M.T., "Il crocifisso del monastero di S. Andrea al Colle in Arpino", in *Il monachesimo benedettino femminile in Ciociaria*, pp. 449-464

Van Cleve, T.C., *The Emperor Frederick II of Hohenstaufen. Immutator Mundi*, Oxford, Oxford University Press, 1972

Van Engen, J., "The 'Crisis of Cenobitism' Reconsidered: Benedictine Monasticism in the Years 1050-1150", *Speculum*, 61, 2 (1986), pp. 269-304

Van Heteren, W., "Due monasteri benedettini più volte secolari (Rieti)", *Bollettino della Regia Deputazione di Storia Patria per l'Umbria*, 12 (1906), pp. 51-55

Van Marle, R., *The Development of the Italian Schools of Painting*, 8, The Hague, Nijhoff, 1927

Vitali F., "Gli affreschi medievali di S. Sisto Vecchio in Roma", in *Roma anno 1300*, pp. 433-447

Volpini, P., Ballarotto, A., *Montefiascone nei suoi monumenti. Guida storico artistica*, Rome, Tipografia Artistica Editrice A. Nardini, 1974

Waley, D., "Colonna, Giacomo", in *Dizionario Biografico degli Italiani*, 27, Rome, Istituto della Enciclopedia Italiana, 1982, online

Wallach Scott, J., "Gender: A Useful Category of Historical Analysis", *The American Historical Review*, 91, 5 (1996), pp. 1053-1075

Walls and Memory. The Abbey of San Sebastiano at Alatri (Latium) from Late Roman Monastery to Renaissance Villa, ed. by E. Fentress, C.J. Goodson, M.L. Laird and S.C. Leone, Turnhout, Brepols, 2005

Walz, A., "Die 'Miracula beati Dominici' der Schwester Caecilia, Einleitung und Text", *Lateranum*, 15, 1 (1948), pp. 293-326

Women and Gender in Medieval Europe. An Encyclopedia, ed. by M. Schaus, New York, Routledge, 2006

Women in the Church, ed. by W.J. Sheils and D. Wood, Oxford, Basil Blackwell, 1990

Wood, J.M., *Women, Art, and Spirituality: The Poor Clares of Early Modern Italy*, Cambridge, Cambridge University Press, 1996

Zaccheo, L., *Amaseno*, Amaseno, Amministrazione comunale, 1979

Zappasodi, E., "Ambrogio Lorenzetti 'Huomo di grande ingegno': un polittico fuori canone e due tavole dimenticate", *Nuovi studi. Rivista di arte antica e moderna*, 19 (2013), pp. 5-22

Zappasodi, E., *Sorores reclusae. Spazi di clausura e immagini dipinte in Umbria fra XIII e XIV secolo*, Florence, Mandragora, 2018

Zappasodi, P., *Anagni attraverso i secoli*, Veroli, Tip. Reali, 1908
Zappi G.M., *Annali e memorie di Tivoli (ms. 1572-1590 c.)*, ed. by V. Pacifici, Tivoli, Società Tiburtina di Storia e d'Arte, 1920
Zarri, G., "I monasteri femminili a Bologna tra XIII e XVII secolo", *Atti e memorie della Deputazione di Storia Patria per le province di Bologna*, 24 (1973), pp. 133-224
Zinanni, D., *Trevi nel Lazio nella storia dell'arte e nelle tradizioni*, Trevi nel Lazio, Edizioni Pro Loco, 1972
Zucchi, A., *Roma domenicana*, 4 vols., Florence, Memorie Domenicane, 1938
Zucconi, P.G., *S. Maria del Paradiso in Viterbo*, Rome, Tipografia Artigiana Grafica Commerciale, 1971

Index of Names

Adrian V, pope 38
Agnes, saint 33, 34, 49
Ait, Ivana 82
Alberic II, king 27, 65, 66
Alberti, Alberto 39 and n
Alexander III, pope 111
Alexander IV, pope 37, 74, 96, 111, 122, 124, 139, 146, 149, 150 and n, 153, 155, 156, 157, 158, 173
Alexander VI, pope 122
Amati, Angelo 122, 123n, 124n, 125n
Anastasia di Sant'Eustachio, 87
Anastasius, pope 55
Andrea da Rocca di Papa, priest 83n, 84n, 86n, 88n, 89n
Andrea de Sancto Eustachio 53, 63
Annibaldi, Riccardo 38
Andaloro, Maria 25n
Angelo Benedetto of Rome 164, 165
Anthony, Abbot, saint 143
Antonio di Ienne 125
Aquinas, Thomas 43, 59
Armellini, Mariano 10n, 33n, 42 and n, 51n, 73n, 83, 84n, 86n, 87 and n

Bacci, Augusto 34 and n
Ballardini, Antonella 34 and n, 35n,
Barclay Lloyd, Joan 23 and n, 27n, 47 and n, 49n, 51n, 52n, 53n, 56 and n, 57n, 61 and n, 62 and n, 63 and n, 64, 65 and n, 67n, 68n, 70n, 172
Barone, Giulia 10 and n, 12n, 23, 28n, 30 and n, 74n, 75 and n, 76 and n, 77n, 82 and n, 83 and n, 86 and n, 173 and n
Bartholomeus from Pisa, artist (Bartholomeus Pisanus) 68 and n, 71, 145n

Barral i Altet, Xavier 23n, 35n, 22n
Batard, Yvonne 135 and n, 141 and n
Bell, Susan 18 and n
Benedetto da Montefiascone 28
Benedict, saint 41, 43, 44, 52, 66n, 102, 107, 108, 110, 115, 116(cit), 117, 123, 136, 140, 157
Benedict XI, pope 30, 77, 85
Benedicta, *ancilla dei* 25, 60n
Benešovská, Klára 24
Bianchi, Alessandro 139 and n, 150 and n, 153 and n, 154n, 155 and n, 157
Binski, Paul 38
Bull-Simonsen Einaudi, Karin 23 and n, 49n, 65 and n, 67n, 68n
Bynum, Caroline 17 and n, 18, 22
Benvenuti, Anna 132 and n
Bernini, Gian Lorenzo 117
Bertani, Benedetto 104 and n
Bertelli, Carlo 157 and n
Boboni, Maria 53
Boccamazza, Angelica 39n, 62
Boccamazza, Giovanni, cardinal 55, 62 and n, 63, 64
Boehm, Margaret 153 and n, 155 and n, 156
Bolgia, Claudia 30, 31 and n
Bolton, Brenda 28n, 51 and n, 52n, 53n
Bonaventura da Bagnoregio, saint (Bonaventure) 66n, 157
Boniface VIII, pope 14, 52, 77, 84, 85, 97, 99, 111, 122, 124, 149
Boskovits, Miklos 48 and n, 157 and n
Bourdieu, Pierre 16 and n
Bruzelius, Caroline 12n, 14 and n, 15 and n, 19, 20 and n, 21 and n, 25, 54n, 56 and n, 57n, 70n, 99 and n, 132 and n, 133n,

134n, 136 and n, 137 and n, 138n, 145n, 152 and n, 153n, 158n, 17 and n
Buglioni, Benedetto 115 and n, 118 (see also Buglioni terracotta 115-116, 128, 173; Buglioni altarpiece 117, 119, 128; Buglioni ceramic 121)
Buonarroti, Michelangelo 78 and n
Bridget, saint 86-87
Breccola, Giancarlo 117 and n
Burns, Jane 18
Burti, Virgilio 82 and n, 87 and n

Caetani, Antima 112
Caetani, Benedetto 124-125
Caetani, Francesco 96, 183
Caetani, Pietro 96
Campaninus, Benedictus 65
Cannon, Joanna 11 and n, 49 and n, 171 and n
Calza Bini, Alberto 151
Capisacchi, Guglielmo 122 and n
Carabotti, Santuccia 28
Carnassai, Panfilo 166
Catherine of Alexandria, saint 164, 165
Catherine of Siena, saint 23n, 41, 62-63, 120
Capoccia, Pietro 84
Capocci, Pietro 37, 38
Caraffa, Filippo 10n, 65n, 93, 94n, 96n, 117, 121n, 122n, 123 and n, 124n, 125n, 149n, 150 and n, 151 and n
Carbonetti Vendittelli, Cristina 10 and n, 11n, 30n, 51n, 53n, 54 and n, 62n, 63 and n, 64
Carletti, Giuseppe 73n
Carocci, Sandro 11n, 25n, 30n, 31 and n, 54n, 76n, 85n, 86 and n, 94n, 96 and n, 97
Cartaro, Mario 66 and n
Cavallini, Pietro 12, 42 and n, 47, 61, 62, 109, 142
Ceccano, Annibaldo 146 and n
Ceccano, Berardo 146 and n
Chelidonia, saint 94
Chiappini, Antonio 164
Cecilia, abbess 102
Cecilia, nun (Suor Cecilia) 53n, 56, 57 and n, 64, 91
Cenci, Iacopa 39n, 67, 68, 91
Charles I of Anjou, king 161

Cirulli, Beatrice 59, 63n
Clare, saint 60n, 67, 74, 131, 137, 139, 140, 150, 153, 154n, 156, 157, 159, 166
Claussen, Peter 37n, 38 and n, 39 and n
Clement IV, pope 122, 146
Clement V, pope 29, 84, 85
Cohn, Samuel 30 and n, 88 and n
Colonna, Giacomo 31, 83-86, 89, 173
Colonna, Giovanni 76, 77
Colonna, Giovanna 53
Colonna, Margherita 31, 74 and n, 75 and n, 76n, 77n
Colonna, Pietro 79
Comparte, Giovanni 155
Consolini, Margarita 53
Constantine, emperor 33, 84
Cordovani, Rinaldo 116n, 117 and n, 118n, 119n
Corvisieri, Costantino 74, 79, 80
Constantia, abbess 25, 39n
Constantia, empress 33
Conti, Corrado 96
Conti, Gemma 96
Conti, Stefano, cardinal 137, 139-140, 145, 167
Cooper, Donal 8, 60 and n

D'Acquasparta, Matteo 77
De Angelis, Girolamo 117 and n
De Crescenzo, Patrizia 83 and n
De Marchi, Andrea 44n, 49n
De Medici, Giovanni, cardinal 118
De Prefetti, Gregoria 87
Derbes, Anne 43 and n, 46n, 141n
De Rubeis, Tuzio 117
Desiderius, abbot 101, 104, 106-107, 109
De Venectinis, Nardus 82, 87
Di Marcovaldo, Coppo 135, 141
Di Nicola, Biagio 125
Di Valeriani, Aquina 124-125
Dominic, saint 52, 53n, 62
Dominic of Sora, saint 95
Donò, Achille 136
Draghi, Andreina 42
Duccio di Buoninsegna 46
Dunlop, Anne 9n, 58n, 59 and n
Dunn, Marilyn 19, 23 and n, 29 and n, 73n

Index of Names

Eckenstein, Lina 17 and n
Elliott, Janis 20n, 21 and n
Emiliana, aunt of Gregory the Great 26
Erminia, abbess 74, 76
Esposito, Anna 22-23 and n
Eudes of Châteauroux, cardinal 37

Federici, Vincenzo 74 and n, 79n, 80 and n, 96n, 122 and n, 123-125n, 150n
Fedele, Pietro 65n, 67n
Fedini, Domenico 117and n
Fallica, Salvatore 82 and n, 84n, 85-86n, 87 and n, 88n, 89n
Ferrari, Guy 26n, 73 and n
Filipiak, Mary Angelina 134 and n
Forcella, Vincenzo 26n, 36-37n, 83
Fiorani, Donatella 100 and n
Formicini, Orsola 67-68, 70, 71n, 72, 89n, 92, 170
Foucault, Michel 14 and n
Francesca, Countess of Anguillara 58-59
Francesca di Sant'Eustachio, 86
Francesco, Count of Anguillara 58-59
Francesco, friar of Santa Rufina 161
Francesco, priest of Sant'Egidio 84
Francesco di Vico, prefect of Viterbo 87
Francis, saint 66, 139-140, 151, 153, 156-157, 164-167
Franchini, Silvana 61
Frederick II, emperor 36, 149
Frutaz, Pietro 33n, 35-36n, 41n, 42 and n

Galeffi, cardinal 125
Gambuti, Emanuele 35 and n, 39n
Gandolfo, Francesco 157
Gardner, Julian 15 and n, 48 and n, 68n, 173n
Gemma from Gallinaro, abbess 102-103
Giovanni, archbishop 150
Giovanni, bishop 111-112
Giovanni of Alatri, bishop 137
Giotto 46, 57n, 108-109, 142, 157
Goodson, Caroline 23n, 26n, 27n, 136, 137 and n, 138n, 142n, 143 and n, 144 and n, 145n
Gordiana, aunt of Gregory the Great 26
Gordiano, father of Gregory the Great 102
Gilchrist, Roberta 15n, 16 and n, 172

Graham, Emily 75 and n, 83 and n, 85 and n
Gregory the Great, pope 26, 35, 136 and n
Gregory IX, pope 28, 31, 54, 66-68, 72, 96, 137, 145, 149, 160, 174
Gerson, Paula 18-19
Giacchetti, Giovanni 73 and n, 74 and n, 77n
Gilbert, Creighton 49 and n
Guido, Simone 82 and n, 84-85n

Hamburger, Jeffrey F. 19-20 and n, 22 ad n, 38n, 70n, 99n, 157n
Herklotz, Ingo 12 and n
Honorius III, pope 28 and n, 52 and n, 55, 66, 84, 131
Honorius IV, pope 62, 74, 76,
Hubert, Etienne 76 and n, 77n, 80n

Iazeolla, Tiziana 135 and n, 136, 139, 140 and n, 142 and n
Ilari, Annibale 94 and n, 95n, 98n
Imperatrice, mother of Filippa Mareri 159
Innocent III, pope 23n, 27, 55
Innocent X, pope 137
Isabella of Castile, queen 85

Jacoba, sacristan 37 and n, 38-40
Jacuitti, Livio 104
Jäggi, Carola 20 and n, 21 and n, 22, 152n
Jerome, saint 26
John of Toledo, cardinal 38
John V, bishop of Alatri 140, 167

King, Catherine 20n
Krautheimer, Richard 33n, 34 and n, 55n
Krueger, Roberta 18
Koudelka, Vladimir 27 and n, 28n, 51n, 52n, 53n, 54 and n, 55n, 64

Laven, Mary 22 and n
Lazzari, Teresa 23n
Lello, artist 12, 41
Leo from Ostia, 104
Leo III, pope 27, 36
Leo IX, pope 95
Leo X, pope 118
Letizia, abbess 125
L'Estrange, Elizabeth 18 and n
Lirosi, Alessia 23 and n, 26-27n, 99n
Lorenzetti, Ambrogio 69n

Lori Sanfilippo, Isa 39 and n, 40-41n
Lowe, Kate 65n, 69n
Lucia, abbess 37 and n, 38, 72, 175
Lucia, nun 86

Mabilia, abbess 96
Macchi, Vincenzo 117 and n
Malleio, Giacomo 28
Marcella, patrician 26
Mareri, Caterina 165
Mareri, Filippa 70, 159 and n, 160n, 163-166, 168
Mareri, Filippo 159
Mareri, Gentile 160
Mareri, Perna 161
Mareri, Tommaso 159 and n, 160-161
Marquand, Allan 114, 115 and n, 116-117, 118n
Marini, Alfonso 10 and n, 11, 21n, 28n, 67 and n, 69, 81-82, 131n, 132 and n, 146n, 159n
Marti, Susan 22 and n
Martin V, pope 30, 49, 82
Martin, Therese 13n, 17n, 22 and n
Marzi, Fabio 147 and n
Mascardo, Giuseppe 118-119
Mathis, Paola 104n, 105 and n, 106-107n, 108n
Matthiae, Guglielmo 45 and n, 51n, 61 and n, 140n, 157n
Medici, Alessandro 34, 35n
Memmi, Lippo 120, 173
Michalsky, Tanja 24
Monferrini Calvesi, Augusta 104
Montanea, Ruggero 159
Moorman, John 132 and n, 146
More, Allison 18 and n
Murat, Zuleika 22n
Murtz, Cherubino 122

Nasimbene da Ferrara 112
Nicholas of Tusculum 54
Nicholas III, pope 28, 38
Nicholas IV, pope 124, 174
Nicholas V, pope 125
Nolan, Kathleen 19

Odericus, artist 38
Odo of Cluny 27, 66

Oliver, Judith 21 and n
Orofino, Giulia 101 and n, 104n, 107, 109n
Orsini, Andrea di Orso 59 and n
Orsini, Giovanni Gaetano 37-38
Orsini, Paola 53
Orsini, Eufrosina 53

Paduli, Martino Francesco 84
Panciroli, Ottavio 71n, 72 and n
Pandolfo, bishop 155
Panvinio, Onofrio 33n, 35 and n, 38 and n, 39, 40n
Paschal I, pope 36, 72
Patrassi, Emilia 111
Paul I, pope 73, 81
Pecchiai, Pio 58n, 59, 59n
Perez Vidal, Mercedes 56-57 and n
Perugino, Pietro 115, 120
Peruzzi, Baldassare 36
Peterson, Ingrid 13n, 20
Philip II, king 151
Philip IV, king 85
Pierleoni, Artemia 53
Pietro da Rimini 48
Pigni, Angela 118 and n, 119
Pisano, Giunta 12, 135, 141
Pisano, Bartolomeo 12
Pius V, pope 89
Pius IX, pope 36, 41-42, 43
Power, Eileen 17 and n
Puccio Boviis, Pucciarello de 58
Pratesi, Riccardo 131 and n, 132, 146, 150 and n
Prehn, Eric 135 and n, 141 and n

Queloz-Agnes, Dominique 104

Ravignani, David 36 and n
Righetti, Marina 15n, 134n
Rinaldo of Rieti, bishop 161
Rita, abbess 102-103
Robertson, Elizabeth 18
Rodolfo of Ferentino, bishop 95
Rogerius, prior 150
Romano, Serena 9n, 10n, 24-25 and n, 28n, 30n, 37n, 38 and n, 39, 40-42 and n, 44-45 and n, 46n, 47n, 49 and n, 51-52n, 57n, 58 and n, 59n, 60n, 61n, 63 and n, 64, 67n, 68 and n, 79n, 80, 98 and n, 102n, 104-105n, 106 and n,

Index of Names

107n, 109n, 139-141 and n, 142, 144, 150 and n, 153 and n, 154, 155 and n, 157-158 and n
Romanini, Angiola Maria 9 and n, 10n, 28n, 68n, 98 and n, 133n
Rosselli, Piero 78 and n
Rubeis, Rinaldo 121, 124
Rusuti, Filippo 47
Rywiková, Daniela 24

Saini, Patrizia 36 and n
Savelli, Steffana 87
Savelli, Violante 89
Salomonia, Domenica 57n, 62 and n, 63
Scaccia-Scarafoni, Camillo 135-136 and n, 137n, 138 and n, 141 and n, 143
Scaramella, Vincenzo 83 and n, 84n
Schleif, Corine 21, 22n
Scirocco, Elisabetta 24
Serena, abbess 26, 36
Seroux D'Agincourt, Jean Baptiste 49 and n
Sheingorn, Pamela 18, 19 and n
Settesoli, Jacopa 66, 72
Sixtus IV, pope 67, 69-70, 122, 125
Sopphia de Sancto Eustachio 39n, 63
Sozio, Alberto 140
Stefano di Anagni 96 and n
Stein-Kecks, Heidrun 48 and n, 99n
Stephen of Fossanova, cardinal 54
Strocchia, Sharon 22 and n
Sulla, ruler 102
Symmachus, pope 35

Tarsilla, aunt of Gregory the Great 26
Tanghero, Antonio 78 and n
Tempesta, Antonio 58
Terzo Maestro di Anagni 157

Theobaldi, Liuto 123-124
Theodora, prioress 37 and n, 38
Thomas, Anabel 21 and n, 99n
Thomassutia de Vallebona 162
Tomassetti, Giuseppe 80n, 122n, 146 and n
Tomassi, Giovanni 112
Tomassi, Pietro 83 and n, 84
Torriti, Jacopo 85, 142
Tortelli, Giovanni 138, 174

Ubaldini, Ottaviano 37
Ugo of St Cher, cardinal 37
Ugonio, Pompeo 33n, 39 and n, 40n, 55 and n
Urban V, pope 29

Vancsa, Stefano 37
Van Marle, Raimond 49 and n
Vanni, Lippo 59 and n, 171
Valdez del Alamo, Elizabeth 19 and n
Velli, Anna Maria 65 and n
Venerando, monk 65
Vici, Francesco 125
Vitali, Federica 51 and n, 62-64

Wallach Scott, Joan 18 and n
Wadding, Luke 66n, 86n
Warr, Cordelia 20n, 21 and n
Weddle, Saundra 14 and n
Wood, Jeraldine 21 and n

Zappasodi, Emanuele 14 and n, 23, 24n, 29n, 57 and n, 68n, 69 and n, 78n, 95-96n, 99n, 104n, 109 and n, 134n, 143n, 150n, 152n, 153 and n, 154n, 157 and n, 172n
Zarri, Gabriella 22n
Zucchi, Alberto, 52n, 55 and n, 58n, 59n
Zucchi, Antonio 59

Index of Places

Acquapendente 187
– Santa Chiara 187
Acquaviva 187
– Santa Maria 187
Alatri 23-24, 70, 95 and n, 97, 98, 100, 111-112, 133-140, 135n, 142-145, 150, 152 and n, 153, 167-168, 170-171, 173-174, 177 and n, 187
– San Benedetto de Plagis 137, 187
– San Pietro 111, 177
– San Sebastiano 23-24, 70, 95 and n, 98, 111, 133, 135-145 and n, 150, 152 and n, 153, 170-171, 174, 187
– Santa Maria in Paliano 177
Amaseno 145, 148, 150, 167, 168, 171, 172, 187
– San Benedetto 187
– San Michele Arcangelo 70, 145-149 and n, 187
– Santa Maria 145, 148
Amatrice 177
– Santa Caterina di Scai 177
Anagni 24, 70 and n, 79, 95 and n, 96-98, 100, 122, 124, 133-134, 139, 142, 145, 149-158, 163, 167-168, 170-171, 173, 177 and n, 178, 180, 182, 184, 187, 190
– San Pietro in Vineis 24, 70, 79, 95n, 98, 133, 139-140, 144-145, 149-158 and n, 163, 170, 188
– Santa Cecilia 177
– Santa Chiara 187
– Santa Margherita al Fusano 177, 182
– Santa Reparata 95

Aquino 102, 178 -179
– Santa Maria delle Monache 178
Ariccia 178
– San Niccolò 178
Arpino 95, 178
– Sant'Andrea al Colle 178
Assisi 42n, 44, 57, 60n, 61, 66-71, 81, 91, 120, 131n, 132n, 133, 134 and n, 135, 138, 140, 141, 152 and n, 154, 157-158 and n, 167
– San Damiano 57, 67, 69, 70, 71, 76, 91, 95n, 134 and n, 138, 145, 150, 152 and n, 154 and n, 158, 167, 172, 189
– San Francesco 44, 68
– Santa Chiara 57, 60n, 61, 133, 152, 154

Bagnoregio 77, 178, 187
– San Cipriano 178
Bologna 54, 56
– Sant'Agnese 54, 56
Borgo San Pietro 69 and n, 70, 134, 152-153, 159-167, 168, 170, 188
– San Giovanni di Terminara 161
– San Pietro de Molito 159n, 160-161, 163
– Santa Filippa 159-167 and n, 188

Capua, Sant'Angelo in Formis 106
Castrocielo 98-99, 101-102, 104 and n, 106-107, 110, 114, 120, 127-128, 145, 170-171, 179
– Santa Maria 98-99, 101, 102-110, 114, 120, 127-128, 145, 170-171, 179
– Santa Maria in Palazzolo 179
Ceccano 95, 97, 146, 179
– Sant'Angelo 86, 95, 179

Cittaducale 179
– Santa Caterina 179
Collepardo 179
– San Nicola 95 and n, 152, 179

Ferentino 93, 95, 134, 178-179, 187-188
– San Benedetto 179, 188
– San Matteo 179, 188
– Santa Maria Maggiore 93 and n
Fiano Romano 45
– Santa Maria in Trasponte 45
Florence 22, 44, 46, 49, 60, 69n
– Santa Croce 46, 49
Frosinone 93, 98, 102, 110, 111 and n, 120, 135, 146n, 149, 180, 188
– Sant'Aurenzio 188
– Santa Maria in Castrocielo 102, 145
– Santa Maria in Palazzolo 98, 128

Guarcino 95 100, 103, 104n, 109, 110-114 and n, 127, 146n, 174, 177, 180
– San Luca 103, 104n, 109, 110-114 and n, 127, 174, 177, 180
– Sant'Angelo 180

Magliano Sabina 134, 188
– Santa Croce 188
Marta 180
– Santa Maria Maddalena 180
Montecassino 15, 93, 102, 105-107, 110, 136, 149, 178-179
Montefiascone 28, 45, 104 and n, 109, 114-121 and n, 127-128, 170, 173, 180
– San Pietro 104 and n, 109, 114-121 and n, 127, 170, 173

Naples 22, 31, 61, 69-70, 93, 98, 101, 106-109 and n, 110, 128, 132n, 133, 148, 152, 160n, 167, 172
– Santa Chiara 69
– Santa Maria Donnaregina 132n, 133, 148, 152, 167, 172
Nepi 94, 180
– Santi Maria e Biagio 180

Orsano 99, 124-125, 127, 147, 152, 171, 174, 180
Orte 77, 95, 181
– Sant'Antonio 181

Paliano 95, 188, 178-183
– San Pietro 179-181, 183, 188
Palestrina 74, 76-77, 86, 97, 124 and n, 134, 150, 181, 188
– Castel San Pietro 188
Poggio Nativo 181
– San Paolo 181
Pontecorvo, Santa Maria de Ripa 102-103
Petrella Salto 152, 159

Rieti 69, 93, 96, 134, 159 and n, 160-161, 170, 174-175, 177n, 181-182, 189
– San Benedetto 181, 182
– San Flaviano 45, 189
– San Francesco de Machilone 189
– San Sebastiano, 179
– San Tommaso 182
– Sant'Andrea 160, 178
– Santa Chiara 151 189
– Santa Lucia in Colle Alto 189
– Santa Margherita 182
– Santa Scolastica 111, 122, 125, 180, 182
Roccasecca, Sant'Angelo in Asprano 105, 106
Roiate 177, 182
– San Benedetto 177
Rome 9-12, 22n, 23-31, 33-53, 58, 61, 64, 65-101, 104 and n, 106, 109 and n, 110, 114-115, 120, 127-128, 134, 136-137, 141-142, 144-145, 149, 157, 160n, 164, 166, 169-175, 179-180, 184, 187, 190
– Aracoeli 9-10, 31, 68, 83
– San Francesco a Ripa 66
– San Giovanni Calibita 29
– San Giovanni in Laterano 68
– San Gregorio Nazianzeno 39n, 25
– San Lorenzo fuori le Mura 34, 74, 78
– San Lorenzo in Panisperna 10, 28, 31, 40, 58, 74, 75n, 79-90 and n, 169, 173, 190
– San Martino ai Monti 85
– San Pancrazio 29
– San Paolo fuori le Mura 68
– San Pietro in Vincoli 40, 184
– San Pietro, Vatican 10
– San Silvestro 10, 28, 31, 40, 45, 58, 69, 72-81 and n, 83, 85-86, 91-92, 127, 143 and n, 172-174, 189

Index of Places

- San Sisto Vecchio 9-11, 23 and n, 31, 39n, 40, 41, 45, 47 and n, 51-65 and n, 71, 72, 81, 91, 170-173
- Sant'Agnese fuori le Mura 9, 26, 29, 31, 33, 35n, 38, 39 and n, 40 and n, 41n, 42n, 43, 46 and n, 47-48, 49 and n, 50, 71-72, 91, 170, 172-173
- Sant'Agnese in Agone 137
- Sant'Ambrogio della Massima 29
- Sant'Andrea de Biberatica 28-29
- Sant'Anna di Marmorata 29
- Sant'Aurea 54, 58, 60, 91, 171-172
- Sant'Erasmo 29
- Sant'Eufemia 29
- Sant'Urbano 29
- Santa Bibiana 28-29, 53, 117, 180
- Santa Caterina 29
- Santa Cecilia 42, 47
- Santa Maria de Cella 29
- Santa Maria di Massima 28-29
- Santa Maria in Campo Marzio 25 and n, 28-29, 48
- Santa Maria in Domnica 73
- Santa Maria in Isola 28-29
- Santa Maria in Iulia 28
- Santa Maria in Ninfa 106
- Santa Maria in Petrochia 28
- Santa Maria in Trastevere 137, 140, 181
- Santa Maria in Tempuli 53 and n, 56-57
- Santa Maria in Via Lata 37 and n
- Santa Maria Liberatrice 29
- Santa Maria Maggiore 9, 47, 83-86, 140
- Santa Pudenziana 29, 179
- Santi Ciriaco e Niccolò in Via Lata 28
- Santi Ciriaco di Camilliano 29
- Santi Cosma e Damiano in Mica Aurea 10, 23, 28, 31, 39n, 48, 65-72 and n, 80-81, 89, 91, 139, 145 and n, 170, 174
- Santi Nereo e Achilleo 55, 73n
- Santi Pietro e Marcellino 34
- Santi Quattro Coronati 36, 43

Segni, San Gregorio 182
Sezze Romano 182
- Santa Lucia 182

Sgurgola 95-97, 181, 183
- Santa Maria in Viano 96, 99, 127, 170, 174, 183
Sonnino 95, 183
- Santa Maria delle Canne 183
Sora 95, 183
- Santa Maria 183
Subiaco 82, 93, 96n, 110, 122, 123n, 125, 135, 144, 149, 183, 189 and n
- Santa Chelidonia 183

Tarquinia 184
- San Giovanni in Isola 184
Tivoli 40, 45, 53, 63, 75, 77, 83, 86, 134, 184, 190
- San Michele 190
- San Pietro 45
- Sant'Agnese 184
Torre Caietani 95 184
- San Benedetto 184
Trevi, San Francesco 190
Trevi nel Lazio 95, 121, 123, 180, 184, 190
- Sant'Angelo Orsano 98, 99, 103, 121-127, 128, 147, 152, 171, 174, 180, 184
Tuscania 44, 71, 190, 79, 134, 152
- San Pietro in Tuscania 106
- Santa Maria di Gavillione 190

Valmontone 134, 184, 190
- Santa Maria in Selce 184
- Santa Maria in Silice 190
Velletri 134, 149, 184-185, 190
- Santa Chiara 151, 190
- Santa Maria dell'Orto 185
- Santa Martina 185
Veroli 95, 112, 135n, 185
- San Martino 185
Viterbo 70, 87, 93, 96-97, 114, 120, 134, 149, 152, 178, 181n, 182, 185-186, 190
- San Fortunato 186
- Santa Maria del Paradiso 186
- Santa Maria in Palomba 185
- Santa Maria in Valverde 185
- Santa Maria in Volturna 186

Finito di stampare
nel mese di settembre 2022
da The Factory srl
Roma